D0149293

985   Baker, Will
Bak   Backward; an essay on Indians, time &
c.1   photography.   North Atlantic Books, c1983.
            286 p.   illus., photos.

        1. Peru – Description and travel
        2. Ashaninka 3. Indians of South America
        4. Campa Indians I. Title
26.45
                            LC 83-17219

YOLO COUNTY LIBRARY
535 Court Street
Woodland, CA 95695
(916) 666-8329

BACKWARD

An Essay on Indians, Time, & Photography

985
Bak
C. 1

by WILL BAKER

NORTH ATLANTIC BOOKS, BERKELEY, CALIFORNIA

Backward, an Essay on Indians, Time, and Photography

Copyright © 1983 by Will Baker

ISBN 0-938190-13-X
ISBN 0-938190-14-8 (pbk.)

Publisher's Address:
North Atlantic Books
2320 Blake Street
Berkeley, California, 94704

Cover and book design by Paula Morrison
Typeset in Garamond by Joe Safdie

This project is partially supported by grants from the National Endowment for the Arts, a Federal agency, and the University of California at Davis, a branch of the State University of California.

Backward, an Essay on Indians, Time, and Photography is sponsored by the Society for the Study of Native Arts and Sciences, a nonprofit educational corporation whose goals are to develop an ecological and crosscultural perspective linking various scientific, social, and artistic fields; to nurture a holistic view of arts, sciences, humanities, and healing; and to publish and distribute literature on the relationship of mind, body, and nature.

Library of Congress Cataloging in Publication Data

Baker, Will, 1935-
  Backward, an essay on Indians, time, and photography.

  1. Campa Indians. 2. Peru—Description and travel—
1981-   . 3. Indians—Government relations.
4. Developing countries. 5. Baker, Will, 1935-
I. Title.
F3430.1.C3B34   1983   985'.00498   83-17219
ISBN 0-938190-13-X
ISBN 0-938190-14-8 (pbk.)

ACKNOWLEDGMENTS

I am grateful to many people and organizations for help in the preparation of this book: to Gerald Weiss and John Bodley for advice and information, to the Fulbright Commission and the University of California for financial assistance, to Kenny Tejada and Padre Castillo for lodging and companionship, to Dianne Kitchen and Brian Ransom for photographs, to Peter Matthiessen for encouragement, to Stephanie Mills for shrewd advice on publication, to Richard Grossinger for keen editing, and to Gary Konas for hours of patient word-processing.

I owe thanks most of all to the people of Otíka and Ovíri, for suffering interminable ignorant questions with forbearance, kindness and good humor. Their grace and beauty deserve a much higher tribute than these pages, and they are in no way responsible for errors and oversights herein.

The author's portion of the proceeds from sale of this book is pledged to the support of the Asháninka people. Such funds, through the auspices of the Society for Native Arts and Sciences, will be distributed equally to Alas de Esperanza and the International Work Group for Indigenous Affairs.

Readers who wish to make similar contributions may send them to the Society for Native Arts and Sciences, 2320 Blake Street, Berkeley, California 94704, United States of America.

. . . . But how is it
That this lives in thy mind? What see'st thou else
In the dark backward and abysm of time?

The Tempest

PREFACE

This book is the record of a long cycle of futility and fascination. The cycle began three years ago when I received a Fulbright Grant for six months of research in Perú. To begin with I had made out an application in haste, concocting some fantastic scheme or other (I believe it was an epic novel on Mongol migrations, to run several volumes), but when the application was actually approved, it was necessary to formulate a more practical plan.

I rummaged through books, and on a dusty shelf in my barn found a collection of photographs from *National Geographic*, the record of an old expedition to the headwaters of the Amazon. The explorers were, as is usually the case in the *Geographic*, a very nice couple, whose earnest but trivial text was more than offset by superlative camera work. In one of the photographs a man in a loose garment the color of earth crouches on a river bank, drawing an arrow to track something beneath the water's surface. The precise, taut curve of the bow and the man's intent squint compelled attention, and more than once in the next month or two I returned to that picture. At the first glimpse it had gone, itself like an arrow, deeply into my being, and there was no wrenching it free.

The caption identified the Indian as a Campa, and remarked tersely that they were a "remote" tribe. I went through library catalogues and turned up only a handful of sources: an 1874 diary by two Franciscan fathers who were preoccupied by the ants and thorns of their journey and the unregenerate greed of their Indian guides; a few standard handbooks on tribes of the continent, whose editors listed the Campa as a fiercely independent people, numbering perhaps 20,000 (a large group by contemporary ethnographic standards), who kept to themselves in the Pajonal region of central Perú; and two studies by anthropologists: an exhaustive compilation of cosmology by Gerald Weiss at the University of Florida and a socio-economic treatise by John Bodley at Washington State University.

I read at first out of mere curiosity. But as I ranged into more general texts I encountered issues that alternately excited me and depressed me profoundly. I discovered that for two generations field workers have labored in a frenzy of despair to document the very last traces of "primitive" cultures, and have suffered with a keen consciousness of their own role in erasing those cultures. Beyond nostalgia and guilt, there was a note of something like fear: fear that these aborigines were taking with them into oblivion a last and dearest treasure, a still-hidden secret, a sacred knowledge of which the world had mortal need.

A few weeks before my scheduled departure (on the last day of the year 1978) I determined to travel into the heart of Asháninka territory—by now I had learned the Campa's name for themselves—armed like so many before me with camera and notebook. I contacted a young filmmaker, Dianne Kitchen, and we made plans to collaborate on a photographic venture later in the year. I reached Weiss, then in Perú, and he most generously notified people in the villages along the Tambo river of our intentions, and advised them to assist us.

By chance I met another anthropologist who knew Bodley, and after an introduction by telephone he invited me to look over his files on the Ashâninka. In a fifteen-passenger Beechcraft I flew through snow squalls above the Wallowa mountains, feeling already quite like an explorer, but two days spent amid the fabrics, utensils and weapons of Bodley's collection brought me back to earth. In particular, his maps stunned me.

I learned that the United States Air Force Operational Navigation charts account for every square foot of the planet. They mark airstrips, mines, ruins, sometimes even irrigation ditches. Blowups of the main sections are available, and provide detail down to the level of small brooks and notable boulders. For the Pajonal area, where few have trod, the *Servicio Aerofotográfico Nacional* offers pictures that capture individual huts in small clearings.

Looking over these materials as well as Bodley's own careful, hand-drawn supplements, I suppressed a wave of dismay. There seem to be no unexplored corners of earth left. All has been photographed, measured, sounded, and probably scanned with infrared devices to check for minerals or unusual topographical configurations which might betray hidden ruins. Nor are there people who have escaped professional attention. Once remote tribes—Jivaro, Negrito, Xingu, Arunta, Tassaday—have all been studied thoroughly, by an international community of scholars with special training.

This was the first swing into futility. What got me out of it was an engrossing paradox.

More and more research is being performed on an ever-vanishing subject, and I suspect that Heisenberg's Indeterminacy Principle also applies to human culture: when we know everything about primitive people and are ready to test our hypotheses about them, they will all be gone. And as there is an impenetrable mystery in the budging of electrons, in the shadows between mass, energy and time, so in the interplay between human observer and human subject there is an indefinable exchange (gifts? poison? souls?), an unsettling transaction that is seldom represented in the "data." And just here, I determined, I would make my research.

I had no hope of undertaking a scientific inquiry. I made it my task to proceed on a mere hunch: that a strange but powerful confluence of memory and yearning, triggered by a single photograph, would impell me to discover, in a distant jungle, the meaning of my own culture and my life in it. This hunch itself threw a disturbing shadow: a suspicion that to understand the primitive, to absorb it fully, I would have to feed upon it, and so become something that both appalled and fascinated me: a white cannibal.

THE MYTH OF *PISHTAKO*

Some years ago a bizarre rumor spread throughout the Amazon basin, a tale still believed in many tribes. It is said the white men come to the selva with their gifts in order to capture Indians, take them to secret places, and render them into oil which is used to power airplanes, motor boats and autos. So fueled, these craft return, bearing more gifts, seeking more Indians.

SNAPSHOT

Lima, near the Parada. A hot afternoon. A boy of perhaps sixteen approaches, a spastic, whose gait is an alternate lunge and drag. His limbs flail and his eyes roll far back into his skull, but somehow he manages a controlled and forward progress. One shoe scrapes sidewise on the pavement, the leather worn through to dirty skin. The face is that of an Inca warrior: a strong beak of nose thrusting from flat copper cheek planes and a wide mouth, drawn askew with his labor. One element is radiant and fresh. Above ragged, filthy trousers he wears a brand-new tee shirt with a crisp decal on the front. It is a picture in red, white and blue, a bird's eye view of a missile snout erupting out of its silo, swelling lethally upward away from blast and smoke. Below this nuclear death's head is emblazoned in letters of fire: STRIKEFORCE.

1

"I hate travelling and explorers."
                    --Lévi-Strauss, *Tristes Tropiques*

I am the only official passenger on the plane that lifts me out of Lima. At the last moment, as we trundle down the runway, a stocky man runs alongside, semaphoring with his hands. The pilot gestures and I open the door. Sweaty and grinning, the man swings up into the cabin to take his place beside the pilot. They are friends, it appears, and this is some sort of informal, *sub rosa* transport service. Ignoring me, they chat as we move beneath rows of *búfalos*, pot-bellied Hercules troop carriers from World War II, camouflaged in mottled shades of olive and dust.

In the air, the plane tilts over the vast sprawl of concrete and adobe below, wheels briefly over the blue water, then begins a long climb inland, slanting up through clouds on the flank of the *cordillera negra*.

On their western slope the Andes receive no rainfall, though fog rolls in almost every day in winter. The landscape is gray and dun, sand and rock. Through gaps in the cover, I watch it begin to buckle and fold. After a few minutes I have the impression that both the plane and the earth are falling upwards, through the clouds. As mountains jut ahead of us, the canyons beneath yawn deeper. We cross a range of pinnacles and I think we must be over the divide, and then beyond another rank appears, rags of snow caught in the peaks. The sharp edges of stone vanish and reappear in the clouds. Looking down, I can see through gray caverns to a thread of silver, a river in a deep notch.

The burly, jocular companion of the pilot catches my attention. He motions me to take down the small plastic tube coiled on the fuselage over my head and inhale the jet of oxygen-enriched air. The altimeter needle is creeping toward its second ten-thousand-foot revolution. The oxygen, and the confusion of land and mist, have me disoriented. The towering banks of cloud seem to be at the wrong angle, as if diving into earth. It occurs to me that I ought to check the I-Ching to find the hexagram for mountain over sky.

Then after cruising between two magnificent snowbound spires the plane tilts sharply downward. We are over the summit. The increased pressure soon has my inner ear squeaking. It is fiercely painful, but I am scarcely aware of it because of the sudden rush of the selva, the famed cloud forest, a green so deep it is a kind of black hole, a luminous darkness that sucks in all the energy of one's seeing. Like the barren land on the Pacific side, the eastern steppes of the Andes are a tremendous abrupt wrinkling of the earth, but here the color and texture of the surface are as powerful as the heave and drop of the landscape.

It is a tufted surface, a carpet partly eaten away to leave portions of thick nap, trees bursting up together like a bomb pattern in the old aerial newsreels, but these explosions are of an intense, glowing life. The smoother areas are expanses of brush, ferns, cane and grass. Occasionally a palm lifts up on slender stalk, delicate as a daffodil viewed from this height. Some large tree is flowering pure white here and there on the mountain slope, like the spatter of a snowball.

We are flying in canyons now, the wingtips below the rim, green walls all around. I notice swatches of cleared land burned into the slope, tree trunks scattered over them like matchsticks, a few still smouldering. An occasional metal roof winks in the sun. Then, all at once, we swoop over a ridge and drop. An irregular dirt strip appears beneath us, invaded by tendrils of grass along its borders. The plane bounds twice and settles to roll, props feathering with a roar. We wheel around on the last few yards of the strip, and taxi back to a clutter of sheds.

The San Ramón airport is a structure of stucco and weathered boards with a galvanized iron roof. A paint job of a ghastly orange hue has mercifully been almost washed away. A couple of mechanics appear and greet the pilot boisterously, while some cargo and my small army field pack are unloaded. Seated on the ground under a little sun shelter of cane poles and palm fronds, a group of women watch impassively. Beside another building there is a single-engine Piper or Cessna, looking like a worn-out toy. Through one of its dusty plexiglass side windows I can see two faces. An Indian woman and the baby in her arms have twisted around to stare at me.

Someone speaks behind me, and I turn to confront a heavy-set dwarf, an old man with one large, soft brown eye and another shrunken and bleary one, ravaged long ago by some infection. His jaw is also deformed, realigning the planes of his face into an expression of sardonic surprise. He is dressed in a ragged shirt and trousers, made soft as deerskin with grease, and his little cap is black with the same ingredient. He repeats his message, which has something to do with a taxi, a hotel, another taxi, and the fact that the plane is not proceeding to Satipo today. He seizes my pack without further ceremony and scurries away toward the back of the compound. I have no choice but to follow: it is clear that there are no accommodations in this aerodrome. In walking past its main structure I get one startling glimpse through an open door. On a concrete apron is the huge head of a cow, beside it a pool of blood and the smoking heap of its own hide.

Behind the building I find the old dwarf has stuffed my pack into a vehicle and is proudly holding its door open. He is not only a porter, but also a *conductor de taxi.* The vehicle itself is a marvel: a station wagon from the early fifties, a Plymouth or Dodge I estimate, but the grill and all traces of trim--the name and company emblem as well as hubcaps, mirrors, aerial and gascap--are missing. Green paint applied with a brush once covered this battered hulk, but rust has repossessed most of the surface.

I climb into the rear seat, noting that both it and the single front seat have been scavenged from a bus, and neither is bolted to the floor, so that one must brace himself carefully to avoid tipping over or skidding about when the thing is in motion. My chauffeur must find the right wires, reaching through the various holes that gape in the metal shell of the dashboard. When he locates them he twists them together and grounds them on the steering column with a shower of sparks. The engine clears its system extensively, and finally reaches a sustained, ratcheting roar.

It rains often in this season, and the track into town is muddy. We slide as much as we roll along it, and I remark that my driver's foot, clad in a cracked, laceless oxford, functions as the fuel pump. He works the accelerator pedal with the same rapid, steady wobble that my grand-mother used on the treadle of her sewing machine. His technique is to reach maximum ground speed, then plunge in the clutch pedal and disconnect the wires on the steering column, coasting until there remains just enough momentum to start the motor by sparking the wires and engaging the clutch again.

In this manner we reach the iron bridge spanning the Chanchamayo river, cross it and arrive at a sleepy plaza in the middle of town. The twisted old Charon who has brought me makes arrangements with another taxi for my transport to La Merced, a town nine kilometers away, where at dawn tomorrow I can catch a collectivo to Satipo. Then he demands his fee--a reasonably exorbitant one--mounts again into his chariot and clatters away without a backward look. Doubtless his work is over for the day.

At the Hotel Crystal in La Merced I unpack, change my clothes, and walk to a pleasant outdoor restaurant around the corner. I order a cold beer and a papaya with the juice of a fresh lime as dressing. It is a balmy evening, a relief after the hot and humid day. There is considerable bustle in the town, as a circus is encamped on a soccer field nearby, and it seems to be a habit here to eat, drink, discuss, and play the radio loudly after sundown. After the fruit and beer I take a black coffee, light up an Inca--the cheapest Peruvian cigarette and an excellent strong smoke--and spread out my notebook.

The first few of the lined pages are crammed with unsteady phrases written on my lap in the airplane, and these must be deciphered, ordered, and expanded before their significance evaporates. What I jotted down then contains a great deal of impressionistic detail and very little secure information: *Bodley... oil... Arunta... snowballs.* I did not, I see, make an accurate estimate of the population of the San Ramón area, nor remark its principal economic activities, nor distinguish the particular ethnic character of its people. Three things only seem to have struck me, and from these I must wring some manner of meaning.

The first shock was the verdant explosion of the jungle: the way streams webbed out of every canyon and draw, threads of boiling froth unravelling from the skirt of the glaciers, and how, from sheer slopes, dense vegetation sprang forth. The clearings I saw proliferating on the approach to the airstrip were a hint toward a conclusion now obvious. The tremendous fecundity of this region, fed by the snowfields of the Andes and the silt and compost of centuries, is a highly exploitable resource. By the time I made a second and third flight over the area, I learned to distinguish the countless small coffee orchards and cacao plantations that scatter along the river courses, and I learned too of the beginnings of bulldozer and helicopter logging, of fortunes made by cattlemen who shot and butchered several beeves a week, loaded the nude carcasses in small, five-seater planes, and flew these cold, silent passengers over the mountains to hungry Lima.

To make the point more formally, I had traversed a miniscule slice of the richest expanse of flora and fauna left on the planet, the largest single terrestrial supply of oxygen for the atmosphere (the irony of sniffing this bottled elixir as I passed over the area eventually occurred to me), and the basin that receives one-fifth of all the fresh water that falls on the face of the earth, and transports it in one mighty stream to the sea. On any topographical map of the world, this basin is an immense, rich clot of green. At its perimeter, the tractor, plow and chainsaw are gnawing feverishly.

The second ineradicable vision was my dwarf chauffeur with the ruined face, and the remarkable taxi he conducted. Taken together, they were an expression of all that is heroic, comical, and sinister about this land. I came to know that the dilapidated green stationwagon, skidding down the road to San Ramón, has its counterparts all over the nation. Ancient delivery wagons in Pucallpa, their milkracks stripped away and board benches installed to convert them into buses, require forty minutes to travel the ten kilometers from the airport to the city. In Lima great gasguzzlers from the fifties bellow up and down the Avenida Arequipa, held together apparently only by the grim will of their passengers. In the highlands one passes trucks limping into their fourth decade. They are ash gray or dust brown, utterly serviceable, without any remaining vestige of comfort or show. Their seats are bare springs, all stuffing and cover gone. Once they were GMCs or Fords or Mercedes, but they have been blasted, bent and rewelded into Platonic forms: they are pure *truck.*

More than once I saw specimens that should be purchased for museums. There are fenders hand-carved from wood, gearshift knobs made from five pounds of solid brass sculpted into a human fist or skull, ignition systems that involve numerous wires, screwdrivers, kicks, sparks and curses. Very often, especially in the front of buses, one encounters pictures of the Virgin with sanguine heart exposed, side by side with Ché Guevara, the two of them encircled by plastic flowers and bits of bright cloth, with here and there a sticker bearing a terse message, patriotic or pornographic. *The people will prevail. Don't swear at me, I may be your father.* And always, even in the most primitive of these vehicles, some kind of radio or cassette tape deck blares cheap Latin rock, songs of passion, betrayal and murder.

What is miraculous, and monstrous, is that the nation moves its people and its goods with these incredible derelicts, and moves them rather efficiently. The bus system in Lima is one of the most thorough and dependable (when not on strike) I have ever seen. The fumes are sickening, pickpockets numerous and very gifted, and transfer points congested, but all the same one may go anywhere in the city at a reasonable cost and in a reasonable time.

It is the same in the provinces. I was to take a collectivo the following morning--a Toyota seven years old--over the narrow ribbon of rock and mudholes that descends the Ene river canyon to Satipo. This teeth-rattling journey of seven hours cost me four dollars and a couple of feet of parachute cord, given to the driver to bind up a dislodged muffler. Until ten years ago, this same route was considered perilous on foot, and except for the Asháninka who lived there it was almost untravelled. It is now possible to reach every major city in the country, except Iquitos, by means of the Peruvian fleet of buses, free-lance taxis, and collectivo companies. This fleet--gasping, backfiring, farting hellsmoke of exhaust, dropping scraps of wire and shreds of tire in its wake; cross-breeding into strange hybrids of engines and bodies and beds; swerving occasionally with terrible shrieks from the rain-soaked roads into awesome crevasses, killing everyone aboard; hauling mangos, bananas, beef carcasses, co-caine, and lumber to Lima and returning with cargos of pipe, plastic buckets, combs, cable, and cases of bright fuschia Inca Cola to the tiniest settlements of adobe at the very end of the trail--this fleet is the glory and the horror of this land, an agency of immense courage and imagination and humor, whose effect on the landscape and indigenous people is an unmitigated disaster.

Another image of unexpected import links up with the San Ramón taxi. The following day, on the trip down the Ene canyon, I saw my first

Asháninka.

Through intermittent curtains of rain, I had been gazing in awe at the green canyon walls and the torrent of the river, its mud-brown waters ripped white by boulders strewn across a steep descent. The other three passengers were preoccupied with their own thoughts. The driver restricted himself to curses and exclamations over the slippery roadbed. They were all *seranos*, mestizo highlanders, immigrants from the brown pastures and thin, cold air of the Andes. For the past hundred years these hungry and bankrupt descendants of the Incas have been trickling in, following the roads, working to "develop," field by field and hamlet by hamlet, the jungle.

Our driver had been pushing the Toyota all he dared, evidently worried that if the rain increased we would find ourselves unable to skate through the mud. One sign of his nervousness was a reliance on the tape deck slung under the dashboard. He played the cassettes at full volume, but the device was so loose on its mounts that the music was recognizable only when he wedged other tape cartridges all around the deck. These wedges were continually shaking loose, with the result that the singers and instruments reverted to a static-filled vibrato, synchronous with the pounding of shock absorbers, until the driver, one eye and hand for the rainswept road, the other pair busy on the floorboards rummaging for the loose cartridge, could shore up the melody again.

I was thus viewing the jungle at first hand through the rain-streaked windows of a metal box, deafened by this soundtrack of fragmented song and brutal noise. Then, skidding around a corner on a steep slope, we came upon a man walking ahead of us, a man from nowhere. We had not met another car or passed by any settlement for many kilometers. He danced aside with an apprehensive look over his shoulder and we were by him in a moment. But even in this swift glimpse I knew he was different. His scarecrow limbs and great startled eyes, like a deer's, had been expressive of some fear beyond the threat of the moment. The ragged rust-brown cushma he wore I recognized from photos as the Asháninka's traditional garb.

When I looked back, the small stick figure had already vanished in the rain. The driver and other passengers looked at me swiftly, and then looked away. Despite the squawking of the tape-player and the rattle of the muffler, there was a stillness for a few seconds, some feeling of expectancy, shame, perhaps curiosity.

But I said nothing. I was thinking of how I had imagined my first encounter with the Asháninka; how the canoe would glide to the river-bank, where the people stood in silent and regal postures; or how the children would run from all over the village to greet the weary explorer with happy cries or even songs. Instead, born along by this insane, miraculous vehicle, accompanied by trumpets and the wails of fatal love, cylinders blazing with oil from Mexico or Venezuela, I flashed by the first representative of the people I had come so far to know. To him I appeared a pale, blurred face in the window of a howling machine that almost struck him down. The myth of *Pishtako* had come uncomfortably close.

The third powerful impression, barely noted in my journal, took months to reveal its meaning: *Proud old man with old camera.*

Arriving in the central plaza of La Merced, I had looked for someone whom I might ask for directions to a hotel. It was afternoon and there were not many people moving in the heat. The lillies burned still as lantern flames, and the roses and jacaranda trees drooped over their own sharp-edged shadows. I noticed one elderly man under a broad-brimmed hat, standing almost at attention beside a large box camera. It was an ancient Zeiss, with brass fittings and a black leather bellows; the kind that produces a plate that can be processed immediately in a small bucket of developer hung from the tripod.

The photographer answered my questions with courtly grace and a touch of imperiousness. Yes it was a very fine camera. It took negatives, which were rephotographed to make a positive image. No, they did not make them like that anymore. Of many things this could be said. On the other hand it was like the Polaroid, was it not? Very new. The Hotel Crystal might suit my needs. For tourists, and two blocks straight off the plaza. We thanked each other ceremoniously and parted. This small incident, as if the grand camera had exposed a plate of it, recurred to me in following weeks and months with greater and greater clarity of detail, as if emerging from a slow developer. Eventually, after considerable travail, I would discover a meaning for this image.

My retouching of the first day's jottings, in which I have become deeply engrossed, is abruptly terminated when the table lurches under my pen. It is not a violent movement, but definite and strong. Some glassware chatters on a shelf. A second shock comes, and I look up to find the other two patrons of the restaurant, men eating dinner alone, staring inquiringly at me and each other. The waiter appears from the kitchen, grinning excitedly.

"*Temblor!*" he announces. The others nod, smiling in return, and for a few moments we share a thrill of anticipation and a temporary, brave camaraderie. The cook is called from her work. Bent over a stove or counter she was too busy to notice anything, and is unbelieving, until the waiter points to the light bulbs still swinging on their long cords.

After a few more remarks, and one man's reminiscence of a *terremoto*, a truly bad quake, we return to our invisible shells of disregard. The men go back to eating. The very slightest of twitches here, this tremor was as strong as any I have felt in my lifetime in North America. When the Andes give a definitive shrug, I learn later, whole cities may disappear, mountains collapse and great rivers change their course. And these shrugs may occur anytime. Perhaps that accounts for the Peruvian attitude of fatalistic opportunism: keep your foot pumping madly on the accelerator, until the earth opens to swallow you up.

Ta Ch'u

The Taming Power of the Great

above	KEN	KEEPING STILL, MOUNTAIN
below	CH'IEN	THE CREATIVE, HEAVEN

THE IMAGE

Heaven within the mountain:

The image of THE TAMING POWER OF THE GREAT

Thus the superior man acquaints himself with many sayings of antiquity

And many deeds of the past,

In order to strengthen his character thereby.

Heaven within the mountain points to hidden treasures. In the words and deeds of the past there lies hidden a treasure that men may use to strengthen and elevate their own characters. The way to study the past is not to confine oneself to mere knowledge of history but, through application of this knowledge, to give actuality to the past.

2

At the airport in Satipo the following day I get some bad news. There is no scheduled plane service to Puerto Ocopa, the Francisan mission at the confluence of the Pangoa and Perene rivers that is my departure point for the Asháninka villages along the Tambo. Since I did not foresee the expense of chartering an *expreso* flight for myself, I have only two choices: wait for other passengers to materialize or find a guide for the ninety kilometer overland trail--a difficult passage in this rainy season, I am told.

Until I make up my mind I will be stranded in this small provincial capitol, so I take a room at the Hotel Majestic. It is a quite decent establishment, with high white ceilings and hardwood wainscotting. The voluble desk clerk supplies information at variance with that obtained at the airstrip: he tells me that *Alas de Esperanza*, the non-profit company that normally serves the back country, has no functioning aircraft at all at the moment, and there are few if any passengers willing to pay the commercial rates charged by SASA (*Servicios Aeronáuticos de Sud América*). He also estimates that it requires a week to walk to Puerto Ocopa.

The next morning I idle around the town, a raw settlement of perhaps five thousand souls. There is a small, unkempt plaza swarming with shoeshine boys and dominated by a church with a steeple sheathed in galvanized roofing. Near the river (the Satipo) a slaughterhouse sends a thin slice of red into the broad brown waters, and at the other end of town a couple of primitive sawmills snarl and thump away. Between these establishments are located several drygoods and hardware stores, three banks, and a large, open-air market.

In the market I spend less than a dollar for all the mangoes, oranges, bananas and pineapple I can eat. As I gorge I wander about to look for articles of local craftsmanship. The saleswomen, however, are all highlanders in voluminous skirts and black mantas; their stalls are jammed with cheap gingham and polyester, plastic buckets and cups, and cartons of Winstons and Chiclets--all at exorbitant prices. Finally I spot in a glass case a couple of the Asháninka's woven *coronas*, with macaw feathers, but they look motheaten and forlorn amid the candy and gum.

At a hardware store I purchase a short machete, and mention to the clerk as he rings up the sale that I may be using it on the trail to Puerto Ocopa. There is none, he tells me with a sudden smirk. One must fly. And there are very few planes. From the sidewalk outside I look back and see the clerk, the proprietor and a customer laughing together. Irritated and disconsolate, I trudge again to the airport--a two-room shack containing a set of scales, a counter and a telephone--and learn by more pointed inquiries that no other potential passengers have shown up for many days. But the chief agent, a fat and surly man in a wilted white shirt, says he has heard of a trail, though it is not one recommended to amateurs.

The overland route, however risky, begins to look like my only choice. I decide to make a preliminary foray into the jungle this afternoon, since I am by no means accustomed to the climate and terrain. Returning to the Majestic, I am intercepted on the front steps by four Indian youths. They are ill-clad and give off the odor of cheap cane liquor. After displays of great friendship, one of them digs in a pocket and takes out a necklace of amber tusks. Jaguar, he says. Four hundred soles and it is mine. Who collected the teeth, I ask. He looks away. It was dead, he says, of disease or old age.

I shake my head. Two hundred soles. I decline, and tell them that I will give them two hundred soles anyway. This move stupifies them for a moment. I cannot identify my own motives, as the old fangs are impressive enough as ornaments, but this beggarly commerce is somehow shameful. I hand them the bill and retreat into the hotel. The desk clerk cheers me a little, as he claims to know where the alleged trail begins, and gives careful directions.

I start off with a collectivo to a bridge where a logging road forks away toward an agricultural district known as Monterico. There a small clear tributary accompanies the side road, as the clerk promised. I strike out along these rough and muddy tracks and walk for about two hours, through alternate jungle and cleared land, getting my first close look at the Montaña. The road passes occasionally near a palm thatch hut, but except for a few desultory chickens and a pig, I see no signs of life. The day has turned sultry, so I take advantage of a convergence of road and stream, find a secluded cove in which to shed my clothes, and slip into the cool water. For half an hour I swim, bask on the bank, watch the huge blue butterflies, and eat the extra orange I have stowed in a pocket. Then I get dressed and return to the mud, mosquitoes and heavy tropical air, heading back towards town.

On a curve I am overtaken by a man, woman and child. We strike up a conversation and walk on together. The man, Aniceto, has an alert face brightened often by a central gold tooth. He is a campesino, a small farmer, about thirty years old, from the Monterico region. They are on their way to some business in Satipo, where his wife and the girl, his seven year-old sister, will be visiting for a few days. Aniceto intends to return in late afternoon to his chacra.

They look me over in a very thorough, but very friendly way. They are most impressed by my boots, a French make of canvas duck over a

substantial rubber sole, and my wide-brimmed leather hat with a head-
band of Lakota beadwork. I, on the other hand, am intrigued by Aniceto's
long hair--uncommon in the provinces--by the little girl's silence and
huge, dark, downcast eyes, and by the opportunity to get direct and
dependable information about the area and the life of its people.

The upshot of our exchange is an invitation to return with Aniceto to
his chacra and spend a day or two before setting out on the trail to Puerto
Ocopa, which, as the clerk guessed, is merely an extension of this same
road. Aniceto hints that he may be persuaded to guide me on the trek. I am
delighted at the prospect, and as certain nerves and muscles in my back
and legs are already hinting, it may be a tactically sound decision to pace
my adaptation to the landscape carefully.

We leave Zenia and Gladiz in the plaza and after I have collected my
pack and signed out of the Majestic, we take another collectivo back to the
logging road at the fork in the river. This time we are fortunate in catching
a ride on an ancient GMC flatbed carrying a crew of lumberjacks. When
they learn I intend to hike to Ocopa, they regale us with many laughing
tales of man-eating *tigres*. We pass my swimming hole, and a short way
further the truck drops us off at a junction of two roads. Aniceto remarks
that we are "not far" from his house, but in the next three hours I come to
understand his small sister's head-down, silent endurance. A conviction is
forming: no one, unless it be the famed sherpas of the Himalayas, can
outwalk the Peruvians.

By Rocky Mountain standards I am a good hiker, and my pack is light--
thirty pounds at most--but Aniceto shook his head and clucked when he
saw it. I soon discover why. The road begins to narrow and deteriorate
rapidly, pitching up and down sharply. I am used to pulling a grade with
frequent halts on the upslope to cool off and recover energy in thin, tonic
air; then ramble down the ridgeback in long, swinging strides. That
system will not work here. This is hot, humid country with a bewildering
topography--long, gradual rises that swoop abruptly into near cliffs, jagged
ups and downs, bogs hidden on hilltops and barren rock at the bottom of
draws. The whole is covered in vegetation that is invariably described as
impenetrable. The trails are a dubious exception, ever in danger of being
swallowed again by an incessant, uncontrollable fecundity.

There is no cooling off, no escape from the heat, not in shade and not
in the rare clearings. A halt to catch one's breath or a thoughtless grasping
at a branch or vine for support gives certain insects and plants the
opportunity for stinging assaults. All this has been said many times before,
in many ways, and two days later on my way to Ocopa I found there is
some truth in the lurid clichés about jungle horrors. There really are
inch-long devouring ants, pitfalls, and deadly predators. It is enough to
say that the first fifteen kilometers of the trip, including a sudden and

torrential rain in the last half-hour, convince me that some extra time at my new friends' chacra would prepare me for what might follow. Also, the next day is a workday, and I mention that I would like to join the brothers in the field, to know a campesino's life as directly as I can. Aniceto laughs a long time at this suggestion, but accepts the offer graciously.

It is a pleasant, though bizarre evening. We arrive, and the brothers materialize from the fields around us. Only one, Nivardo, is a brother by blood; the others are spiritual kin. The last to appear is a child, or so I first thought. Upon drawing near enough for a handshake, I perceive that he is a man in a child's body. He does not possess the large head and torso of a dwarf, but he is no larger than an eight year-old, a kind of withered cherub. The others call him *Hermanito*--little brother--and introduce him with a special, shy care. All of them are members of something called the Congregation of the Israelites of the Universal New Covenant, and are zealous readers of scripture. And all wear their hair long, evidently in accordance with an article of the faith.

The farm itself, they explain to me, is quite typical; about 30 *hectárias*, the legal limit unless you are connected somehow to the ruling military establishment. Chacras of this size support families of from four to ten or even a dozen souls. The standard structure, for humans and livestock, is the palm thatch roof on a frame of poles, the whole lashed together with tough grass rope. This roof covers a bare earth floor, and in human habitations, a platform of staves made of split bamboo or palm. The platform serves as a combination settee, table, and bed. There may or may not be walls of the same material, and often there is a sleeping loft, with ventilation and a wooden ladder for easy access.

Throughout most of rural Perú there is neither gas nor electricity, so cooking is generally done over an open fire, the smoke wafting through the slats of walls and roof. Sometimes, as in this home, a kind of mud stove contains the flames, with a piece of flattened metal as grill. A few old boxes serve as cupboards, and pots hang from the roof on bent wires.

Surrounding the buildings is a stretch of bare ground, where range the dogs and chickens. The former seem to be an emaciated and furtive breed, sharp-nosed and short-haired. The chickens, on the other hand, look like miniature ostriches; they are long-legged, fast and tough. More than once I saw them face down the dogs over some bit of offal.

Beyond the bare zone is the cropland, not laid out in neat sections as is our custom, but planted seemingly at random: here a few papaya trees, their green scrotum-like fruit bunched under an indecent skirt of leaves; there a clump of bananas sprouting up in huge, glossy fans; an occasional orange or lemon tree; somewhere a large, irregular tract of the brown, oversized indian corn; and, underfoot and in and around everything, the yucca, or manioc--the potato of the jungle. This gawky plant with its hand-like leaves and long, tubular roots is the principal item in the diet of the population east of the Cordilleras. From two to twenty acres are usually planted in coffee, the common cash crop. A campesino begins with an acre and tries to add another each year, the average being from ten to fifteen acres in current production.

The animal life takes some getting used to. Dogs, chickens, *cuya* (guinea pig), pet parrots and various insects live and eat in the main house along with the rest of us. A hen, I notice, has laid an egg on the bed while we talk around the kitchen table. It is evening, and when the kerosene lamp (a rag wick stuck in a bottle) is lit, huge thrumming moths appear, swooping in and out of the light. Hermanito begins to talk to me of God's way, his small, eager face illumined like a Rubens in the yellow glow of the lamp flame. As I watch him, the wall just behind him seems to move. I lean forward and discover that it is alive with cockroaches, so thick they are swarming over each other's backs. He notices when I recoil, and explains with a shy smile that they are harmless; they clean away debris and do not carry disease, as flies do; they are among God's good creatures. I relax and go on listening to the high, childish voice, speaking of how the commandments are very clear and must be kept through simple faith. There is some extraordinary power of poetry and mystery in the whole scene, the face of the aging cherub in a flickering light, and behind it, a halo from the shadows, the crawling mass of insects.

Later, I think of how wrong Rousseau was to leave out of his portraits of pious rusticity all the flea-bitten curs and scrawny chickens, all the filth and ferment of real life. For in this very context, surely, faith shines forth with a particular splendor. The men of Galilee, builders, fishermen, and herdsmen, knew that the life of peasants is not particularly simple, orderly, or even healthy. It is, rather, a life of grim perseverance, and of necessary courage and compassion. As the good Book says:

Many times in my journeys I have known the danger of rivers,

the danger of thieves, the danger of my own people, and of Gentiles,

the danger of cities, the danger of the desert, the danger of the sea,

the danger of false brotherhood;

In toil and weariness, in many vigils, in hunger and thirst,

in fasting, in cold and nakedness;

If it is a duty to rejoice, I rejoice in my want.

II Corinthians (11:26-30)

In the morning I climb down from the loft, stiff from a long sleep on the hard palm slats. Hermanito has fanned up the fire and Juan Carlos is preparing a great pot of boiled yucca and bananas, while Aniceto strips a few ears of the coarse red corn for the chickens and Nivardo sharpens a

machete. I also am greeted cheerfully as *hermano*, and given a hot cup of
tea. During breakfast, conversation is lively despite my halting Spanish.
Mornings are clearly the time for discussion of things of this world, and I
find myself besieged with questions about the price of things in the
United States. How much are autos, knives, chainsaws, shoes, soap,
movies? And on and on.

They are puzzled that I own a car, a pickup, and a tractor, though I am
not related to anyone like John Wayne. I do not even know George
Peppard personally. Their knowledge of American actors rivals that of our
suburban moviegoers. I am asked about Eastwood, Bronson, Brando,
Welch, McQueen, Fonda, Ford, James Arness, Gene Autry and many
others. Certainly their knowledge of film is far in advance of their command of political history. Nixon is the only president they have heard of in
recent times. He was perhaps the most Latin of our leaders.

I fend off further questions about prices by turning the tables, and
collect the following facts about their household economy.

Coffee production is calculated in *quintales* (56 kilos) per *hectária*
(2.5 acres). Aniceto's three *hectárias* yield, in a good year, 45 *quintales*,
each *quintale* selling for 7,000 soles ($30-$35 U.S. dollars). The price per
quintale can fluctuate dangerously, he warns me, but as a part-time
California almond grower, I am fully aware of how farmers are at the
mercy of obscure manipulations of the market. This family can expect,
then, a cash income of a little over $1500, rather less, for the five in the
household, than the $580 per capita listed as the standard by our State
Department's specialists in the area. The sum could, as the winds blow in
Wall Street, dip below a thousand or rise a little beyond two.

Yet, by local standards, Aniceto and his brothers rank as well-off. They
possess land, and therefore an assured source of staples. And as I was soon
to discover, there is a connection between the heaps of smoking starch--
boiled bananas, yucca, and corn--and the effort required to cultivate a
crop. They have also the promise of increasing the production of the
chacra year by year, at some point doubling or even tripling their income.
Finally, acquired free from the government as a homestead, their small
plantation has now an equity value proportional to their effort, a value that
will augment to offset the runaway inflation that haunts Perú.

One of the millions of landless dayworkers in the country, however,
must do the same kind of backbreaking labor for 200 soles per day, often
sin comida. One dollar, or slightly less; and no midday meal. To grasp the
impact of this figure, a few prices of vital goods and services should be
kept in mind. Potatoes are 10 cents @ pound; milk, 25 cents @ liter; a
meal in an ordinary restaurant, $1. For imported items, especially tools,
the prices are breathtaking. A Homelite chainsaw goes for around $800; an

ordinary single-load shotgun brings $250; and a small set of Thorsen wrenches is worth $100.

Even everyday items like aluminum pots, axes, and files are very costly. After buying such necessities, and a little salt, oil, sugar and spice, a family has little left for decoration and diversion. Peruvians seem to make two herculean sacrifices to achieve what they imagine is a better life: they purchase a radio and a wristwatch. An occasional movie and a bag of sweets are the only other luxuries most families can aspire to, and any unexpected expense--a need for glasses or dental work or minor surgery-- can wipe out an entire year's profits. In the case of the landless laborer, there is no possible margin. His eyes go bad, his teeth fall out, or he dies.

Later in the morning I discover that there is not, in any case, a lot of time for idle diversion. It rained lightly for an hour or two after breakfast, and while we were going over the statistics given above, the sun broke through. It is now time to start the day's work. We set out for the field, machetes flashing, with a lot of banter too fast for me to follow.

The crop is often planted on a steep slope, and some tall trees are generally left in the field to provide shade because coffee does not respond well to direct sun. The plant itself is a bush that sprays up in several limber branches to a height of eight or ten feet. The branches droop when the beans ripen, somewhat like a lilac or pussy willow in bloom. Cultivation is simple. The surging jungle must be hacked into submission over and over, to prevent it from swallowing the orchard. This is done with a heavy-gauge machete, two and a half to three feet long, swung in an arc close to the ground while the worker is crouched under the overhanging branches.

In the green tunnels formed by rows of the orchard the air does not move, though breezes may sway the tops of trees high above. In this rainy season the humidity is like live steam. In seconds my spectacles are a blur of moisture, my shirt soaked and dripping. The steep pitch of the slope causes me to lose footing often and send the blade into the damp humus or ringing against rocks. But I keep swinging, conscious of the steady *chuff, chuff* a few rows over, the strokes of Aniceto and Nivardo.

Soon I have to discard my glasses as useless. They will not dry, and the only remedy I can imagine is a tiny set of windshield wipers, an absurdity that brings a grim smile. A few feet further down the row after this decision I am stung sharply on the hand and cry out. Aniceto moves up to investigate and points to a large plant with a silver fuzz on the underside of bright green leaves. "*Shalanca,*" he says, and taps with his finger, as if touching a hot wire. I do the same, and jerk back at another, slighter sting. "*Se pique,*" he laughs, and indicates the red blotches forming on the back of my hand. He cuts a forked stick then, something like the crude hook we used to fashion as a makeshift fish string, and shows me how to use it with my left hand, probing the uncut area ahead, lifting up sagging or bent stalks, while cutting with my right. It is also useful in dealing with *culebras*, the common venemous serpent in these parts.

At the end of three hours, shortly before noon, I am operating in a more or less dream state. I feel as if I am actually under water--and it is warm to hot water at that. The machete rises and falls in deepsea diver motion. The intense discomfort of working continually bent over at hips and knees has faded, either dulled by the heat or lost in the pain from my hands, the one red and throbbing from the *shalanca*, the other, wrapped around the machete handle, aflame with several blisters that have broken and are being cured in salt. I have been saved from an even worse fate by Nivardo, who spotted ahead of me a low-slung nest of wasps. I must surely otherwise have slashed straight into them, and in my myopic and fatigued condition I would have been far too slow to evade a furious swarm.

I am most grateful for this warning, not because of the averted disaster, but because I have to leave off cutting for a few minutes and make my way around the wasps to find another row. Seeing the delay, and smiling, Aniceto and Nivardo stop work too and saunter over. They too are streaming with sweat, but otherwise alert, with spring in their stride. I am trembling all over with exhaustion. The hot, damp air feels like a physical burden on my shoulders and neck. It occurs to me that without the rain in the morning, we would have been at this work for five hours. Just half a day's work. Were I a Peruvian field hand, I would have earned the grand sum of fifty cents, provided Aniceto would hire someone as slow as I.

The meaning of poverty in this country has become much clearer. When we reach the house for lunch, I am glad to sink down to my bowl of chicken broth and my plate of boiled yucca--I am ravenous for just this sort of thick, starchy meal--glad not to be in the steamy green tunnel, with the endlessly rocking blade in my hand; glad that I can offer, in my inadvertent groans and sighs, some comic relief for these poor, generous, friendly brothers of mine. They are laughing at me, not in ridicule, but in understanding.

Hermanito, who has beads of sweat on his brow too from working over the stove to prepare this dinner, gives me his radiant smile. He brushes a half-grown chicken from the table, and sits beside me. It is so, is it not, he says, that we come to understand the meaning of life, through suffering? Life, I repeat dumbly after him, slurping at my soup, life. And more suffering, more understanding, no? offers Nivardo, with a playful look. We cut this afternoon too, Señor Weel?

I look up and smile, a little savagely. *Si, hermano,* I agree, *se puede. Pero por dos cientos soles? Nunca!*

They laugh uproariously at that, and I do too, white teeth all around the room. But not for a dollar a day, brother. Not on your life.

3

The next morning there is rain until about ten o'clock. Then the clouds burn away suddenly, and the earth steams. After last photos and hearty farewells from our brothers, we shoulder our gear and make off. We must return to the main road, follow it for some distance on the way to Mazamari, then break off on the trail to Puerto Ocopa. At the juncture of this trail and the road there is a small store, a thatch shed some farmer has stocked with the most basic goods. From his phlegmatic wife we purchase two cans of tuna, hardtack, candles, and a couple of meters of plastic to serve as Aniceto's raincoat.

Our first day's destination is Shanki, perhaps 25 kilometers distant, which is described to me as a large hacienda, where the trail breaks away from the Satipo and crosses a range of mountains to the Pangoa river. For the first few kilometers the route climbs gradually, and though the humidity is oppressive I manage to get a second wind and keep within sight of my guide. These mountains are rugged and thickly forested, but not high. My Air Defense Navigation map--despite the warning caption "Relief Data Unreliable"--notes a few crests of six or seven thousand feet. The most difficult passages are those where the slick red clay is sown with boulders and half submerged roots, or those where the air is stifling in a green tunnel of leaves and vines. Fortunately, there are brooks or dripping springs in many draws, and we pause often to drink and dash the cool water over our heads.

In these interludes I have time at last to wipe the film from my cursed spectacles and enjoy the play of sun, water, and leaves. As we catch our breath, we converse.

I have Follett's smallest pocket dictionary, and must search often for the right word. The result is a castillean stiff and pompous, without being grammatical. From Aniceto's frequent signs of mirth, I conclude that the combination is comical. But he is interested in the discussion, much of which turns on spiritual or political matters. The night before in our dinner table talk I was asked what faith I followed, and travelling in other parts of Perú later I was to be posed the same question. Caught off guard, I found myself claiming a sort of indefinite status as a Buddhist sympathizer. Aniceto was curious about so strange a position and plied me with further questions which I had to answer with the little patchwork of notions I had pieced together from desultory readings in Suzuki, Alan Watts, and Gary Snyder. The notion of sitting still and trying to think of nothing in order to learn something unspeakably glorious Aniceto found most bizarre and much less attractive than his own belief in direct prayer to an attentive God.

I on the other hand am fascinated with my companion's Israelite faith, which I soon determine has nothing to do with Judaism. It is fundamentalist, intensely local--the chief prophet is a Peruvian living somewhere in the highlands--and decidedly populist. To perfect himself in the creed, Aniceto has committed great chunks of the Bible to memory. He keeps a small notebook crammed with a verse by verse listing of what has been learned, and studies it to keep his mastery and to cross-reference various concepts. I will look up often, in the days ahead, and see him on the other side of the moth-buffeted candle, lips moving as he repeats some passage to himself, pen poised to enter any correspondence that might occur to him; and the irony of myself, offspring of a Socialist and a Mormon, nursing a feeble impulse toward Zen, and this descendant of the Incas and their arrogant Catholic conquerors, who sings evangelical hymns at the dinner table because his tiny sect has no church--both of us deep in a dark jungle on a journey to meet Indians whose priests are tigers--such an irony would drive me to a kind of exhilarated bafflement. What were we doing, and who were we, that we could entangle ourselves in such incongruities?

Shifting to political matters gave the discussion greater substance, but no greater simplicity. At our lunch of hardtack, raisins and cold water, we fell to wrangling about the Franciscan Mission of Puerto Ocopa, our destination for this first leg of the journey. My only knowledge of the place stemmed from a brief conversation with a child psychologist in Lima; she had worked with nuns who collected medicine and cast-off clothes to ship into the Campa country. I had learned it was a major outpost, with a chapel, a dispensary, a school, and--my only concern--an airstrip. My friend had offered to put me in touch with the good Sisters, who might be able to give me guidance, but I declined, having read in Bodley's account of the territory that the missionaries themselves began the destruction of Indian communities. They thoughtlessly taught them cooperation with and dependence on "civilized" agencies, eradicated pagan traditions, and then withdrew to leave the natives to the mercy of unscrupulous *colonos* who moved in next.

This process--early penetration by missionaries, erosion of traditional aboriginal life, subsequent exploitation by commercial interests--has not, however, been entirely successful among the Asháninka. That is the reason I am here. I know from my reading that the history of the area includes several notable massacres of Franciscan missionaries, and there is a statue to these martyrs in the central plaza of Satipo. After a hundred years of encroachment into the Pajonal, and the construction of major missions at San Ramón, Satipo, Tarma, Quempiri, and Ocopa, the Francis-

cans and Jesuits were forcibly expelled in 1740 when the Indians, under
the leadership of Juan Santos de Atahuallpa, a half-breed magician who
claimed to be the last Inca king, revolted and wiped out these settlements.
For the next century and a half the highlanders left the Asháninka alone.
The difficulty of maintaining supply lines over the formidable barrier of
the Cordilleras, the risk of ambush along the few arduous trails into the
Pajonal, and the notorious ferocity of the Asháninka kept out all but a few
intrepid explorers, who stuck to the rivers and did not stay long.

This period of stability ended after Bolivar's revolution, when Perú
began a period of aggressive development of its trade resources, and an
extensive resettlement policy for the highland peasants. The climax of
this movement occurred at the turn of the century, when rubber became
the most valuable crop in the Amazon basin, and hordes of *caucheros*
drove up the rivers by steam launch to ravage the forest for the *oro negro*.
Routinely, these prospectors imported Barbados Negroes or bribed the
more war-like tribes to make slave raids among the Putamayo, Shipibo,
Machiguenga, and Campa. The unwilling were shot, the women captured
for the usual reasons.

Still the Asháninka managed to survive, retreating along impassable
tributaries or retiring into the rough terrain of the interior. But their
territory was sharply reduced and fragmented by new trails and roads, and
after a last uprising in 1913-14, when they killed 150 of the interlopers, the
Indians abandoned a policy of resistance. The bow was no match for the
repeating rifle. Then, following the reestablishment of the Franciscan
missions and the immigration of refugees and renegades from World War
II, the area underwent a second boom. Aniceto tells me that about twenty
of the most affluent local families, those who run the coffee warehouses
and sawmills, or hold large coffee or cattle plantations, are gringos who
entered the country at that time. Poles, Germans, Australians, Yugoslavs,
and Canadians--Communists and ex-Nazis alike--were encouraged to
homestead the Chanchamayo, taking advantage of the road the Franciscans had finished in 1919. They were also armed, he adds, and allowed to
enforce their own labor law among the local Indian population. Now no
such crude methods are necessary. Many Asháninka have collected around
settlements such as Satipo, forming the most destitute element of the
population, willing to work themselves to death for a few baubles of
polyester and plastic. Although, Aniceto shrugs, "they don't really care to
work, like civilized people."

I have little doubt that the Peruvian government is an oppressive
one,* though less brutal than the Brazilians and Bolivians are reputed to

*In 1979, General Francisco Morales Bermudez was President,
having served as Prime Minister under the previous President, General
Juan Velasco. Currently there is a democratically elected chief of state,
Fernando Belaúnde.

be. Certainly everyone I have talked to so far--taxi drivers and waiters in Lima, doctors and teachers, Aniceto and his brothers--speaks bitterly of the fantastic wealth of the military class, which they believe is accumulated by profiteering, and the abject poverty of much of the populace. At the same time, the man-in-the-street is for development of everything, immediately, and thinks of the selva as a wasteland ripe for colonization. And Bodley is surely right that the ruthless exploitation of Indian peoples has been aided, however unwittingly, by the missionaries' subtle, preliminary pacification.

Aniceto, however, portrays the situation as far worse. He decided to accompany me, he confesses, partly in order to protect an innocent. Rumor has it in Satipo that Ocopa is a kind of armed camp, part of a Catholic policy of securing the area against any intruders. The Franciscans, he insists, have their own planes, modern weapons, and live like the petty lords of private fiefdoms. Their policies are all profit-oriented: the medicines and clothing collected in Lima are used to bind the Indians as serfs, with debts so huge they can never work them out; and it is not unknown for the Padres to give the mission girls as brides to tribesmen from the interior in exchange for a lifetime of labor. Finally, there is a breath of more obscene scandals: concubinage and cocaine traffic.

I express strong reservations that the Church could be a shameless partner in such a business, and Aniceto admits that not all the clergy are corrupt. One of his own populist heroes is Padre Solomon Bolo, deported a decade ago for publishing some hard facts concerning the Generals' salaries and perquisites. A friend of Ché Guevara and John F. Kennedy, he is a much respected polemicist, still publishing his attacks in other Spanish-speaking countries. But about the Franciscans in the jungle Aniceto remains adamant. They are *capellanes*--a military order--not as powerful as the junta of rapacious generals, but formidable all the same. Deeper in this hill country, Aniceto claims, these missionaries are a law unto themselves, and can back up their decrees with bullets. We must be circumspect, forceful in asserting that my proposed research is only educational and in no way political.

I cannot believe the Franciscans are such ogres. Yet as I swing my pack up and settle the web straps, now dark with sweat, against my shoulders, I feel a little less secure in striking out fifty miles through territory I know only from books ten years old, with nothing but a Pentax, a brand-new machete, and a letter from an obscure office in Lima to maintain my position.

The afternoon heat has become oppressive, and I am wringing wet from head to foot. The clay has caked on my boots and sucks at them incessantly. The straps of my knapsack create a burning friction against my shoulders. Worst of all, of course, is the hot blur of my vision. I imagined during my flight over the cloud forest what an exciting time I would have examining the trees, flowers, vines, insects and small animals of the region. It was one of the reasons I persuaded myself to walk from Satipo. But to move more than a few steps in this boiling air will send rivulets of sweat into the eyes, and heaven help the bespectacled, whose world is transformed into the work of a sloppy impressionist trying to paint in a rainstorm.

I saw more in my brief walk from the hotel in Satipo, a few steps over the bridge and into the trees. There was a dark blue to purple flower startlingly like the lupine of the Coastal Range in California, and another that reminded me of cinquefoil. Then, along the riverbank, I discovered the delightful sensitive plant, a little runner with leaves formed of tiny blades along a stem. When the plant is touched, the bladelettes fold and the stem droops, the crumpled leaves reveal a brown underside, and the organism appears dead. The variety of vegetation was everywhere overwhelming. Beside the road I picked at random a square meter of ground and tried to count the different plants in it. There were thirty-odd, none of which I could identify. To test how representative my sample was, I took the adjoining square meter and started again. I had not covered half the second block before finding eleven varieties not present in the first square.

Now all this richly differentiated life has run together in a watery green wall, and doomed are my hopes of acquiring enough detailed impressions to flesh out my account and give it a proper ring of authority, the precision of a competent explorer. I try to listen, too, for specific birdcalls, but the insane racket of crickets and frogs drowns out most other sounds. The insects sing in choruses, a sound that builds to a crescendo of dry, ratcheting harmonics. The frogs call more intermittently in small, clear burps. The combination grows maddening, and for a kilometer or two I fight off irritation by searching for the exact metaphor to represent these noises. The crickets, I decide finally, are really a tape loop of thousands of tiny Groucho Marx clones laughing in the bushes, while the frogs remind me of John Cage's plops occurring in vast electronic caverns.

One bird I do see a time or two, a stubby-winged black one with yellow markings. It looks quite like a large blackbird with lemon instead of scarlet chevrons, and has a similar obnoxious squawk. When I happen to be close to Aniceto when one flies, I ask him what it is called. He shrugs. "*No sé.*"

By mid-afternoon I care nothing for the riotous life around me. It is only a vast, perverse impediment. I proceed doggedly, head down, intent only on threshing my way through to the next point of rest. Once, slithering in the mud, I reach to steady myself on a slender young palm by the side of the trail, and yelp in pain and outrage when my hand sprouts a cluster of black needles. Aniceto, who has taken to waiting for me every few hundred yards, humming some popular tune under his breath, waves the machete reprovingly and calls out a warning. It is fortunate that he has the blade, and not I. My companion reminds me of the small Ford tractor I use at home to mow the weeds in an almond grove. Its primitive transmission is such that one must come to a full stop in order to shift gears. Aniceto must likewise stay with the range of velocity he starts with, and he seems to possess only two speeds, overdrive and dawdle. His concern for my discomfort and physical condition--he is constantly whacking off overhanging branches that would catch my pack--is genuine, I know, but it has become infuriating. I seethe at his cheerful compassion, at the straps biting into my shoulders and numbing my arms, at the stupid, invincible power of the earth to interfere with my progress, at the Fulbright Commission for some obscure crime, and, most of all, at myself for permitting such pettiness to mar an experience I have anticipated for months. Finally, as my mind, thus tortured, drifts under the spell of seductive little fantasies of self-pity, vengeance, and escape, my blind foot skids on a slimy stone and I stumble and fall off the trail, headfirst into a rock-choked ravine.

4

In the middle of the journey of our life
I came to my senses in a dark forest,
for I had lost the straight path.

--Dante, *The Inferno*

Shock. The *roshi's* flywhisk whapping the shaven head of the novice.
Wake up! A sharp, clean pain from my knee empties my mind, and my
torso, head downward, is wedged tightly between rock faces so that I can
scarcely move. In the dazed moments after my first croak for help, a
memory flickers, a memory of another walk four years ago when I was
driven into the wilderness by a profound and desperate need, and when I
believed I learned the real function of walking: that is, to walk *out* of
oneself. A risk of such motion, of course, is that one will step off a brink.

Each summer for many years I had visited a friend's ranch, a remote
five hundred acres located on a flank of the Continental Divide in
Montana. Several clear, cold creeks full of trout and grayling crossed the
property, and a string of saddle horses was always in the corral. To earn my
keep I worked moving cattle and building fence, but there was plenty of
leisure for fishing and hiking, reading and writing. Summers in these
mountains and high pastures had always served to quicken the deep and
vital currents of being. I felt not only energized by the clean air, wild
country and hard work, but transported, altered, in contact--though briefly
and imperfectly--with a stratum of self long buried and denied but still
very potent. It was the nearest thing I knew to what others seemed to be
talking about when they talked about religious ecstasy.

Then, four years ago, the connection failed. Even when I rode a good
horse under the white brow of a mountain, a blaze of sunset on one
horizon and lightning forking on the other, these displays became no
more than, as Coleridge has it in his ode on dejection, a "peculiar tint of
yellow green." I had been restive for a few months, depressed for no
reason I could discern. I held classes, delivered lectures, spoke with
students quite as usual, but inside squatted an observer alternately frightened and cynical. Sometimes, reaching for a glass, listening to a colleague,
or even shaving, a trapdoor would open beneath me, and though I always
caught a fingernail-hold on the edge, I got a whiff of some cold horror
beneath, the frozen hell of Prufrockian routine, a death of the spirit. Now

that ghastly mood had invaded even these cool, flower-strewn meadows.

The famous "mid-life crisis" was offered as an explanation, both in careful discussions with loved ones and in casual banter with friends. At forty many men hit an unexpected streak of wretchedness, and so change careers, get divorced, explore therapy or the like. According to Jung such measures are a response to the realization that our life energies are waning, an attempt to reaffirm will and potency. At the first perception of this twilight, one may develop a conviction that he has not "gotten enough" out of life; he may lunge wildly at some new challenge, yearning for rebirth or enlightenment or fulfillment. I was urged to consider the currently recommended cures for this condition: a sabbatical, psychotherapy, trips to exotic lands, meditation or light training in the martial arts.

None of these contemporary nostrums appealed to me. Nor did I feel this crisis was an entirely personal one. It was true my despair bore some relation to a condition symptomatic of adolescence, what Erikson describes as an identity crisis, a sense that one is still a stranger to oneself, or that several strangers are quartered uncomfortably in the same body. At puberty, a boy feels himself confronted by a bewildering variety of possibilities, of potential selves. A middle-aged man may panic at the shrinking away of these possibilities, at his gradual petrifaction into a monolithic personality. Both are desperate to choose, as if time were running short: the boy yearns to become some kind of man, to resist being overwhelmed by the welter of alternatives; the man suddenly calls into question all that he has been and thought, and may reach after last, far-fetched choices.

But even this sort of individual funk seemed to me the mark of a wide vein of rot in the culture around me. In wealthy industrial nations people fret about "self-fulfillment" and "opportunity." When they have automobiles or airline credit cards they pine for the places they are not. When Hollywood and Madison Avenue tantalize them with visions they discover the shoddiness of ordinary life, and nurse consuming ambition or take refuge in various intoxicants and sexual experiments. As mindless insects in the hive of a complex technology, they must grow hard shells that insulate them from the sufferings of others, from the mad violence that erupts daily in cities.

The decadence of the Western World is an easy, fashionable, and cheap rationale for petty discontents, and I had been guilty of many a boozy jeremiad on the subject. At cocktail parties one heard whines of protest at pollution, congestion, bureaucracy, nuclear disaster, crime and hypertension. These litanies began to betray a shade of tedious hypocrisy. But at the core of all the clichés there was a hard truth: gasoline and electricity cannot generate peace of mind; in fact our obsession with speed and light seemed to be hurling us into a sinister, ominous future. As the rocket America accelerated, as its ambiguities and stresses intensified, I began to feel the gravity of the past, a powerful pull toward original mysteries.

The dominant figure in these mysteries was a Red Man in his Green World. I had grown up in a tiny logging town in Idaho, and my first notions of spiritual life were the wonder, fear, and delight I knew in the woods. On Sundays an old Scots farmer extolled the majesty of God in our little church, but I felt no great interest in his tales of desert wanderers, cruel Pharoahs and angels. Only when he once delivered a sermon on the Maker and Mover of our own mountains and rivers did I experience a thrill of recognition. So, I thought in childish triumph, I know who He is.

At about the same time I discovered Indians. There were jokes about them, and somber stories too. A very old grandmother, one of the first settlers in our valley, had survived a massacre as a girl and bore the scars of an arrow wound. These fierce people, I was given to understand, had roamed these forests, living on wild game and fish, before there were cattle ranches or lumber companies, possibly even before there were Pharoahs, and they had nothing to do with the angels.

My father and uncles introduced me to the legend of dark blood in our own lineage. Some Texas ancestors, they said, had mingled with Quannah Parker's people. They brushed off my insistent questions by telling me that the drop or two of Comanche in my veins was nothing to be excited about. But I stopped going to Sunday school, and spent my spare time in the woods or reading cheap novels where the Noble Savage flourished in his most blatant form. I cherished secretly my connection to these swift, strong and taciturn heroes, and tirelessly mimicked scenes from the texts, creeping along the banks of Goose Creek with turkey feathers in my hair, looking for broken twigs.

We lived in Nez Perce country, and one of my earliest memories is the sight of their tipis--disappointingly of patched canvas and old blankets--clustered near the hot springs a few miles outside town. For years a local rancher gave them permission to camp in a pasture near the holy water. I dreamed of running off with them to a life of hunting and horse-stealing, but was troubled by their ancient, battered pickups and reputation for drunkenness. I of course knew nothing of the grim reservations to which they were condemned. Then one summer they failed to appear, and never returned.

This infatuation with the Red Man persisted into early manhood and became finally a half-serious study. I read many accounts of Joseph's War, including Yellow Wolf's fine memoir, and delved into erudite compilations of the folklore and mythology of various Western and Plains tribes. Occasionally I mailed a check to agencies committed to improving the lot of Native Americans, as they were coming to be called, and when militant actions were undertaken a few years ago, I was there to help as best I might.

Yet I was increasingly aware--and the experience at Wounded Knee drove the point home with considerable force--that my library studies and good intentions were not bringing me much closer to understanding these vanished cultures. The books told me what they once ate, what they once wore, what they once worshipped, but no life-blood moved through these facts. References to "anthropomorphism," "animism," or--a typical mouthful-- "mythopoeic consciousness" served more to confuse than to enlighten. I came to mistrust profoundly the anthropologists' claim for the exclusive merits of objective research. On the contrary I suspected that only through a sympathetic reliving of the old ways could one grasp their significance. Reenactment was the only possible revival. Vacationing with an archeology text in one hand and a fly rod in the other was no longer enough. I had to move deeper into the woods.

So, in this time of unrest in my own life, already associated with the torment of adolescence, I determined to undertake a vision-quest of the sort that is widespread in North American tribes. To become braves, boys must submit themselves to a period of isolation in a remote area, where they endure cold, hunger, and darkness as they seek a signal--a dream, vision, or visitation of some animal spirit. The experience, unique for every individual, will guide him throughout his life, yielding in time of trial special strength and powers of understanding.

I felt foolish when I announced this plan over breakfast. I was afraid my family and friends would be amused or contemptuous, would find a grown man playing at being an Indian a silly diversion from the hard-headed business of getting on with life. But there was no laughter, no silent ridicule. To my surprise everyone supported the notion of such an experiment, some (the children) most enthusiastically.

At dawn the following day I walked away from the ranch toward the Continental Divide, some twenty-five miles distant. I carried a sleeping bag, a pocketknife, and a few matches. The luxury of fire I excused on grounds of my lack of prior conditioning. I planned to be gone at least four days, and carried no food. There was no fixed destination, other than away from the cattle ranches scattered over the valley.

For two hours or more I hiked as I have always hiked in this country, in spurts interrupted by rest periods at points that commanded a view. It was August, and though it could be warm during the day, many of the bushes and grasses had already started to turn: blades of rust and gold were scattered on the hillsides, and the wild timothy in open stretches was a delicate honey color. The game trail I followed wound into a draw where a small creek ran. Beavers had been at work, creating a chain of ponds, black mirror surfaces that dimpled as trout rose to feed on insect larvae.

Between these ponds, the creek became white noise around boulders and dislodged trees. Small birds flicked in and out of the willows tangled along the bank. I saw an ouzel bobbing on a rock with his characteristic motion, like a diver springing up and down to test the board. Little by little, insensibly, I slowed my pace to accommodate my eye, intrigued by the play of water over stone in the sun.

I plodded on, glancing at the trail occasionally, and entered a region of tiny waterfalls and pocket-sized meadows. The sun had not reached here, and the clearings were like cool, gray caverns whose floor of moss and dense grass was still silvery with dewfall. I wandered idly along the edge of one of these open spots and an instant before I passed by it I saw that it was occupied. A large reddish-brown stump with a white scar at the top balanced on its roots, then swayed. It was not a stump, but the rear end of an elk. He was cropping the tender roots beneath the cutbank of a spring, his head out of sight except for the great rack of horns.

I froze for long seconds. He was not more than ten strides away, perhaps less. I could see droplets of mud and wild oat burrs in the buff hair of his throat, and, when he raised his head to look about, the tendrils of root dripping from his jaws. He was immense. The sharp tines of his rack were higher than my head, and in my automatic hunter's calculation I put him in the four-hundreds, dressed meat. But of course there was no question of that. Or if there was any killing to be done here, he was much the better equipped to do it. His large, soft brown eyes passed over me, returned to dwell for a moment, then went on. But this time, when he lowered his head to feed, he stepped around broadside and I saw that he could, literally, keep one eye on me, even though his muzzle was buried under the bank.

We remained so, he cropping methodically, I stuck in mid-stride, until my limbs began to ache with strain. But before moving I spoke. "Hello, brother elk," I accosted him. The great ears came up sharply; he tensed and held as still as stone, except for the slow working of his jaws. "Don't be afraid," I urged. It was no avail. He gave a little snort, and I could see a muscle in his shoulder quiver. I moved my hand, as if in greeting, and with a tremendous crashing of branches he was out of the clearing and gone into the trees.

I expelled a long breath, and discovered that I too was trembling with relief and exhilaration. Never had I seen a large wild animal so near--near enough that, had I been careful at the outset, I might have touched him. Counted coup. Perhaps the elk was my totem? But we had not engaged in a dialogue and my reaction had been one of ecstatic contemplation rather than kinship. At any rate I knew this journey was not like others I had undertaken. In years of hunting deer, elk, and wildfowl I had never stalked so well as now, when I was proceeding absolutely without destination.

By nightfall this insight was confirmed beyond doubt. I had seen at least a dozen mule deer, two of whom never caught sight of me, a cow moose with her calf, two mountain goats, and various smaller creatures: a muskrat, several fool hens--a local variety of large grouse that depends on camouflage for its defense--a sharp-shinned hawk, mountain bluebirds and jays, and--a first--a large marmot, caught napping on a great slide of jagged granite. I felt myself in the presence of some mystery. Without a gun, without any conscious attempt to sharpen my awareness, I was seeing more game than ever before in my life.

I made cold camp beneath the rock slide where I saw the marmot, in an alpine meadow where the snowbanks had disappeared only a few weeks ago and where a few wildflowers were still blooming white and purple. Gazing over the rising field of granite blocks and slabs, their edges sharp and naked as if just broken, it occurred to me that I had come to one of the last regions on the continent that yet existed in anything like a pristine state. The glacier retreated from these slopes perhaps as recently as ten thousand years ago, certainly no more than twenty, and the rocks are still jumbled together precariously. Sometimes, walking on the spongy mosses at the base of these slides, one can feel the edges of stone beneath the skin of humus and rootlets, and the next morning, clambering over the steeper part of the slide, I felt one of these titanic blocks, as large as a railroad car, shift a little under the pressure of my gnat's weight.

We had gotten dramatic proof of the inviolate nature of this mountain range a few weeks before. Fishing a pair of high lakes twenty miles or so to the north, some of our party had elected to climb a nearby peak. On a narrow bench of rock fragments, apparently a protected place, a young lady found a perfect flint spearhead. It was notched, but not fluted, and lay on the surface, bright and sharp as the day it was made. How many centuries had it endured there? At this altitude there is no game but mountain sheep and goat, and the Nez Perce hunted these animals with horn-backed bows and arrows tipped with much smaller, triangular points. It was likely that this weapon had been hurled by a man whose people followed the retreating ice, hunting the woolly mammoth, reindeer and American horse, bison and greathorned sheep. I had seen in museums similar points, classified as Magdalenian, and dated from ten to twenty-five thousand years ago.

Night fell, and I lay under the stars, lightheaded from hunger and fatigue. No vision had come to me yet--but what privation had I known, beyond missing one day's meals?--only an extraordinary number and variety of animals. At least I had learned that an aimless search may have special advantages, and I resolved (not seeing the irony, the error!) to pursue the same strategy in the days ahead. Tomorrow I should pass the ten thousand foot level, the snow line, and find stretched before me the backbone of the continent. From there I could strike what way I wished: west to the Bitterroots, north to the blunt, barren mountains above the buffalo plains, or south to yet higher and colder peaks.

5

I woke to find the little meadow and my sleeping bag coated with the thinnest of rime, a frost so delicate that when I breathed on the nylon cover the crystals evaporated at once. The peaks around me were tinted rose, and the immense, empty sky had taken on the steel and gold of dawn. No birds or squirrels stirred. The only sound was the breathing of wind through the stand of lodgepole pine bounding the clearing. I had only to shake my bag from its cover and spread it over a log to dry, while I had breakfast--a few mouthfuls of the spring that trickled from beneath granite blocks. The water was numbingly cold, and had no more taste than air.

The bag dry and tightly rolled, I set out to climb the rock slide. I was jaunty and energetic; on this second day hunger pangs seemed to have diminished and I felt agile and easy on my feet, at home as a goat on this glittering white stone peppered with flakes of obsidian. A time or two there was a thrill of terror and a frantic scramble when the precarious, broken mass grated and shifted slightly under me. An accident here might be the end of all my quests.

There were still pools of shadow in the valleys far below when I reached the last ridge that rose to the spine of the Divide. Along this crest nothing grew among the stones but bunches of tough brown grass, and here and there a cluster of tiny white flowers. I had passed the timberline and the way was open to the top. I strode along, drawing great lungfulls of the cool, invigorating air. In a few minutes, the fresh and brilliant day scarcely begun, I stood in a saddle between two peaks, their flanks still heavy with snow, looking westward into Idaho, and eastward toward the great plains. There was nothing between me and two mighty oceans but a curve of space.

I sat on a rock and for perhaps a half an hour gloried in this high spot. But the mind, in its insatiable desire for verification of itself, sought metaphor and exclamation to pose against the vast mystery of the world. I tried to describe to myself the appearance and the meaning of what was before me. With each effort the vigor and joy of my ascent waned a little more. I began to fidget, tapping my boot against the mountain. Thirty miles away, where the Big Hole river looped through its great basin, I saw a wink of light: the sun flashing from a metal roof or the window of a passing car, a heliograph reminding me of what swarmed between these mountains and the sea. Glancing in the other direction, I could see a line, ruler straight, along the flank of a foothill: a logging or fire road.

All at once the world shrank. This pristine wilderness was no more than fifty miles across. From its very heart one could see the track of man on the perimeter. If I suffered some mishap, I could pile green boughs on a fire, and the smoke would guide the helicopters. The animals that had seemed so wild and unafraid yesterday were living in a narrow corridor, hemmed in by humanity on all sides. Perhaps they were *used* to visitors like myself, stumbling hikers, fishermen, and amateur naturalists. They had to adapt, to buy time. The saws bit deeper every day into the forested slopes; companies were forever prospecting here for the material of industry.

Restive and preoccupied, I decided to aim for the highest peak I could see, a splinter of iron-red stone to the south. I thought I could see corridors through its girdle of snow. Up there, if anywhere, I might expect my moment of enlightenment. I moved along the saddle onto higher, more broken ground. The ridge to either side grew precipitous, and I reached a point where landslides had erased all trails. It was necessary to retrace my way, drop a few hundred yards down the slope, and work around under the cliffs.

It was one of those rare days in late summer when the wind failed and even at this altitude it grew uncomfortably warm. The pure atmosphere also telescoped distance. The peak I had chosen, after three hours of hard up and down climbing, seemed no nearer. Sometimes, when I dropped into deep notches, I lost sight of it altogether. At what I judged to be high noon, I was exhausted, drenched in sweat, and weak from lack of nourishment. But I could not rest; a grim, stubborn and stupid urgency had taken hold of me. I dug boots into the mountainside and lunged on, no longer trying to pick a natural route, but driving as directly as I could at the goal.

In mid-afternoon I leaned trembling against a sheer stone face, up to my knees in heavy, wet snow, as coarse as gravel. The rust-colored spire looming above me remained invincible: what had appeared from a distance as minor nicks and broken edges that would provide access in easy steps to the top turned out to be impassable clefts and overhangs. Without special gear for ice and rock and experienced companions, there was no way to proceed further. I had wasted the entire day: after the few minutes of rejoicing in early morning, I had known only pain and frustration. Even the animals had deserted me. Or almost. Gazing unhappily out over the tremendous panorama of mountain, foothill and plain, I caught sight of a speck almost motionless in the air between crags. An eagle. He sloped and hooked with maddening ease, near the naked stone. To traverse the same terrain I had covered in half a day, he needed only to trim his wings for a few moments and in one slashing glide he would be across the canyon.

I turned away in disgust. There was no totem here. This carrion-eater was alien, aloof, mocking. In my silly delusion I had hoped that some fierce predator--eagle, falcon, mountain lion or wolf ranging down from Canada--would appear to me as a brother, and revelation would flash from its topaz eye. But there was nothing. Only soreness, ragged breathing, and anger. The calm and delight of the previous day had dissipated like the wraiths of cloud that moved up from the west and vanished in the blue sky overhead. With a stride leaden, graceless and bone-jarring, I retreated the way I had come.

It was dusk when I reached again the alpine meadow at the foot of the rock slide. I had sweat through my shirt and levi jacket and the sleeping bag was damp, so I hung it full length from a high branch. To ward off the chill of the ground, I set about collecting bough tips from surrounding trees to make a crude mattress. Moving through the still, darkening air, I thought for the first time of bear and mountain lion. Both are found in this country, and in certain seasons can be dangerous. The peculiar silence of this small clearing, broken only by the tinkling of the spring, was all at once ominous. I hurried from tree to tree in a random way, cutting the boughs and piling them in an oblong heap at a level place. I was thinking of a yarn in a worn paperback at the ranch, a trapper's tale of a long night spent hurling flaming brands at an incensed grizzly. Tonight, vision quest or no vision quest, I would have a brisk fire.

I bent over beside a tree to pick up a handful of dry needles, balancing my armload of boughs. A gust of wind roared in the branches overhead, and as I rose and turned, from behind the tree appeared a black shape. It loomed high over my head and bulged toward me, silent, huge. The terror inside me was so sudden and so intense that I gagged. Another second or two and I might have fainted, but in the space of two thundering heart-beats I recognized the shape as that of my sleeping bag. Circling about through the trees, I had lost track of its location, and the wind had for a moment given it a threatening life.

My knees gave way and I sat down in front of the empty bag, three pounds of down fluff, and began to laugh and cry at the same time. I let the hysteria have its way, and whooped and bawled until the rocks rang around me. There was no one to hear; no one to record that the warrior-in-training had broken down. When the relief and self-ridicule at last subsided, and the silence returned, I was no longer lonely or alarmed. I now knew the benchmark of fear; I had seen for a split-second the bulk of a mighty, ravening beast, and had discovered that its power was my own creation.

Far into the night, easy on my fresh bough bed, I mused over the meaning of this shock. All the day long I had gone in circles, thought in circles. Civilization appeared to me to have surrounded this little patch of wilderness, trapping within the dying species; I had climbed to an impassable edge and grumpily descended to my starting point again; all was boundary and circumference, containing senseless struggle. I fretted over such waste--a further waste--and so spiralled down to the ultimate point of disorientation and anxiety, a dizziness of the soul. And just then, from the gloomy thicket of my own imagination, bear-spirit leaped forth and scared this living hell out of me.

In how many ways, for how many years, had I been cursed with circles within circles! Our skull is the cage. In that chamber a few inches across we can pace out a whole life. Always the same sad bowl and mat, stains and smells, the same idiot faces leering. We worry our own limbs, peck at our own livers, prove again and again Satan's adage: "I myself am hell." I had seen some of my friends driven to divorce, suicide, or nervous breakdown by nothing more than this fatal habit of doubling back, and back again, over the quirks of self, limits of being or understanding familiar for years. My quest was a lunge to shatter such patterns, as much as anything, and by great good fortune (and the effects of walking steadily for two days without food) I had learned that some part of the mind--the "unconscious" I suppose, though the word is a poor tribute to an agency of salvation--may collaborate with a trick of light and shadow or a chance warp in the predictable sequence of space and time to create a new perception, a perception shocking enough to smash the bars and release us into the power and turmoil of the imagination, terrified but free.

The lesson, hard-earned, was easy to forget. On the morning of my third day, restless energy still galvanized me and I strode and clambered some miles in the other direction, away from the red peak toward the barren domes just south of Anaconda. The giant smelter there had sifted arsenic over the land for twenty miles or more, turning it into a waste of eroded sandstone and skeleton trees. The wind had dropped again, and the southern slope of the ridges trembled in the heat. I toiled uphill and jogged down, thinking of this and that, cabbages and economic systems, failure and fame, my child, my blisters, my books, and the like. This circling, however, was idle and remote as that of a lazy bird of prey. I had at last reached a state of weariness that took the venom out of reflection. One contemplates his checkered past, his possible death, with equanimity. There is no energy for regret.

And finally even this low-level static died away. Lifting my boots and planting them gently in the dust or pine needles was a full, sensuous pleasure, without consciousness of itself. I moved over the landscape the way moss grows over a stone. When I once more reached a chasm of fractured strata that I could not pass without a long detour, I turned back without a thought, absorbing and interpreting the information with my feet. In this manner I wandered from the ridgetop and discovered a minute basin, screened all around with jackpine and stunted fir, where was a lake no more than thirty yards across. At the edge coarse marsh grass sprang from a rich, black mud, but trees had fallen into the water for years and their bone-white trunks and roots like twisted claws made inter-locking bridges by which one could walk out onto the surface.

Squatted on the back of one of these logs I stared into the motionless water, at the layer of fine, gray sediment that covered the sunken limbs and stones like a nap of velvet. Periodically the water wrinkled, and I noticed the squadrons of water-spiders skittering over the surface. Hither and thither they darted, small ovoid bodies and cocked, hair-fine legs doubled in shadow beneath them, perfect in scale. They moved so quickly they seemed invisible except for brief hesitations in discrete loca-tions, as if frames had been cut out of a movie. There were hordes of them, over the entire lake, all moving in this random, miraculous jig. The lines from the Yeats poem came to me with a new, quite different significance:

> Like a long-legged fly upon the stream
> His mind moves upon silence.

I stretched full length on the log, so I could observe them from inches away--these common and familiar companions of every mountain fishing trip I had ever taken. I saw a mosquito hover and touch, swirl and fall again, struggling on the surface. One of the spiders appeared over it, and the tiny, fluttering form all at once diminished; then the spider was gone and there was nothing but a tremor in the water, a kicking leg or two and one still, transparent winglet. Fascinated, I watched this fierce dismem-berment again and again. There were also nearly microscopic clots on the surface which the spiders took in. Larvae.

The day was waning so I rose, reluctant, delighted and amazed with my discovery. After nearly forty years of looking at these insects I finally saw and understood the simplest and most obvious aspect of their being: their peculiar beautiful movement was their way of surviving, and their predations were a benefit to every suffering fisherman or lakeside camper who must battle the dread hordes of mosquitoes in this high country. The long-legged fly was a brother to be cherished.

I returned to my viewpoint in the saddle between white pinnacles. The miles seemed to be consumed in the period of one long breath in and out, though I was moving more slowly than before. The sunlight slanted in long shafts through the tiers of cloud moving out of the west. These thunderheads were in their hour of glory: shadowed gray on the underside, they rose in great ramparts and towers, canyons and overhangs, to an edge of irridescent silver that would soon darken to bronze. Then the whole mass would go dolphin gray with a flush of fire along the top.

I sat in this last light, the shadows of small boulders pointing long, blunt fingers eastward. There was a great, peaceful emptiness without and within. I noticed a tiny plant, a succulent hugging the ground, which had produced a spark of flower, startlingly red as a serpent's tongue. I had walked within a step or two of it twice, had sat here the morning before for thirty minutes without registering its presence. Or perhaps it had only this afternoon burst into bloom. At this altitude, its flowering would be a matter of hours. Now it was burning strongly, dominating the whole tremendous range of mountain and sky.

Then a flickering at the periphery of vision interrupted all contemplation. On the slope below me, the eastern face of the saddle, bouncing lightly in the steady breeze, rode a butterfly. It was a Monarch, most common of the midsummer species. The familiar halloween colors, pumpkin and soot, were dramatic against the ochres and duns of the earth. It drifted back and forth in its characteristic graceful staggering, sinking to flutter on the face of a rock, then hopping up an invisible ladder in the air. In the slightest gust it dropped back a few feet, but gradually, inexorably, it progressed toward me, until it was dabbling all about my head. I held my breath. It reeled on, and in its nonchalant, aimless progress crossed the Continental Divide and floated out over the abyss on the western side, where the cliff dropped away sheer for several hundred feet. The wind quickened there, and it leapt away on the stream.

I let out my breath, and tears ran down my face. The vision, not as I expected it but unmistakeable all the same, had come and gone. Not by perseverance, not by the stretch of muscle and bone, and not by intensity of search, but in the dead calm of exhaustion. I laughed, too, at my high hopes for identification with the swift and the strong. My message was of quite a different sort. The message I never wanted to hear, and suppressed at every opportunity: the great barriers of self are not conquered by frontal assault, the tiger's spring; they are crossed without design, in idle, blind indirection, in happenstance, confusion, and fortuitous weather. So, I imagined, had those early hunters wandered across ten thousand miles of wilderness, crossing two continents, hunting well because they hunted without expectation, driven in desperation beyond the perimeter of their own circles, addled as butterflies.

6

The fall was a bad one. My hip is bruised, and one knee soon swells and stiffens. Probably I have separated a ligament already weakened from an old injury on the basketball court. Aniceto descended the ravine gingerly to pry me out, for I was jammed head downward between two rocks, my pack half wrenched away and binding my arms. We go on to the first convenient resting place and take a long breather. Aniceto is worried, and keeps asking if I am able to walk.

There really is no choice. It is mid afternoon, and he might not be able to go on alone and return with help before dark. We redistribute our goods to give him most of the weight, and move on again, more slowly than ever. I must place both hands on the bad knee and shove to make climbing steps. Going downhill is not so bad, and fortunately we seem to be losing altitude gradually. Aniceto thinks we are near, and in fact in a little over two hours we see the first broad leaves of a banana tree ahead.

Shanki is, however, only a grassy clearing in which are three large thatch houses and one with a sheet metal roof. A few children peek at us and a woman washes clothes in a creek. She and Aniceto exchange greetings and when he asks about lodgings, she shrugs and points down the trail. It is another kilometer or two, apparently, to a place where we can find a bed. I shoulder my pack grimly and limp onward. Within a few hundred yards the trail drops along the river, still the Satipo, but now larger and muddier from the rain.

There we find a huge mango tree. The floor of the cavern made by its hanging branches is littered with ripe and rotting fruit. A few have fallen in the mud of the riverbank and are cool to the touch. I fumble out my pocketknife and strip away the purplish-green hide. The flesh is a little fibrous, but explosive with sweet juice. Every mouthful seems to go to the marrow of my bones. While I eat two or three, Aniceto forages on the other side of the trail and returns with a shirtful of huge, pale lemons, hard, dark green limes, and some other fruit with a tough, sunflower-yellow rind. The lemons are sweet ones, bland and without any of the expected puckering acidity. The limes are an excellent dressing for mango, and the mystery fruit splits to expose large, black seeds covered by a succulent pulp with a flavor similar to passion fruit.

We stuff ourselves. Juice and bits of pulp turn my three-day old beard into a sticky mat, and my lips sting with the combination of oily nectars and sharp lime. Aniceto vanishes in search of another armload. A few moments later I glance up from the mess of pits and rinds where I am hunkered and find myself face to face with a stranger. A stocky Indian in ragged knee-length trousers and a shirt without buttons has come down the trail soundlessly on bare feet. He carries only an old pisco bottle half full of water, stoppered with a wooden plug, and a machete. He is looking at me with undisguised amazement.

We greet each other and he asks my destination. When I tell him Puerto Ocopa he looks not only dumbfounded, but apprehensive, as if he had stumbled into the presence of a dangerously deranged being. He is staring at my hands, my feet, my pack underneath the mango tree. When Aniceto comes back he feels he must give a plausible account of my existence. The film is mentioned, and the fact that I am a *norteamericano* not accustomed to the climate. Finally I get some inkling of the impression I must create. The leather hat, now heavy and drooping with moisture, the bleary spectacles, mud-caked boots, and sweaty, grizzled, bespattered face must be an apparition dire in effect. When I rise I tower over both of them, a great anthropoid in blue denim, at whose feet are the remains of a considerable sacrifice of fresh fruit.

The Indian gives some information about the trails ahead. The pass over the mountains, which we plan to take, is *muy malo*, he says, slippery and circuitous. He has himself followed the river. There are two or three treacherous passages and the machete must do its work, but it is more direct. On the other hand, with the señor to take care of... He shakes his head. We must do as we think best. After a final stare he pads away down the trail, and we shoulder our packs and go the other way.

Shortly we come to an abandoned shed. The roof appears tight, and the floor is clean but for a few heaps of cow dung and scraps of wood. We sweep the place bare, shake out our bedding, and I kindle a fire with the bits of wood. Aniceto is entranced with my aluminum cooking kit, and the little perforated teaspoon with which I make tea. The mosquito net is another marvel, and I offer to set it up for him, even though there are few mosquitos here in the high selva.

I rig a frame of twigs to serve as a rack before the fire, for nothing will dry in this humidity otherwise. We break out a can of tuna and a package of dried soup, and in a few minutes, after a change of clothes, I relax over a hot meal. Rid of the cumbersome hat and boots, stretched out on the packed, level earth, I feel myself the fortunate object of a small miracle. This frame of poles and dried fronds, livened by a small blaze, has the charmed character of those inns and huts and caves which materialize propitiously for the far travellers of children's adventure stories.

In the distance we can hear a dog bark, and the shrill cries of small children, but around us nothing is visible but the jungle, growing denser as the light empties from the sky. The air is soft and balmy, no longer a burden, and the little Groucho Marxes have toned down their jeers. I hear a bird whose exquisite call is to become familiar and beloved in the months ahead. It sounds like three or four smooth stones striking clear water at the bottom of a deep well: *Plunk-a-blub-TINK.* A little reminiscent of the meadow lark at home, though much louder and more resonant under the canopy of great trees.

Our few dishes rinsed and propped before the coals we turn to our studies. Aniceto retires proudly into the net to review his notepad full of biblical references, while I scribble in my journal. Occasionally my companion helps identify material in Spanish: the yellow fruit is *maracuya*; *mal paso*, bad spot; *limon dulce*, sweet lemon; *resbaloso*, slippery. Other notes: "Aniceto like Ford tractor," "combination of day-dreaming and irritation can make you foolhardy," "lesson I should have learned (Montana)." Then an ironic comparison of my accoutrements and those of local travelers:

Gringo Gear	*Indian gear*
sleeping bag	water bottle
mosquito net	machete
nylon cord	
matches and candle	
machete	
Swiss Army knife	
xtra pants, shirt, socks	
cooking kit	
camera, notebook	
film, pens	
dictionary & maps	
toothpaste, brush	
hairbrush, razor	
soap, towel	
poncho	
first aid kit	
raison nut mix	
tea	
sombrero	

The final entry:

"I write this by the light of a candle stuck in my tin plate--one hand to cup the flame away from a light breeze, the other to hold the pen."

*   *   *

A heavy mist swathes the mountain when we wake. Water glistens on the leaves, and drips steadily from the edge of the roof. Aniceto shakes his head. We are in for another wait. My hip has a purple bruise the size of my hand, and my knee is painfully stiff, so I am secretly pleased. Also, the clothes so carefully dried the night before are already limp again with the humidity. I make a mental note to add plastic or rubberized bags to my list of trail gear, then cancel it, remembering that I can barely carry what I have already.

Over cups of hot spice tea and hardtack we speculate on the history and destiny of men, topics of endless fascination for my companion. He adheres to the old belief that the Indians of the Americas are descendants of Israel, wandered far from their homeland. In the course of demonstrating some argument he mentions Homer, and it develops that he has read both the *Iliad* and the *Odyssey*. I have a sudden vision of him, in his cheap polyester bell bottoms and ragged sport shirt and mud-caked rubber brogans, reading the saga of Troy by the crude light of the can and wick in his thatch hut. Out of these scraps from the Bible, an old Greek poet, the novels of Ciro de Alegria, John Wayne movies and newspapers, he determinedly constructs a system of belief. I am touched, and awed, by his efforts. The work of wresting an existence from this riotous, steaming jungle is back-breaking and mind-numbing, and the printed word is impossibly dear--the thinnest paperback costs more than a day's wages-- but he perseveres, a true scholar, cherishing knowledge in the face of any adversity.

He questions me closely on my theory of the settlement of the continent. If the Asiatics migrated over the landbridge to the north, might they not have migrated previously from Jerusalem? I must grant that it is at least possible, geographically. He knows too of the belief that the Aztec and Inca owe elements of their culture to Egyptian influence. The Nazca lines are mentioned, and--as in the case of my Lima friends-- Aniceto entertains seriously the hypothesis that these were signals to alien travelers in space craft.

Later, on visits to the sites of pre-Incan civilizations, these and like speculations acquired for me greater passion and penetration. Amid the vast and labyrinthine walls of Chan Chan, or the fierce, monstrous stonework of Chavín, the imagination must race and expand to meet and grapple with powerful specters from the past. The cautious and detached opinion one finds in the works of eminent archeologists does not touch the living heart of the mystery. In the case of the theory that some of the early Americans had contact with extraterrestrial beings, or at least an extrahuman intelligence, it is not enough to seek factual proofs for or against the myth. It contains a great truth beyond the challenge of fact.

In simplest terms, this truth is embodied in man's faith--or intuition or hunch or even desire--that time may be transcended. In our Christian system, this principle was presented by Boethius as God's fourth-dimensional omnipresence: He contains all of history and can enter past, present, or future, at will. An interesting variation of this belief in God's control over time was the nineteenth-century attempt (by Edmund Gosse's father among others) to explain evolution as the Lord's recent forgery of a fossil record in order to test man's faith.

In other cultures, the yearning for transcendence is expressed in myths of the messiah and the apocalypse, in tales of adventurers who escaped the earthly cycle by means of heavenly potions, sky-ropes, or animal guides, in a belief in ancestral ghosts who trouble us with unfinished business, or await us at the end of life, where old attachments are renewed. For holy men of the East, techniques of breathing, posture and concentration can annihilate the constraints of temporality: all that has been and all that will be are equally not present. Our contemporary fantasies of time-machines or time-bending travel in and out of galaxies offer a similar, if only playful, release.

The clearest and most comprehensive formulation of this universal element in the human psyche is Mircea Eliade's discussion of sacred time, the time-out-of-time, which is at the center of religious ritual and achieves its most intense manifestation in the ceremonies of primitive peoples. In these ceremonies, Eliade believes, mortals feel they "return" to the moment of first creation, when their world was made, and participate in that primal mystery--not "again," but always for the first time. In the transubstantiation of the wafer and wine, in the act of communion, Christians know an experience like that of the Arunta of Australia, who enact the first birth of the witchety-grubs that have always sustained them. But "enact" or "participate" are words that imply a separation between agent and event, which those possessed by the experience do not know.

Our own age--that is, from the onset of the industrial revolution to the present--is unique in its reversal of the directional meaning of time. Our myth of progress or "development" teaches that time tends towards, rather than away from perfection, and that the past is mainly valuable as an emerging pattern whose ultimate configuration will work itself out in the future, shaped at least to some degree by human choice. So it is we have "planning commissions" and "development boards" and "progress reports."

Yet there is in our progressive society, with its countless new and improved products, its climbing graphs, its tremendous engines, a powerful undertow of doubt, a still vital current that draws the mind backward, toward a memory or dream or phantasm scarcely perceived, a ruined city on a mountaintop vanishing in the clouds. However tedious their descriptions may be, however dusty their glass exhibition cases, however comic or incongruous the bright tour buses and picnic debris, however costly the taxis and restaurants, the crumbling monuments of past civilizations draw a steady tide of pilgrims. They see much of the scene through viewfinders, paw dutifully through misguiding booklets, and betray a woeful ignorance of even the most elementary archeological method, but their curiosity and wonder are authentic. At times they reveal a troubled awareness of some challenge to their own code of values.

SNAPSHOT

Lima: The Museo de Antropología y Archeología. A party of middle-aged Americans, clucking and querulous, peering at the floor-to-ceiling stacks of stone and ceramic ware, the thousands of Mochica heads, each as individual and striking as a passport photo. One man lingers. He is tall, white-haired, dressed in expensive sport clothes. He gazes through the glass as if hypnotized. He is talking to himself in a stentorian whisper that conveys the rasp of many board meetings and much bourbon. "Hunnerts of years," he is saying, "hunnerts of years. Hunnerts and hunnerts and HUNNERTS of years. . . ."

Of course like the overwhelming majority of civilized people, this man will recover from his spell. At the hotel he will drown the memory of the blank stone eyes staring back at him through the dusty glass, shake off the hunch that some secret is shrouded there. He will say what we always say. "You can't turn back the clock." This slogan is perhaps the cornerstone of our culture, especially if we include as its primary corollary "Time is money." For the most part, we live at a forward, upward tilt, climbing the years toward some treasure. There are many with the same goal, so we are encouraged to hurry.

But the power of the old stones is not so easily dismissed. Even when the romantic balderdash of the tourist brochures is stripped away, we have to admit that cultures of awesome enterprise and talent have flourished before us, often in odd and unlikely places. Some have then vanished without clearly visible cause, and their spirit has been transmitted only by inferior imitations. They have left for us to ponder tremendous, ambiguous statements: the portrayal of grotesque beings performing cruel acts, the plan of graceful and opulent cities, records of precise observation and imaginative genius. The shock comes when Eliade calls our attention to an obvious point: the amazing energy, organization and dedication of these societies was directed yet further into the past, toward mythic events at the beginning of time, or toward legendary feats of god-heroes who lived on a grander scale than the celebrants. Sometimes the attitude of these "high" civilizations toward their predecessors was, like our own, ambivalent. The Incas were not anxious to preserve the rival mythologies of conquered peoples with traditions more ancient than their own, but they revered and preserved the ruins of Tiahuanaco and Chavín and Pachacamac, succumbing to the fascination of the indecipherable past.

So the board chairman from Nebraska does not see a mirror image of life as he knows it and lives it. These strange people do not face into things, do not have familiar postures of truculent aspiration, do not appear to have been caught up in the lift and drive of life as we know it. To be sure there is captured in Mochica ceramicware every aspect of daily affairs, in a startlingly realistic way: disease, pornography, domestic routine, high ceremony--it is all caught in marvelous detail and informality, like snapshots in clay. But there is nothing like our futuristic sculpture, our "artist's conceptions" of onrushing splendor, nothing like our constant yearning for the new.

The busts and statuettes in the museum are all turned the wrong way. Our observer should really look over their shoulders, as the Inca craftsman must peer around the Mochica, who in turn confronts the back of a Tiahuanaco artist whose eyes are fixed on the Chavinoid sun god, who faces away toward heaven....And what is it they are all straining to see and express more definitively, to freeze forever in their art? A vision? A vast city of light? Proof that the "ruins of time build mansions in eternity"? Nightmares from the unconscious? Or is it possible that at the edge of the last outpost, a city that is barely that, so crude are the temples and streets and gardens, men gaze nostalgically into the wilderness, troubled by memories of a time before their time, a time that was somehow perfect. That perfect condition, a memory so potent that it has touched age after age, culture after culture, galvanizing whole populations into spasms of conquest and creation--could it be the state of those shadowy creatures who came out of the north with their spears and pelts, leaving us nothing but a heap of cracked bones and char? Could these spear-throwers have come from fields of ecstasy whose shadow still haunts us, from a dimension of being that appears to us now as virgin, cold, dark and mysterious as the reaches of outer space?

7

Aniceto is looking at his watch, and grumbling. The mist may or may not have lifted slightly, but the morning is wearing on, and if we are to reach Puerto Ocopa in a day's march we must soon decide to leave, or wait out the day where we are. I am tired of confinement and feel rested enough and restless enough to move on, so we pack up our gear and strike out. During our long and wandering discussion of aboriginal migration, a latter-day descendent of those far travellers came by and gave directions for the trail to the mission. When Aniceto determines that we have found it, we begin climbing.

At least the fog screens out the sun's heat, and though vines and shrubs that invade the narrow trail drench us with their cargo of droplets, we are making better time. Then, at the top of the first range of hills, the trail brings us to an abandoned chacra. The thatch has fallen in, a frame of poles has weathered to the gray of old bone, and vigorous, coarse grass is reclaiming the clearing. A cluster of grapefruit trees, unpruned and over-grown with creepers, still produces a heavy crop. The fruit is huge, thick-rinded, brilliant yellow. On the other side of this desolate site, the trail forks twice. We explore each route, and they both peter out within fifty yards of the clearing.

We tramp back down the mountain in disgust, to a place where we can hear voices, and finally locate a house where an Indian woman listens to our complaint and plea for help with ill-disguised, malicious joy. She cackles over our mistake for a long time, and then makes up some directions of her own. We set out again, and after another half-hour, by a somewhat different route, we find ourselves again at the collapsed roof and bright globes of fruit. The mist has intensified to a fine, slow rain. I don my poncho and Aniceto wraps his two yards of fluorescent plastic about his shoulders. We stand, dripping and disheartened, and eat some of the sweet grapefruit. We can retrace our steps to the cowshed and wait out the weather, or push on in hopes of striking the right trail. Aniceto confesses he knows nothing of the lay of the land to the east of Shanki. We finally determine that we will go on, but we must have a guide.

Back at the farm at the bottom of the slope, the woman is again overcome by mirth, this time with an edge of contempt. We finally bribe her with twenty-five soles and she sends her nine year-old along to guide us for an hour, until we are securely on the trail. The boy, silent and quickfooted, leads us through a labyrinth of what appear to be game trails, ignored on our first ascents, to a wider track that leads over the brow of the hill and to the next and higher range. He indicates the direction to take, stares at us briefly, then turns homeward at a swift trot.

Angry, wet, and thoroughly depressed, we hurry as best we can along the slimy, winding track. It is already noon, and there is little hope of reaching our destination before nightfall, especially in foul weather. Aniceto says the woman has thrown into her gratuitous tirade the information that there is another, larger chacra about two hours away, but neither of us has much faith in her words. We have received wildly various estimates of the time and distance we must cover. The Indian we met yesterday beneath the mango tree intended to make the trip in a single day. He started, however, at three in the morning, travelling light over familiar territory. The loggers who gave us a lift on the Monterico road guessed four or five days, given the rain, providing we were not eaten by jaguars, and Aniceto himself ventured an estimate of two long or three short days. By my Air Force map, the crow need fly only fifty kilometers from Satipo to Puerto Ocopa, but the path of the river and the ruggedness of the terrain dictate a tortuous route, nearly twice that distance. We must gamble on finding some sort of lodging this afternoon, and hope for an earlier start tomorrow.

The trail grows steeper, exposing smooth rocks and twisted roots that must be traversed gingerly to avoid another serious fall. My knee joint is grating audibly, and though some of the stiffness has been worked out, it feels undependable. We slog onward, Aniceto waiting at intervals for me to catch up. He politely suggests that I am suffering a *choque de clima*, understandable in one who comes from a place so cold and dry as North America must be. I gratefully add this justification to my list, which now includes age, physical condition, myopia, excess baggage, and ignorance of the terrain.

In mid-afternoon we discover that the old witch at the trailhead was not deceiving us. We break into a large tract of recently cleared land, five acres or more covered with charred tree trunks. On the opposite hillside is another field with stands of corn and yucca, and at its edge a long building where woodsmoke curls and drifts. A creek winds between the two fields. We cross it by means of a huge, burned trunk and approach the house.

As is usual in the selva, there are no walls to the place. A frame of poles supports the steep roof thatch and a low platform of slender staves that serves as table, bench, and bed. From crossmembers hang pots, clothes, and sacks. We can see a woman in the shadows beneath the roof, bending over an open fire, and a ring of children around her. She has seen us approaching, and has hurried to heat food, partly out of hospitality and partly out of embarrassment, to put her work between us. She wears a highlander's full skirt, dirty and patched, and a blouse and shawl that are no more than artfully connected rags. Her greeting is warm and shy, delivered between vigorous fannings of the fire with a blackened pot lid.

The usual interchange takes place. We relate our origin and destination, our ages, and our business. I, especially, am described in detail. The simple joy with which she accepts my marvelous presence unnerves me. She is amazed (and I am suddenly guilty) at the contrast between my age and appearance; people here are often wrinkled and toothless well before forty. After the mention of my role as a maker of literature and the cinema, there is a period of respectful awe. When Aniceto mentions the trials of our journey, the *choque de clima* I have suffered, and our uncertainty about the trail to Ocopa, she begs us to pass the night.

Her husband is *macheteando* in fields nearby with a crew of Asháninka, and will be back later in the afternoon, perhaps soon if it rains as it threatens to do. The soup is nearly ready, so we excuse ourselves to wash up in the creek. Two of the children tag along and pretend to play on the bank in order to watch. They are no more than four or five years old, still with smeared faces and taut, round bellies. Just as we are finishing our ablution, the rain comes in a rapid, drumming crescendo, and we sprint back to shelter, the children shrieking and scampering ahead of us.

The lady of the house delivers to each of us in turn a steaming earthenware bowl of soup, and a huge iron spoon. It is a thin but zesty combination of yucca, corn, peppers, and bits of chicken. As we eat she chatters on, her shyness gone in a flood of enthusiasm for company, which must indeed be rare here. The children continue to observe us, alternately giggling and gaping. Whenever I smile back at them they squat or fall over. The impact of such attention leaves them breathless with fear and delight.

I am surprised to learn that this family has come from Lima less than a year ago, lured by the promises of a friend who had already secured employment as a sharecropper. The promises were quite false, she says with a shrug. Her husband gets only the standard 200 soles a day; in addition she must daily cook for her husband's friend and the crew of three Indian boys, as well as her own family. To obtain land, they must first work for three years to expand their employer's holdings. They had been told they could begin at once on their own chacra.

Still she does not regret leaving Lima. They were starving, she says matter-of-factly. Three families lived in two small rooms, and tensions began to develop. They fought over food for the children. Better to try the jungle, whatever hardships they encountered. She laughs heartily. On the first day they reached the chacra at eleven o'clock at night, after walking since dawn from Satipo. Before that there was an eighteen-hour bus ride over the Andes. She and the children were all in tears begging to go back. But they stayed and she is glad. *Hay a comer!* she states triumphantly, sagely. Aniceto nods vigorously over his soup. He too, he informed me in one of our conversations, has tried a stint in Lima. *Hay a comer!* That is the advantage of the jungle. There is always food.

I am still thinking of this tiny, ragged band--the smallest member barely three years old--marching over that formidable trail all day long and well into the night. Not only was it an act of considerable courage, but nothing drives home to me more powerfully the misery of the slums in Lima. There is a final irony to the anecdote: this family is a rare exception, and more typical are the *andinos*, who pour daily into the Parada, the foul heart of Lima, with nothing in their sacks but old clothes and a crust of bread. For them, the scraps in the gutters offer more than the cold plateaus they leave behind.

Soon after arriving in Lima I visited the television studios at the Catholic University, where a couple of young men had done a documentary film on the *invasores*, the squatters who spread in settlement after settlement over the barren lands around the city. There are nearly three million of them, well over a third of the population. The settlers dig a hole in the hard clay for sewage, throw a few boards over it, and surround this crude floor with a frame, to which grass mats are lashed. A pair of sheets of galvanized metal make a roof. Water is purchased out of tank trucks at fifteen soles a bucket, but there is no electricity or gas, no schools or hospitals or fire engines.

In the interviews recorded amid these wretched hovels, the *invasores* spoke of their pride and renewed hope, now that they possessed a home. Gaunt and careworn, surrounded by the mouths and glittering eyes of children, they nevertheless spoke vigorously, glowing with a newfound integrity and independence. *Mi casa*, they said again and again. *Mi casa.* Oh yes, a sociologist confirmed for me some months later, they are very, very happy there. To those who have had nothing, the smallest advantages can bring joy. Four walls and a shithole of one's own.

8

The men arrive at last, long-legged shadows moving swiftly through the heavy veils of rain. They are drenched and grinning, their machetes bright with water. The day's work has been mercifully interrupted; they are home early for their soup. Children squeal and hens explode out of corners where they have brooded unmolested all day. The newcomers wring out shirttails and kick the mud from between their toes. We shake hands.

The husband is tall, thin, and gap-toothed, with kind, melancholy eyes. His friend and the *patrón* of this enterprise is sharper and wears an officious little cap. The three Indian boys, all about fifteen years old, are wiry and small, with immense black eyes and protuberant white teeth. They look at us with alternate expressions of insane glee and solemn indifference. The *patrón* ostentatiously produces a cheap, battery-powered radio and suffuses the scene in a wash of static and distant music. To this refrain the soup is served. Politely, though of necessity loudly, we begin to converse, repeating the information we have already supplied to the woman. Again I am the featured attraction, and shift uncomfortably in the role. Aniceto inventories some of the treasures in my pack, and I produce the cooking kit and my Swiss Army knife, to considerable effect. The tiny folding scissors are held to be particularly *lindo*.

The discussion gravitates naturally once more to the mysteries of international economics. I tell of the fantastic prices and wages that are common in my homeland. An ordinary laborer like themselves may earn thirty and sometimes fifty dollars a day. Ten thousand soles. They are thunderstruck. I explain that on the other hand the little knife costs the equivalent of five thousand. No matter. To have and spend such sums seems the privilege of gods, and their faces are wistful and ecstatic to contemplate such a possibility.

Perú is not *desarollado*, they say, and lacks everything. A backward country. I try to explain that this is the very reason I have come, because I believe that these notions of *desarollo* and *avancado* are topsy-turvy, that a fatal haste to industrialize and produce the gimmickry of affluence may destroy the human race's last hope of recovering its dream of a natural paradise. The Incas, I remind them, fed everyone very well and maintained the roads. They try tactfully to hide their unease. It is not seemly, I finally understand, for a gringo who has flown over the mountains with a sackful of wonderful toys, a jaunty Santa, to engage in this anguished carping.

The problem, they agree, is the Generals. They take everything worth having. In Lima there are fabulous estates in the foothills, with fine horses and swimming pools and Persian carpets and color television, where the Generals live as they please, and care little enough for the sufferings of the people. But how can it change? They have the guns. The men nod in agreement. Without guns nothing can be changed. Can they be obtained? The *patrón* sighs. Very difficult. There are a few old sixteen gauge shotguns, a handful of Winchesters. Nothing to match the helicopters and machine guns with which, they mention respectfully, my government has equipped the Peruvian army.

Ten years ago, in the time of Che, there was a moment of enthusiasm. Embryonic guerrilla units had materialized in this very area, not far from Satipo. But the *búfalos* and *helicopteros* descended; there were burned huts and bodies, a microscopic Vietnam. Then the CIA and Bolivian Army finished Ché, and the spark was extinguished. In any case, revolutions often went awry, as Belaunde's had. At bottom, the problems are economic. But also, Aniceto interjects, men do not keep the commandments. A very complicated business.

The hot food and the steady battering of rain on the thatch have made me drowsy, and I am aware again of the Indian boys laughing at me. They have kept up a soft, turbulent conversation in their own language behind our talk and the roaring of the radio. Their observation of my every movement has been unflagging, intense. When I reach into my pack and produce a ball of string they erupt into excited whispers. And I do have a surprise for them.

I had learned that the Asháninka are fond of, and famed for their string tricks. My daughter and her classmates a couple of years back had gone through a craze for these stunts, so just before my departure I got her to teach me a half-dozen figures: witch's hat, Jacob's ladder, crow's feet, and the like. I thought I would be able to establish some common ground that way, perhaps impress and please the people I wanted to know.

Pretending to be idly doodling while listening to the conversation, I make a loop and begin to weave it between my hands. The boys burst into excited whispering, and when the crow's feet finally appear, they break into open hilarity. The man of the house speaks to them in a show of irritation but they pay no heed. Their faces radiate all the rapture visible in young girls when the kings of rock music push through the crowd. I do the ladder, a more complicated figure, to further claps and cries.

I proffer the string next to one of the boys, who dissolves in giggles. A second grins fixedly at a point just above my head, and hides his hands in his armpits. The third, a little older, serious and sly, picks up the string, though the effort makes him dip his head to mask a loose, embarrassed smile. For a time the string is draped limply in his hands. I indicate by gestures that I want him to do a trick, and would be delighted if he did. He demurs, and the others begin to hiss and poke at him. This urging goes on so long I turn back to the discussion in Spanish, which has moved to the prices of corn and coffee.

After a bit there is a plucking at my sleeve, and I turn to see the older boy complete a figure rather like the ladder. I utter several emphatic *buenos* in appreciation. The second trick comes easier, the brown fingers stitching swiftly and surely, a flat, webbed structure. *Cama!* One of the boys crows, and slaps the platform under us with his hand. There is a hurried discussion, and after a moment's thought the older boy, whose name is Marcos, embarks on a more extensive construction. Back and forth, in and out; then when the hands are charged with a tense net he picks out a line with his teeth and hooks it over a little finger. Finally a last loop is slipped and--the whole dissolves into a homely knot. All three are pulverized with mirth. Failure is, if anything, more joyous than achievement.

Marcos looks sheepish, and gathering himself again, repeats the motions, this time even more rapidly, his eyes empty with concentration. His hands are as unconscious and sure as spiders, and in moments the thing is done: *casa*, a rectangular cage containing within the replica of a house, its roof properly slanted. After an instant of appreciation he collapses it, and hands the string back to me.

I do two of the three figures that remain in my repertoire, both much simpler than the *casa*. No matter, they watch as intently and happily as ever. The conversation behind me has grown peevish, so I force out an apology for my inattention and pass the string back to Marcos. Yes, I have noticed that there are two kinds of corn, the large-kernelled red and a white. The former, I am instructed, is *maíz campa*, Indian corn, good only for chicken feed. The other, *blanco de sierra*, is for the table. The ears of both, I cannot help observing, are coarser and less sweet than those in my own country.

Again the plucking at my sleeve. This time Marcos does a series of rapid, dazzling tricks. The string draws into a tight knot; he claps his hands and the knot vanishes. He throws a loop over his head, pulls it to make a garotte, and in a sudden movement the string twangs through his neck, leaving him free. The others feed him words and he does the figures as soon as he hears them, without reflection. His hand is tied fast, with one corner of the loop protruding. I am ordered to pull it, and with the mazy motion of a snake the cord slips free again.

The *patrón* with the absurd little hat snaps out a command, and, rolling their eyes, the trio manages to stuff their merriment back within bounds. Now there is, however, a pact between us. Though I make a final, futile attempt to think of something to say about corn, and the *patrón* stalks over to turn up the radio as far as it will go, when a toe touches my ankle I give up and turn to find that Marcos has made a much larger hoop of string, and is creating giant pictures involving his hands, toes, and teeth. Some of them are animated. I watch in fascination as a huge butterfly strokes his wings. A saw goes through a log. The tail of a bird spreads. A monkey climbs a treetrunk.

All at once I too am unable to restrain shoulder-shaking laughter, and the three faces opposite me arrange themselves like refracting and intensifying mirrors. They are peering at me, and into me, in a way that is unsettling and exhilarating in its intensity. All at once one of them emits a sound that is between a cackle and a great whoop. I will recognize this cry many times in weeks ahead. It is a feature of life in Asháninka villages as constant as the sepulchral croaking of the treefrogs at night, or the call of the beautiful, invisible bird that I named the water-in-the-well bird. It occurs wherever people gather to share a bowl of masato or sit in the shade to converse, and it will make me conscious of my own laughter, and that of my countrymen--the near silent hissing between bared teeth, the catching of one's breath as if air were thin, the sound that sometimes recalls the sob, or strangulation.

At dinner that evening Marcos offers to go with us to Puerto Ocopa on the morrow. He attends classes there when they are in session, so he has travelled the trail many times. Aniceto and I are greatly relieved, as we have supplies enough for only one more day, and would not like to blunder about in this region without food. We have contributed our last can of tuna to this meal. It is clearly a luxury item, and the woman reverently and carefully divides it so that each of us has his morsel.

There is an exciting moment midway through the meal. We are seated around a rough-hewn table in the light of the kerosene lamps when one of the Asháninka boys shouts *"Culebra!"* Everyone except me erupts from the table. I sit still holding my spoon, peering into the night, where nothing is to be seen. One of the soupbowls is upended, and drips onto the packed earth floor. The Indians have seized their machetes and I watch them doing a wild dance in the flickering shadows from the lamp, hacking at the ground and shouting. I get up at last and walk out to observe at first hand. They are grouped around something at their feet, whispering excitedly. I see a serpent's tail, perhaps a foot long, writhing on the ground. It was a big one, they tell me, but it slipped away in the darkness after this one lucky blow.

But Aniceto has told me the culebra is not venemous. So why bother them? I ask. They find this point of view hilarious. *Most* of the culebras are not deadly, they correct me. At night it is better to kill them all. I grant the logic of this approach. Also I wonder how the children must feel, if these great vipers glide at the very edge of their living room. It appears now that they return quite happily to their soup.

The rain has stopped and the overcast has broken into swift racks of low cloud shuttling before the moon. It is not yet nine o'clock by Aniceto's faithful watch, but here the day is done. The master of the house throws a heap of musty coffee sacks on the floor beside the fire coals, and indicates that this is the guest bed, a choice location especially for me. Everyone gathers to watch me unroll the sleeping bag. They are plunged once more into that lively and open amazement that strikes me as child-like, perhaps because in my own land a sense of wonder is held almost unbecoming in an adult. A whole bed, they say to one another, complete, and out of that little sack! They insist that I demonstrate its use. Somewhat self-consciously, an actor on this very tiny and remote stage, I remove my boots and shirt, stuff them under the hood of the bag, and zip myself into the downy cocoon. The children become spastic with delight, and the adults coo in admiration.

The friend of the family takes his radio and hangs it reverently from a crossbeam directly over my head. He turns up the volume as far as it will go, with a deferential nod and smile. Another honor, I understand, has been conferred on me. I am forgiven for the string tricks. For a few moments I look up, from flat on my back, at a ring of contented, joyful faces. Then the woman tactfully withdraws her reluctant children, and the friend herds the Indian boys up a ladder into a sleeping loft. Everyone else retires to a blanket on a wooden platform.

When I wake periodically during the night, the scene is eerie. The moon, nearly full, sails high through banks of dark and glowing cloud. The jungle is an intricate pattern of pearly light and stark shadow, with tiny shimmering diamonds of moisture clinging to the broad leaves. Fireflies drift here and there like dying sparks. And the station in Pucallpa, blathering and pumping out its raucous music, fades and swells according to sudden, mysterious warps in the atmosphere. The radio sounds often as if it were underwater. Occasionally, querulous, a bird tries to answer.

There is an obscure poignancy here: the dark hulks of my new friends, stilled in sleep, their precious batteries dying through the night to produce for me this strange incantation; the huge and silent growth surrounding all of us; somewhere in a nearby thicket a serpent tailless and suffering. It occurs to me that there is no way to ever film such a moment and arrest it, and abruptly there flashes into mind the image of the photographer in the plaza at La Merced, his legs set well apart like those of his tripod, his bearing courtly, face impassive under the shade of his hatbrim. I can make no sense of the beauty of this moon-drenched night and this fragment of memory, so I hunch back into my bag and let the radio, like a cararact, drive me into sleep.

9

The morning breaks cool and overcast but without rain. For the first time we have decent weather in which to travel. We breakfast together on baked yucca, the root simply thrown on the coals, and spice tea I have brought from California. The men leave for the fields while we make up our packs. Marcos, I note, carries only a little flour sack with a bit of cord for a sling. He has put in it a change of clothes and a few pieces of the yucca wrapped in banana leaf. I press two hundred-sol notes into the woman's palm, and she accepts them with shy graciousness. The children are as enthralled by our departure as they were upon our arrival, and stare us out of the clearing.

We move much more quickly and surely with Marcos in front. After the first few rest stops, he takes from me my small camera bag and the machete. The trails, I realize, are made for light-boned people not over five and a half feet in height, for he moves along them without pause, at a glide that reminds me now of a snake, now of the low clouds that steal swiftly through the trees at the ridge tops. Even Aniceto appears clumsy and slow now, and I see his bent back and driving feet as better suited, as my own pace is, to steep, barren country.

Marcos has told us that he will take us on a slightly longer but easier route that will bring us near his brother-in-law's chacra. There is not a single trail to Ocopa, as I have been led to believe. The Asháninka know many, in various conditions. Some are good for rainy weather, some for dry, some for hunting along the way. At one point in mid-morning he pauses by a trickle of water that winds through a benchland. The trees are very large here, and the undergrowth somewhat less dense. It is a hunting place, he announces, and points to the clay of the stream bank, where tracks of deer and pig are visible. Then he draws our attention to a spot just off the trail. When I look closely, a tiny domed hut materializes out of the tangle of vines and ferns. Made of palm fronds draped over saplings bent into a frame, it resembles a wickiup. There is a small window, perhaps six inches in diameter, facing the trail, and an entrance just wide enough to crawl through at the back.

The hunter sits in this *chosita* to wait, Marcos explains. When the animals come they are led to a certain spot by means of cleverly arranged branches and vines on the opposite bank. He indicates these fences, and I am amazed at their ingenuity. A few bark fibres, at most, are used to hold up tough vines or tie together low branches; and these, in conjunction with fallen logs or thorny bushes that constitute natural barriers, lead the animal insensibly to a place visible from the window. The angle is such that as the quarry bends to drink, it exposes the front shoulder and flank that are the bowman's target.

Marcos tells us that "many people" live nearby, but we have not seen sign of them, nor heard dogs and children. As far as I can determine, we are already in the heart of wilderness more desolate than any I have heretofore known, though Marcos seems to feel himself merely on a walk through a familiar suburb. Perhaps two or three kilometers further, when we have climbed from the benchland to a long, high ridge, he stops, and when we have come puffing to his side, tells us that we will drop down the other side to his *cuñado*'s place. There, he says solemnly, we will visit only for a short time. When we move on he goes slowly so as not to outdistance us, and after a few moments utters a low call, a single, mournful note like a quail's. After listening for a moment he continues, and in a few strides we reach a small clearing.

The earth here has been swept absolutely bare, and three small thatchhouses are positioned around a central fire. From their beams hang woven baskets and bottle gourds, and I see a bow and bundle of arrows stuck under a rafter. A woman and two small children squat near the fire. The woman's long hair, black as obsidian, hangs down her straight back. The roomy cushma, a simple brown sack of a garment with holes for head and arms, covers her body entirely except for her bare feet, flat and broad on the earth. Although she has surely seen us, she faces away, peeling yucca with a machete on the woven mat before her.

In the gloom of one of the houses, an arm lifts and a head rises from a pile of bedding. After a brief stare, a young man steps from the platform into the light and shakes himself. He and Marcos greet each other with a nod and a word. He regards us. Though only a little taller than Marcos, he is heavier through the shoulders, spare but well muscled under his ragged shirt and trousers. He wears his hair cropped short in the Asháninka fashion. The eyes are alert and unsmiling.

Aniceto and I greet him and extend our hands. After an instant of hesitation he reaches to take them. He does not squeeze and pump; the fingers are dead in my grasp. Perhaps he is not accustomed to the gesture. Marcos indicates that we are to sit in the smallest of the houses, which seems without any furnishing, though it perches on the edge of a slope and commands an impressive view of the mountains ranged to the east. There is fog far below us, lying in dense white banks between peaks, and the air is noticeably cooler. We must be well above three thousand feet now.

When we are seated to face this prospect, the man calls to the woman at the fire. She rises and moves to a wooden trough, shaped like a miniature canoe. Removing two or three banana leaves that serve as its cover, she begins to dip a reddish-purple liquid into bowls made from gourds. I have prepared myself for this moment, my first draught of masato. The drink is brewed from steamed and mashed yucca, with a bit of *camote*, a dark red sweet potato, for flavor and color. A share of the fibrous yucca is carefully chewed by the women of the household and the pulp is then spat into the wooden trough. Water is added, and bacteria from the saliva act to ferment the mixture overnight, yielding a strong, rich beer.

I am unprepared, however, for the beauty of the young woman. Civilized writers of the last century, including some who lived among the Asháninka, circulated notions of filth, smells, and disease, of blackened teeth and protuberant bellies. The woman who comes to us over the level earth, libation-bearer, is as graceful and delicate as a young deer. Her motion in the long, full cushma recalls to me the phrase in Herrick's poem, "the liquefaction of her clothes." The face, perfectly still with downcast eyes, is fine-boned and elegant. Her color is dusky, if the term's connotation of twilight softness and dark roses can be resurrected. Around her smooth, lean throat is a necklace of amber jaguar teeth, some of them as long as my middle finger.

We thank her for the bowls and drink. I am conscious that Marcos and his *cuñado* are watching us closely. The liquid is cool, with a sharp sweet-sour flavor. I find it refreshing, and my sigh and spoken praise are genuine. We try to exchange a few pleasantries with the *cuñado*, and though he is attentive, he does not respond. Marcos tells us that he does not know much Spanish. They talk in their own tongue for a time, and Aniceto and I sit quietly, sipping the masato. I look at the woman again, as she fusses about the fire tending a child, and catching Marcos' attention I point at her and then at my neck. Where did the teeth come from, I ask, smiling.

The man shifts his posture only slightly, but in that instant I know I have done something wrong. His eyes are wide, boring into mine, and though he does not crouch or lift his arms, I sense an invisible tension, quick as a drawn bow. He got them himself, Marcos says quietly. *Lindo, muy lindo*, I say with a nod to the man. Tell him they are *muy lindo*. But Marcos says nothing. He looks away. I look away too, careful to turn from the woman. When I glance again at the man, the ferocity has evaporated. He waits, alert but impassive, as before. He is waiting for us to leave, I realize, so we drain our bowls, thank him, and after a last, lifeless handshake, make our way out the the clearing and down the slope.

Across the deep canyon is another high ridge, its top combed by the clouds. We must cross there, Marcos indicates, to another lower range, and beyond that the Pangoa flows to its juncture with the Perene. He estimates that it is thirty kilometers to the mission at Puerto Ocopa, and we can do it "easily" by this afternoon. If his calculation is correct, we have made no more than fifty kilometers in the previous two days of travel. Here the trail is better, Marcos assures us, although for the last half of the journey there will be no water to drink.

At first, to the bottom of the canyon and across the creek there, we make good time, but the climb up the steep ridge to the clouds is arduous. Once again I am far in the rear, and periodically lose my footing and skid to my knees. Marcos says nothing, but I can sense his boredom and impatience. He varies the routine by padding on ahead and waiting for us on a convenient log or moss-sheathed rock. We proceed in this fashion for hours, crossing the greater and lesser ridges, then following a gradual descent through a forest of huge widely spaced trees where the undergrowth thins out a little. This is the dry region, and perhaps this knowledge whets my thirst. Although we drank deeply at what Marcos said was the last spring on our way, the cloud cover has burned off and the sweat is steaming from my shoulders again.

Finally we reach gently rolling terrain, where the brush is again thick, and I expect to glimpse the river at any moment. For better than an hour we do not stop to rest. At each query Marcos replies "*cerca, cerca.*" For a stretch of two hundred yards or so we take a side trail that he clears with the machete. Here the air is close and motionless, the heat intolerable. Where our short-cut rejoins the main trail there is a clearing in which stands the ruin of an old chimney of stone. I can go no further, and collapse at its base. Marcos, who has bounded ahead and out of sight already, returns at Aniceto's call.

They crouch over me. "We are near, Señor Weel," Aniceto says hopefully. I remind him that Marcos has told us that we have been "near" for the past two hours. I am exhausted, suffocated by the heat, and, finally furious at the continual failure of these people's predictions and reckonings. I take perverse pleasure in the dismay I see in their faces when I slip off my pack. I am taking a rest, I announce, a good long one. Perhaps half an hour. Perhaps I shall spend the night here. They squat in silence for a few minutes. Marcos looks glum.

"There are oranges," he says finally. "Lots of oranges, very near."

"Very near?" I hope the tone of scathing irony comes through my Spanish.

"Very, very near. *Cinco minutos, no más.*"

"Oranges?"

"Lots."

Aniceto looks at me pleadingly. The vision of oranges, once engendered, will not be suppressed. I sigh heavily and reach for the pack.

10

It is true. Minutes later we arrive at the edge of a large orchard and stand under an immense, lone mango tree. Before us are row after row of oranges, several varieties, some as big as grapefruit, others small and brilliant of hue. For a fleeting moment I hesitate, wondering about the local notions of trespass, but Marcos and Aniceto are already scooping the ripe fruit from low branches, and I join in.

Nothing has ever tasted so good. I find a few mango that have fallen intact in soft grass, and take alternate bites of their smoth, sweet, slightly oily flesh and the tangy, explosive citrus. I look at Aniceto and we burst into laughter. We are a study in smears and rivulets and bits of pulp. The fresh, sweet juices sluicing down the throat prompt us to gasps and sighs of ecstasy. At first we merely split the oranges and mash their contents into our mouths; later we separate the segments and savor them. It seems a miracle that in the midst of this jungle, full of strange, bitter and dangerous pods and berries (for I have asked Marcos as we encountered them, and invariably they were forbidden), someone has prepared this Edenic grove, where nourishment and refreshment come to hand without effort.

I ask Marcos whose orchards they are. These are the oranges of Padre Castillo, he says. They belong then to the Mission? *Sí*, he replies. The Mission, Padre Castillo. They are clearly the same in his mind. All at once I recall Aniceto's warning about the militant fathers, and grow a little uneasy. The orchard appears deserted, and no buildings are to be glimpsed nearby, but I feel vulnerable, sprawled on the grass with peelings and mango stones strewn everywhere about. It is also late in the afternoon, and I would like to clean up before arriving at the Mission, especially if our introduction there is a touchy matter. Marcos tells us the river is only a few steps away, and the main buildings no more than another half a kilometer.

The Pangoa is twice the size of the Satipo, and the rains have made it unruly. In a shallow eddy bordered by a beach of pebbles and fine sand we strip and bathe quickly. The water is surprisingly cold. I change my shirt, though the one from my pack is nearly as damp and wrinkled as the other I have worn for three days. There is not time to shave. I clean my glasses, square my leather hat, and with a hitch of the trousers and a John Wayne here-goes glance at Aniceto, I walk the last of the ninety kilometers to my destination.

The principal structures are the church and the refectory, both simple rectangles of brick, with high, arched windows and galvanized iron roofing. These are supplemented by one huge pole-and-thatch building, a dormitory for the students, and several lesser ones, well-spaced, that serve as classrooms and storage areas. Mown Bermuda grass, hedges, plots of roses and hibiscus, coconut palms and bougainvillaea adorn the grounds. The place seems almost deserted. Across a soccer field where a handful of half-naked boys are toying with a ball, there is a small village of huts, where smoke from open fires threads into the air and vanishes. As it is January, Marcos has told us, most of the children are home for the seasonal vacation. Classes do not begin again until April.

Marcos meets another boy on the path, asks him something, and then motions us to follow him around the church. The window shutters are open, and I see the spacious, whitewashed interior, plain wooden benches, a few rudimentary murals of the Madonna and Infant Jesus lined with a bit of gilt. Behind the church there is a nook shaded by a riotous purple bougainvillaea, where a covered cistern of rough stone forms a low circular platform. A man seated there considers a chunk of porcelain on his lap, and a float bulb and flush handle mechanism beside him indicate that he is repairing a commode. He wears faded trousers rolled to the knees, a shirt without buttons, and a large straw hat whose brim has unravelled.

When we approach the hat tilts up to reveal a pair of thick spectacles in frames of heavy black plastic, and behind them a ruggedly handsome face. He gets swiftly to his feet and removes the hat. I see that his luxuriant gray hair has been shaved at the crown. He is apparently a lay brother of some sort, clearly a highlander and unusually tall for a Peruvian, taller than I am. He shakes our hands cordially. I relate quickly our purpose; I mention Weiss, my hope to make a film and write a book, our intention of finding transport to Otíka. He nods and using the straw hat like a broom, ushers us down a pathway to a covered courtyard.

He calls a few words through an open door and then leads us to a sparely furnished dining room. A fruit jar full of roses rests on a long table covered with a white cloth. A shelf bears a lamp, a portrait of the crucifix, and a pair of candles. When we are seated he departs, and a few moments later an embarrassed Indian girl enters with a tray of coffee and bread. I lift an eyebrow and Aniceto shrugs. The coffee, a black and powerful brew, and the wheat bread are a welcome change from the tea and hardtack we have had for days. We have devoured half when the tall, bespectacled man enters again and takes a seat at the head of the table. The girl follows, this time with plates of boiled yucca and steamed fish.

We must eat in haste, the man says apologetically, for a boat is leaving downriver within the hour, and he has arranged for our passage on it. He would like to be more gracious, and learn of our plans at length, but these opportunities must be seized when they appear, for there is no dependable transportation on the river. With a shock, I understand that this man is indeed Padre Castillo, the head of the mission. He gestures at the plates of food. Eat, he urges, eat quickly.

Between mouthfuls Aniceto and I manage to explain that we are out of supplies and need to procure more. The Mission has a small provision store, Padre Castillo reassures us. He will have it open for us when we finish. He eats and talks furiously, giving a brief history of the Mission, which he has headed for twenty-one years, inquiring discreetly into my origin and background and the state of my homeland, digressing into speculations about the Manson case, Hollywood, and the cops-and-robbers politics of the Nixon period. Toward the end of the meal I relax enough to make a few rejoinders, and somehow we find ourselves deep in a discussion of Dostoevsky.

Then Castillo springs to his feet. We really must go, the light is failing. With an admonition to enjoy our coffee nonetheless, he bounds out the door and we hear his progress through the courtyard as a series of fading orders. I glance sardonically at Aniceto, who is examining the rim of his coffee cup with great care. "No guns," I say. He grins sheepishly and shrugs.

"Still, Señor Weel . . ."

"How could it be?"

"How can he be fifty-one years old? It is not natural. He looks younger than you. The Indians must do all the work."

"He works. He was fixing the toilet."

"Still . . ."

We hear Padre Castillo returning, so we rise hurriedly and move to meet him at the doorway. *"Adelante!"* he cries. "This way, to the store."

In one of the board and thatch buildings behind the refectory there is a room divided by a rough wooden counter. A plump, somewhat severe nun in a white, winged cap is selling a bar of soap and a few jellybeans to an Indian girl. A couple of men in oily clothes, somewhat nefarious in appearance, lounge about. Behind the Sister I can see canned goods, sacks of rice and beans, candles, soap, batteries, rope, a few cheap articles of clothing. Castillo speaks rapidly to the two men. As well as I can follow their exchange, these river rats, known as *regatones*, have the boat that will carry us downstream, but they claim not to have sufficient gasoline for the trip. Castillo offers a certain number of gallons from his own barrels. The men shrug and roll their eyes. There is quick calculation of miles, currents, engine efficiency. The men shift uncomfortably. Castillo is alternately imperious and wheedling. Finally the older of the two men, who has no teeth but many cunning wrinkles, nods.

Castillo turns to us. "Buy your things, quickly, before he changes his mind. They are leaving right now. The Sister will help you. I will be back to bid you farewell."

"Wait," I call. "The gasoline. How much--"

"No matter. Don't preoccupy yourself."

In a few long, athletic strides he is gone, the ragged straw hat vanishing in the twilight among the buildings. The two old pirates who will be our skippers fall to wrangling with the good Sister over the price of a quart of oil. They pay reluctantly, bill by bill, trying to renegotiate with each installment. Then it is our turn, and we buy cans of tuna, a kilo of rice, a kilo of beans, more candles, salt, sugar, and some caramels for gifts to the Indian children. When these items are stowed in our packs, we thank the Sister, who is already closing off her smile with the shutter over the entrance to the little warehouse.

Padre Castillo intercepts us in the courtyard. He heads a small brigade of Indian boys, who are to act as our guides to the boatdock. We thank him as warmly as we can, given that he is already shooing us away through the roses of the yard, toward the airfield. In a sudden access of conscience, I mingle with my gratitude for the gasoline a confession of our secret gluttony in his orchard. He tips his head back, gives a great gust of laughter, and claps me on the shoulder. The oranges are there, he says, precisely for that purpose, to provide refreshment for the people of the selva, among whom, apparently, I may now count myself. He commands one of the boys to gather a shirtful of oranges from one of the trees on the grounds, so that we may have them on our journey.

Then he is gone again, and the boys, whispering and giggling, wrench our packs from our hands and set off rapidly in the darkness. We follow them across the airstrip and through a banana grove to the river. A moon shimmers on its surface, which appears smooth, but we can hear the silken hiss of swift water. The boys swarm aboard the canoe and Jaime, the toothless pirate, gives gruff instructions for the stowing of our packs among the heaps of goods already amidships. There are two shadows hunched over the motor in the stern, arguing in Asháninka, while a small group observes the scene from the bank. One of them carries a storm lantern, and its pool of yellow light reveals small children with huge, intent eyes peering like lemurs through the legs of their elders.

Aniceto and I are directed to seats between the motor and the cargo, where clearly we are out of the way. Two teenage lads handle the sweep, and Jaime and the other old one crouch in the prow. The craft is very long, very narrow, hewn from a single log with an added sideboard to draw another six inches. There is just room enough for passengers and cargo, and the gunwales are not more than four inches from the water. After a dozen or more trials the *motoristes* manage to start the engine and keep it running, so we cast off and move swiftly with the current, away from the bank, to a chorus of soft calls from the people clustered about the lantern.

The motor is a nine-horse Briggs and Stratton, a tried and true workhorse, ugly, squat and dependable. The propeller shaft is very long, and extends at a slant into the water, because it also serves as the rudder. A steering handle of reinforcing bar steel is used to swivel the engine and the shaft as a unit, a method of control that seems cumbersome, though it does do away with all gears, pulleys, or levers. Once the first catches and coughs are ironed out, the motor reaches a rhythmic stutter and we surge steadily and evenly ahead. The people call this form of transport the peki-peki, an apt onomatopoetic term.

Now the two pilots in the bow are standing up, gesticulating and shouting directions to the boy on the sweep. I gather we are avoiding rapids, half-submerged logs, or sandbars, but the arm-waving and pointing seem confused and even contradictory to me. The banks have receded to distant shadows, and the river reaches vast around us, its surface in a slow boil. Sometimes, ahead of the canoe, the water seems to bulge; at other points a vortex appears, a migrating black hole at the bottom of a dish-like depression. Occasionally I hear the slap and dash of rapids and see to one side white plumes of foam, but we glide effortlessly, rising gracefully on the bulges and skimming over the whirlpools.

We pass the mouth of the Pangoa, and less than an hour further intercept the Ene, where the watercourse becomes the Tambo River. Up to this point, the streams are represented on my map by single lines which would normally be reserved for creeks. Even the Perene and Pangoa, however, are larger than any of the mighty rivers of my home state of Idaho--the Salmon or Snake--and their confluence produces a stream at least as great as the Columbia or upper Missouri. Yet we are still a thousand kilometers, and many more tributaries as large or larger, from the Amazon.

It is easy to see why men travelled this country primarily on the rivers. The balmy wind, the columns of moonlight breaking and reforming on the water, the simple delight of swift, unencumbered movement would be enough to justify the trip, but there is the added benefit of being able to transport heavy loads with little effort. Donald Lathrap, who has written much about the watersheds of the region and their populace, concudes that the history of human migration on this continent--at least from East to West and vice versa--is merely the pursuit of and struggle for the rich plant and animal life that occurs on bank and delta. The remains of early man are concentrated along the waterways, and tribe after tribe has displaced earlier arrivals only to be themselves pushed out by war canoes bearing newcomers.

The rivers of this tremendous basin thus form an arterial system for the body of the continent. They connect the great vertebral ridge to the interior plain and delta. Pottery, cotton, flint, gold and feathers travelled far on these waterways, as trade and booty. People circulated too, as voyagers, war parties, slaves. For--again like the blood system--these branching streams may transmit the pestilence of invasion. When the first waves of *colonos* moved down the Urubamba, Chanchamayo and Perene, the people of the Amuesha, Conibo, Piro, Machiguenga and Asháninka tribes retreated as from an advancing virulence, fighting as they went. The first three of these populations have almost disappeared, victims of the usual triad of war, plague and "cultural assimilation." Only the Asháninka and Machiguenga, who knew not only the rivers but the rugged interior of the Pajonal as well, have survived in some strength.

For how long? I remember the last letter from Professor Weiss, received only a few days ago in Lima. The professor mentioned rather curtly the death of two of his most beloved informants--one drowned in this very river--and the vanishing of many traditions. His brusqueness of tone was, I guessed, a way of handling grief. A phrase from the letter was etched in my mind: *a culture in an advanced state of collapse.* Again the irony of direction and purpose: the advance of collapse, the progress of disintegration, the evolution of destruction. Is there not implied in these twisted metaphors a shadow of a possibility of going backward to whole-ness, of a regression to health?

The river is bearing me to the scene of this collapse. It would bear me further, if I let it, to the raw and booming jungle port of Pucallpa; to the fever of Iquitos, with its ornate, faded elegance now overlain by an oil rush; to Manaus whose grand plaza and Opera House made it the most "advanced" city of the continent during the rubber trade; finally to the Atlantic Ocean and thence to the capitols of Europe. But this stream touches all these places only to leave them, and it makes many motions at once. Gnawing at one bank it may reveal the bones and shards of a distant past, doing excavations for the archeologist far beyond the scope of the most generous grants. At the same time other sites vanish under the silent mantle of tons of silt. In flood stage it sweeps all before it, mindless, obliterating. The rest of the year it is a causeway for a brisk trade in kerosene, cheap fabric, and steel blades. Through its net of tributaries it fosters the vast canopy of the jungle, that hides and protects the survivors of many rare species of animals and men, preserving them like a living memory, a germ or seed that could flourish again as a green antiquity, a throwback.

Professor Weiss did his original work on the Tambo in 1960-64, and published seven years later a "monograph" in the Museum of Natural History's anthropological papers. A mighty compilation of the Asháninka myths of cosmology, it was at once exhausting and exhilarating to read. I will begin to understand, a few days later, the reasons for its fanatic comprehensiveness, for Bodley's similar zeal, for a peculiar attitude of grim thoroughness and concealed pain that I have sensed before in anthropologists, without realizing its source or explanation. The Weiss monograph presents the river as a primary aspect of the Asháninka world view. The people describe their world as bounded by "river's beginning" and "river's end," and they have not, until recently, concerned themselves with what might lie beyond those frontiers. Like the river through their land, things appear, are, and then are not.

These notions are of course familiar to us in Heraclitus, in Taoist thought, in the common expressions of "the river of time" or the "stream of events." But at this moment, moving past occasional red points of fire on the bank, a sign of small settlements, I am acutely conscious of the fact that I will soon appear out of the river for these people. My history, motives, and plans will become manifest--a prospect that suddenly daunts me. I will be an apparition who claims to wish to capture their lives on pages or in a little black box, so that they may be transmitted beyond the river, for the delight and instruction of strangers.

The whole expedition suddenly transforms itself in my mind into an act of sinister piracy. I am aware that concealed beneath my grant application there were motives of personal aggrandizement. With luck this book and movie could make for me a reputation as a daring documentarist, a foundation for further travels and adventures. Now it is not the slave raid the native must fear; now we spurn their persons and rob only their images, which may be conveniently transported to distant lands, where civilized people, comfortably seated, enjoy a touch of nostalgia, a brief and idle dream of another more "natural" life. My notion that the Asháninka may teach us something, reveal to us the value of their way, seems shallow and presumptuous, and I sense, as I did when I gazed on the beauty of the young woman who brought me drink the day before, that my motives are as murky, treacherous, and driven as the dark waters surging around me.

11

After an hour or two on the Tambo, we curve into the bank and the boatmen begin unloading a few things. Here, we are told, we will stop for the night at the house of Vicente, the second of the old pilots. Jaime departs in the canoe without further explanation, as soon as we have taken out our packs. With the noise of the peki-peki receding in the night, we climb a steep sand bank to a hut where a low fire burns. There the boatman's wife serves us a bowl of masato and a portion of soup. Two men have come from nearby houses to eat and talk, and one of the engine boys is with us.

Fortunately they are conversing in Spanish, so I am able to learn that our voyage on the river is not as easy and casual a matter as I first assumed. The bulges and black holes in the water have claimed lives and property before. With considerable mirth, the old man relates an anecdote about two German women who arrived a year ago with a great deal of camera gear. Another pilot of his acquaintance offered to take them downriver, and in the very stretch we have just traversed the canoe capsized and sent their bags to the bottom. They lost the cameras and lenses, money, passports, and clothes. The young men are ecstatic with hilarity at this reminiscence. Though I suspect that some of this banter is undertaken mostly for its effect on Aniceto and me, I make a silent vow to lash our packs to the gunwale henceforth.

Fatigue has overtaken me, and the conversation has shifted to the idioma, as the Indian tongue is called here, so I ask for directions to a bed. Aniceto and I are bunked together on a narrow slat platform, so narrow that when one of us turns over the other is obliged to follow suit. For the past three nights I have lodged in such odd places that even this hardship does not succeed in keeping me awake, and I am very soon in some twilight state that is not really sleep, but at least a restful approximation.

The next morning is spent in renegotiating passage downriver. Once beyond the frontier of the Padre's authority, the boatmen claim that they have not enough gas to proceed. We pull in at another village where a man owns a peki-peki, and for 2000 soles he agrees to lend it to his son-in-law to carry us to Otíka. The closing of this bargain is hastened by my tossing in four Lomotil tablets, as the canoe owner claims to suffer from a digestive disorder. Aniceto believes that one of his wives is birthing a child, and as the Asháninka practice the *couvade*, the illness the man professes may be more symbolic than real. He appears grateful for the medicine--somewhat indiscriminately so--and I suspect that the Lomotil may be given for any complaint that happens along: malaria, snakebite, tuberculosis or ringworm.

The contrast between the canoe's owner and his son-in-law, our new pilot, is striking. The older man wears a fine cushma of hand-woven cotton, white with broad black and orange stripes, and his cheeks are covered with tattoo lines, like cat whiskers. Samuel, the son-in-law, receives us in a house that has been modified from the standard by the addition of walls and a couple of cheap wooden chairs. He is clad in polyester slacks and sport shirt, and displays a huge gold-plated wrist watch with an audible tick. Immediately after greeting us and offering the chairs, he starts up a plastic, battery-powered cassette player, and we are treated to a loud Protestant hymn in Spanish. Samuel summons his wife, and together they stand proudly beside the machine, smiling, while the mournful music of sin and redemption in blood rises around us, at an uneven speed.

When this ritual has been repeated three or four times, and we have been served the customary bowl of masato, he changes quickly into tattered shorts and blouse and we set off for the canoe. A boy of perhaps sixteen accompanies us, to man the bow. They take no gear of their own, except for an extra can of gasoline, for they say they will be able to drop us in Otíka and return home before nightfall.

The sun has hammered the river into a burning plate. We slide along it near mid-stream, the brilliant labyrinth of green to either side, blue mountains and rolling white clouds beyond. A swallow with a blue-black hood and snowy underbelly skims the surface of the river, rolling and swooping like a stunt plane. Before long we enter a low canyon. The vertical walls of rotting white limestone are festooned with creepers, shrubs and trees whose roots clutch crevices where a little groundwater seeps. Huge formations of a darker stone protrude into the river, which has scooped and channeled them like swiss cheese.

Imperceptibly the stream has grown swifter. There are no rapids, but I can now see what was mercifully obscured the night before: the dread *remolinos*, the whirlpools. These vortexes occur in certain places where, because of some bend in the river's course, or the sudden inrush of a major tributary, or an obstruction on the bottom, a confluence of strong contrary currents persists. At the outer circumference the brown water gyrates slowly, like a frothy syrup. Then it drives more swiftly near the center, either forming a sudden black hole or dashing in upon itself to make an ugly chop or a hump like the emerging back of some great, brown beast.

The tearing force of water in these places is apparent in the uncertain wobble and bob of the canoe when we skate across the outer edges. I recall again Weiss's cryptic mention of his old friend's drowning in this river, and finger the parachute cord that now lashes my pack to the gunwale of the canoe. Samuel moves up to squat beside me, leaving the youth in charge of the tiller. He points to a notch in the distant mountains, calls my attention to the long silver thread of a waterfall that drops from the clouds about the mountain's brow to disappear into the forest at its base. A beautiful place, he says. There are many ghosts there.

Have we noticed the *mal pasos* here in the river, he asks, grinning. Indeed we have. You understand, señor, that if the motor fails in such a place, it is *muy malo?* He begins to laugh aloud. I assure him that I understand. *No hay salvación*, he shouts gleefully. *No hay salvación!* He searches our faces for signs of comprehension. I find myself smiling and nodding. *Entiendo!* We would be lost, utterly lost. The stutter of the Briggs and Stratton now seems a frail racket behind us, and the wavelets that dash on my hand, gripping the sideboard, have the cold sting of vipers' tongues. Samuel gives a final, sardonic whoop and springs lightly along the rocking canoe to the engine. He cranks it up a notch, and settles back to smile and signal at me with his eyebrows.

Shortly after midday we arrive in Otíka. The village is perched on a low bank, perhaps twenty feet above the river, which is broad and shallow at this point. A few women and small children in brown cushmas appear on the bank where we are unloading our packs. They watch impassively as we bid farewell to Samuel and the crewman, who only nod and cast off summarily for their return voyage.

We march up the bank at the first house, which is a large empty structure apparently used for storage. The platform is strewn with coffee sacks, empty plastic bottles, and rusted machine parts. A hen amid the rubble departs with a huffy outburst. On the other side of this building is a broad clearing somewhat overgrown with tough grass but quite level. Apparently it is the landing strip, for on its opposite border, housed in a long, open-ended shelter, is the battered fuselage of a small plane, the paint still bright and new. Around the airfield, nested among sprays of broad banana leaves and clusters of balsa and papaya trees, there are roof peaks and from a few of these rise pale, evaporating ghosts of wood-smoke. Small, brown forms appear then at the edge of the field and begin to filter across it. We drop our packs on the platform of the storage building, and soon are surrounded by a ring of children. Their forearms and ankles extend like birdbones from a capacious cushma that flaps when they run. Their heads seem larger than usual, and their features, framed in jetblack hair in a bowl-cut, are extraordinary: all white teeth and lustrous black eyes, radiating mad joy. They are like tiny suns; it is hard to look at them for very long. They whisper and giggle when we mop our brows, open a pack to secure a comb, scratch ourselves.

Then a party of adults arrives, one of whom extends his hand and greets us in good idiomatic Spanish. He is a handsome man, despite the lack of four upper teeth, with uncharacteristic wavy hair and a small beard. It is Matías, whom Weiss advised us to contact for help with our project. He tells me Gerardo, as Weiss is known in the Tambo country, has notified them that I might arrive, and has discussed the film project with them. Matías says they want to help, and we agree to discuss the whole business soon. I mention that Weiss has offered the use of his tent, which I see is still set up on a platform beneath a hut across the airstrip, so we are escorted there. I glance inside and note that things are quite as the Professor and his wife left them: bottles and spray cans of medicines and insect repellents are grouped between air mattresses; a couple of books and a few cans of foodstuffs as well. I unzip the mosquito net flap and raise one corner of a mattress, and a terrified mouse bolts out.

This tour of our quarters completed, we return to the large storage shed where we disembarked. A few other men have gathered. There is Martín, whom Weiss mentioned as the official president of the village. He is squat, powerfully built, with a wide, impenetrable smile. Two young men, silent and watchful, hang in the background, and an old fellow, his cushma ragged and dark with grease, leans on one of the houseposes, working a hard knot of coca leaves in his cheek, which bears the cat-whisker tattoo lines. They ask me immediately why I have come here. The question is without malice, but unsettling in its directness.

The prepared little speech, the invocation of book and film, sounds hollow and stumbling in my ears. Aniceto adds deferential touches, an encouraging echo, and occasionally a discourse of his own. We stress that a primary purpose is to find traditional Asháninka tales, those they are especially fond of, and shape our accounts around them. As if, I say in what I think is a flash of insight, they wished to tell the outside world the stories which best represented them.

This lengthy offering is received in silence. What, then, I ask, are some likely stories? Matías shrugs. The old man has paused in his methodical coca-chewing; his eyes are half-closed. We know no stories, says Martín, and looks away. But, I remonstrate, my friend Weiss has collected dozens and dozens of them in this area. That was ten years ago, Matías says, and many of those tale-tellers were old then and are gone now. We do not know those stories. It occurs to me that perhaps they expect *me* to provide some mysterious import to things, to bring to them a new meaning for their lives.

What of the story of the god who holds up the world or the one about the woman changed to stone, an outcropping still to be seen on the river, I go on desperately. Martín smiles a little. I have heard them, he says, but I cannot tell them. The story of the man who rode a raft into heaven, I persist, and became the cluster of stars, the Pléiades. It is supposed to be very common, known to all. Yes, Martín nods. There is that one. Briefly, he and Matías relate it.

PORÍNKARI

Porínkari became weary of his life. He drank much *ayahuasca*, for three days, and gave the visionary drink to his wives and children as well. They all sat upon a large *balsa* and sang and played the flutes together. So they rose, and voyaged into the sky where they may be seen now. They are happy there, and have no duties or cares.

They add the corollary tale of Porínkari's brother, who followed him to heaven and lodged there as the three bright stars we know as Orion's belt. Then there is another addendum: still more disgruntled Asháninka tried to ascend a rope let down by the first voyager, but these were bad men and the rope was cast loose. They fell back to earth and were transformed into the different animals. This sky-rope I recognize not only from other versions in Weiss's book, but also from Hopi mythology, in which a spider-being provides a web for a similar ascent. Is this an especially important story? Matías shrugs again. Not especially.

In those old days a man grew weary of his life. How is it now, what are the people's cares? Again silence, and downcast looks. I repeat the question: the key word is *preocupaciónes*--worries, concerns, cares, problems. Finally Martín turns his fixed smile on me. We have none, he says. No *preocupaciónes*. But that is impossible, I expostulate. Everyone has them. All people. Martín's smile does not alter. We have none, he repeats firmly. The two young men laugh and nod.

I return to the matter of the stories. It is most necessary for us to record the matters important to the Asháninka. They live in a way different from that of my people, a way that may teach us something. In these days many of us have the feeling that we should know something, but we don't know what it is. The Asháninka have lived in the selva for a long time, and have therefore a special knowledge and a unique life. For that we have come.

It is twilight now, and more difficult to see faces in the deep shadow under the roof. The old man pushes away from the pole, weaving slightly, and belches. The sky is a clear vault, bordered on the horizon with a rank of leaden clouds, a violet glow at their edge. From the river comes a hoarse whispering. The men shift uneasily. My last words, crude flattery in a language I barely know, have made them quiet and evasive. At last Martín speaks, low and swiftly, but I hear him. *No somos como antes.*

12

These Chunchos, or 'Campas,' are evidently the remnant of a very barbarous and low caste race of untameable savages, recognising no laws, and killing each other with as little compunction as we kill our rodents.

--Arthur Sinclair, *In Tropical Lands* (1895)

We are not as we were. The statement is delivered with averted eyes, a head bowed in shame or dogged defensiveness. In subsequent conversations I am told how much better it is now, better to live in peace on the river, better not to be fearful of raids by the pajonal Asháninka, who once killed the men and spirited off the women. Matías even claims that it will be still better when his people are completely civilized, and possess the mechanical saws and music-makers that we whites so casually take for granted. Those who have adopted Christianity likewise hasten to assert its merits over former beliefs in demons and witches.

Still, the regret of that simple statement is sincere and profound. These people are embarrassed that they cannot (or will not) summon for me a recollection of their original nature. Perhaps they grieve over its diminishment, yearn for its renewal, are puzzled and disturbed by those like myself who come to them seeking the remnants of an abandoned culture and bearing, as barter for these scraps, the overpowering new magic of machines. And I am in turn troubled by my mission as corrupter and preserver.

This huge, simple-minded paradox will grow more insistent in subsequent weeks. What I never perceived at the time, what now supplies some comfort if no solution, is that the Asháninka live at the heart of this paradox too. I believe it is now the central, inescapable condition of human life, along the Amazon as in the suburbs of Los Angeles. No specific intellectual act is required to bridge a gap between the primal peoples and industrial civilization, to bring these cultures into meaningful relation; they are already rushing into each other with a speed and momentum beyond control. Everywhere on the planet human communities are uneasily aware of this acceleration, of the fascination of new machines and the threat they pose to old ways of life.

Of course there is a difference of perspective. The ethnographer and folklorist have tempered the onslaught of colonist and missionary, who aimed to convert the Indian to a cash-for-labor economy and supplant his old superstitions with a new faith. The modern invaders encourage the primitive to maintain his traditions; they strive to protect him like a hothouse plant, so as to provide authentic material for study. For the social scientist is now aware of his need for difference, for the "other" as an aid to comprehending his own systems and even as a vital supplement to them. He suspects that the data are more than information, more than structure; are in fact living substance, glowing and consuming itself like a bed of coals. This realization brings agonizing qualms, for the researcher knows that he fans this blaze, hastens the transformation to ash (his books). He carries with him flashlights, beads and steel knives to trade the future for the past.

As this past recedes, vanishes, it becomes more precious. The civilized man feels a nameless nostalgia, a temptation to romanticize, eulogize, daydream, mourn; also a haunting suspicion that this barter of kitchenware for sacred stories involves incalculable, irredeemable loss. The myth of Pishtako reveals a metaphorical truth. Our own substance is aflame with the ravening appetite for oil. And what is oil but the ancient jungle? With it we fuel our quest for knowledge of the living land and people, who in their turn are encouraged to become not only the object but a functioning element of that search, so that the Indian and his whole green world are being transformed by and into the energy of quest, discovery, invention, development, civilization, and finally, closing the circle, the commemorative documentation of what this process destroys.

The Indians, for their part, both detest and desire this outcome. They revel in machines with a fierce ardor, aware of their magical dimension in a way we seldom are. We would react similarly if a shaman demonstrated to us conclusively that he could send his soul flying far away to spy on distant happenings, or could change himself into a jaguar. A young man in the Tambo region will travel several hundred kilometers and work for months as a woodcutter in order to obtain a small, cheap radio that will break in a year or two. The radio is a medicine object of great power. Often no one listens, for no one in the household understands Spanish. The wash of static drowns almost all sense anyway. The sound serves only as a ritual drum or prayer wheel, to evoke or placate or entreat a distant and unknown spirit world.

In their mournful moods, the Indians recite to us a weary and sentimental litany: the *colonos* are taking our land; once we were a free people; they will cut all the trees and dam up the rivers; we have enough to eat and good water, but the young people will not stay; in the towns they make fun of Indians; *we are not as we were*. Of course it is all true, and incidents of armed resistance are recent enough to make the older people conscious of their current hopelessness and softness. Their pride suffers obscurely, even as they delight in buying a handful of sweets at a market stall in Satipo, or in gazing voraciously at the plastic goods in the stores. They know that they once walked there as lord and master, and fought the Spaniard to a standstill for three centuries.

The Americas have always presented disturbing ambiguities. Columbus believed he had discovered the Garden of Eden, and the Spaniards found their wildest dreams of golden cities surpassed in reality, but the early chroniclers also recorded their fear of the vast wilderness into which many an expedition vanished without a trace, and of the strange, bloodthirsty people who made a home there.

The Indians, similarly, wavered between viewing the whiteskins as gods who came to save and regenerate them and as demons who would exterminate them. There was evidence for both theories. In the confrontation of European and aborigine it appeared at first as if the Indian suffered by far the greater shock. In a generation whole tribes disappeared; in two or three, most of those that remained lost their religion, language and custom. Except for a few hundred thousand souls precariously existing in the rarest, most remote corners of the world, there are no sovereign Indian cultures left. Everywhere the tide of western, scientific, industrial society is running at the flood, and the turn was centuries ago.

The impact of Indians on the European mind has been less visible, has operated primarily on the imagination, but for that very reason may outlast such ultimately perishable things as iron, alcohol and germs. The ghost of the Redman has not drifted away, but continues to haunt our literature, our popular mythologies, our dreams; he still inspires a few visionaries, malcontents, poets, and revolutionaries, and retains a powerful hold on children--all through the universal appeal of that sentiment Martín implies in one sentence: *we are not as we were.*

How has this simple, wistful notion survived? And how could it weigh significantly against those awesome dogmas that have inspired our dominant civilization? Dogmas like *The sky's the limit, Ever Onward, The future is ours, Bootstraps,* and *Annual Growth Rate?* To answer these questions, we must review the story of how this small, nagging nostalgia was revived, how the Redman's ghost migrated across the Atlantic, buoyed by the exaggerations of early explorers, to whisper his charm through periwigs and lace and find at last a prophet, in the very bosom of progress.

*   *   *

One very hot day in 1749, an impecunious and unknown Swiss music teacher trudges through the suburbs of Paris. He is on his way to pay a visit to his friend Diderot, the brilliant and eccentric editor of the *Dictionnaire Encyclopédique.* Diderot is, momentarily, in jail. The royal authorities have put him there because they detect, in his compendium of new knowledge, a powerful and dangerous undercurrent. The Encyclopedia's trenchant definitions harbor, implicitly, an assumption that has inspired most subsequent libertarian movements: human reason, not divine revelation, determines truth--determines it as a matter of fact and measurement--and the search for such truth produces an infinite progress.

By "progress" the keen men of the Enlightenment at first intend only the eradication of poverty, ignorance and disease; but grander dreams ensue, dreams of equality, dreams of what we would call a "free and creative lifestyle" for everyone. The abolition, in short, of caste, privilege, and degree. The shrewdest minds of Church and State spot the Encyclopedia for exactly what it is: the striking of a match. The fuse, three decades long, terminates in the cannons of revolution.

Our dawdling music teacher, however, has no inkling of these momentous consequences. He has his own problems. Though he has made himself useful as an editorial assistant in the project, he nurtures secret reservations about the marvels of this new learning. Jean Jacques Rousseau is, by nature, given to inordinate introspection, to alternate bouts of self-pitying despair and arrogance. His life's work--an idiosyncratic theory of musical notation--appears to be a matter of indifference to the scientific community. Approaching middle age, he is still ensnared in a liaison with a plump, provincial matron who bears him unwanted children and supports a household of predatory relatives. Above all, he is burdened with the ignominy of having to beg his bread from patrons who are his intellectual inferiors.

Far from feeling himself poised on the threshold of a new age of boundless plenty, Rousseau has reason to suspect that his civilization promises a lot more than it delivers. No one could doubt the splendor of the French court, the power of its armies, the cunning of its clocks and cabinets, the wit and elegance of its arts. But one could not be blind either to the dismal lot of the peasantry, to the scandals of bribery and wife-peddling among the nobles, to the hypocrisy of a clergy in gold trim.

Perhaps to take his mind away from such gloomy contrasts, Rousseau fumbles out of a pocket a new edition of the *Mercure de France* to read as he walks. His eye is drawn to an advertisement by the distinguished Academy at Dijon. They are spnsoring an essay contest, open to all. The topic: *Has the restoration of the Arts and Sciences had a purifying effect on morals?*

What happened to Rousseau when his mind registered the opportunity presented by the advertisement is best described in his own words:

> If ever anything resembled a sudden inspiration, it was the disturbance that occured in me when I read that notice: all of a sudden I felt my mind dazzled by a thousand illuminations, hordes of vivid ideas

materialized at once with a power and confusion that threw me into an incalculable disruption; I was seized by a dizzyness like intoxication. A violent heart flutter struck me, swelling my breast; no longer able to breathe as I walked, I fell beneath one of the roadside trees, and spent there a half-hour in such agitation that in arising I saw the whole front of my waistcoat wet with my tears, without having realized that I shed them.

Rousseau never recovered from this particular bolt from his unconscious. Articulated finally as a *Discourse On the Moral Effects of the Arts and Sciences*, it indeed won the Dijon prize, launching Jean Jacques on his stormy career as an international celebrity. Fame brought him, among other things, dyspepsia and paranoia, a confirmation of his own insights. The chief of these insights, that for which Rousseau is most remembered, is quite simply that civilization, as we know it, corrupts us from a state of "natural" goodness. The more we learn, the worse we are.

The idea is not new, as devout Bible readers are quick to assert, but Rousseau's argument is secular, even political. Springing as it does from the context of scientific and technological revolution, his message has special resonance for our own time. Rousseau is the grandaddy of hippies, the first modern oracle of such doctrines as simpler is better, cities are earth-cancers, Indians have the answer, the rich go bad, and so on. His success as a philosopher--and in his century that title carried the kind of clout that high-energy physicist does today--in the very community he was castigating, evokes a familiar irony. I think of Rousseau when I see an earnest face in a newspaper photograph, or on a flickering screen, making a plea to the public for the greening or dieting of our little planet, the preservation of the environment or ecosystem or biomass, or when an advertisement on a plastic bottle promises that the contents will revert to a harmless or even useful breed of molecules in a short time, or when I race in my petrol-powered vehicle toward the high, clean air of the mountains.

In Rousseau's day the paradox took the form of the elegant *bois* at Versailles, tailored by skilled horticulturists and landscape gardeners to look exactly *like* a wild, bosky dell. There the court ladies could dress as shepherdesses and poke prettily at some freshly laundered and beribboned lambs, brought in for the occasion. We used to laugh at that scene in graduate school, and then pack up our books for a weekend at Yosemite, where the deer nibbled candybars from our hands.

Rousseau and many of his contemporaries knew this pastoralism was phony. The truly natural man, they also knew, was to be found in the New World. There, deep in the Florida swamps and dense forests of Canada, lived a simple but heroic race that remained uncorrupted by the artifice of civilization. For two centuries after the "discovery" of Columbus, voyagers spun one glowing account after another of these amazing aborigines. They were alleged to know nothing of murder, adultery, or treason; they disdained gold, using it as mere kitchenware; they spent their lives roaming free in Nature's bosom, laughing, dancing, singing; they talked to animals; they were swift as deer, strong as panthers, keen-eyed as eagles. One analogy occurred over and over to these fabulators: the American Indian enjoyed something of the condition of unfallen man in the Garden of Eden.

There were of course those who sought to qualify this beautific vision: the Spaniards told ghastly tales of Huizipochtli's blood-spattered altars, of the Caribs, headhunters and cannibals; a close reading of early chronicles revealed that the Atahuallpa Inca surpassed his fellow Sun King in France for rigidity, authoritarianism and pomp; and trappers reported warfare of unprecedented brutality among the Huron and Mohawk. But this sort of information was not popular at the zenith of discovery and conquest. What the sophisticated urbanite of the eighteenth century wanted to hear was the story of Paradise, and the "explorer" with his eye on the market wrote accordingly, adding dashes of sadism and gore only for piquancy.

We are again indebted to Mircea Eliade for the ultimate ironic twist in this chain of misinformation, fable and paradox. He has sifted through the mythologies of aboriginal tribes from every corner of the globe, and has documented that these "simple" folk posit their own primeval paradise, and perform their most sacred rituals in order to restore, temporarily, a condition of perfection which existed "at the beginning of things." In other words, "the 'good savage' of the travellers and theorists of the sixteenth to the eighteenth centuries already knew the Myth of the Good Savage." No less than Rousseau, moping over the filth and depravity of his society and dreaming of a purer, more primal America, the Indian himself believed he existed in a world degenerated from the beauty and virtue of an earlier time.

For the early settlers of the New World, of course, there were some very rude shocks. Fruit did not fall unbidden to the hand; every seed sown did not bring forth bounty; the forest did not yield to the sway of rhetoric. The journals and hortatory works of residents, as opposed to tourists, often took on quite a spiteful and gloomy tone in describing the marvels of America. William Bradford, debarking from the Mayflower, shuddered to contemplate a "hideous and desolate wilderness." After a hundred years of toil with axe and plow, Cotton Mather could still spook the seaboard colonies with tales of "Droves of Devils" and "Fiery flying serpents" lurking in the trackless interior forests of the continent. And the same Indians who appeared to cultivated Europeans as a chosen people (they held them to be the Lost Tribes of Israel), were savages, brutes and devils to the settlers, who feared them above all other dangers in their new homeland.

For the first two centuries of the white man's penetration of North America, these two myths--the romantic notion of a Garden of Eden and the sinister vision of a hostile wilderness--existed side by side. For the believers in Paradise, America promised escape, regeneration, a trans-cendence of the iniquities of an older civilization; for those who viewed the new land as an enemy, there was challenge, an opportunity for the conquest of the unknown, the alien, the evil. And even those who feared the wilderness were lured by its mystery. Something--possibly super-human--called them in great droves from the ordered life of city and village.

Eliade's postulate of some deep, archetypal memory of a Golden Age, a "holy time" of harmony with nature, can explain both these powerful visions, which still exist--though radically transformed--in contemporary life. For the romantic purists, nature untouched is most sublime, closest to that distant original; for the conquerors, the wilderness must be altered by hard labor to become a paradise of plenty. The struggle goes on still, pitting the radical environmentalist against farmer, fisherman and logger, but now there is another element in the equation: technology.

Like the conquistadors of previous centuries, the settlers of North America thought of themselves as bringing not only faith but the light of knowledge. As they proceeded systematically to exterminate or drive off the natives, it was convenient to develop further the doctrine of the rightness of shaping nature with tools--Rousseau's arts and sciences. In his inaugural address of 1830, Andrew Jackson demanded "What good man would prefer a country covered with forests and ranged by a few thousand savages to our extensive Republic, studded with cities, towns, and prosperous farms, embellished with all the improvements which art can devise or industry execute?"

We can note in passing the automatic opposition of "good man" and "savage," but the important emphasis here is upon the principle of progress through the ingenuity of industry. If there is a primary theme in American thought for most of the Republic's history, this is it. We prosper by digging, cutting, smelting, and putting together; nature is a raw material, which human reason and imagination can turn into the useful and the beautiful. It is too outworn a story to recapitulate in detail--the hurling of two thin rails across the continent, the springing up of great cities with their roaring factories, the magic of human voices shot through wires, then the human image recomposed in light--what we must con-front is that Jackson's position is still essentially our position, as a matter of fact if not of faith.

Rousseau had a tremendous vogue as a thinker, as a conversation piece in the salons of Europe, but he did not turn his century around. The Captains of Industry prevailed, and still prevail. For two centuries the intense and dangerous political controversy in the world has not been over the value of technology, but over its control and the distribution of its benefits. The *encyclopédistes'* belief in the primacy of science and the perfectibility of the world through reason has spread everywhere, and in continent after continent the bearers of this doctrine have displaced earlier civilizations, destroying or transforming them into crude copies of industrial states.

By the middle of the twentieth century, the desolation and horror of the primal wilderness had largely evaporated as well. Nature could still prove intractable (floods, earthquakes, volcanos, and new strains of virus presented a challenge from time to time) but she was familiar: a middle-aged, somewhat befuddled dowager whose vast wealth was at man's disposal. He felt empowered to administer her affairs, and apart from occasional, perverse benders, she seemed to acquiesce. It was even claimed that man had an obligation to use her resources, alter her features to improve them, replumb and rewire her system, breed her for special hybrids and changelings.

This notion of the manipulation and transformation of nature is deeply ingrained in the American mind. Consider the implications of a full-page ad in the *Atlantic Monthly*, sponsored by something called the American Forest Institute. "Modern forestry," we are first told, "has found new ways to make Mother Nature more productive." What are these ways?

> Superior seedlings that will grow stronger, faster, are being raised by the millions in special tree nurseries run by companies like Weyerhauser, Georgia-Pacific, Simpson and Pope & Talbot. When they are two years old, these hearty seedlings are hand planted in a newly harvested area, giving the new forest a five-year head start over natural regeneration.
>
> As the trees grow, they're protected from insects, fire, and other natural enemies. Slow growers and competing brush are thinned out to give the best trees room to grow. And helicopters are brought in to deliver the extra nutrients that will give the young forests an added burst of growth.

The message is dramatized in a large central photograph of cross sections from two trees, showing Mother Nature a poor second to the "forest product" managed by man. Her work is small and discolored. His is big and uniform. The conclusion is self-evident: "The result is a better quality forest, often more than twice as productive as the generations before it."

Our technology has here only extended to the conifers of the Northwest the same advantages given earlier to many other animals and plants. Cattle are fatter, stupider and more manageable than buffalo; corn, squash, and potatoes (developed by the good savages) are juicier and larger than wild seeds. So the nursery-bred, chemically purified and nourished fir tree is "better quality" than its stunted and deformed ancestors.

An American billionaire, said by *Time* magazine to be the richest American alive, has launched a project to clear nearly 6000 square miles of jungle in Brazil--an area larger than Connecticut. He wishes to plant a forest of fast-growing trees from Burma to be harvested for pulp. There is no suggestion anywhere in the article that this new crop is anything but a legitimate and admirable extension of man's authority over the wilderness. In fact, the project's directors announce that their reforestation is "revitalizing the rain forest's mineral-deficient soil," a direct and simple extension of the Jacksonian frontier philosophy.

The commitment to this principle of man's stewardship of all nature seems to hold universal sway. It connects the advanced technological states and the "emerging" or "developing" nations. In Perú the word *desarollo*-development--occurs in headline after headline announcing government policy, grants from foreign nations, hopes for the future. In less articulate form the attitude occurs in native villages, where small planes and peki-pekis bring exciting goods, tangible promise, and the first of the endless stream of colonists, bureaucrats and sight-seers.

Still, the pursuit of progress has not been as ardent and unqualified as the newspapers make it appear. There are odd stumblings, backward glances, moments of doubt, contradictions. A taxi driver in Lima discoursed to me at great length on the value of the selva to his country. Such a huge, rich, virgin, uninhabited place--it would provide such material for *desarollo*! Wood, minerals, perhaps even oil! Not exactly uninhabited, I remonstrated. *Nativos* live there. A good life. He looked at me suddenly, this poor man in a dirty and decrepit vehicle, laboring for bare subsistence in this hot, crowded, criminal city. Ah, he said, it is not like life here, is it Señor? It is beautiful there, no? They say it is beautiful? I nodded, ashamed. I had seen it, and he, in his whole life, probably would not. We drove on in silence, the ghost of Rousseau in the back seat, sobbing in ecstatic nostalgia.

13

I never learned to like the dogs of the jungle. In Otíka they were even smaller, mangier and more cowed than in Satipo. They seemed to have no function beyond yapping at nocturnal predators. Monkeys, toucans, parrots, and a large and bold turkey-like bird with a white head were more common pets. All these animals, as well as less agreeable ones like snakes, vampire bats, and even jaguars, roam at liberty and may visit any household. Three weeks before our arrival, in a dwelling on the outskirts of the village, a woman was attacked by a jaguar. She did not die, Matías said. Her foot was badly mauled and she was dragged a few yards before her husband's shouts distracted the cat.

In the face of such hazards, Otíka has made an effort to concentrate and organize itself. "Streets" have been formed by hacking a straight path perhaps three meters wide through the undergrowth, parallel or perpendicular to the airstrip. But the older system of randomly dispersed homes connected by winding footpaths persists, and the village simply diffuses deeper into the jungle, the last "residents" living as much as five or even ten kilometers away.

The population is now around thirty families, large by local standards, and Otíka has a school and a soccer team as well as the grass airfield. There is a plan for a medical post in the near future, to serve several villages, for tuberculosis and malaria are rife in the area. These diseases, according to a pair of medical authorities from Pucallpa, occur mostly as a consequence of the concentration of population. In the interior of the Pajonal, the usual settlement is a group of no more than half a dozen families, and maladies do not spread and recur. So ironically enough the medical post, spoken of proudly by Matías and Martín as a mark of advancing civilization, is no more than a necessary corrective for the suffering that this "progress" entails.

Perhaps there is a further irony, or an element of hypocrisy, in my enjoyment of Weiss's quarters. We bivouac at last in relative comfort. The tent is equipped with screened vents at front and rear, and is large enough to permit us to recline on air mattresses with our books, papers and pens beside us. We build a fire near the entrance to boil our rice and make tea, and with an additional candle inside, we have plenty of light and no insects. Some twenty yards away our predecessor has rigged a folding stool over a latrine in a tiny clearing, the whole screened by bushes and vines, so daily eliminations will be free of the usual scratches, stings, and sand.

I wake rather late on the first morning, after a deep and untroubled slumber. Aniceto has already fanned up the coals and a pot of water steams ready for the spice tea. Mist clings to the mountain slopes and hangs in banks over the river, but high in the east the clouds are dazzling white, disintegrating before the sun. On the far side of the river, where dawn lingers in the dim light under the canopy of trees, some variety of parrot screeches as if in outrage, and across the green airstrip I can see figures moving in Martín's compound, and hear occasional voices, even a modest whoop of laughter. Though I have not learned the routine of the village, I can already sense a quiescence, almost lassitude, in the movements I can see. Eventually I realize that midmorning is actually mid-day for the Asháninka; the fishermen and hunters are already home with their quarry or their stories of failure, and the women have come back from the fields with their baskets of yucca or bananas. After a meal and perhaps a nap, the time of drinking and visiting will begin, and by nightfall some will be asleep, and others well into revelry.

After our breakfast of hardtack, conserves and tea, Matías appears, a little deferential and hesitant. He would like us to visit his home and converse further. We put away our cups, and I slip a Bic cigarette lighter into my pocket for a gift at the opportune moment. The path leads along the airstrip, past the thatch shed where the battered fuselage of the Cessna is housed. An unexpected gust of wind caught it, Matías tells us, and flipped it over on the third bounce of a landing. A child was cut on the head, but not seriously.

It is an *Alas de Esperanza* airplane, not SASA, and another like it is laid up in Satipo for repairs. Otherwise I would have been able to fly in rather cheaply. Alas, as everybody calls the organization, is a Canadian-based philanthropic agency which flies into remote jungle areas at cost or less, freighting coffee bags, sick Indians, or adventurers. It is much revered by the local people, who otherwise are confined to river transport.

When we arrive the family is finishing a meal. A gang of children and Matías's wife, Hermania, squat at the fire digging steamed yucca and plaintains from a large aluminum pot. The two teen-age boys, Heraldo and Alejandro, dress western fashion, though without shoes or buttons on their shirts. The two small boys, Zacarías and Antonio, eight and ten years old, wear ragged cushmas, as does their sister Heorihéna, an ethereally beautiful girl of thirteen. Hermania unloads the youngest boy, a two year-old, from her hip and stands to greet us. She is a small, pretty woman with an anxious look.

Matías directs us with a magisterial touch to the two metal folding chairs under his roof. There is also a small matching table with a formica top. It is several visits before I realize that these are among his most prized possessions, a mark of prosperity and advancement. The house is a large one, with an extensive overhead loft. The furnishings are a mad mixture of woven baskets, cheap suitcases, bows and cane arrows, a derelict sewing machine, various wrenches, pieces of pipe, cast-off cushmas, bunches of feathers and clumps of fur, plastic buckets, gnawed bones, banana skins, empty cartridge casings, old books and magazines mottled with mold, stray chickens, and eviscerated tin cans. Near the table a black box stands atop an abandoned crate; it is connected to two storage batteries frosted with corrosion, and a long wire runs from it to a tall, bare pole. The radio, Matías says with modest pride, catching my look, but it is not operating just this moment.

Hermania returns from the yard, where the canoe of masato and gourd bowls are kept on sturdy shelves shaded with palm fronds. Masato, it appears, is taken at any time of the day or night. Aniceto and I sip politely; and slowly, circumspectly, the conversation develops. We begin by talking about Weiss, or Gerardo as he is known here, and I am embarrassed to confess that I have never seen the good professor. Matías does not seem surprised, but proceeds to tell me of his friend.

Weiss first entered the region in 1961, and spent more than three years among the Asháninka in the ensuing decade. He speaks the idioma fluently, Matías says, and knows many, many stories from his travels up and down the river. Once, Matías adds in awe, Gerardo brought his own motor for the canoe, and ranged far indeed, finally losing the engine and many of his belongings in a rough stretch on a tributary. He is a very good man; everyone up and down the river knows him; it is hoped he will return in September. Much of his camp equipment has been left here. He has also given fine gifts.

Matías produces from beneath a heap of dirty clothes a transistorized portable cassette player. Immediately the children are around us, chattering and giggling in anticipation. Heraldo, the oldest boy, covers his eagerness with an expression of lofty nonchalance. He receives the machine from his father's hand and snaps an order to one of his younger brothers, who flies like a squirrel monkey to rummage for a handful of flashlight batteries. Heraldo is obviously the manager of this machine, and, once the batteries are installed, twiddles its controls skillfully.

The first cassette we hear, from a jumble hidden under rags, consists of songs in idioma, with interspersed commentary from Weiss. It is strange to find at the end of the melodies, some sweet and mournful and some raucous, translations in a measured, scholarly voice in English. A maiden sings, we are told, a song of love "of the blighted variety." Then there are pieces played on the panpipes, tootlings and breathy honks, and finally an eerie, high, skittering music, like nothing I have heard before. This, says Weiss, is the mouthbow, an instrument peculiar to the Asháninka. It is very moving and I ask for particulars. From Matías's description I can gather only that it is a stringed device played in the mouth. I imagine a kind of jew's harp.

After this concert, which has come to be an obligatory welcoming ceremony in the selva, we discuss our project again. I am unsettled when Matías tells his wife that we are to make a *película* so that the whole world will know the Asháninka. I hasten to qualify that assertion, and make clear that our intent is to record their way of life and present that information to people in the outside world, both in written and photographed form. We will not, however, reach everyone. I mention also that I wish to learn certain matters that the advanced nations have forgotten. Matías appears nonplussed and a little disappointed, and again I know a twinge of doubt and guilt about my role here.

Occasionally, in a flash of detachment, I see the two of us as too ludicrous to command the respect of even the most untutored. Aniceto, in his mud-spattered bell-bottomed trousers and rubber shoes, long hair under the little billed cap, is quite unmistakeably an ordinary happy-go-lucky campesino. Graying and grizzled, with my ponderous leather hat, spectacles, and little field pack, I am far from convincing as a representative of the mysterious agencies of literature and cinema. I feel that the little Pentax, compact and definite, with its neat rings and tiny numbers, carries all by itself whatever authority we possess. Aniceto treats it with great reverence, and when I set the camera aside, the children will stare at it for minutes on end, as if expecting it to fly away.

At some point, while I am describing the theaters in our great cities, and how many kinds and levels of films there are, Matías mentions that he has seen some of them, many years ago. I am taken aback, and ask him how this came about. He says that when he was seventeen he left his homeland and made his way to Lima. There he signed on board a freighter and worked as a seaman for a voyage or two; he visited the ports of Seattle, Tacoma and San Diego. He is pleased at my surprise, and I see behind his happy, toothless smile a reason for the difference I have already detected in his presence, a touch of vacant, unfounded melancholy, a look now and then of sad understanding, as if we possessed a mysterious kinship.

He has walked on the streets of stone, seen the hurrying vehicles and the mighty buildings, entered one of the dark palaces where the huge, life-like shadows stride across a blank white wall. In that time it must have been Humphrey Bogart, Randolph Scott, Myrna Loy, Rita Hayworth, or Abbott and Costello. I am too amazed even to laugh. My rough, loud, horrific homeland is known to him, at least as a distant memory. Here he sits now, in his grass hut, surrounded by the debris of cultural collision, ready to act as guide and instructor to one who comes from that roaring, stinking, alien world. And he does not mock or despair or temporize, though he, of all the people here, must have more than an inkling of the magnitude of the task, and its dubious feasibility. Out of a kind of shocked shame, my own faith revives.

14

Next Matías proposes a tour of the village. Hastily I press upon him the cheap, disposable cigarette lighter. He accepts graciously, tries it out, and we adjust the variable butane flame. When I explain that it is not rechargeable, he nods and with considerable tact remarks that the old-fashioned model employing flints and fluid is perhaps a better investment, though these materials are difficult to come by in the selva. Perhaps, he suggests, when we return to do our work we could bring the old kind and a supply of replaceable materials. I promise to do so. We bid Hermania farewell and set out on the main pathway through the village.

We pass by the first few houses, exchanging brief greetings with the women or children who squat by the fire. The men are apparently off together in some other house, perhaps Martín's, drinking and relaxing. Our first stop is at an old woman's place. Martín introduces her as Tia Rosa, his aunt Rose, a widow who has survived two husbands. An old crone in a filthy cushma and a hood modeled I suppose on the mantilla, she looks fierce and shrewd. Her face is a complex weave of achiote rouge, wrinkles and tattoo lines.

Matías tells her at some length who we are. At the end of his speech she snorts, steps nearer, and tweaks the fabric of my shirt. Then she fires a question into my face, along with a breath of sour masato odor. I glance appealingly at Matías.

"She asks if you have a machete."

I confess that I do.

"She says give it to her as a present."

I grin tightly and raise my shoulders.

"It is the only one I have. I need it." Rosa does not need the translation. She snorts and delivers an apostrophe that I am glad I do not comprehend, then asks another question.

"What else do you have?"

"Tell her I have some smaller knives, other things. But . . ."

Matías is smiling sympathetically. He enjoys this interchange without detectable bias, I perceive. Aniceto is grinning too.

"Tell her we will come back later."

The old woman listens, gives me a final and not very favorable examination, and returns to her fire. We continue then to a wide clearing, in the center of which is a long house competely enclosed with walls. A trimmed pole before the entrance and an official seal painted on a wooden slab identify the structure as the village school. We glance briefly inside at the facilities: handmade wooden benches and tables; a larger table bearing a heap of faded, dog-eared books and a few boxes containing paper, crayons, and rulers; a soccer ball on a shelf. The earthen floor is swept and the two or three hens strutting over it seem to be enjoying the shade rather than seriously pecking for tidbits.

The Professor's house is just beyond the school, and we chat for a few moments with his wife. The Professor himself is away in Satipo, but expected to return soon. His wife, Natalia, is a buxom, mischievous woman. Her face is flatter and rounder than most; later I learn that she is half Conibo. She speaks rapid and idiomatic Spanish, clearly proud of her position as the Professor's wife. I note that she wears a dress and has a plastic comb to hold her hair back. Part of the house is walled in, and this household also boasts a table and benches, perhaps purloined from the classroom. A silent radio rests on the table. At one point Natalia glances at it and I hear the word for batteries. I infer that there are no freshly charged ones, and our hostess is apologizing for her inability to provide a proper welcome.

At the professor's and at the next two or three houses we take a quick bowl of masato, and the day slows to a crawl. The mist has burned away from the green banks of trees in the river canyon and the sun pours down a steady heat. We pass houses where everyone is asleep, then retrace our steps, take a fork toward the river, and make a final stop at a large compound where three houses are grouped together. This is the dwelling-place of Margarita, Rosa's daughter and also a widow, and her two daughters and their husbands. Only the three women are at home. Margarita is tall for an Asháninka woman, and of regal carriage. Like Matías, she projects, beneath gracious good-humor, a sense of deep, ineffable sadness. Her black hair reaches below her waist, and despite deep lines of care she is a very beautiful woman. Her daughters, one fifteen and the other eighteen, are also striking. The elder one has daring eyes, above the child of a few months balanced on her hip.

We are talking desultorily in the shade of the main roof, immobilized by the heat. Margarita offers us a plate of steamed yucca along with the bowls of masato. Except for a wheeling vulture or two, the birds have folded away into the silence of great trees, and when conversation lapses the only sound is the buzz of flies and a little clucking from the hens. Tobacco plants near the house lean motionless, their shriveled leaves hanging as if in exhaustion. When we finish the food, Matías yawns, lies back on the platform and closes his eyes. The daughters wander off, and Margarita, without a word, moves to the adjoining house to continue plaiting a tough grass into some kind of mat or perhaps basket. Aniceto and I are left thus to our own thoughts. I feel vaguely restive, as if I ought to be more intensely involved. After all I have come ten thousand miles to be here. But I sit passively and watch nothing in particular, sluggish from the masato. How would it be, I wonder, to live day after day under this sky of bottomless, indifferent blue, weaving some pattern of forgotten significance, over and over; or waiting for someone to come with the batteries, so the magical sounds of the distant, invisible world would be heard again?

After a time Heraldo comes, shirtless and carrying a bow and handful of arrows, in search of his father. Matías rouses himself, and indicates that he must return home. We get up to leave also, and as we do so I make motions at the bow and ask Heraldo if he can demonstrate its use. He is shy, like Marcos with the string tricks, until his father prompts him. He points to a small banana tree a few yards away and nocks one of the arrows. Then in a single, smooth motion he draws the bow into a taut curve, hesitates an instant, and releases the shaft. It hisses across the yard and drives into the tree with a solid thunk.

Aniceto and I laugh and nod appreciatively. "Otro," Aniceto says. Heraldo selects a second arrow, draws it back, hesitates a moment longer than before, and sends it into the trunk not more than four inches from the first. We applaud enthusiastically. Heraldo grins with head twisted aside and eyes downcast. He is a handsome boy, well-set but agile, with perfect, dazzling teeth. He hands the bow and an arrow to me and steps back, expectant and mirthful.

Both the arrow tip and the bow are trimmed from a hard, close-grained, almost black wood. If my authorities are correct, it is the heartwood of the chonta palm. The cane shaft is very nearly true, and the fletch of black and white feather is spiraled neatly at its top. The bow seems too short for me, but is sturdy and resistant to the draw. When I try to coordinate the two, aiming merely at the ground a few feet ahead of me, the arrow goes wide to the left. Heraldo retrieves it happily, and gestures toward the banana tree. Stretching and testing the weapon once more, I recall suddenly that I have done this before, as a boy, and once even with an Indian bow.

A bookworm--at least by the standards of small logging towns in Idaho--I absorbed many a cheap romance about cowboys and Indians, and at the age of seven or eight years I was given archery equipment. Diligent practice over some months netted a few groundsquirrels and robins, but nothing edible. A neighbor who noticed my enthusiasm called me in one afternoon to show me the Indian bow. It was probably Bannock, or perhaps Nez Perce. I was first awed, then disappointed. It seemed small and not very much stronger than my own manufactured model. It was a plain, tapered bow of some dark, springy wood, and when I tried to shoot with it I was bothered by the lack of a handgrip with a flanged or notched top to cradle the arrow. After a day or two I mastered the trick of holding and guiding the shaft with a crooked index finger, and aiming to compensate for the deflection this technique caused.

Now I remember to lay the arrow across the shaft of the bow to align it, then to secure it lightly with the index finger, and finally to draw my bead well to the right side; the memory is wordless and dissolves into a certain set of the muscles and rhythm of breathing. When the feather touches my cheek I release the string, and the arrow flies straight and swift into the tree, a foot above Heraldo's darts. The solid, wet sound of its striking and Heraldo's cry of surprise give me an extraordinary jolt of delight. "*Zero!*" cries Aniceto, also impressed. Matías looks amused. "*Otro,*" he commands. He thinks it is a fluke.

I receive the second arrow, and remember something else, true of bowling, golf, and basketball as well. If you are hot, don't think. I nock the arrow, breath in measure, draw and release and the second shaft whips home. Heraldo gives a boy's version of the Ashaninka drunken whoop, Matías laughs aloud and Aniceto beams. We rejoice together for a few, pure moments. I am proud of myself--inordinately but without guilt. Aniceto is proud of me too, and the Ashaninka are delighted in their own amazement. Many months later, reviewing the memories of my time here in the river villages, I find only two or three other experiences that match these moments, when the alcohol of childish triumph ran again in my blood.

Before we set off for home, Matías proposes that I come again tomorrow, as Heraldo plans to make a batch of arrows, and I would have the opportunity to observe how this is done. Later, after lunch, we might wish to see Martín's work on a new canoe. The Ashaninka indicate time by lifting an arm to demonstrate the angle of the sun's rays, and Matías appears to be setting our morning appointment for shortly after sunrise. I agree, and we separate. For the remainder of the afternoon we scavenge wood for the fire, carry water from the river in borrowed aluminum pots, and make the tent tidy and secure. Several times people materialize at our hearth, greet us shyly or impassively, and then merely stand and watch or run fingers light and quick as spiders over a spoon, buckle, or notebook cover. Usually the children arrive in small groups, three or four at a time, and giggle as quietly as possible. Their interest is so frank and complete that I am not embarrassed, but joke with them and occasionally squeeze a shoulder or pat a shock of the straight black hair. A few ask for cigarettes--I have brought none--or items that especially please them, and I explain as well as I can that the small pack contains all my possessions, that these things are necessary to my work. My little stock of caramels from the Mission is soon gone, as word spreads among the youngsters.

In the evening we are left to ourselves, and talk a little over our notebooks. The night sky is full of cloud caverns and rare pools of stars. Out of the black jungle an increasing clamor rises: cicadas, frogs, and birds begin a concert; a clattering and burring and barking, with an occasional pure and plangent call from the well-water bird. At Martín's a low fire flickers and there are periodic bursts of laughter and ki-yiiing. There are many sounds, at many levels--even the rustling of our pages and the sputtering of the candle emerge in the foreground from time to time--but the selva is immense, and fills every interval with a vast and perfect silence.

15

When I arrive in the morning Heraldo is already at work, two completed arrows by his side, another in his hands. Matías excuses himself, having other pressing business to attend to--he is in charge of mowing the grass on the airfield--and Aniceto volunteers to accompany him. The other boys, uninterested in our task, set off on more promising adventures. Hermania and Heorihéna move about doing desultory chores with knives and string and water, quick and quiet and unobtrusive. Left to ourselves, Heraldo and I sit side by side at the fire and the class begins.

The cane shafts have been peeled and straightened already. They are kept in bundles of perhaps two dozen, gathered by a loop of twine near one end. After extracting six from the group, Heraldo gives the bundle a quick, skillful spin and it arranges itself into a loose cone, a teepee skeleton, which keeps the shafts apart and dry. Next he takes a bunch of feathers and a roll of twine from the inside of the roof; the thatch and cross-bracing provide a convenient storage place for many items, the equivalent of our cupboards and shelving. When the feathers are carefully matched in pairs, he begins trimming and stripping them in the following pattern:

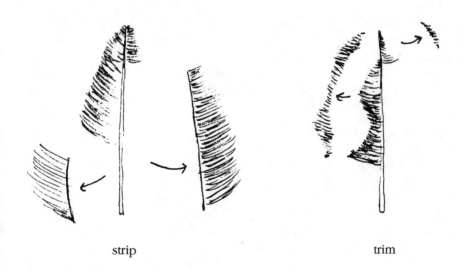

strip   trim

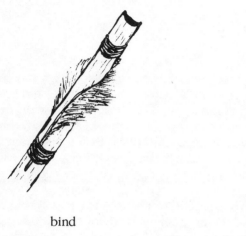

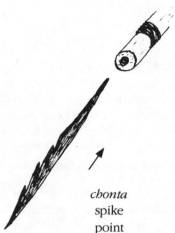

bind

chonta
spike
point

His tool is an ordinary table knife that has been whetted against a smooth stone, and he is very adept with it. Bracing the slender spine of the split feather against his thumb, he turns fine gray shavings from it, flattening it to fit against the shaft. After making a shallow notch in the top of the shaft, he picks up a tube made from a hollow section of bamboo. It contains a dark resin with which he begins to coat a length of twine, held taut between toe and one hand while the tube of resin is stroked along it. The resin comes from a tree, Heraldo tells me, and his mother spins the cotton twine. He dabs resin on the shaft and sticks the pair of trimmed feathers to it, then binds the fletching tight at top and bottom with the thread. He gives the feathers a twist, so that they spiral symmetrically around the shaft.

With the same knife, Heraldo splits a handful of long splinters from a chunk of the dark, hard chonta. The Asháninka call the palm the *kiri*, and it is the dominant presence in more than one old story. Its most salient feature, aside from the invaluable hardwood heart, is a bark covered with needle-sharp, two-inch spines. The *chakopi*-arrow--of the common sort is simply this barbed splinter pushed into the soft center of the cane shaft. Heraldo scorches both the point and the haft in the coals. He says the fire hardens the tip, and the heated haft sinks into the cane pith, melting it to a sort of glue which hardens when the arrow is set aside to cool. The final touch is a few turns of the twine just above where the haft enters the cane, to keep it from splitting.

The whole process, excluding the time necessary for gathering the cane and chonta, takes no more than ten minutes. In a morning a boy can easily make twenty arrows. But it is not uncommon, Heraldo says, to expend all twenty in the afternoon, trying for the numerous and elusive small animals around the village--lizards, rodents, birds, snakes, fish, and monkeys. I ask about some of the other kinds of arrow, which I can see stuck in the roof above our heads. The trident I guess is a fish-catcher, made by binding three of the barbed splinters around the shaft with a wooden plug to spread them. *Cempokirenci* it is called, and Heraldo confirms it is for fishing, or for ground birds. Another kind, *taharonci,* has a heavy blunt wooden point. It is used for small tree birds and squirrels. The point stuns the creature, but will not stick high in the trees. *Kapiromeni* is used for heavier game; instead of a chonta point, a sharpened bamboo blade is bound securely to the cane shaft. It can bring down deer or *shintori,* the wild pig, if the hunter is skillful enough to strike the lung and heart cavity behind the front shoulder.

Matías and Martín, I learn, have shotguns, and most of the men own one or can borrow, rendering part of the kill as repayment. The bows and arrows I suspect are largely toys and symbols. Every boy in the village seems to be equipped, and they are constantly flitting in and about the undergrowth along paths or at the riverbank, hissing and shouting at one another, drawing and firing at anything that moves.

Now and then a man passes by with a bow and a handful of arrows, perhaps on a long walk to a friend's house; he may hope to pick up a fat quail, a razorbill dove, or even a *sahini,* a sort of huge rat, as tasty as pork.

We get up from the fire, stretch, and move off to try out our batch of new arrows. I have managed to do the fletching on two of them, and in that work I am surprised into a paradox. Making arrows is easy; knowing how to make them seems impossible. All the materials are easily obtainable: the cane grows everywhere along the river; cotton is a common and ancient crop; the bark fiber that has been twisted into the bowstring is from a common tree, Heraldo says, and so is the resin; one parrot supplies enough feathers for dozens of arrows. The technique of assembly is not complicated--I have mastered it in one sitting--and with a little practice any ten year-old could make perfectly serviceable weapons by the stack.

But who would think of a bow and arrow in the first place? How many generations would be required to locate the best woods, to invent the twist in the feathers that gives the arrow a truer, spiralling trajectory, to discover that a treatment in fire hardens the tip? The pragmatic, manual intelligence, the capacity for neural speculation involved in these advances is astonishing. Watching Heraldo's sure hands repeat patterns that are thousands of years old, I am as amazed as when I look through the plastic porthole of a jetliner at the shining wing surface and imagine the nests of wires and tubes beneath it, the calculus and calibrations, the formulae and circuitry that maintain us smoothly, drowsily, miles high. Out of the wild, indiscriminate profusion of this jungle, into which every plant and creature fits in a complex harmony, this lad picks just those bits that may fuse into a precise instrument, whose employment entails a further knowledge of weather, topography and animal behavior. He is demonstrating a complex, highly elaborated and advanced technology, an impressive human achievement.

Not far from our tent we find a small banana tree that will serve as a target. The almost forgotten knack I recalled the previous afternoon has deserted me, and only after an hour or two of hard practice do I find the rhythm again. Also, each arrow is slightly different: the cane is seldom perfectly straight, and the weight of the tip varies. After a few practice shots, it is possible to correct the aim for each shaft. Finally I hit a hot streak, and Heraldo and I have a contest, each man shooting a set of four arrows. It goes two and two, two and three, two and one, back and forth. For a last round, I predict, like Babe Ruth: *quatro y quatro, los dos.* He grins, takes the bow, and quick and regular as a machine drives all four darts into the trunk. I step to the line and am lucky on the first shot. Then a pause, and I manage to reach the state of mindless care that is necessary, and the last three arrows follow the first. The banana tree has become Saint Sebastian, and we laugh at it.

The session is over, and the midday rest is upon us. Off and on we have heard the Briggs and Stratton sputtering, and looking far down the strip I have seen Matías pushing the cumbersome claptrap mower, cutting no more than half a dozen swathes. Now Matías and Aniceto, sweating and coated with chaff, return to the tent and we talk a little while we are preparing lunch. Our tuna and hardtack are supplemented by yucca someone has left by the fire.

When Matías leaves we sit and eat slowly, the air hot and heavy but clear around us. The brilliant green foliage is slashed with sharp black shadows, immobile as paint. These silent, soporific afternoons are vaguely depressing. Also, Matías seems distracted and a little crushed by circumstance, perhaps by our presence. He has mentioned that in a day or two we will voyage downriver to another and larger village, Ovíri, which he says is more *avancado* than Otíka, and probably a better location for our work. The professor in Ovíri is a man of considerable parts and influence, and could assist us greatly. He studied with the *lingüísticos* in Pucallpa, Matías says. The *lingüísticos* are the American missionaries from the

Summer Institute of Linguistics, the agency which for forty years has worked to translate the Bible into various Indian languages throughout the Amazon basin.

Our enthusiasm for Otíka is further clouded an hour or so later, when a young man with a sour smile appears at our tentflap and launches immediately into a language lesson. He claims to be Weiss's old teacher, and brags of how much he taught the gringo professor. Soon he is demanding a pronunciation drill, pointing imperiously at various objects in view and giving the name alternately in Spanish and in idioma. Then he begins interjecting into the lesson requests for gifts: a knife, my pen, the machete, Aniceto's extra shirt. Señor Weiss, he remarks pointedly, gave him many special gifts for his services. Unlike Señor Weiss, I tell him, I am not at the moment studying the idioma formally. In a couple of months I intend to return and will probably undertake lessons of some kind then, when I have more time. He falls silent for several minutes, merely observing us as we wash our plates and cups, then begins to ask for smaller items: a handkerchief, a piece of notepaper, a bit of the hardtack. Wearily I hand him a biscuit, but thereafter meet every request with a curt refusal, and ignore him pointedly.

At last he leaves, and I discover in the ensuing measure of relief how tense the interview made me. It was a shock to encounter an Asháninka whom I could not like; obviously I held a naive delusion that everyone in the tribe would be gracious and considerate. There is also a conflict of cultural values: I recall that Bodley wrote of the importance of generosity to the Asháninka, and of their insistence on trade as a necessary cement in human relations. Clearly our visitor believed that the stock of new words he brought and presented to us ought to be recompensed, while for me the right to refuse, to rebuff a merely verbal overture, could cancel any such debt. Aniceto's shrug and single observation ("They don't have much, Señor Weel.") further humble me. I see that it is easy to take for granted the restraint and good manners of these villagers; their grace is achieved in the face of poverty and hard work, and a few individuals chaff at their lot, and perhaps go sour.

16

I make a few notes in my journal and then retire into the tent for a nap. It is after sundown when I wake and find Matías standing at our fireside, his face daubed with patches of bright orange achiote. He weaves a little and reeks of masato. There is a celebration at Martín's, he tells us, and when we have had our supper we may wish to attend it. Only if we wish. I assure him that we will be very glad to accept the invitation, especially if there is some of the music that we heard on Weiss's tapes. Matías says that Rosa will sing for us, most certainly, and Martín may even be persuaded to render his ayahuasca songs. They will expect us then. With dignity, Matías weaves away into the dusk.

During a light supper we hear occasional whoops of merriment from Martín's, where two fires are burning, but when we present ourselves, in clean shirts and--in my case--a face newly and painfully scraped, the affair seems to have calmed down considerably. A couple of the kerosene can-lamps give only a faint illumination, so most of the figures sitting on the house platform are mere shadows. I can determine that they are all male, but I recognize only the old fellow who smells of coca and belches periodically. Some youths--Heraldo probably among them--recline on the platform giggling and holding hands. Only Matías knows very much Spanish, and when Martín or others try to talk to me he must interpret. Again I find myself subjected to a language lesson, in the form of a slow and stilted conversation. Its topics are trivial: how the rains are here now, what Lima must be like, how long we expect to remain.

Some of the men drift away, and all at once Martín stands up, seizes the box he has been using as a chair, and indicates to me to follow him. We set off at a smart pace across the airstrip; he calls over his shoulder that we are going to Margarita's where we will go on with the fiesta. At Margarita's, true enough, there is another gathering, mostly women, with their children of various ages running in and out of the darkness about the fire. Tía Rosa is present, and addresses to me a long and unintelligible but apparently friendly harangue. A group of young men arrives then, wearing fine, clean cushmas. They greet us rather guardedly, a formal acknowledgement followed by studied indifference.

The masato is flowing freely, and the women will not allow us to nurse the drink; they wrest the gourd bowls from us half-full and return them brimming. The young men down the stuff steadily with much smacking of the lips and manly eructation. Matías has not accompanied us here, and I find myself confronted with face after face, open and sincerely inquisitive, gusts of meaningless words passing between us. Then some of the women join arms and begin to sing, at first shyly, but soon quite lustily. They too are drinking a good deal of masato. The songs sound melancholy to me, like a high and keening lament over lost loves "of the blighted variety."

As I watch and nod encouragement, a tiny boy who seems to be in Rosa's care, a mite no more than two or three years of age, comes to embrace my leg. When I lift him into my arms, he seems light-boned as a small bird underneath his cushma. He is very dark-skinned, and the little stick legs look gray, perhaps from fine ash from the fireside. He does not smile, but his huge eyes, dark as water in the dead of night, do not swerve from my own. Immediately we are comrades, for he too understands little enough of what is transpiring here. For the rest of the evening he keeps near me, in my lap, between my legs, or seated silently beside me, his hand like a fallen leaf on my arm.

All at once the singing stops, for two girls have run up to the house shouting excitedly. There is a hurried conference; anxious looks are exchanged. I try to get out of Martín some notion of what has happened, but he shakes his head and looks away. In a few minutes he and two other men leave as unobtrusively as they can. Aniceto whispers that he thinks there has been a fight. The little boy climbs into my lap again, and I hold him firmly and talk to him in my own language. The young men in new cushmas have continued indifferently with their drinking, and after a while Rosa starts another song. She stands before me with a happy leer, swaying as she croons, a bowl of masato held to her distended belly.

Matías arrives, now quite drunk. When he bends forward to talk to me, I see a bruise at his hairline still oozing a little blood. After a few pleasantries he announces very firmly: "I am indebted to nobody. Nobody." I make some sound of accord, a generalized endorsement. "I owe no one anything," he repeats with a gesture of great finality, and this movement seems to restore him. With his gap-toothed grin, he beckons Heraldo from the group of young men. He sends off his son with some instructions, and in a few minutes Heraldo is back with a Coleman lantern and the cassette tape machine. One of the cassettes is a blank, Matías says, and now they will record the music.

When the lantern is fired and the soft, yellow glow of the kerosene has been erased in its calcium glare, Heraldo loads the cassette and poises a finger over the record button. Everyone has gathered excitedly around him, and his face is a study in pride and pleasure overcoming adolescent bashfulness. Without understanding a word of the language, I am quite certain that the women are teasing, pretending to refuse to sing, hiding their faces in their hands, giggling and ducking. Finally Rosa can stand this coquetry no longer and grabs another woman in a hammerlock and begins her chant.

Asháninka dances hardly deserve the name. I thought in the beginning that the staggering, reeling run that accompanied the wailing was simply an example of drunken amateurishness. But I found the performance the same in every village. The women (men have very few dances and execute them rarely) simply clutch each other about the neck or shoulders and rush ahead for several yards, then back, then ahead, and so on. When the fit is very much on them, they will continue for hours, drenching their cushmas in sweat and spilled drink, singing at the top of their lungs the whole time. They often form a sort of snake-dance, six or eight in a row with linked arms, always in order from the tallest at the head of the line to a child at the tail. But of pattern, of repetition of steps, or even of graceful improvisation, I see no hint.

The singing, on the other hand, is full of vigor and variety, and is clearly music. There is a strong flavor of the middle east in it, and I can imagine zithers or tympanis in accompaniment. At one time such an association would be ruled an idle fantasy, but modern anthropologists have been compelled by their own evidence to entertain speculations on such correspondences. Odd and highly suggestive parallels turn up in the mythologies of widely separated cultures--Indonesian and Scandanavian for example--and the possibility of Precolumbian transpacific contacts, once a notion ridiculed by scholars, has now become a strong likelihood, if not a certainty. So, watching the old woman reeling and wailing, I imagine that I may be hearing melodic lines or key changes brought by seagoing canoe thousands of years ago, from another jungle half way around the world.

All at once Heraldo cries out, first in idioma, then in Spanish: *"Bastante, bastante!"* Rosa stumbles to a halt and the song dies away. The women disengage themselves and everyone gathers around Heraldo while he rewinds the tape. Then he plays it back and everyone listens, rapt and still, even the small children. Rosa nods approvingly from time to time and mutters commentary, perhaps self-criticism. We follow the song until we hear Heraldo's small electronic ghost shouting *"Bastante!"* Then there is an interlude of bright smiles and chatter. My opinion is consulted and I also voice praise for the performance.

Then Heraldo rewinds the machine and begins to play the song a second time. His audience is no less mesmerized than before, and they rejoice at the end of the performance with cries which, I fear, are an urging to repeat the playback yet again. I gesture animatedly for a return to live music, encouraging Rosa to do another from her repertoire. She complies, and when she is through one of her daughters, a strapping saucy woman with a baby of a few months on her bare breast, volunteers another tune.

When she finishes, two teenage girls shuffle coyly forward offering to contribute a duet, but Heraldo waves them away imperiously and replays Rosa and her daughter. The tape is not long enough for the latter, and there are exclamations and outcries when the recorded version is nipped off abruptly. Still, we hear both songs through twice before Heraldo is willing to audition the teenagers. They have fled into the darkness on an errand, which turns out to be that of bringing another large canoe of masato from a neighboring house. The bowls are immediately full again, and the young men have loosened up enough to whoop their appreciation.

Martín is persuaded to attempt his ayahuasca songs. A pair of the young men, cheeks aflame with achiote, have grown convinced that I am eager to learn their language at this moment, and are bombarding me with alternate words in idioma and Spanish: *aviro--buenos días, shima--pescado, shirompári--hombre*; so that I can barely hear Martín's thin falsetto. He shakes his head and grins defensively, embarrassed. He is not in voice, he says. One must have ayahuasca to sing properly. I ask where the songs come from, and he is surprised. They are my songs, he says. Others downriver confirm this tradition for me later: people habitually invent and refine their own material.

I find myself growing irritated at Heraldo's continual interruption of the singers. Each time the music seems on the verge of real intensity and passion, when the women are near ecstatic transport, he cries out to interrupt them and everything stops for the replay. The performers are not bothered in the least by this peremptory treatment. They listen as avidly and indefatigably as everyone else. The playback, unlike the living artists, is treated with great respect; children are shushed and Rosa's ramblings discouraged by looks askance whenever her tinny, scratchy reproduction is in progress. Finally the batteries weaken, and the songs begin to drag and wow in a lugubrious parody. I hope that the celebration can at last be spontaneous and unrestrained, but Heraldo rouses Matías from a stupor, secures permission for supplementary batteries, and one of the younger brothers is sent scampering off for them. He wears the fierce, intense expression of a warrior-hero.

My head feels like a huge, soft bud, the effect of the masato. The young men have abandoned the translation into Spanish, and are simply shouting words at me, waiting for me to repeat them. I try to shout them back, miming the pronunciation. When I am succesful they nod enthusiastically, although I have absolutely no idea what I am saying. One of this group of young men has maintained his aloofness. He is tall for an Asháninka, perhaps five feet eight or nine, wide through the shoulders, and his flat, strong face has a great deal of intelligence and reserve--except when he laughs. Then he exposes a row of oversized buck teeth, perfectly white, and emits a tremendous, dumb lowing. After such displays he reverts instantly to his distant, impassive calm.

On an impulse I approach him and make the gesture of fitting an arrow into a bow. "*Usted- cazador?* I inquire. He nods curtly, watching. "*Arco y flechas, por mi?*" I mime the making of the weapons. I indicate that I will trade or pay for them. He seems to understand, but I am not certain. I introduce myself as Weel, and he responds, Carlos. There is something different about his manner, but I have been too confused by the masato to isolate and identify the source of the impression.

Rosa has taken up a position in front of me again, her fierce old eyes now quite red from drink. She indicates forcefully that it is my turn to sing. The others around second her zealously. My musical talent extends no further than a half-dozen old folk tunes that I can plunk crudely on a banjo. But here, surrounded by happy inebriates who speak an unknown foreign tongue, I have no qualms about launching into "Old Plank Road," and then a rousing chorus or two of "She'll Be Comin' 'Round The Mountain," complete with hack-hacks and scratch-scratches, hand-claps and foot-stomps. Rosa is delighted. She throws back her head and emits the most ear-splitting cackle-whoop I have yet heard, and I am moved to try "Old MacDonald Had A Farm." Rosa even tries to imitate the quack-quacks and oink-oinks, with surprising success. My tiny companion hovers at my knee, so awed he touches me lightly, like a hot stove.

But this fine moment does not escape the inexorable Heraldo. As soon as the new batteries are installed, he insists that I repeat the songs, and with rather less gusto I comply. Again, of course, I must listen to myself twice through; and only by dint of forceful remonstrance do I escape a third playback. At last Heraldo has to confront a dilemma, a technological (and perhaps metaphysical) barrier: so far he has erased each recording to make way for its successor; every resurrection has been doomed; but now he wishes to keep these new songs in English. Reluctantly he decides to be satisfied with what he has, and to transfer the batteries to a radio.

Soon the din of terrible latin rock from Pucallpa washes over us. Some of the young men have gone off; Matías has passed out; and the children are rubbing their eyes or have curled up asleep on the platform. The most recent batch of masato has an unfortunate consistency, and has grown tepid, so that I have been unable to get rid of the recollection of its origins. The women, however, no longer press the stuff on me or anyone else. One has to gesture aggressively to obtain a refill, in fact. The drink has done its work and they doubtless see no reason to waste it. My conversation of sound and fury with the men has fallen off to an occasional grunted repetition of the three or four simple words that I have retained.

It is time to go. When I turn to look for Aniceto, he is behind me, dancing with the elder of Margarita's daughters, the one with bold eyes.

The dance is a very subdued, very discreet boogie. An Asháninka boy in ragged pants is doing something indescribable behind them in belated imitation. They do not look at each other, but their bodies are growing gradually looser, more fluid. The Coleman has begun to run out of air pressure or fuel, and its light waxes and wanes in long gasps. Sometime ago Rosa lurched off to her own house, taking the little boy with her. Three or four women sit at the edge of the light, talking quietly.

The blood has begun to thud dully in my head so I rise to bid farewell. No one notices. With a final glare at the black box of the recorder, I stumble out of the hut. Overhead the stars are few between dark and rolling clouds, and the air feels damp. A thin rasp of music follows me, and as I walk the frustrations of the evening finally condense and ignite. In one of those occasional moments of clarity known to late revelers I understand that I am jealous of Aniceto, who avoided the interminable language lessons and struck up a flirtation with a pretty girl. I also am aware that the girl has a child, probably a husband somewhere, and that we may be compromising our position in the village. But more than anything I resent the power of the cassette machine, that captured and contained these people's lively spirit simply by throwing them back a few moments in time.

I am astonished out of my stupor by a sudden notion: the tape-player is a psychic *remolino,* a whirlpool that traps the impulse to celebrate freely, keeps it in tight orbit, and eventually swallows it. Performers are quickly transformed into the audience, again and again, and it is the nature of this oscillation to inhibit continuous creation--and to spoil good parties. Each time the singers clustered around Heraldo and cried out in glee at the miracle of a fragment of their own being objectified, they lost an opportunity to expand that being, to sing directly out of themselves into the hearts of others.

In my own culture most music is electronically processed. It comes through our radios or television sets or record players, produced by amplifiers hooked to fingers and voices. The performer is invisible, unknown to the millions who may listen to his songs, except as a cinematic or phonographic phantasm. This ghost, however, has tremendous power and range. I saw tee shirts in Satipo bearing the imprint of John Travolta and the Grateful Dead, and heard music by many others. A performer from my culture is one of many thousands who have striven with tremendous energy to become "stars," people of diamond and flame, prancing in glittering costume, generating waves of music and giant images that can cross continents instantaneously. For all but a very few of my countrymen, these stars produce (and sell) whatever music is available, and that music is so potent that it invades and possesses us everywhere; we hum the tunes--even those we detest--or sway to their rhythms while shopping in a market, waiting for the doctor, working at our jobs, even in elevators and rest rooms. The great whorl of this manufactured sound holds us spellbound; we do not often play as children do, chanting nonsense verses; most of us never perform for the people around us; we compose no personal songs, our own creations.

And what is the content of our music? Not only love of the blighted variety, but passion, betrayal, lust, jealousy, regret, confession, delight, nostalgia, humor--a complete emotional life--detached from any personality or particular community. We can be stimulated in almost any waking hour to re-experience some incident of our past that was once charged with strong feeling. The song is consumed like a tablet, one of the quick-chew kind, a light stimulant whose impact may be shrugged off if traffic grows heavy. The effect of the drug is simply to stir a shallow pool of memories and idle fancies.

Between "numbers" we hear the dynamic and mellifluous disc-jockey, whose ultimate message is that we are spinning free in this great effluvium of trite emotion, able to dip and soar through life and love in terrific style. His jargon stresses the "new" and "now" and the pace of delivery seems eternally accelerating, taking off or rather blasting off, and the flow of sound is continuous, incessant, day after day and year after year. In fact the music, its salesmen, attendant products, and vast symbiotic circuitry only act to keep us "with it" or more accurarately in it, without our ever achieving enough centrifugal force to escape this eddy of shallow feeling to the outer reaches of the self, to the state in which creating one's own song is a psychic necessity.

Beneath the shimmering cloud of electromagnetic sound that envelops the planet, a dense impacted atmosphere of wails and coos, there bubbles a black lagoon of oil, the old dead jungle burning off into impersonal song and chatter, musical smog. The whirlpool reaches then, across hundreds of millions of years, to connect this small whine of steel guitar, riding the night air of the forest, to the black blood of ancient life, and to bring the people of the river into its current--in both senses--so that they may be new and now, drown their individual melodies, produce the wood and coffee and feathers whose sale will give them money to consume radios and batteries, completing the cycle.

But there is a transformation from water to fire. Once the virus of civilization was carried from the sea up the riverine arteries, and gold, hides, and rubber were its prey. Through trade, word-of-mouth, and migration the aboriginal people were introduced to iron, whisky, cheap cloth, and Jesus. They began to forsake their old ways for these new goods and ideas. Now the process has been tremendously accelerated by the electrification of the planet, and the vortex is of fire: the fire of foundry, refinery, and generating plant at the literal level, and the incandescence of television and quadraphonic stereo and cinema at the metaphoric. These metaphorical flames consume minds and souls and issue them trans-formed, smelted into a uniform substance: pigsoul, on the analogy of pigiron. Pigsoul is the raw stuff of humanity in large cities, where the movies and tapes are accessible even to the poorest. The urban typology, worldwide, is uniform: the furtive and rapacious thief, the unctious manager, the barkers, blarneymen, and hot-eyed whores of advertising, bored bureaucrats, and especially the anonymous workers, faces uninha-bited and bodies collapsing, all moving like dumb swine to their stalls and trough, the same trivial tunes and conditioned lusts stirring within. Each day new ideas, new products circulate through the popula-tion: skirt hems go up or down, automobiles lengthen or swell, other peoples, distant and imaginary, are embraced or reviled. Through the immense compact energy of the ancient jungle, circling back to us after many millions of years, all the people of earth are being pulled into this mighty, pulsating whirlpool, a psychic force-field.

We owe to Ortega Y Gasset the remarkable perspective from which this new universe of apparent mobility, power and plenty actually pro-duces a primitive being, a *Naturmensch* who can absorb products and styles and opinions as they are produced, and forsake them at will, a being without a past, unencumbered by culture, tradition, or any sort of ances-tral furniture. The Spanish philosopher exaggerates and twists this notion under the pressure of his own hatred of the vulgar, but it is surely true that the usurpation of a culture and its values, once the result of brutal conquest, occupation, and oppression, can now be accomplished almost at the speed of light, through the manipulation of electromagnetic waves. And once the usurpation begins, it is immediate and incessant. Flick the switch at any hour of the day or night and the genii of new and now will speak to you.

What Ortega Y Gasset does not conceive is the miraculous dimension of this fiery tornado, the hypnotic and galvanizing force of it. He is himself victim of it, concluding his treatment of the issue with an appeal for an even newer newness, complex and aristocratic in its rejection of the "primitive."

> There is no hope for Europe unless its destiny is placed in the hands of men really "contemporaneous," men who feel palpitating beneath them the whole subsoil of history, who realize the present level of existence, and abhor every archaic and primitive attitude. We have need of history in its entirety, not to fall back on it, but to see if we can escape it.

The irony is that these archaic modes of life and thought are vanishing into the electromagnetic vortex; they are being transformed into pigsoul.

For the *Naturmensch* is no true primitive--that is, a creature with a special deer-spirit and his own songs of power, with knowledge of stories perhaps as old as any on earth and spells that may sprout seeds, summon rain, or inflict death. Pigsoul lives only in and for the great current of the new and the now, the drama of shampoo, the addiction of money, the carnival horror-show of politics and war, broadcast live. Paul Radin has said that primitive man lives "in a blaze of reality," in the constant presence of the mystery and terror of a spiritual life. Pigsoul lives in a blaze of artificial visions, manufactured and purveyed to supply him with an identity and to galvanize him to feed these flames, variously named a "movement," "a trend," "the nation," "the economy."

So intense, so magically extendable and transmittable are these visions that the true primitives are ready to sacrifice themselves, willing to become fuel, in order to be possessed by them. They fear the Pishtako myth with good reason; they are everywhere tempted to confirm it. It is within them already.

17

The morning is gray with a fine rain coming from banks of mist over the hills. Aniceto returns to camp with cap and shoulders drenched, and downcast eyes. I try to joke a little with him, but he has withdrawn into silent penance. This is the day we were to go downriver to Ovíri, but unless the clouds lift we will be confined to our books. Both of us have hangovers, however, and the prospect of an idle time is welcome. I have made tea, and we fall into our comfortable routine: he mutters numbers and verses, and I pore over my notebook, trying to organize the confused impressions of the previous evening. After perhaps two hours the mist grows dazzling white, then rends to reveal patches of cobalt sky, and soon the sun strikes through to set the grass steaming.

Matías arrives, and announces that he is ready to take us downriver if we wish to go. He too appears a little subdued and hung over, but his politeness and consideration are unflagging. He answers me frankly and says he would prefer to go today, as he has work to do in a few days at his chacra upstream. He signals at the sky to appoint a time an hour hence, and leaves us to gather our things. This is no great chore: we take only a clean shirt, towels and soap, cigarette lighters and hand mirrors as gifts, and the camera. Everything else we secure inside the tent.

Before midday we have loaded the canoe and push off, Matías steering with a paddle from the stern, his wife, the two year-old and his eldest daughter in the prow, and Aniceto and I amidships--the position of no responsibility. It is painfully hot and bright on the river, yet exhilarating too because we escape the small pool of shade under our thatch and the steaming growth that surrounds it, gliding effortlessly on the wide waters. Only a few hundred yards downstream we pass a great rock, the size of a steamboat, and I recognize one of the formations Professor Weiss listed in his compendium. Like many outcroppings along the river, it figures in a legend. Once when the white men were making their raids along the watercourses in search of slaves, the trickster-god Avíreri intervened on behalf of the Asháninka and transformed a mighty vessel full of armed men into this stone, now called *Manihironi.* I query Matías about the story, and he recognizes the name but says he knows no details of the account.

The surface of the rock at the waterline has been sculpted into remarkable contours: knobs, whorls and small natural stone bridges and columns. I snap a few photos here and also in a following smooth stretch where we pass near the bank beneath thick overhanging branches and trailing vines, the sun fragmenting into golden flecks on the water and moss- sheathed stone. But for our own sporadic chatter and an occasional squawl from the parrots there is no sound but the hiss of the water, an occasional slap of a wave on the gunwale. From time to time we glimpse behind the fringe of cane along high, sandy banks a rooftop or spray of banana leaves, or a thread of smoke rising straight in the still air. I tip my hat over my eyes and doze. My dreams, brief and incoherent as the caverns of shade and dappled light we drift through, are all about my previous life, odd people and places: an abrasive New York feminist, spacious barns and gasping old John Deere tractors, and Frank Sinatra singing a song I cannot quite recognize.

When I rouse myself, we are only a few minutes away from Ovíri. The entire trip has lasted no more than two hours, and given the number of encampments we have passed, I am persuaded that we are in the heartland of the riverine Asháninka. According to Matías, most of the villages are only a little over a decade old, and before that time existed only as periodic settlements or campsites for a nomadic population. Now it appears that the major towns have stabilized and extended the population living between them, forming a series of interlocking neighborhoods.

Ovíri has a reputation as the most developed of the new villages, and I am curious to learn more about it, not only as a possible location for our work, but because Matías speaks of it with such deference. At our debarkation point, there seems to be no village at all, only a corner of pole fence and a path leading into the undergrowth. We unload our sacks and baskets, and Matías and Aniceto beach the canoe, securing it also with a heavy vine rope tied to a log which is in turn anchored with sizeable stones.

I ask about the fence, and Matías reports that Professor Nicolás has cows, seven of them, and two bulls. This inventory is announced with some pride. Ovíri possesses the only cattle in the area, and there are high hopes for its development as a source of milk and meat. The breeding stock was brought in, Matías says, by the *búfalo*, one of the Peruvian Air Force cargo planes that I saw parked at the Lima airport. It flies once a month through the area. I am amazed that such a craft could land on these tiny grass airstrips, and also that the Peruvian government manages to supply this service, when it cannot furnish such modest advantages as quinine and schoolbooks.

Two hundred yards along the path and we emerge into a large compound where are one small and one large house only a step apart, with a cluster of orange, grapefruit and mango trees at its perimeter. A group of women and children peer at us from a doorway, and in a moment Professor Nicolás comes out to greet us. He is a broad stump of a man, with an open grin and gracious bearing. He wears slacks and a flower-print sport shirt, a little soiled, and like Aniceto he has gold at his wrist and in his teeth. We are seated comfortably on the spacious platform beneath the main roof, and begin our conversaion.

Nicolás speaks good Spanish, woven skillfully around frequent, hearty laughter. He tells us the story of the cows, which he says he obtained for the community, and of his studies in Pucallpa. He was there for three years, and assisted in the important work of translating the Bible into idioma. North Americans are no strangers to him; he has seen their generators and power drills and houses with wooden floors. Here he is working to teach his people Spanish and arithmetic and a little history, so that someday they may have such advantages themselves. He understands that we are interested in making some pictures and wishes to know our plans in more detail.

I outline our project, trying to stress gently our interest in traditional aspects of Asháninka life, and he listens attentively. Aniceto has learned my spiel rather well, and several times contributes clearer or more elegant phrasing. Therefore, I conclude, we are surveying the Tambo region, recommended to us by Gerardo, in search of a site for our work. Very good. After a meal Nicolás will be pleased to take us on a tour of the village, which lies some distance away across a small river. We can visit a few of his friends, and see what housing might be available should we decide to return with our notebooks and cameras.

Two shy girls arrive with hot soup and baked yucca. Nicolás, aside from his garb and manner, seems to live like all the Asháninka. Sitting cross-legged, he takes the smoking yucca with his fingers, and wipes them on his trousers. After the meal, he and Matías talk, occasionally in Spanish, and I gather that they are discussing local matters of no particular moment. There is mention of Nicolás' wife, away for a medical checkup. It is the midday period of idleness, and I see that no one is in a great hurry to visit the village, so I move out of the shade of the platform to stroll around a bit.

Sampling the Professor's grapefruit, I mark an extra advantage to this location. They are ripe and sweet, and though the Indians seem indifferent to them, I find the keen juice a welcome complement to the starch of the usual meal. At the fence I catch a glimpse of the famous cattle. They look like Charlay or Holsteins, rather incongruous against the background of dense jungle. In the heat they move seldom, preferring to stand immobile, jaws working slowly and steadily, in a grass that is like green fire. They must represent considerable wealth here, or at least influence. I was told at lunch that none have so far been butchered; the Professor has taken only milk. But with a salary and these cows on his side of the river, he clearly feels as if he can speak for the whole village, and the casual expansiveness of his manner is tribute enough to the power of these huge, lethargic beasts.

When I return to the house the others are ready to proceed. Nicolás leads us along well-travelled trails through groves of large trees. Where there is a steep pitch down, logs have been driven into the mud to make crude steps. After perhaps a kilometer we arrive at the banks of the little river, itself called the Ovíri. The water is milky with debris, and quite rowdy. Nicolás admonishes us to roll up our pantlegs and follow him with care across the ford. In dry season, he says, the stream is perfectly clear and can be crossed on a chain of rocks.

A low cliff rises on the opposite bank, and the village lies on the plateau at its crest, commanding a view of the river that winds away toward the blue mist-shrouded mountains. It is a lovely spot, more spacious and open than Otíka; and beyond the proximity of fresh water for drinking and bathing, this location also can supply fresh fruit--I spot a large grove of orange trees beside the schoolhouse. The airstrip is cropped closer than the one at Otíka, and appears larger. Several houses are visible along its edge and we make our way slowly among them.

At each house we speak to the men and drink masato, while the women sit apart with young children and the chickens wander everywhere. Nicolás and Matías provide me with spot translations and I ask a few questions. Ovíri is now fourteen years old, and the people say it is a good place to live. Game, however, has grown scarce because so many families are gathered in one place. The fishing also has fallen off considerably. Everyone seems to have a small coffee orchard, and this is the only consistent cash crop. Sometimes they can sell corn, but this year the price is so low that their small harvest is going to the chickens.

I am beginning to get used to the pace of these visits; this requires calming the restless social behavior of my own culture: there are no bookcases where I can scan titles, no television set in the corner to use as fleeting relief from the chatter, no rugs or cabinets to inspect and admire. The Asháninka lie or sit at perfect ease, leaving long pauses between interchanges, occasionally breaking into their whoops of merriment. The women too grow lively sometimes, and trade comments with the men. I do notice that unlike the sessions in Otíka, in which no personality seemed to dominate, our group centers each time around the Professor, who is by turns genial, mocking, and discursive. Probably my presence is responsible for this arrangement, which is familiar enough, the official host and the distinguished visitor.

The termination of the visits, however, is not easy to foresee, and is swift and uncomplicated. All at once, when the mood of inertia seems well established and the gourd bowls are still half full, Nicolás and Matías rise quite naturally and in a few moments we depart with a last gulp and few words. Often when we walk past the edge of shade into the bare compound our hosts of a moment ago are already back at work on a fishnet, or turning away to doze. I have noticed the same behavior even when a canoe is departing on a considerable journey. When it leaves the bank there are a few noncommital words. Then the oarsmen and passengers set faces to the wind and rarely look back. If they do they see those they have left, standing motionless and without expression, simply watching. If someone calls out it is a kind of afterthought, some piece of minor unfinished business, an undifferentiated fragment of the preceding conversation. Yet I know too that at this season there is a not unappreciable chance that the voyagers will not return. Perhaps it is felt that to treat the moment of departure differently would be an admission of such risk, and therefore a subtle enhancement of it. And perhaps our traditional expression of false light-heartedness--the smiling through tears--is a similar attempt to avoid casting shadows on the future. By striving for neutrality, the Asháninka compromise themselves less.

At one dwelling the leave-taking is unusual. After we have set out from a man's house he calls us back and presents me with a necklace of brown seed-shells fastened to a cotton band. He is a thin man in middle age, with a shy, sweet smile. I have no inkling of the motive for his sudden generosity, and in some confusion ask the Professor to ask him what gift I could bring him upon my return. After some hesitation and signs of embarrassment, he mentions the tiny varicolored beads that I have seen a few times on the wrist or at the throat of people here. I promise to search for them in Lima, and thank the man again for the necklace.

At the Professor's we take a leisurely dinner and retire early. I have trouble sleeping because of a ring of red welts at my beltline. They itch furiously and when I examine them the next morning I find my fingernails have brought blood. Nicolás and Matías laugh knowingly and explain that the tiniest of the jungle predators are the most persistent and ferocious. A nearly microscopic insect called the *isango* has attacked. It is very active in the damp weather, and the Indians are not immune to its bite, though they have developed a certain resistance to local strains. Matías says that moving more than a few kilometers up or downriver affects this resistance.

After breakfast we finally discuss the details of our project with Nicolás. He tells us he will find us a house, locate an interpreter, and direct us to those in the community who can remember old stories. The interviews of the previous day have given assurance that people will cooperate in the work. In turn I offer to pay rent and a salary for those who wish to help, or to bring goods to exchange for these services. In deference to Matías, and also because I believe Otíka has an intriguing lack of sophistication or community purpose, I indicate that we will probably spend time in both villages.

Our business succesfully concluded, the Professor summons some boys to carry our few bags, presents us with a stalk of fresh bananas, and accompanies us to the canoe. We are quickly loaded, for Matías believes that it will require all day to return to Otíka. We shake hands with the Professor, Matías regarding us like a good student. He casts us loose and pushes off with a slender ten-foot pole, this time taking up a position in the stern. Nicolás has donned a white shirt for the day, and when I look back I can see it moving up the bank and through the trees.

18

The long reach upriver begins. Hermania guides us near the bank, skirting snags and submerged bushes, sometimes putting us through the cavern of overhanging branches. The two year-old is slung from one shoulder in a wide loop of handspun cotton fringed with the small, flat bones of some animal, in which are burned a crosshatch pattern. One breast is bare, ready for the child's need, but otherwise she pays him no mind, turning and dipping her paddle expertly with a wiry, alert strength. Matías provides the force to move us against the current, plunging the pole to the bottom and pulling us along hand over hand, then giving a final shove at the very top of the pole before lifting it smoothly up for another bite. His bare feet are spread wide and his shoulders twist gracefully so that he seldom has to change position. We move slowly but steadily along.

The route along the bank has two advantages: the current is not as strong there, and periodically there are back eddies that carry the canoe upriver even without our propulsion. It is not long, in fact, before Hermania calls to Matías and steers us away from the bank. He lays the pole in the bottom of the canoe, seizes another paddle and the two of them drive hard to bring us across the river to one of these countercurrents near the opposite bank. Fine discrimination and a thorough knowledge of the river are necessary for such manoeuvres, since one does not want to lose in these crossings more than he gains, either in distance or effort.

We procede in this fashion, crossing the wide and turbulent waters many times, and by late morning Matías' body glistens with sweat when he twists on the pole. I snap photos occasionally and converse with Aniceto. He has also been impressed with Ovíri, especially the hospitality and neatness of the households, and believes as I do that Nicolás is an able, dynamic sort who can greatly assist us. Many of his conceptions about the Ashaninka have changed, Aniceto further remarks, proving again that one must see things with his own eyes. I am touched once more with the poignant knowledge that this adventurous and enterprising young man might never have known the people on the other side of the mountain, except for our chance meeting on the road. The Ashaninka who drift into Satipo, like the obsequious, ill-smelling and shifty-eyed youths who tried to sell me a jaguar tooth necklace, are all too frequently the highlanders' only vision of the Indians of the selva.

Inching along this way, we see more, contend with more. Matías stops once to nab an arrow washed down from upriver and caught in the reeds, and again to pick off a small freshwater crab trapped in some debris. We pull over to the bank where I notice a streak of red in the soil, and he scoops several handfuls of mud into the canoe. Off and on Aniceto and I have had to bail with a gourd because of cracks in the canoe bottom. Matías packs the wet red clay into these cracks and soon the leaks have diminished to an ooze of a few drops.

In one stretch of swift water we fail to make headway. After several minutes of leaning hard on the pole, while Hermania flails with the paddle, Matías has managed only to keep us even. He gives up in exhaustion and seizes a branch jutting from the bank to hold our position. There is another pole in the bottom of the canoe, somewhat shorter but still serviceable. I take it and offer to help. Matías nods and, releasing the branch, tells me we will float back downstream a few yards to match our strokes and gather a little momentum before another assault on the rapid. He warns me that I must not shove too hard, or I will lose my balance and fall out of the narrow canoe. This time he intends to skirt very near the shore. If the bottom scrapes he will leap out onto the bank with the bow line and drag us over the rocks.

Though I use the pole gingerly and miss a stroke or two, the bit of force I contribute is enough to get us through the swift place. On the other side I keep on, enjoying the stretch of muscles long cramped from sitting amidships and the simple rhythm of the work. The plunk of the poles, sometimes exactly together, their long travel to the shock against the bottom, and the plume of water raised by their withdrawal is hypnotic. Squinting against the glare and the sweat that soon fills my eyesockets, I concentrate on the shift of the canoe under me, the pressure of the current that sometimes sets the pole to thrumming audibly, the synchronous drive of our strokes, and scarcely look around me until Heorihéna shouts. Matías glances up, points, and I blink at the branches overhead. A band of monkeys glides and dips there, keeping pace with us for the moment. Their fur is rust-colored, and the small black faces flash as they glance back and forth between our canoe and their darting, zig-zag path through the tree tops. They are red howlers, I learn a few months later, when I hear their incredible cry for the first time. Matías makes an imaginary gun with his arms and aims at the monkeys, rather wistfully, and they vanish into the leaves.

At one of the places along the bank where we can see banana fronds and the peak of a roof, Matías indicates that we are pulling in. A good friend lives here he explains, and we will have our lunch. The friend, Kenchori, is tall and narrow for an Asháninka, with also an uncharacteristic hawk nose. He greets us warmly, jokes passing swiftly between him and Matías, and makes a place for us on the shaded platform of his small house. Hermania and Heorihéna gravitate immediately to the fire to gossip with Kenchori's wife and another old woman, a mother or aunt, who are busy there with pots.

We talk of Gerardo, since Kenchori is apparently one of the important informants for his research. With considerable pride, Kenchori tells me that Weiss three years ago took him all the way to Lima to identify birds in the national museum. He is a sort of unofficial *sheripiari* (shaman) as well, and later I find in Weiss's book a picture of him ten years ago as one participant in an ayahuasca session. Kenchori does betray a certain sly shrewdness, with a thread of the madcap in it, without compromising his friendly hospitality. His Spanish is much less facile than Matías's, but there is a special blend of devilish humor and reserve in his eyes.

When the large pot is steaming hot we are served a rich stew: yucca, plaintain, a bit of rice and chunks of a savory dark meat. I ask the name of the animal, and Kenchori replies by fishing its skull out of the pot. *Shintori*, he says. By the tusks I guess it is wild pig (Matías confirms the inference) and agree that it is very tasty. He takes a stone from beneath the platform and proceeds to knock the curved tusks out of the jawbone, taking care not to split them. When the two ivory crescents are free and wiped clean of grease, he hands them to me. This will be a memento of my visit, he says. I am grateful and embarrassed, for after distributing the cigarette lighters and mirrors in Ovíri I have nothing more to give in return.

Our party is, however, able to render a small service. Soon after the soup we begin to organize our departure, and it develops that Kenchori and his wife wish to travel with us for a few kilometers to visit another chacra. She takes a basket of yucca and bananas and Kenchori carries his bow and arrows. The canoe sits very low in the water when we push off, and several times in the rapids ahead we have to unload everyone and haul the craft upstream by its bowline. But these are occasions for merriment and volubility--the women hop along the stones, slipping and teetering, while the men look for animal tracks in the mud. Once, approaching the shallows of a back-eddy, we see the water bulge over a mighty back and there is a loud, sucking swish.

"*Zungaro!*" Kenchori exclaims. "*Grandasso.*" He stretches his arms wide to show the probable length. These giant catfish doze in quiet backwaters and occasionally may be harpooned from a stealthy canoe, but they are very difficult to subdue.

A few days later, checking schedules at the Satipo airport, I see a little five-passenger Cessna land and taxi to the main building. Two men climb out and begin to wrestle one of these leviathans through the narrow doors of the airplane. It is all they can do to stagger a few feet away with their burden, return and lift out a second fish. They have come from somewhere near Atalaya with their catch, well in excess of four hundred pounds. In response to my query they say that the *zungaro* were beached the evening before, perhaps twelve or fourteen hours ago. When I glance over at the two huge creatures, their pale hides beginning to wrinkle in the direct sun, I see the whiskers of one twitch, and all at once its gill plates open and close, open and close again, revealing the wine-red latticework inside.

Perhaps an hour further upriver, Kenchori and his wife debark and set off on a trail into the jungle. Typically only a casual sentence or two passes between him and Matías. Their business completed, the couple will borrow or quickly build a balsa, the crude rafts of from four to eight logs spiked and lashed together, and float back to their home. They can cover the distance we have travelled so arduously in a matter of minutes. We have yet two hours to go, Matías says, so it will be late afternoon before Otíka is in sight. Travelling by pole and paddle, one must figure the upstream trip at least three and sometimes as much as five times the length of the voyage with the current. Even in a peki-peki the time is at least doubled.

Matías has cut me a new pole, longer but green and heavy, and for the rest of the trip I work with him. I am surprised at the energy it requires in this climate to keep steadily at a physical task, and I am grateful for the reprieve of the back currents when we can rest our poles and glide effortlessly ahead. Also I am filled with humility, realizing that Matías was willing to take on this journey by himself, and would if necessary draw out of his small frame the power to propel all six of us up the river for many miles. To ease his burden after the long day, I strive to take a longer haul on the pole and push off harder at the end of the stroke.

When I make this effort we have just left a long reach on a back eddy where the water is shallow and large low trees hang far over the bank. Concentrating on putting forth more power, I do not see a branch above my head and do not allow for the proximity of the river bottom. In a moment the pole is fouled in the leaves and wedged into the mud below. Then the sky rocks crazily and I have time for only one squawk of surprise before flopping into the placid water. When I stand up, spluttering and groping in futile rage after the gunwale with one hand while I keep my spectacles clamped on my nose with the other, the canoe has drifted broadside to me and I hear shouts of laughter. Matías's grin is especially wide because of the missing teeth, and he is unable for the moment to wield his pole. His wife manages to bring the canoe within reach, without interrupting her squeals, and Heorihéna can look at me only for split seconds, which are enough to give her paroxysms. Aniceto does his manful best to register concern and help me back into the canoe. After the first flash of irritation, I am pleased to provide such entertainment. Even though I am soon dry and back at my post, for the rest of our voyage whenever I catch Heorihéna's eye she claps a hand over her mouth, shaking with silent giggles, and tries to disappear inside her cushma.

19

During the night, despite my heavy-limbed exhaustion, I wake periodically to the sharp rustle of rain and the crack of lightning. The morning begins in a steady downpour, and we resign ourselves to another day of reading and note-making. The gray weather brings melancholy reminiscences from both of us, it seems, because we soon stray from our books to the fire, the teapot and conversation. A discussion of our recent trip leads Aniceto to a wild and quite incredible tale of a lost city in the north, inhabited by dwarves no more than a meter high. I press him to tell me where he has really been, what he has really seen.

Like the refugee couple on the chacra and like Kenchori, like many Peruvians I will meet in odd corners of the country, Aniceto has spent some time in Lima. In fact, he has done time in Lima. For *un delito sexual* he was confined to the city jail for a month. The girl's father had some influence, and after a hasty hearing Aniceto was placed in one of the subterranean tiers where "no one knows whether it is night or day." The cellblocks are only rows of cages on a concrete floor, Aniceto says, with a gutter running through each row. Twice a day the gutter is flooded to remove waste, and food is ladled through the bars. He learned from other inmates that some men had spent as long as two years in this underground prison, never seeing the light of day. Release is possible only if there is a relative or friend working through bribery or persistent cajolery to have one's case processed.

Aniceto expains that he had been working as a waiter in a rather posh establishment. Gringos frequented the spot, big spenders, with gorgeous companions and thick bankrolls. They spent the equivalent of a month's pay in a single night. Not a good example, he remarks ruefully. He began to carouse in dives after work, spending whatever he made. After a few months he became embroiled with the girl and found himself in that sinister tomb of concrete and steel. Fortunately a couple of sympathetic friends managed to extricate him. He worked until he had paid off his fine and a few debts, then left for Satipo to work as a woodcutter. There he met members of the Israelite sect and converted fervently to a new life. He married and through a bargain struck with a local landowner, traded a year's diligent labor for his ten hectares of land. The selva, he says, has been his salvation: enough to eat, and a community of spiritual brothers.

Lima emerges again as the villain of the piece. Yet with the fascination of a villain too, with the villain's tremendous, restless, compelling energy.

As in Shakespeare's plays, this extraordinary combination of corruption and flamboyance, lust and ambition, seems to be the motive spring for what happens. In this country it is the aggressor, the shaker, the challenger, reaching high into the great mountains and now over them into the green slopes for its fix of raw materials and power. Most Peruvians are at some point in their lives drawn to it, and all are at least affected by it. For Aniceto it seems to have served as the principal trial of his soul, a journey through sin and the ultimate purgation of punishment to a rebirth in Eden.

On the other side of this pretty conceit, of course, are the Asháninka lads who vanish downriver to Pucallpa, a dirtier and more brutal version of a city, and never return. A kind of circulation, perhaps, is occurring. The metropolis is like a heart (or perhaps more fittingly a kidney) that absorbs the desperate and driven, while it pumps others out into the land as wastes that must be regenerated before reabsorption. In the case of the Indian populations, this metaphor is merely an extension of the Pishtako myth, and has operated since the arrival of the Spanish conquerors. For these four centuries the aboriginal people have been herded or have themselves fled into the coastal cities-- Chimbote, Lima, Trujillo--or the rubber ports of Iquitos and Pucallpa, where in a generation or two they have been assimilated into the colonial culture. After a few years of marginal existence, reduced to a new level of penury and depravity, a few of their offspring strike out to return to the provinces. This time, however, they arrive without knowledge or skill to live independently in the forest: they must cart with them the tin and gasoline and plastic of their new culture and create tiny, ramshackle Limas on the fringe of the wilderness, shrines whose evil reaches only to the pathetic, where in the great city there is at least an appalling grandeur.

After lunch the rain ceases and patches of sunlight alternate with the swift shadows of cloud scud. Matías comes by to ask whether or not he should try to radio Padre Castillo and secure a peki-peki. It comes as a shock to realize that already our journey is drawing to its close. But Matías is right to nudge us into that awareness. We are low on supplies, can offer nothing more in exchange for the generous support of the village, and in this uncertain weather we must take advantage of whatever transport may be moving on the river in the next few days. If we hear an engine approaching, Matías emphasizes, we must hurry to the bank and signal vigorously. No official passenger service exists, so all is luck and beggary.

For three days the pattern remains the same. Matías has discovered that his batteries are exhausted and no contact with Puerto Ocopa is possible, so we must depend on a canoe happening by. There is a rumor in the village that a pair of local men are expected soon, in transit from Atalaya to Ocopa. Aniceto is a little nervous, since he fears that one of these men may be Margarita's daughter's husband, but our growing impatience soon overrides all qualms. Fretfully we idle away our time, fishing with Heraldo, taking pictures, staring into the fire while the rain rattles on the leaves. Our meals are built around the last of the hardtack and spice tea, with some oranges brought back from Ovíri for dessert. Since we have no further projects or gifts, the villagers largely ignore us, except for casual individual visits. Occasionally I look up from my notebook to find that an Asháninka boy or young man has materialized at the fireside to observe me or my moving pen with patient curiosity. We greet each other, and I return to my notes, he to his observation. When I look again, he is gone.

One afternoon we are invited to watch Martín and his sons-in-law working on a new canoe. The site of construction is perhaps two kilometers from the river, and the men walk to it whenever there appears to be a significant break in the weather. On the ground lies a tremendous trunk, like the half-gnawed femur of an antediluvian giant. With axes the men are shaping it gradually. They work in shifts, no more than two at any one time, while the others sit in the shade, drowsing or talking. The tree is *caoba*, a wood relatively light but hard and close-grained, and the canoe will emerge as a single piece from its heart. At the base the trunk is a good six feet through, so they must trim a long foot from each side and more from the bottom.

I try my hand with the axe and after a dangerous skid or two, which elicits whoops of laughter from the men, I acquit myself credibly. It is hard, slow work and I have trouble believing Martín's estimate of one month to complete the job. It is explained to me that although the rain continually interrupts the work, it is desirable to keep the wood wet; it cuts more easily that way and does not crack in the sun. I learn also that the shape of the craft is achieved by matching two center spines from huge palm fronds and laying them on the flattened top of the log in opposing curves. The slender, graceful craft, perhaps thirty feet long and four feet across, is buoyant and strong.

This canoe will be the largest in Otíka, and I gather that Martín intends to make it available to any competent navigator in the community. It is a considerable investment in effort and time, requiring not only the brute force necessary to cut and section the huge tree, but great skill in the final trimming. By means of a small hand adze--a very much prized tool in the selva--the center is hollowed out until the thickness of the sides is an even two and a half inches and all surfaces inside and out are smooth. Then careful engineering is necessary to skid the craft down steep hillsides and through the undergrowth to the river more than a mile away. Ropes and short lengths of log serving as rollers are employed in this task, which will itself require several days.

There is no sign of a boat on the river. Hour after hour it slides by, a huge, rustling serpent, its opaque back reflecting an empty sky. Twice on the second day of our wait we hear an engine and race to the bank wild with excitement, but both times the boat is going downriver. We watch it dejectedly, small in the distance, the crouched passengers turning toward us and then away. I have to labor almost moment by moment to quell impatience and frustration, though I realize full well that my schedules and responsibilities in Lima have no bearing on this place, can exert no force, and ought to be forgotten. I am even aware that within days of returning to the rude hurly-burly of the capital I will begin to dream of returning here for a much longer stay. But these contradictions are not resolved by mere exposure: the vicious little red insects keep me physically restive, the damp weather softens all my clothing and renders it odoriferous, and my notebook has become a scatter of petty maunderings and rootless images. Quite simply, my limited and half-formed purposes have been overwhelmed by the reality of the place. Scenes and anecdotes skitter through my mind, then collapse under the impact of this dripping, green profusion, these people who stand and watch as stupidly as mushrooms, and the anxiety and boredom of waiting.

Late in the afternoon of the third day the expected travellers from Atalaya arrive, two young men and a plump young woman, a toucan and a tiny black monkey, and the following morning we embark on the long upriver voyage to Puerto Ocopa. Our leave-taking is swift and noncommital. I cannot tell whether Matías and Martín believe my assurance of a return in May, when the dry season is expected to set in. Many visitors have passed this way--missionaries, surveyors, explorers, anthropologists, hunters--leaving promises of salvation, roads, dams, cartridges, knowledge and the like. Certainly not all have been kept.

Without the slightest suggestion of reproach or suspicion, with no qualification of their fundamental politeness, the people of Otíka have greeted us, entertained us, and watched us depart, their faces blank as mirrors to my eager search for hope or approval, enthusiasm or doubt. As the river appears in the world, then vanishes at its other rim, my plans and purposes--perhaps the plans and purposes of all men--have their brief existence, give shape to a few days, and are gone into both the past and the future, as memory and as possibility. For the Asháninka I do not think existence has that wide margin of promise which in us generates so much effort and turmoil; for them life settles on the back like the yucca basket, resonates up the bones of the arm from the axe handle, leaps from the fingers like an arrow.

20

Or throbs through one's backside as the Briggs and Stratton pounds away to move us upstream. Several times in rapids it seems we are making no progress at all, merely fighting to stay even, and finally one of the boatmen takes a pole to edge us forward through such stretches. Though the motor appears old, caked with grease and grime, and periodically develops hiccups, the two young men remain sunny. *No hay problema*, they shout at us whenever we bear into a racing stretch of river and the engine begins to labor. Like Matías, they elect to cross the river often in order to take advantage of the back eddies. In this quieter water they feed us fresh mangos, a giant variety shaped like a beef heart, bright green with a scarlet flush near the stem. The flesh is light peach, cool and deliciously sweet, without any of the fibrous or pulpy quality that marks the smaller, more common fruit.

After perhaps three hours, as we round a bend, one of the men gives a strangled shout and waves furiously for his companion to kill the motor. The canoe glides into the bank and the two of them peer over the brush, whispering excitedly. I finally spot a red deer, a good-sized one, grazing on a sandspit some two hundred yards ahead of us. I have brought with me an old bow and three arrows purchased from one of the village boys for fifty cents. One of the men gestures and I hand it to him. He is gone into the undergrowth. For perhaps forty-five minutes we wait, sweltering in the sun, while the toucan works incessantly to force his great banana beak through the stitching that closes his basket cage, scraping and rapping it against the side of the boat.

Finally there is a shout. The boatman and his girlfriend laugh, shake their heads, and the engine is started again. We pick up the luckless hunter on the sandspit. He is dancing with excitement, breathless to begin his tale. Waving the slack bow he pantomimes just how the string snapped at the moment of release, sending the arrow a foot below the deer's neck. I am struck again at how pleased these people are simply with what happens, whatever the outcome in terms of success or failure. We stop a short distance further on at a good-sized settlement and spend an hour describing our adventure to our hosts there.

One of these, a young man with the impressive status already of professor, tells me a little of the uneasy relations between river Asháninka and those of the interior Pajonal. The mountain people are still not civilized, he says, and have given up raiding only because the villages are too large now and the government's ability to retaliate too formidable. When he was a child he travelled with his father and some companions into the hills, taking a cross-country route to visit friends on a distant tributary. They were attacked and driven back by a group of the mountain warriors, who did not pursue them far because there were no women with them.

More than once I am to hear of the *Pajonalistes* craving for women or female children, for many told me that the raiders made off with girls of six or seven years. These tales recall others from the world over: woman-stealing is second only to stock rustling as the favored enterprise of ambitious young braves. In my own culture, undergoing upheaval at this time over the issue of women's roles, these tales would be shocking proof of the primal oppression of men, and could serve to fuel the polemics which flare up regularly in the popular press.

The people of the interior, however, differ only slightly from the river tribes. The dialects spoken by the two groups are mutually comprehensible. A woman's lot is essentially the same: brewing masato, weaving the cushma, dressing and cooking game, digging yucca, rearing children. I cannot help wondering whether some young women did not secretly yearn for the excitement of abduction, as a spice to the otherwise lifelong routine of their lives in a small village. A half-century ago the Asháninka still held to their belief in witches, and according to Weiss, if preliminary chastisement and isolation did not bring an end to bad luck, the unfortunate girls cast in this role sometimes were killed outright, or sold into slavery. Other tribes had provisions for marrying off widows to a brother-in-law, or trading daughters for advantage, or otherwise narrowly defining the pool of available mates. It appears to me possible, even likely, that in such cases the prospect of becoming the captive of a total stranger, even an alien of another tongue and faith, may have seemed an acceptable or even glamorous alternative.

There is also a disposition to deny nowadays an aspect of female psychology that has a long and substantial tradition. Many species of animal life reproduce in complex patterns involving battle between males as a precondition to copulation. Among horses, seals, lions, gorillas and other large mammals one dominant male may assemble a harem which he must defend against periodic challenge from aspirant males. The principle of "raiding" may therefore have some biological foundation, to test the mettle of the bearers of vigorous genes or to hybridize a population. Further, in many mythological systems gods, demigods and heroes spend a great deal of time raping and philandering; they may disguise themselves as animals--eagle, bull, swan, coyote--but the offspring is usually of human form and often gifted with special powers. The Immaculate Conception of Jesus by the Holy Ghost may be viewed as such a raid. And many civilizations have cemented their conquests of weaker peoples by enforced marriages or concubinage as a means of binding new subjects firmly into the social fabric.

The assumed passivity of females in these complex equations of sexual and social behavior may be a semantic illusion. Among animals, oestrus is an indiscriminate signal which *initiates* the whole cycle of aggressive display and conflict among males. Whatever the outcome, the egg-bearer will survive and perpetuate her influence. Were the abducted utterly recalcitrant and vengeful, or utterly abject and spiritless, it is doubtful that their captors would risk life and limb to secure them. Similarly, although it would be easy to read the myths of divine ravishment as the projections of masculine fantasies of lust and promiscuity, surely the maid who is the object of such celestial attention may occupy a superior position on earth: she surpasses all others in grace and beauty, and becomes sometimes the origin of a new cult or race of heroes. She has only to commit an act of daring availability, a calculated misstep, a sign perhaps of the priceless genes of courage and imagination.

SNAPSHOT

A footpath, in disuse except during the worst rains. It skirts the perimeter of a settlement, leads to a small stream where the purest water may be drawn. Dawdling because of overwork and secret resentments, an adolescent girl bearing a large urn moves along the path. It is twilight, later than she should be abroad because a visitor from a nearby village has carried ominous news of marauders from the mountains. But the girl does not think about this danger; her heart is full and hot with anger at her old father who gave her to another old man who is her master, and the other wives of his household, who conspire against her.

When she reaches the pool the girl sinks the lip of the urn under its shimmering surface and allows the vessel to fill slowly. She splashes a little, idly, and begins to sing. Her song is about a young girl whose lover has gone off hunting and how lonely she is without him. In the gathering darkness the mournful notes give the singer a strange buoyancy, a daring, and she leaps lightly across the stream and follows for a few steps one of the faint trails made by the deer who come to drink there, and by the hunters who pursue them. She knows she should not be so bold, but as she walks and sings the rage in her heart begins to transform itself into a kind of fierce joy. Her disobedience is a tonic, and when once the shadows move and her heart leaps, she has a vision of a man with a strange face, a man who moves through the forest as swiftly and silently as a snake, travelling far, a man with a body as smooth and strong and sweet as cedar wood, a great hunter.

The other wives, when the broken urn is discovered, will insist that she ran away with a jaguar--the jade, the witch!

When darkness falls we are still some kilometers away from Puerto Ocopa, though we have cleared the mouth of the Ene and are proceding up the Perene. The water is shallow and swift, moving now between low hills, now around nearly submerged islands and sandbars, where bushes and small trees nod violently in the current. Against the tinge of yellow and burnt orange of the sky to the west, they gesticulate like warriors in a frenzied dance. One of the boatmen poles steadily now, groaning at times with the effort. I peer at the fringe of shadows on the bank and can no longer detect any forward movement at all. The bratting of the motor indicates continuous strain, and I remark that its attendant has begun to whistle, swatches of the tune faintly audible through the throbbing. Sometime ago the last of our gasoline was poured into the engine tank, and though at the time I believed we would have plenty for the last leg of the journey, progress through these rapids is painfully slow. The boatmen and the girl no longer joke among themselves, and even the toucan has ceased his infernal rapping and scraping. I suspect that we dallied too long at the last village, and the crew is now anxious at the prospect of some mishap which would force us to make a cold camp in this black place.

The color drains at last entirely from the horizon, and we have only a skyfull of stars to light our way. Several times the man on the pole cries out sharply and we swerve to dodge half sunken logs that hurtle down upon the canoe. Once we scrape one and I poise in the rocking craft, my fingers knotted around the camera bag. As usual, the Asháninka men laugh immoderately. At last we see for a few seconds a distant fleck of fire, and there are cries of excitement and relief. *Ocopa!* the motorist exclaims, breaking off his shaky whistling. But it is a good twenty minutes before we have fought to within a few dozen yards of the blaze, which lights a small circle of beach where another canoe is drawn up and a handful of people await us with calls of encouragement. Just then the engine dies, and we coast in free and dying flight for the last few boatlengths to the bank.

Out of gas! the young man exults, and the people at the fire whoop. I express frank incredulity, but the man unscrews the cap, plunges in his dipstick, and shows me by firelight that the tank is dry. It happened once before, he remarks, just that way. The last drops gave enough momentum to glide into safe harbor. *Que suerte!* But that was not at night. As we unload our gear and tread up the bank to cross the airfield I mull over the probabilities, and decide that a different kind of calculation may be at issue here. Without reference to gauges or numbers, these river travellers must judge the current against the boat, make the choice of crossing or not crossing the river to ride a certain eddy, listen to the slosh of fuel in the tank, pole nonchalantly or furiously, and finally whistle and pray to a very fine margin of error indeed.

In a few minutes we are waiting nervously on the veranda of the

Padre's quarters at the rear of the church. Inside the small boy's voice is too faint for us to catch his meaning, but I hear the good man groan and say, "But child, it is the middle of the night! Where are my spectacles?" When he shuffles out to meet us, tall and a little spectral in the light of a storm lantern, he has recovered his good humor and with swift tact ushers us to spare quarters above the dormitory. It seems a luxurious suite: a pair of narrow iron beds, a nightstand with candle, a plain table, a pitcher, a basin and chamber pot. While we murmur a few words of apology and gratitude, the small boy appears with two nuns who have brought us sheets and blankets. When the beds are made Padre Castillo bids us a good night. Aniceto and I exchange a wondering grin and stretch out to a fine, deep, and untroubled slumber.

21

The next few days are easy and enjoyable. I wake to the early, slanting light and Padre Castillo's strong baritone resonating in the chapel. He sings mass each morning at six o'clock to the thirty-odd orphan children who remain at the mission over the holidays. The nuns, a wizened old lay brother who assists him, and a few villagers also attend. Once I slip in to listen and to take in the simple, clean space. The walls and high ceiling are whitewashed stucco, with sparely decorated alcoves for the stations of the cross. The shutters of the arched windows are thrown wide, admitting the coolness and a heavy fragrance of roses and bougainvillaea. Padre Castillo is imposing in his cassock and surplice, the handsome hawk face solemn but benevolent. He speaks of Sin and of Satan, but as well as I can follow, given my Spanish and the echoes of the room, these are not rendered as abstractions, but as the incarnation of temptation and irresponsibility, the monstrousness that appears when men resort to lies, theft, and brutality. The little Asháninka boys for the most part attend patiently, round-eyed, though a few of the smallest yawn and once in a while an older boy folds in upon himself with silent, mysterious mirth or embarrassment.

Our day is organized around the meals, which always last a minimum of one hour and are the nearest I have ever come to the high table conversations of cloistered dons. Padre Castillo discourses at length (in reply to a query of Aniceto's) on the location of the soul--it does not reside in the blood or brain, but is an immanence of the corporeal, present everywhere. We talk of the atom, the concept of half-life--with numerous puns and conceits--of Carbon 14 dating, and beekeeping. Sometimes Castillo regales us with tales of his jungle adventures: jaguars, bushmasters, the warrior ant, as well as more modern thrills: dope-runners, guerilla raids, and vagabond travellers from the four corners of the world. His enthusiasm for information is boundless, and though I often lose the gist of the more rarified and metaphysical points, he invariably condenses and summarizes like a good teacher, often with the phrases *cosa tremenda es...* or *cosa curiosa es...*, delivered with a frank and penetrating gaze through his thick, Buddy Holly glasses.

A jar of fresh roses, the white tablecloth and the good father's wit transform this humble refectory into a salon. Under our feet the floor is bare, packed earth and overhead are musty beams bearing the mark of the axe, but the atmosphere is a combination of the seminary and the supper club. At intervals the crude but natural ways of the selva interrupt my concentration. The old lay brother, owlish behind his wire-rimmed spectacles, finishes stripping the meat from a chicken leg and without pause utters a sharp monosyllable and tosses it over his shoulder. The huge German shepherd that dozes on the floor is instantly on his feet and snaps the bone right out of the air. A few quick crunches and the dog drops again to lay his muzzle in the dust.

So it goes, through breakfast, lunch and dinner. Nietzsche, the Spanish revolution, Carlos Castaneda. Black holes, Hitler, and Howard Hughes. The gastronomic fare is simpler: chicken or fish, corn and yucca, bananas and oranges. There is coffee, however, served serano fashion as a cold concentrate to which one adds hot water, and sometimes sweet bread. Like most Peruvians, Padre Castillo likes to eat and talk, the two activities reinforcing each other, and I have to make an effort to master the art of integrating them. Often I am left with half a platefull, the fork forgotten in my hand, while the others are launching into unrestricted discussion and the kitchen girl clears away their dishes, throwing nervous glances at me. I would be last in any event, as Castillo has taken to keeping a bowl of fresh grapefruit at the table to serve my predilection, and I finish each meal with this succulent dessert.

Following breakfast, Padre Castillo rushes away to record the information at his weather and seismographic stations. Then he works in his rose garden or oversees some work in one of the orchards, or a project to build a laundry. In charge of this last undertaking is a happy, shambling old man from the highlands who has all the mannerisms of a town drunk. I see him several times a day crossing the grounds with a wheelbarrow or a beam across his shoulder. Each time he touches his fingers to the brim of his shapeless hat, calling out a hearty greeting. Castillo tells me that he was in fact a hopeless drunk ten years ago, but came to the mission at the father's urging and has remained his most trusted and energetic workman.

After lunch there is a siesta of two or three hours, and then the father works at his books until dinner. After dinner he has no duty except the eight o'clock radio contact with Satipo and Atalaya, and through these stations with Lima. I have asked him to try to arrange for a flight to Satipo if a plane happens to be passing through, as I do not want to pay the expresso fare and do not want to walk the ninety kilometers again. Nominally at least we are waiting here for that purpose, though the rest is very welcome whatever the excuse.

To while away my own time I have expressed interest in Padre Castillo's library, and he gives me the principal histories of the region from the point of view of the first Franciscan missionaries. Armed with my tiny pocket dictionary I approach these formidable tomes: José Amich, *Historia de las Missiones del Convento de Santa Rosa de Ocopa*, written in 1771; P. Dionisio Ortiz, *El Pichitea y el Alto Ucayali, Tomo 1*, a 1974 compilation from the preeminent Peruvian historian Raimondi, Izaguirre, and Padre Biedma, the first dependable source of ethnographic observation in this region. With nothing to expect but the next meal and its heady context of ideas and anecdotes, I find it pleasant to browse in the works of these earnest clerics. When I glance up from the veranda which separates Castillo's quarters from ours, I can look out over the tidy grounds, the flowers and shrubs varnished and fixed in the sun. Now and then a group of boys wanders through, or the happy workman, or a pig.

The temper and pace of the community possess a charming calm and informality. Padre Castillo is on the best of terms with everyone, from the smallest boy--perhaps four or five years of age--to the Mother Superior. The pressing business of the community is to repair the commodes, maintain the radio, prepare the football field for Saturday's match, and build the laundry. There is also an eternal wait for parts for the generator and tractor, which have not operated for months. The generator especially worries Castillo, because without it he cannot run the ancient movie projector which provides the children's most favored entertainment. One of the few useful tasks I can perform is the cleaning of this antique, a model with a ventilated bulb chamber perched like a lighthouse between its long fixed arms.

All this is indeed a contrast to the saga of the intrepid soldiers of the cross who first descended the Eastern slope to penetrate the selva. Raimondi remarks with some puzzlement that although the gold-mad conquistadors explored almost the whole of Perú for a century, they did not penetrate the jungle directly to the east of the main cities of Cuzco and Lima, and the first report of the Asháninka people is provided by missionary parties in 1631. Fathers Jeronimo Jimenez and Cristobal Larias established Quimíri (now La Mercéd), the first mission in the area, and in 1637 were massacred and martyred. A rumor of gold brought a small expedition to the abandoned mission in 1645, a motley lot of adventurers including a few men of the cloth probably interested more in wealth than in soul-saving. Travelling down the Perene, they were ambushed by Asháninka who killed all but two of them. One survivor married an Asháninka woman, and the other, a certain Villanueva, became a trusted adviser who was given charge of the tribe's defenses when a second expedition of 46 Spaniards headed by Francisco Bohorquez invaded the area.

Attempting to cross the Chanchamayo, Bohorquez was surrounded by Villanueva's warriors. The two arranged a truce and came to an agreement. They combined forces and Spanish and Indian marauders struck back into the mountains to raid highland settlements, taking cattle, grain and women. "Of the gold they set out to find there was not a trace," as Varese observes.

This unusual alliance did not endure long. The viceroy Conde de

Salvatierra sent troops who soon routed the bandits and captured the two leaders, who were sent to prison in Chile. This mild punishment indicates that the authorities tolerated a certain attitude of lawless opportunism in frontier districts, perhaps recognizing such freebooting as merely an extension of the crown's overall colonial policy. The government in Lima also had to arbitrate the pragmatic interests of several holy orders who were competing for control of various aboriginal populations. The Limeños were quite aware that a franchise to construct missions could be a political plum; the settlement of an area opened up many kinds of resources, including the right to raise funds--ostensibly for the salvation of souls, but in practical terms for the production of foodstuffs, cotton, hardwoods and animal hides.

The doughty friar Manuel de Biedma thus spent the first dozen years of his career as evangelist in the arduous labor of combatting the Jesuits, who were pressing into the upper Ucayali from Cuzco. He divided his time between intrigues in Lima and expeditions to contact the tribes along the Perene and Tambo. Biedma allied his Franciscans with the Conibo early in his travels, while the Jesuits had enlisted the support of Piro settlements, and neither order actively discouraged its charges from preying on the opponents. The Conibo survived principally through piracy, not even bothering to weave their own clothes but raiding to procure what tools, garments, food or wives they might need. More than content to make their forays in the service of the ambitious ecclesiastics, these fearsome corsairs were apparently at once a powerful escort for the good friar, and a guarantee against any resistance from other tribes. In 1686, however, returning from a major expedition--at least 20 canoes and 100 warriors--Biedma was hurrying to Lima to contest a new threat from the Jesuits when his detachment was ambushed by Piros near what is now Ocopa, and he died in a shower of arrows. Nor, the historian Izaguirre remarks mournfully, was this tragedy the last of the trials of the indomitable Franciscans.

> "This is the story which will be repeated for the three centuries of missionary work which we are going to describe. The heroism of the missionaries who succumb to the savagery of triumphant indians; the solicitude of the selfless which multiplies an affectionate industry in order to win indian souls, and the indolence of this latter which frustrates all expectations of the self-denying apostles."

One may balk at describing the Conibo slave-raids for which Biedma's expedition provided the excuse as "affectionate industry," but certainly the eulogy of the friar as a man of vigor and a tireless explorer is justified, and his successors seemed no less intrepid in their determination to subjugate the people of the Montaña.

Several more attempts to penetrate the territory of the Asháninka and Machiguenga also failed, but the mission at Quimíri was active more often than not by the end of the first quarter of the eighteenth century, and smaller outposts had been established in the Pajonal. The reports of trouble and sometimes massacre in these areas assume a monotonous pattern. The early chroniclers first write enthusiastically of the Indians' docility and cooperation: a church is built, houses laid out, fields planted, Bible work begun. Then the people grow sullen and demand more gifts, or abruptly depart from the community. The historian then laments their fickleness, their childishness, their addiction to unhealthy and dangerous superstitions. In more than one instance, the friction develops over the priest's insistence that an Asháninka man give up his extra wives. This custom especially seems to have galled the missionaries, but I suspect that the Indians were quite as scandalized by the celibacy of the interloper --who nevertheless expected them to do his cleaning and cooking.

Despite these petty grievances the Asháninka tolerated the missionaries for years, until the newcomers' overall strategy at last became clear. For of course the evangelist does not rest until the faith has percolated into every corner of life, and driven out all trace of heathen custom and philosophy. Invariably, just as the friars thought they were beginning to save souls, the Indians sensed that they were losing theirs. The confrontation is very clear in a moment of high drama in 1737. Padre Manuel Bajo had built his mission with the help of an Asháninka chief, Torote, whom he rechristened Ignacio. After a series of misunderstandings, Torote descended on the mission with a group of warriors. Bajo, two other friars, and a few frightened servants fled to the chapel, but their former disciple did not respect the sanctuary. He hunted them out and shot them where they knelt to pray. An Asháninka boy witnessed then an exchange between the chief and the priest, which Izaguirre reports:

> "His body pierced by two arrows, Father Manuel Bajo said to Torote: 'So, Ignacio, why do you kill me?' The criminal replied: 'Because you and your people are killing us every day with your sermons and lessons, taking our freedom. Now you can preach that we ourselves are the fathers.' And with their war clubs they finished off the three principal ecclesiastics."

It is easy to imagine the horror, revulsion and rage that would ensue when the Indians grasped that these strangers came not merely to exchange gifts for labor, nor to solicit help with house-building and crop-raising, nor even by means of force or trickery to carry off goods and women. These pale beings in black robes were after nothing less than the Indians' souls, a necessary nourishment apparently for their own existence. They were ghouls who ate spirits and thus converted others into their own substance.

A secular version of this psychic vampirism is still active, in the form of plans for "development" of the "emerging" nations. The governors of many of these countries have themselves been converted to the religion of progress through industrial technology. Educated in Europe or the United States, where they acquired a taste for television, fighter planes, and hair spray, they approach the tribal people within their borders as a political problem to be solved by assimilation and resettlement, but also as a more profound challenge, a reminder of a lost world with its echoes of paradise, and a living demonstration that people may live simply and peaceably without any commitment to civilization.

The vigor and enterprise with which modern societies pursue the subversion of these vestiges of primitive culture argue that more than mere material advantage is at issue. The tribespeople represent the last traces of doubt in modern man, who wishes to convert them to his own path because he can then hurry to his destiny with no more backward glances. A century ago colonial powers were content to exterminate the natives or push them onto preserves unless they were willing to accept economic slavery, but now, rather like the inexorable padres who journeyed to the heart of the selva, we insist on all sorts of projects and programs to integrate our minorities into the dominant social order. Of course many of these educational programs are highly sophisticated in their apparent benevolence, and urge the preservation of "autonomy" and "traditions," by which is meant usually songs, dances, myths, and decorative skills. But these are coveted not as vital and viable ways to live, but simply as charming museum pieces, a belated gesture of humanism.

In fact it is the western anthropologist who is most active in seeking out and recording the vanishing primitives. An exactly contrary impulse motivates his work: his doubts are about his own culture, which, as Levi-Strauss observed twenty years ago, he renounces in favor of the study of alien peoples, even though in this way he makes himself an incompetent observer of either. Among the Sea Dyaks, Arunta or Nambikwara he explores a negative vision, a search for all that has been purged from the world men have constructed for themselves in Paris, London, or New York. This bias insures that his findings will be of no use to his own society--they may in fact be toxic there--and also prevents him from seeing the intrinsic value and function of the native's culture. Ineffectuality is compounded with bitterness when the ethnographer realizes that he and his trade exist nevertheless only as a function of and at the pleasure of the very industrial civilization that is greedily consuming his subject matter. His grants come from government or philanthropic foundations whose revenues are the effluvia of the complex factory and trade system that has spread everywhere its net of road, rail, pipe and wire, and that draws into its vortex not only wood, coal, oil, diamonds, uranium, copper, bananas, coffee, rubber, cotton, and so on, but the deer-souls of those few remaining human habitants of the forest as well.

So it was true as Torote saw that sermons may kill as surely as arrows, and it is true still that the souls of Indians are fodder to the juggernaut of civilization. For modern government planners, as for the priests of three centuries ago, each conversion of a deer-soul into a productive Christian citizen confirms and enhances the myth of progress; while for the anthropologist this same transformation creates anxiety and despair, for the vanishing population he wishes to study has become at once his justification, his hope and his doom.

22

One afternoon, by some miraculous recombination of old parts, the unofficial mechanic from the village succeeds in resurrecting the generator, and the Mother Superior has a box of photographic slides which have not yet been shown, so Padre Castillo decrees an evening program with the magic lantern. After dinner there is a distant cranking and coughing, and in a few seconds a dim yellow light pulses out of dark bulbs strung here and there through the kitchen and dormitories. The excited shouts of the children echo in the courtyard, and Castillo bustles off to collect his projector, cords, and screen. The new light fluctuates erratically every minute or so, and the old lay brother shakes his head dubiously, but the general enthusiasm has achieved an indomitable momentum. We assemble on the crude wooden benches in a classroom, and after considerable fussing the Padre has his equipment ready: another antique projector, a cumbersome black box that accepts one slide at a time, which must be inserted and withdrawn by hand, and a pale, wrinkled bedsheet on the mud plaster wall.

The children's babble of joyful anticipation pauses for an instant as the first slide clicks in, and then becomes a great sigh of ecstatic contemplation. It is a picture of the mission grounds, with a few figures small and indistinct in the background. There is excited discussion and laughter. We wait for minutes until a chorus goes up: *Otro! Otro!* Another slide drops into place. Now the courtyard outside the kitchen, with a few chickens and peeking children. Again the universal sigh, the sound of the very thirsty after a long, sweet drink. There is commentary, seemingly on every chicken, child and brick in the wall.

A little further along and the Padre, perhaps not strictly by accident, inserts a slide upside-down. The response is that kind of wide-open screaming that I remember from cartoon matinees when I was a child. Later a variation of this effect is achieved by tilting the projector at a forty-five degree angle, and this gesture also generates shrieks and applause. Finally a shot of the smiling Mother Superior walking down a path on the grounds brings near pandemonium. I do not see the reason for this revelry, unless it is the simple mystery of that foot apprehended aloft in mid-stride, a homely version of the Grecian Urn, but the laughter and cheers are genuine, and when Padre Castillo finally removes the slide there are groans of disappointment.

The show concludes with a promise that if the generator maintains its

health the whole performance will be repeated soon, and this announce-
ment seems to mollify the spectators, who still gaze absently, wistfully, at
the blank sheet. Then in a few moments they dash outside in the courtyard and begin to sing *huaynas* and dance in the gasping light from a few
bulbs strung there. When the machine is packed away and the good sisters
have recovered their sheet, we step outside and watch for a little while.
Here too only the girls seem to dance, while the boys lounge against the
wall and call out encouragement or mockery. The Padre makes a sally or
two and there is an interlude of banter and merriment before we stroll on
to our quarters.

It is eight o'clock, the broadcast hour, and soon the set is crackling
and hissing. The incoming transmissions are only harsh electronic honks
to me, except for a rare common phrase-- *"cambio"* seems to mean "over"
or "ten-four"--but the Padre's side of the conversation makes everything
clear. Although he adopts a radio voice, flat and stentorian, the messages
are all charmingly routine: Has Father Jimenez come back from Tarma yet?
Was the road rained out? How much is a sack of cement in Lima and would
it pay to ship from there? We have a man here--a nice gringo--who needs a
lift out, if anything is flying. I listen to the radio's squawk, the distant
singing of the happy children, and the frogs and night birds of the
surrounding jungle, trying to connect it all with the dismal speculations
evoked by my reading of the early chroniclers.

It is impossible to view Padre Castillo as ghoul, oppressor or exploiter.
Crouched over his microphone in his ragged smock and thick glasses,
chatting about a distant brother or a few sacks of cement, his orphan flock
laughing now from darkness (the generator has been retired), he strikes
me as a redemption of those first centuries of aggressive missionizing.
Since there is no escaping the great remolino of civilization, of the radio
and the roads and airstrips, the Indian's best hope of survival is some
knowledge of its currents. No gentler emissary and navigator can be
imagined. I have noticed how the boys beam when Castillo strides near,
or fall into a quick step of their own to keep near him, venturing their
Spanish, their minds, their hearts. The good father too is energized and
uplifted; he jokes, lectures, and commands by turns, always with an
underlying compassion and good will.

On the following day there is a soccer match pitting the older boys
against men from the small village that adheres to the mission. A few days
previously the teams worked together with machetes to clear the weeds
from a grassy field bounded by orange trees. The spectators sit on an
immense bench made from a tree trunk cut in half. The gallery includes
Castillo, Aniceto, myself, the nuns and a few of the boys too young to play.
After the main match two teams of girls square off, and Padre Castillo
seems to delight most of all in this contest of kitchen and laundry maids.

He cheers especially a very fat forward, whose short, thick legs propel her with awesome momentum. *Gol! Gol! Gordita!* he shouts. (Come on Tubby! Score!) And with an expression of intense, total dedication she begins to move the ball. Several times it is stolen, but she always recovers, sometimes not quite legally it appears to me, and thunders back down-field. The Padre bellows his encouragement at every hard-won step and at last she mows through the last pair of guards like a little tank and whacks the ball through the posts. Castillo pounds his knees with his fists and delivers the Latin American victory cry: *Go-o-o-o-l! Go-o-o-o-l!* It is a triumph to balance the murderous sermons of Padre de Bajo.

23

At lunch on the following day, in a brief lull in our conversation, Padre Castillo looks up suddenly with vacant expression. *Avion!* I strain to catch the sound. Just as I perceive the faintest of vibrations, he rises and begins to give orders. It is landing, he says confidently, and you must hurry to the airfield. He sends the serving girl out to fetch some boys to collect our things. I have just begun a cup of coffee so I only nod my understanding and murmur a promise to make haste. Padre Castillo is positively dancing around the table: all right, finish the coffee, he says, but hurry. The Mother Superior looks in at the door, breathless. The plane is indeed landing. She looks alarmed. Children, you must run! she admonishes.

Aniceto and I get up then, exchanging a look of surprise with a touch of suspicion. Perhaps the good father has indeed, despite his impeccable manners, grown tired of entertaining us. When we reach our quarters a gang of boys has already stuffed everything we own into my pack and Aniceto's flour sack, so we stream down the steps at a half-trot, a line of tiny porters staggering under their loads, the Padre shooing us along like a great mother crane. We say our farewells as we go. I promise to check at the American Embassy to find out why they no longer send their free propaganda films to the mission, and to bring when I return a handful of tape splices for broken film. Castillo embraces me quickly, calls me brother and tells me to run.

I try, but it is a very hot, unclouded day, and parasites have at last found a path to my digestive tract. I can proceed only at a hurried, tight-kneed walk, my bowels sloshing audibly with each stride. The airstrip is better than a quarter-mile distant, and soon I am the last of our straggling train, accompanied by a heroic lad no more than six years old, who bears my sleeping bag and keeps his reverent smile turned to me like a searchlight. As I reach the end of the lane where a little thatch shed for storage marks the beginning of the field I hear the motor of the plane revving. The group of porters surrounds our heap of baggage, jumping up and down and gesticulating. Streaming with sweat, my glasses riding precariously on the tip of my nose, I jog heavily to the edge of the field and see the wheels of the little Cessna, white with orange trim, lift away from the grass. With a roar, wings waggling, it flashes by and in a few seconds banks over the river and begins to diminish rapidly into the hot blue sky.

I look down at the children gathered around and see that they are delighted, expectant. What fun to gather up these strange and wonderful articles, run with the huge gringo in hide hat to watch the airplane bound away! I dig out a small sack of Chiclets and distribute them. The little man with my sleeping bag suffers no diminution of his adoration, but trudges back beside me as proud as ever. Too shamed to grumble, I must force a smile on this long retreat and when we have deposited our things again in the room, shake the hands of my cheerful helpers. When I have unpacked I take a bar of soap and a towel to the river to wash away the sweat. The lay brother squats beside a mango tree, sharpening his machete on a flat rock. He greets me with a dour nod, and between strokes observes, "A fine opportunity lost." A few strokes later, "You'll have to order a plane now. Otherwise you could be here for weeks."

It strikes home to me that he is of course right, and we are in danger of outstaying our welcome. The plane came to deliver some part or supplies to the ElectroPeru station, which is located across the airfield from the mission. It is an experimental station, measuring the annual flow of the river and making calculations for a possible hydroelectric installation. There are diplomatic contacts between this settlement and the mission, but they are diffident and tenuous. To hitch a cheap ride on one of their flights would involve presenting my credentials to the director of the station, perhaps undertaking a probationary friendship, or at the very least checking each day for rumors of an incoming flight. And the SASA pilot might very well insist on charging the expreso fare for hauling us back to Satipo, instead of to San Ramón, his usual destination.

With great tact, Padre Castillo has refrained from suggesting an expreso order. I realize that our economies during the trip have led him to believe that we are nearly destitute, a common condition in Perú which everyone tries to ignore. Actually, I have the money for the full fare, but it will mean taking a bus over the Andes to Lima, a grueling eighteen- hour trip--if I am lucky enough to hit a gap in the rains--and a sharply reduced farewell gift to Aniceto.

At dinner that evening our flight and failure are the subject of merry elaboration; my suspicion of tension in the Padre evaporates. He seems glad to have us back, yet concerned that we find a way to return to our usual lives. With the best grace I can, I assure him that I can pay for an expreso, and would appreciate his radioing for a plane as soon as possible. As things fall out, the Mother Superior, a visiting nun from Lima, and an Asháninka woman and her seven year-old must have a plane on the following day, and the shipment of cement has arrived but is too much weight for a single trip. So it is arranged that the Cessna will bring half a load from Satipo tomorrow, fly the party of women out on its return, then come back for us with the rest of the cement. We will receive a slight reduction of fare by paying for the incoming cargo only, and the Mother Superior can use the receipt for tax purposes.

So, after eight days of uncertainty and anxiety, we see the plane arrive promptly at nine the next morning. It is unloaded with swift efficiency, while the pilot in his crisp white shirt with black and gold braid receives a freshly punctured coconut from a woman of the village. Clearly he is the royalty of the selva, still a kind of divine visitant for the Indians, who gather at a respectful distance to admire for the hundredth time the miracle of flight. As soon as the sacks are out of the cabin he oversees the boarding of the Mother Superior and her charges, securing the safety belts and stowing their baggage. The village woman recovers the empty coconut husk and with a jaunty wave the pilot clambers in; after an experimental flop of ailerons and a blast of air from the propeller the plane lurches around and trundles away for takeoff.

Within the hour it returns and the ritual is repeated. Padre Castillo has come to see us off, and we are allowed a more leisurely and expressive farewell. His warmth and magnanimity are unflagging, the character of one who has guided and loved a flock of four dozen children for twenty years. Then we are locked inside the little cabin, and in a few minutes bump along the grass, flash by the small group of waving villagers around the white-smocked pillar of the Padre, and slide into the air. The river and the bright metal roofs drop away as we climb over the rugged green slopes. Aniceto is tremendously excited, for this is his first flight ever. I am impressed too, after our three-day trek over this territory, at the effortless sailing that brings us back to Satipo in a matter of minutes. The shock and disorientation when we walk again in the market is greater than that I have experienced on transcontinental journeys, and the noise and stink, the cunning and opportunism of the place provoke a strong revulsion in me.

Our parting is hasty and sad, a little clouded by the cramping of my generosity. I am able to afford--ironically--only the dollar a day minimum wage, since even by taking the bus I will have to economize in order to survive for a day or two in Lima while I arrange to draw funds from the Fulbright office. Still, I believe my sturdy Sancho Panza has gotten an eyeful. He will be able to speak with some authority about the place of the mission in the selva's economy, about the ways of the Asháninka, and about the marvels of air travel. I have taken him further east than he has ever been. I promise also to try and find him when I return. With a quick handclasp we separate on a street-corner, and I watch him become one of the townspeople on the sidewalk, striding along with his tractor-like determination, the flour sack over his shoulder bulging with the comestibles he has bought in the market--salt, rice, flour, and beans--on his way to the little shack in the hills where his wife and brothers await him--with some impatience I would presume.

My return to Lima was a queer combination of pain and delight, of the psychic bends, demonic hallucinations, and sensual gratification. The bus trip over the Andes was a nightmare of discomfort. It was a muggy night, and the vehicle was stalled twice for hours behind a line of trucks that had to be towed one by one through awesome mudholes. Every seat was filled to overflowing with passengers, offspring, baggage and blankets. The aisle was impassible, jammed to the armrests with additional cargo. There was even a rooster, I discovered at three in the morning, in one of the baskets heaped at my feet. He crowed lustily every half hour thereafter. Sometime before dawn it got very cold, and I saw the reason for the blankets the passengers had carried with them. We had been in low gear for hours, crawling back and forth up the face of a mountain, and the dense canopy of trees had given way to stone and clumps of frost-scorched grass. Seeing my misery, the young man next to me offered a corner of his thick llama wool blanket. We huddled together through a long dawn, the rooster's raucous shriek marking its advance. But shortly after a breakfast stop at a fly-blown, greasy roadhouse we were hurtling down the grade into a layer of dense, warm, coastal air; and when we reached the outskirts of Lima I was sweating again.

The bus terminals are all on the edge of the Parada, the gullet and bowels of the city. Into this district pour truckloads of produce from every province of the nation, as well as the collectivos and buses bearing desperate immigrants. From other banlieus, taxis, handcarts and pickups move in to feed daily on the arriving swarm. The hot, acid breath of the place is overwhelming. It is at once the main market for the entire country and a vast foul slum, a labyrinthine warren of mudbrick, galvanized iron and scavenged boards where the poverty-ridden, dispossessed highlanders eke out a miserable existence. Many arrive here, their dreams of plastic and neon visible only a few blocks away, but never leave. They squat on the sidewalks before a wretched stock of cheap combs, pencils, stolen auto headlights or hubcaps, and at night crowd into dirt-floored hovels or sleep in alleys. It is a den of thieves, many of them children, with its own codes and language, where outsiders venture at their peril through a gauntlet of quick, hungry eyes.

I helped the Mother Superior and her charges debark, keeping a sharp lookout for light-fingered would-be porters, while they secured a taxi. I was too hurried and numb to register many impressions, but already through my revulsion at the dust, stench and noise I was experiencing the first pangs of desire--desire for cold drink, for tobacco, for chocolate, for the lovely women of Lima, for brilliant, glowing, gigantic images of all these things. When we were installed in the taxi, and moving into the anarchic full-throttle traffic, I turned to chat with my travelling companions, since we had scarcely been able to see each other in the chaos of the bus. I noticed then the face of the seven year-old from Ocopa. It was strangely blank, the expression of the blind, or severely retarded, and his whole body from the waist up was rigid as a doll's. His mother held him fast, whispering intently into his ear.

I nodded at the boy, tacitly questioning.

"He's never been out of the selva," the Mother Superior said confidentially. "Not even to Satipo."

I could see then that the boy was paralyzed by a terror beyond screams or convulsions, a mind-freezing terror. His eyes were wide, but I could see no flicker of cognition in them, and could only imagine the avalanche of information thundering into his brain: the monstrous, greasy buses lowing and charging like bulls, the hordes of strangely dressed, sullen people--more in one glance than he had ever seen in his whole life--and the looming concrete cliffs all around.

"He'll be all right at the convent," the Mother Superior said hopefully, crossing herself.

I nodded, but I knew that the boy would never recover. He was seeing hell, beyond the grave, a stark vision of the fate of his race, and such things are not forgotten.

PART II

24

There are profound questions to be raised in contemplating the peculiar geography of the Americas, and the campsites and ruins that mark the crossing of these continents. North America, broad and fertile in its midsection, is feminine. The great curve of the Gulf, like a womb, and the stumpy outflung arms of Alaska and Newfoundland give it a shape reminiscent of the crude clay dolls that symbolize the awesome fecundity of the earth. And the grasslands, from the Rockies to the Appalachians, from Alberta and Saskatchewan south to the high deserts of Mexico, are indeed one of the planet's most bountiful regions. Yet North America descends from ice and cloud; its dreams are born out of fierce and storm-laden gales; the essential strength of its character is conservative, a cunning adaptability, and its strongest drives are toward propagation and self-perpetuation.

Its first inhabitants, nomads of a physical power and endurance beyond our comprehension, moved with that icy wind at their backs and a yearning to know every inch of the land before them. In blizzards, sudden thaw and flood, they learned to waste nothing, to move without rest, to leave the old and weak behind, to be ever alert to temporary advantage. Like hundreds of other life-forms before them, they did not stop until they had passed through that tremendous womb, to be born anew in the southern continent.

South America has the tight wedge shape of a man, held erect by the vertebral column of the Cordilleras. From this spine of rock extends the arterial system of the Amazon, creating an alluvial plain like a puffed-out chest. Through this basin flows the mightiest river in the world, nourishing an uncharted richness of plant and animal life. It is a continent of unrestrained and dangerous powers: the backbone shrugs periodically, and mountains fall or rise. The green surge of the jungle swallows itself endlessly, and ingests everything else as well--water, stone, air. Here and there, in pockets and strips, the men from the north found a temperate clime and workable terrain, but for the most part they faced a land of seething, violent, unmanageable energies. The characteristic mind-set of Latin America is profligate and explosive. Its volcanoes are symbolic of orgasmic civilizations, whose hour is brief, but whose accomplishments are awesome. Its strongest and most basic urge is toward splendid sacrifice.

The first intriguing problem involves the distribution and concentration of aboriginal populations. The scholars of the neolithic period tell us that groups of Asiatic origin crossed the Bering Straits on a bridge of land or ice during a glacial age. Some, considering the rigors of such overland crossing, speculate that settlers also came by seagoing canoes of wood or walrus-hide. A common date for this event is about 12,000 years ago, at the end of the last Ice Age, when long corridors of tundra opened between the tongues of the retreating glacier. Others have argued recently that the first travellers must have come no later than 20,000 and perhaps as early as 40,000 years ago.

A great deal of painstaking attention has been devoted to fixing this immigration in time. The wrangling over dates and methodologies (stratification, tree rings, carbon dating) seems to derive from a set of assumptions. First it is assumed--often tacitly--that in "prehistory" man--or an early rude sketch of him--was merely a kind of very intelligent animal, driven to migrate by changes in the climate and food supply. Then, with the development of agriculture, human beings "advanced," underwent a neolithic revolution which culminated in the "high" civilizations of Meso- and South America. In the case of these advanced cultures, scholars undertake analyses and comparisons of tool complexes and patterns of diffusion of products, techniques and customs; they muse over a rich iconography and its religious, social and political implications. But the earliest traces of man--the spear-thrower and meat-eater--appear too crude and fragmentary to warrant such speculation, and the primary challenge is therefore to deduce, from bits of chipped stone, charred hearths, pollen grains and animal bones, a defensible chronology. As if, for these creatures, to know when is to know all.

It is easy to see why most archeologists have preferred the "richer" more recent cultures--Olmec, Maya, Toltec, Aztec, Chavín, Tiahuanaco, Nazca, Moche, Inca--with their treasures of pottery, weaving, carved stone and wrought metal. Here are the giant images of bloodthirsty gods, intriguing hieroglyphics, significant fragments of myth gathered by the first chroniclers, temples and tombs with their intact mummies, icons, and weaponry. Books on such material can be illustrated with beautiful color plates, and the writer may ground his theories in a dense stratum of tangible artifacts and the accounts of early explorers.

Before these high cultures, most authorities agree, bands of "primitive precursors" roamed far, equipped with little more than fire, spear points, baskets and perhaps garments or tents of hide. They are generally given credit for two achievements, which stand also as a kind of explanation of their nomadic nature. They were, above all, formidable hunters. They killed and ate the largest of the mammals: the mammoth and mastodon, an early (and outsized) bison, and the great cave bear. Their second extraordinary feat was to pursue these animals across hundreds of thousands of square miles of alien territory, and then, when familiar game thinned out, to learn how to capture quite different creatures in a quite different climate. The motive for this tremendous journey, we are encouraged to believe, was the simple need for a full belly.

This chapter in the history of humankind is variously called prehistorical or preagricultural. The scholars imply, with this inevitable prefix, that for perhaps thirty thousand years the human race incubated in darkness: bands of ferocious killers merely subsisted; their harsh life provided little margin of leisure in which to develop a culture; in a series of tiny, gradual, painful steps they progressed finally to the gathering of wild seeds, the domestication of animals, crude basketweaving and pottery. Then, the implication is, they were ready for really important business, and in a sudden acceleration of inventive and organizing skill, based on a more refined agriculture, civilization burst into flower.

It is true that for prehistory few facts are available and these must be used ingeniously. Geologists and paleobotanists can tell us a little of early man's environment. Rummaging through his garbage heaps we learn of his diet, and comparing garbage heaps gives some notion of his itinerary. From projectile points we can infer certain degrees of manual skill and the diffusion of such skills. There are a few dramatic advances: pressure-point flaking, the *atlatl*, ritual burial, drawing for fun.

Yet even these few obvious facts cast mighty shadows, evoke mysteries as awesome as those arising from the temples of the first civilizations. Consider the discoveries at the Larina-Cocha caves in the eastern *montaña*. These human remains are at least 10,000 years old, perhaps older. If we assume that man entered the Americas from Siberia some two or five or even ten thousand years before that, we confront a remarkable achievement. With nothing but small stone tools and his cunning, this primitive precursor made his way through two continents, crossing swamp, jungle, mountain range and desert. He learned the habits of monkeys, seals, lizards, bears, alligators, moose, flamingoes, salmon, sabertooth tigers, eels, bison, otters, boa constrictors, camels, eagles, grasshoppers, clams, foxes, mammoths, worms, giant sloths, sea urchins, musk oxen and many, many others. He knew when these animals bred, when they migrated, when they ate and slept, what their bones, feathers or hides were good for. In the next few millenia our precursor acquires knowledge of the properties and uses of beech, pine, spruce, palm, balsa, mugwort, pigweed, corn, cotton, caoba, squash, potato, sage, jimson, achiote, papaya, seaweed, peyote, curare, gooseberry, ayahuasca, tan oak, buckeye, sourgrass, cane, prickly pear, and thousands more. Some of these he will domesticate. From others he will make houses, medicines, spices, cosmetics and visionary philosophies.

As he ranges over 16,000,000 square miles, one-third of the land area of the planet, he will leave progeny adapted to local environments. Here, unencumbered by orthography, the fertile human brain will produce hundreds of different languages, from Aleut to Zapotec, and thousands of dialects, each with a body of stories, myths, songs and incantations. For languages as we know them have no primitive precursors. The remnants of neolithic cultures available to modern scholars speak tongues as complex and expressive as classical Greek. All that we know of the speech of "primitive" people indicates that they were capable of articulating dream and recipe, humor and terror, religion and philosophy. If there were no other evidence, we would have to assume as much in order to explain the sudden invention, in the last five thousand years of this odyssey, of civilization: the creation of cities where artists produced fabrics, pottery, metal and stonework as fine as any in human history.

That this amazing adaptability and creativity can be ascribed to the urges of a mere hungry animal seems to me incredible. A number of obvious inconsistencies occur as objections to such an explanation. The Eskimo has survived into our epoch with a material culture surely little different from that of early migrants from Asia. The similarity of custom in tribes all along the northern edge of the world, from the Chukchi and Koryak in Siberia to the Eskimos in Greenland, proves that these snow-country hunters could evolve a stable and lasting equilibrium with their environment. If the northernmost Indians were late arrivals, after the mastodon hunters, why did they not follow their predecessors on the long trek south? If the very first big game hunters exhausted the resources of the glacial steppes, why did they not remain on the plains, feeding on the practically limitless buffalo and antelope herds, since this game supply would approximate the life they had known for 20,000 years? Why did they enter the deserts and tropical rain forests, and from these strike again into the high, cold terrain of another continent?

It might be argued that in each environment, inevitably, an expanding population, natural disasters, and shifts in climate drove some members of a specialized culture to migrate and adapt to new conditions. But if a group could adapt from tundra to plain, from plain to desert, and from desert to forest, then surely it could pass from forest to desert, desert to plain, plain to tundra, and if the impulse to survive was a primary motive, a group with a tentative hold in a new environment would forsake that niche for a previous, more secure one at the first opportunity. We may note that the reindeer does not migrate to the Amazon, nor the buffalo to Tierra del Fuego, nor the moose to the Andes.

Some animals--deer, rabbit, and many birds--have indeed managed to penetrate diverse regions, but very slowly, through speciation. It is interesting that big cats and birds of prey have also been successful hunters in a wide range of climates--from timberline on the mountain slopes to desert scrub and jungle--and both creatures figure prominently in the first icons of the Americas. The eagle and the tiger have perhaps been our rivals and brothers-in-arms for a long, long time.

Still, no other single species has demonstrated the mobility and adaptability of man. No others have travelled so far, so fast. The erect apes who were his ancestors required two million years to explore a pair of continents; man accomplished the same feat in one one-hundredth that span. Now he has also walked upon the moon. But the long trek across the Americas and the sea journey over the Pacific, and most especially the amazing variety of culture spawned during these passages, overshadow our exploration of space, as an example of endurance, daring and imagination. It seems likely too that these Mongol nomads and sea-going Asiatics were driven not by hunger pangs or the sharp winds, but by much the same urges that inspire our rocket probes: restless curiosity, the desire to know something new, the need to test mind, will and body against unforseen challenge.

25

Our own American civilization has peculiar notions of time. Events become "historic" almost immediately--the word is often used as a kind of promotional device in the vending of current political strategies ("In a historic gesture last week . . ."). The Second World War has already acquired a somewhat ghoulish fascination: the quaint propeller-driven airplanes, the naval battles, beachhead assaults, and strutting dictators are locked in film archives and reanimated regularly. The dress and jargon of the thirties and twenties likewise appear dramatically different, and the inhabitants of the previous century, in their bustles and coonskins, possess an almost archetypical resonance. To read, then, of a thousand years, or ten thousand, or a hundred thousand, is without meaning in terms of a direct, personal sense of events lived, changes seen, habits acquired or shed. For our sense of history is conditioned by the span of a single human life, especially since we now experience time not as a vista but as a series of dense nodes. Our major units are decades--the '60's, '70's, '80's--but we are primarily engaged by what happens this week and what may happen the next, as "news" breaks. Our most popular magazines (*Time, Life, People, Us*) say as much.

One way I can grasp time as a function of life is to consider grandparents. My own were born in the third quarter of the last century--the twilight of the coonskin age--and the children of my children may survive well into the next. My grandfather exists in my memory only as a tall figure propped up by a cane, his pockets hiding candy; then as a form in a white bed surrounded by bottles and tubes, and finally as someone dressed up asleep in a box. (Even these few scraps of memory, however, tell me a good deal about old age, disease and death in my culture.) Later, from grandmother, father and uncles I heard a good deal more. To his own sons William Jess Baker appeared as a considerable man: he punched cows on the Chisholm Trail, was one of the first to strike sign of galena ore in the Deadwood Basin, and brought a rumor of Indian blood to shake the family tree. They knew him in Idaho as Axehandle Bill, for the width of his shoulders. He knew hay, trees, stock, guns and ores, how to swear with inspiration and how to use his fists and boots if the occasion demanded.

Until I was grown that was the only portrait--artfully shaded--I had of him. Then my grandmother, in a series of final, intimate interviews given in her ninety-fifth year, revealed another side of his character. He was, it seemed, unable to witness the birth of his own children and twice fled the snowbound ranchhouse at the crucial moment, leaving my grandmother to cut the cords herself. He also lacked prudence. The Baker homestead, a hundred and sixty acres of fine high pasture, with a slope of jackpine for posts and house logs at the back and a large clear creek full of trout through the front, was lost for good when grandfather sold the stock--cattle, pigs, and chickens--to buy a 1934 Chrysler. There may even have been a motive for this purchase more ignoble than ostentation. My uncle once mentioned in an aside that Axehandle was inordinately popular with ladies at other ranches down the valley.

So old Will is by no means a figure legendary and aloof, and my acquaintance with him humanizes and illuminates the world he lived in. I can still, in a restricted way, experience that world. He bequeathed me a few artifacts: a sheetmetal sheepherder stove, a wooden-frame packsaddle and a shaving kit--strop, stone and straight razor. Of these I have learned to use the first two and with practice I believe I could master the art of the last. Through my father I became familiar with other tools and processes of that frontier period: diamond hitches, crosscut saws, sourdough mix, and placer claim law. This scatter of archeological remains in my own mind (and closet) is enough to make a whole age part of my immediate experience, for my grandparents were the contemporaries of Mark Twain, Sitting Bull, Queen Victoria, and Darwin, who must perforce have been no less--and no more--human than my personal ancestors.

By the same sort of projection I can savor the future as my own grandchildren will know it. Already I see its outline in beehive condominiums, laser holograms, microchip circuitry, endless, mindless jogging, whale cults and the dissolving family. My descendants will doubtless hold me to be a charming anachronism--the old man with his gas-powered car, hand-operated typewriter and goosedown jacket. If I survive until their age of reason and reflection, I can tell them of my grandfather and his life (pass on the packsaddle as a den ornament) and thus extend and bind human experience into a two-hundred-year span--a Grandfather Age.

This period is a key to the comprehension of time. It involves simply introducing one's grandparents to one's grandchildren. The Sioux call the oldest and wisest spirits the Grandfathers, and we are all familiar with the curious magic that gathers around these characters, something beyond the novelty of mere relics. This charm is a function of our realization that through these immediate ancestors we reach beyond a lifetime into what we call history, that through them the past, which otherwise remains a realm of cold textbook abstractions, and the future, otherwise a terrifying void, are made human, are bound together and to us.

It requires but two and one-half of these Grandfather Ages to bring us to that time before the Europeans had a foothold in the Americas, before the printing press, gunpowder and the compass, to the very time of castles and knights-in-armor, a flat world bounded by darkness and dragons. Ten such Ages and we are a little before the birth of Christ; twenty-five and we have reached before the pyramids to the dawn of civilization. Eighty of them takes us to the moment when the first human sets foot on American soil; a time when nowhere on the planet is there any sign of a city, an instrument of metal, any glyph or crude design inscribed by man. And as my grandfather knew his grandfather, and as my grandchildren will know their grandchildren, each of these eighty ages is linked intimately to the others.

If we give the skeletons of our eighty grandfathers to a physical anthropologist and force him to judge by dimensions and configuration alone, he will not be able to distinguish the last from the first. If we revive them all and assemble them in a quiet glade, they will soon establish common fields of reference. The last twenty-five, for example, may recognize their common "civilization." The Hindu astronomer, Greek mathematician, Mayan chronologist, Roman engineer, French philosopher and American anthropologist, would develop a pidgin tongue in which to converse. Others, by star picture and numerical system, would establish the communication of abstractions.

The other fifty-odd grandfathers would discover a similar bond, I think. But instead of numbers and ideas they might trade songs, images, stories, dreams, ghosts and gods. Given their character, they would not be inclined to stay in the clearing for long. One wonders whether the twenty-five representatives of civilization would judge them as childish, inattentive, and dull-witted, and so again justify their enslavement and annihilation (perhaps over the vehement objections of the French *philosophe* and the American anthropologist). At any rate there would probably be a rift, a need for a special act of translation and understanding to join those whose achievement is to travel very far on very little, and others who stay put and try to heap stone to the skies.

The vocabulary of archeologists expresses a clear bias in favor of the stone-heapers: the "dawn of civilization," the "emergence" or "development" or "flowering" of "high" or "advanced" culture. For modern thinkers our imaginary clearing contains only twenty-five grandfathers; the rest crouch in distant caves, grunting and scratching, perhaps chipping a little rock. Their culture is described as "simple" or "rudimentary" though the professors confess that they really know very little about these creatures.

So it is that in most accounts of the tremendous aboriginal migration and settlement an extraordinary mystery surrounds this shift from a nomadic brute existence to highly organized cities. One solution to the problem involves extending the time frame during which the primitives precursed, and admitting the possibility of oceanic or even transatlantic influences. For Lévi-Strauss, the common belief in a settlement period of around 10,000 years, during which successive waves of nomads crossed the land bridge, is untenable.

> ... we had to explain how, in the few thousands of years at our disposal, these nomads settled down from end to end of the Western Hemisphere and adapted to different climates; how they discovered, domesticated and propagated over such vast areas the wild species which, thanks to their diligent efforts, were to become tobacco, beans, manioc, sweet potatoes, potatoes proper, peanuts, cotton and--most important--maize; and lastly how successive civilizations of which the Aztecs, the Mayas and the Incas were the distant heirs, came into being and developed in Mexico, Central America and the Andes. To succeed, we had to whittle down each development until it could be contained within the compass of a few centuries: the pre-Columbian history of America thus became a succession of kaleidescopic images, the details of which constantly varied according to the whim of the theoretician. It was as if American specialists were trying to impose on primitive America that absence of depth characteristic of the contemporary history of the New World.[1]

But even with the addition of another ten thousand years of "development" the mystery persists. He who reviews the history of the New World finds what amounts to a great cliff in time, whatever the extent of the two plains separated by this upheaval. On one side is civilization, the fixed walls and temples, the rich gravesites, the invaluable chronicles of the first eyewitnesses; on the other only bits of bone, shell heaps and crude lithic tools. High culture appears to spring, fully formed, out of the primal darkness. Listen to the director of the Museum of Anthropology in Berlin:

> If the dates obtained by the radiocarbon method are reliable, there is a gap between the time when plants were first cultivated and the first visible signs of the emergence of a high culture. About this period we are still so much in the dark that we cannot define its limits exactly. There is no bridge, no direct transition from the early beginnings ... to a period of cultural history that embraces the whole of Peru. This era seems to appear quite suddenly; and it was one in which, more than in any later period, works of art were produced that were inspired by profound religious feeling ... in my view there was at no time an age more brilliant than this ...[2]

It would be one thing if civilization had appeared in a rude and half-finished form, like the sketches of a child learning to represent his world. But the scholar encounters, in the Olmec heads and the statuary of Chavín, an unerring naturalism and a sophisticated, highly stylized craftsmanship.

The history of art, in fact, is often curiously at odds with the notion of "advancing" culture. Both the Roman and Inca civilizations are striking testimony to this anomaly, for though both are often labelled "mighty"-- masters of great empires who left their mark permanently on peoples they conquered or absorbed--both produced a derivative art, inferior to that created by their predecessors centuries earlier. They achieved distinction not through the power of original imagination, but rather as assimilators and exploiters of the work of others. Roman roads are built from Greek geometry; Roman statues are overblown copies; Virgil must acknowledge the precedence of Homer. The Incas, similarly, cannot touch the pottery of the Moche people, nor can they match the barbaric splendor of Chavín sculpture, or the mandarin intricacy of Paracas weaving, though much of this extraordinary work was done a thousand years or more before the stones were laid for the Temple of the Sun in Cuzco.

In the end archeologists have been driven to explain the peerless art work of the earlier civilizations in terms of two nerveless abstractions: agriculture and social organization, the two being interdependent. It is well known that husks and seeds and pollen grains of cultivated plants, primarily corn and cotton, appear in association with the first great monuments of civilization, and common sense tells us that a dependable and abundant food supply must fuel any major human effort. Efficient crop-raising and domesticated animals yielded such nourishment, in most cases, but they do not "explain" the sudden brilliance of early American art or its unique character.

It is also obvious and undeniable that legions of workers had to be brought together, regimented and kept at their tasks in order to erect such colossal structures as the Temples of the Sun and Moon near Chan-Chan, or the temple at Chuquitanta, one wing of which is a quarter of a mile long. But this insight does not entail the conclusion that urban, stratified populations will "naturally" produce mighty architecture and elaborate art. For one thing the temples at Chuquitanta and Rio Seco--among the largest ever erected in human history--arose in the rather thinly populated and extremely arid central coast where shellfish supplied the principal staple. According to dependable radiocarbon samples these structures must be at least four thousand years old.

> It is not easy to understand the appearance of temples and pyramids on the central coast at this time. . . . in a region of relatively sparse population . . . and of minimal consumption of cultivated plant foods.[3]

At Chavín de Huantar the surrounding settlements also seem too small to account for the size and excellence of the temple, and scholars have assumed that workmen and supplies must have come from a widely dispersed net of small communities. Only at Chan Chan, with its immense walled city, six square miles of interlocking compounds that contained perhaps 200,000 inhabitants, do we find a clear connection between cultivated fields, irrigation systems, concentrated population and a monumental architecture.

The civilization at Chan Chan, however, immediately preceeds the conquest of the Incas, and therefore occurred two or three thousand years *after* the flourishing of the first "high" cultures of Perú, and a thousand years after the rich period of Moche and Nazca art. We know through the .diffusion of Chavinoid motifs and styles and later through the dissemination of Tiahuanaco and Huari art that the coastal and highland tribes traded goods and ideas, but there was no automatic formula for the development of a society, no invariable explanation in terms of corn-farming and city government, above all no evidence that the extraordinary art of four millennia shows progression at all, at least in the sense of a linear series of improvements and refinements.

26

In April we journeyed to the mountains to visit the ruined house of our twenty-fifth grandfather, he who stepped so abruptly out of the shadows to show us "civilization." Our party included my thirteen year-old daughter Willa and Dianne Kitchen, the filmmaker from San Francisco who had arrived to work out a plan for a documentary on the Asháninka. To reach Chavín de Huantar one takes a bus or long-range collectivo to Huaraz, situated in one of the high valleys between the Cordillera Negra and the Cordillera Blanca, not far from Huascarán, Perú's highest mountain. A gravel road, with occasional washouts and mudholes, connects Huaraz with Chavín, which perches on the eastern flank of the mountains; and several small companies offer daily service to and from the ruins: a ten-hour trip with three hours in the middle for the studying of stones.

Huaraz is a city a bit less than ten years old. It was constructed in the aftermath of the terrible earthquake and avalanche of 1970, which completely buried the city of Yauya and its 40,000 inhabitants, most of whom have never been disinterred. We are accustomed to think of mountains as symbols of the permanent, the "pegs of the world" in the phrase of a Moroccan folk tale. In this valley one is conscious of their precariousness. Clefts and notches in the rock spires create overhanging walls thousands of feet high; the planes of shadow and leaning cliffs of ice are incised with such clarity against the sky, a dark and glowing azure, that they appear to be only a few steps away, though in reality it is a journey of days on foot. Sometimes, stepping out of the hotel, I am stricken by a giddyness, a sudden, inexplicable pang near the heart, at the startling brilliance of these jagged towers, glittering motionless in the thin and perfectly transparent air.

The three of us joined two German doctors to rent a Plymouth sedan with a driver. The car had been raised on its springs to provide enough clearance to navigate the ruts in the road, and the driver appeared to know his business. We chatted for the two hours during which we crossed the valley, and then the doctors unlimbered their cameras and fell into their own technical discussion of aperture and focal length. We climbed toward a pass in a range of white peaks which appeared intermittently through a mask of cloud. The landscape was treeless; only tough grasses grew among outcroppings of granite. Above the shores of a small lake, clear as emerald, the first dirty fingers of glacier gripped the hillside near the road. Near the top we entered a tunnel, perhaps three-quarters of a mile in length, hewn through solid rock, and emerged on a slope that dropped steeply to a stream far below. Here and there patches of brighter green or gold lined the watercourse, and in the distance were lower mountains blue-black with vegetation. We were here passing to the eastern montaña, a region of higher rainfall, and the waters boiling far below us would end in the Atlantic ocean as part of the vast watershed of the Marañon, main tributary of the Amazon.

Soon, the driver tells us with an encouraging smile. He has managed the climb well, driving as swiftly as the grade allows, but with great concentration. A few times he unloaded us to charge on his own across mudholes with high, congealed ruts. The surface of the road on this final descent is better, and within the hour we are at the metal gate to the ruins. One other high-clearance taxi and a dusty tour bus are parked nearby, but through the fence we can see nothing but an undistinguished stone wall overgrown with weeds.

From behind a very small shed, evidently the office, a man approaches. He is dressed in soiled, baggy khakis, and has the hawk nose and shaggy, straight black hair of a highland Indian. Reeking of *chicha*, the native corn beer, he regards us with faintly suspicious boredom, and announces that the monument is not officially open until noon but we can wander over the grounds if we wish. We are not to dislodge or write on anything. Photos are permissible. For seventy-five cents we purchase our tickets and are instructed to follow the arrows painted on boards along the trail. We arrive thus in a large, open courtyard before a raised terrace at the foot of a small hill. The courtyard is lined with rectangular blocks of stone, and on the terrace are two cylindrical columns, one black and one white, support-ing a huge horizontal plinth, the whole forming a portal. Figures are inscribed in both the roof-stone and the columns.

A small flock of French tourists circles about these exhibits, and a Peruvian family that includes several children plays on the steps, nibbling from a bag of salted plantain chips. Dianne and the doctors elect to wait for unobstructed shots of the terrace, so we drift to the opposite end of the courtyard, and there discover a stone-lined tunnel perhaps a hundred yards long, with side shafts too narrow to admit passage. It appears to be a drainage system of some sort, though the stones were fitted and smooth beyond the requirements of an ordinary sewer.

The sun is strong even in this thin air, and when the tourists at last move on we find the great columns warm to the touch. The figures in relief appear to be identical winged creatures with intricate decorative motifs suggesting fanged jaws and serpent bodies. These motifs are coiled and nested everywhere on limbs and torso: the creature's crest was a fan of snakes; its plume became eyes and teeth. The overall effect was of a being bristling with sinister, symbolic force. Whatever sacred mysteries once lay within the temple, these guardian demons cannot have inspired the original visitors with a sense of tranquility. The care exercised in their execution and the extreme stylization of the figures contrasts sharply with their ferocity. It is vaguely reminiscent of certain oriental scrolls in which scenes of brutality are rendered with exquisite, distracting craft, and the viewer is startled into admiration, fascination and dread.

We speculate for a time on the probable origin and date of the monument, deplore the condition of the wall against the hill, and finally drift idly about, the doctors clicking their cameras at intervals. I remember from my reading in Lima that this site is the earliest substantial ruin on the continent, except for the excavation at Kotosh, which is thought to be of Chavín origin also. One of its chief artifacts, the Raimondi stone (named for the preeminent Peruvian historian) was excavated in 1840 and used as a table top for thirty years before being recognized as a priceless archeological exhibit. It resides now in a museum in Lima, along with what pottery and portable sculpture were salvaged by Tello before a bad flood in 1948.

Still, after an hour, we seem to have seen what there is to see, and impressive as the portal may be, we are all a little disappointed. Willa has brought a couple of oranges, so we sit on the sun-warmed steps and share them with the doctors. The Peruvian family has taken up an emplacement nearby and breaks out more packages, also cans of soft drinks, while the children launch a noisy game of tag. Though they have disappeared from immediate view, the French are gabbling around the corner of the hill, where they have discovered something worth discussion.

Now the ticket-taker appears, shambling at his leisure toward the family. He asks perfunctorily if they desire the services of a guide. They decline, and he next approaches us. I shake my head; then as he turns to trudge away I inquire about the tunnel. It was for waste water, he says. There were others for fresh water and air. He points to the hill. The two wings of the old temple had outlet channels that carried the flow along gutters on each side of the courtyard. A headgate controlled the stream, so that the whole temple and terrace could be washed periodically. They were very clean, and very efficient.

So there, at the portal, is the center of the original temple? I ask. No, that is the new temple, built on the south wing of the original one. Let me show you. He shuffles away, head down, and reluctantly we follow him to the wall behind the columns and he begins to explain its design. A couple of the children are pulled into our wake and clamor for an account of the demon figures on the columns. Patiently he describes them, calling them "angels" as he smiles to himself, and identifying the motifs as those of the jaguar, the condor, and the serpent, representing power, vision, and wisdom. Nearly all the principal figures of Chavín art integrate these three beasts; often they are grafted onto human forms, or divinities with human features. The heads of the two bird-beings, for example, are feline, and many cat mouths may be seen elsewhere, at the joints of the ankles and along the edges of the wings. His gnarled finger, white at the end with dust, traces over the patterns, and all at once a number of additional faces take shape, nested into this larger form and into each other, for sometimes two heads share a mouth, or sprout snake-hair that intertwines.

Upon closer inspection the figures lose some of their symmetry. The black one is a hawk, the ticket-taker notes, from its head-markings and raptorial feet; the white one probably an eagle. The space between the white eagle's legs is vacant; the black hawk extends there a tiny, sharp tongue. One is therefore male, one female. The rest of the family has by now joined the audience, and the paterfamilias says something which makes the children laugh. The ticket-taker smiles slightly. Always at this point there is a little joke, he observes, and moves on past the collapsed stairway behind the portal to a walled canal that borders the hill.

Here, on the top step of three that lead to the bottom of the canal, he shows us a remarkable little carving. An arrow has been chiseled in the stone, bent in a curve downward and away from the terrace. For the profane, the ticket-taker says. It was even stained red when we uncovered it. To warn them away from the temple. For there were surely high priests here who performed rites not meant for ordinary eyes. There were two kinds of ceremony, he continues, one for the people, which must have been held there on the terrace between the great columns, and one for the priests. But access to the public ceremony must have been through the main courtyard. Also, there may have been visitors from far away, speaking other languages, and this little arrow tells them they must not enter here.

I am dubious about such a convenient extrapolation, though my companions nod earnestly enough. The Germans snap closeups of the arrow, and then we return to the portal. Is there any interest in seeing a few things I have helped find and excavate? our guide asks. The family has grown restive at the lecturing. They move away, back to their games and snacks. The French pass by on their way out, still arguing, and also decline the invitation. We are game enough, though I suspect that the ticket-taker wants to lead us to a few drawers full of contraband shards or stone tools which he can clandestinely sell. He leads us to the end of the wall, which has been dug out at the base, and down a flight of crude steps to a small, padlocked wooden door.

When we step through the door I realize that until this moment we have not really seen the temple at all. In the first few stabs of the flashlight beam it is clear that the hill is not a hill at all, but a thin shroud of soil and vegetation over a great rectangular stone honeycomb. In most places the passageways are high enough for me to stand upright, and the blocks of stone remain neatly fitted, making a smooth surface. At various points there are smaller, transverse shafts at various levels. These are part of the elaborate system of plumbing and air conditioning, the ticket-taker explains. Fresh air was led in through shafts, perhaps over moving water, and circulated throughout every room and passageway. Each room had access to a conduit of potable water, and a separate system carried away floodwater and provided also a method of flushing out the various levels of the temple. Another set of vertically inclined shafts let in sunlight. Even now the air is perfectly cool and moves in a detectable breeze even in the pitchdark depths of this structure, which covers approximately the area of a football field.

At a main intersection of two corridors we come upon the first of the finds our guide mentioned: a group of human heads, some better than two feet in diameter, the features done in startlingly realistic style except for a coiffure of serpents. The eyes are wide-staring, a round pit drilled to represent the pupil, as in Greek statues, and from the nostrils of two of the heads thick rope-like strands protrude. When these great, leering stone faces first started forth from the darkness our conversation stopped. Now they stare back at us, these half-ton toys of our grandfathers, grinning or snarling or yowling in silence.

"My God," someone says.

"It looks like they have runny noses," Willa bursts out.

When I translate the remark the ticket-taker laughs. It is true, he says. The nose runs uncontrollably when one eats the San Pedro cactus, a strong drug known for a long time in the highlands. One sees things. Later I will show you a carving where a god is holding one of these plants. But first we must have a look at the great *lanzón*. We thread our way through the corridors, down a short and narrow flight of steps, and enter a chamber in the form of a cross. A shaft in the roof admits a faint, gray luminosity, and by this diffuse light we can see the outline of a great stone. It is some fourteen feet high and three feet thick, elaborately carved with the same cat and snake motifs we have seen on the columns. The top of the stone is narrower, like a blade or finger, and it rests on a blunter, broader base. The extension at the top is covered with twined serpents and jaguar jaws. The makers of this image have preserved the contours of the original granite formation. The central face is formed around a slight narrowing and projection of an edge, which makes a beak or nose in profile.

The ticket-taker points out to us a groove which runs all the way down the high crest, over the brow and nose, to the bared fangs of the mouth. The remnants of an altar on the roof of the temple, directly above the aperture leading to the lanzón chamber, suggest that sacrifices were made there, and the blood allowed to course down this groove. What was sacrificed we must guess. The jaguar and the serpent are among those creatures deadly to man, as is the cayman or alligator, which figures prominently in another icon, the eight-foot Tello obelisk. And the condor feeds upon the corpses of all. Certainly this figure before us seems calculated to inspire terror, and it is not difficult to imagine its awesome mouth drooling with human blood.

We finish our tour with a look at some more heads, these with rectangular pegs at the neck, tenons which were locked into sockets in the original temple walls, and a few tablets with stylized engravings thought to represent a bat, a monkey, and possibly a rabbit. Outside again, blinking and stretching as if emerging from a dream, we are led to an excavation of a kind of small amphitheater, lined with thirteen stones representing the familiar beings that combine feline, reptilian and bird-like features. One of these indeed bears a ribbed cactus in hand. Just above him, the ticket-taker observes gently, there in the dry earth of the hillside, is a living example of the San Pedro. The similarity is obvious: the blunt, dusty green thumb with a fuzz of spines is reproduced a few feet away in stone, the work of some unknown craftsman whose bones have mouldered for four thousand years.

I inquire as tactfully as possible how Marino--at last we have exchanged names--has come to be the learned custodian of these ruins. I worked with Tello, he says with pride. In the circle of Peruvian archeologists, such an apprenticeship is the equivalent of working with Maxwell or Planck in nuclear physics. Tello was the first to challenge Uhle's theory that the high civilizations developed out of coastal fishing settlements. He suggested that they may have had jungle origins. After Tello died, Marino remained to continue the excavations at Chavín, working often without funds or recognition, or attaching himself to expeditions from foreign universities. He unearthed a great many of the tenon heads that had fallen from the temple walls, and restored the architecture of the great portal and the stairways and platforms around it. After the terrible flood and landslide of 1948 he had to begin all over again, and even so many valuable artifacts were swept away and never recovered.

Our driver has come to intercept us, impatient to return to Huaraz, and Marino hurries us around the hill to a rear wall to view the one tenon head still in place. It glares out from its socket in the high stone parapet, surveying the gravel road that winds away over the barren plain, bringing two or three times a day the tour buses and rented cars. But in this intact fragment something of the order and power of the original temple is visible, and we grasp dimly what an awesome thing it would be to see everything in place, a fusion of severe grandeur, in overall conception, and cunning elaboration of detail.

Returning to the gate in earnest conversation, I think to ask if it is possible to make contributions to forward the work of maintaining the site, and Marino allows that it is. I present him with five hundred soles which he pockets in a gesture of dignified gratitude. We bid him farewell and watch him shuffle away to his plain adobe dwelling by the gate. I see no one there to greet him but the few chickens around the doorstep.

For thirty years he has ministered to the stone angels and the grinning god in the catacombs, has pondered the mysterious and sinister grandeur of this spot. It is an impressive commitment. I think I understand a little the sadness, the boredom, the stoicism of his manner. The pittance the government gives him--about thirty dollars a month, I learn later from an American archeologist friend--permits him to survive and do a little desultory work on the chief monument of pre-Incan civilization, but allows no major additional excavation or restoration. The generals do not care. Probably no one, not even the eminent foreign scholars, cares as he does for this ruin. I wonder if late in the afternoon he walks about the temple, musing on the mythological beings that haunt it, picking up bits of cellophane or aluminum cans, running a finger gently over fang or plume, reflecting on his days with the great Tello, when he was young and knew the heart-shaking enthusiasm of finding such treasure.

On the way back to Huaraz, driving again past the snow-draped spires of granite, now turning rose in the sunset, we are all lost in our own thoughts. The Germans snap a last shot or two of the mountains, without comment. Dianne turns to us all at once with a wry smile.

"You know," she says, "I just realized that he probably planted that cactus there."

I think of how casually I dismissed him as a bored functionary, a ticket-taker with perhaps a sideline trade in petty illegal artifacts, of how narrowly we escaped following the French, of how indirect, even nondescript our grandfather's disguises may be. For a few months I recall Marino wistfully as an unsung hero, until the American archeologist in Lima gives the whole experience an ironic turn, handing me a copy of Professor John Rowe's definitive monograph on the art of Chavín de Huantar. On the title page I read

Dedicated to Marino Gonzales Moreno
Savior of Chavín

27

I was intrigued by the stone faces, howling and running snot, and the taloned birds with cat heads. Back in Lima I undertook an intense, if amateur study of pre-Incan cultures. My quarters were in the household of Doctor Kenneth Tejada, a psychiatrist at the Victor Larco hospital, who had a fine trilingual collection of books on the ancient art of Perú. I borrowed also from the wide knowledge and compact library of Richard Burger, an American archeologist in charge of a dig near Huaraz. I have since supplemented that reading with modest research in the libraries of American universities, but in what follows I do not pretend to launch a professional analysis of the subject; I aim only at some informed speculation.

At first I pursued a single question that fascinated me: what was the relation between the Asháninka, who had maintained vestiges of an ancient and rudimentary way of life and this first "high culture," so busy to incise awesome deities in stone? Many scholars venture to theorize on the problem but despite their intelligence and exactitude, most commentaries leave unexplored some questions which seem to me primary. It is perhaps arrogance to believe that a casual visitor to a ruined temple can perceive matters in a new light--an arrogance explained simply enough by ignorance of scientific procedure--but it is also possible that the emperor does indeed lack some items of his wardrobe.

The ruin at Chavín traditionally raises three problems. Professor Disselhoff has already posed half of one of them: this complex culture develops with an inexplicable suddenness.[1] Tello supplies the other half: "This period of classic Chavín disappears almost completely after having reached, as did no other American civilization, so vast an area of propagation and a high degree of development."[2] The same kind of mystery seems to surround other advanced civilizations, notably the Tiahuanacan and Olmec. After millennia spent as "hunters and gatherers," groups of humans all at once conjured elaborate cultures which flourished for a few centuries and then abruptly vanished.

It might be argued that this "problem" is simply an illusion created by gaps in the archeological record, and a modern disposition to underestimate the creative energy of earlier civilizations. There are, however, attendant puzzles that complicate things. Archeologists have logically enough sought to trace the roots of these advanced people, to discover whence they came, hopefully to unearth vestiges of an intermediate development. In the case of the Chavín culture, Tello claimed that settlers came from the Eastern jungles, having migrated up the tributaries of the Amazon after passing onto the continent through Central America. Thirty years ago Carl O. Sauer argued convincingly that these migrants were already skilled farmers and fishermen, Arawak speakers like the Ashá-ninka, and had developed their special knowledge in the temperate highlands of what is now Colombia.

Whatever their origin, those who built Chavín had to possess or invent new, sophisticated methods of crop production. That is the keystone of the classic position on cultural evolution, and leads to the second major problem. It is assumed generally that a kind of breakthrough in tech-niques of planting, irrigation, and organization was necessary to provide the calories for such tremendous expenditures of human energy.

> *Agriculture of a superior type* is what fosters what is called the "neolithic revolution" (Childe). It engenders all high culture. No high culture in antiquity, therefore, has any other basis but agriculture.[5]

> In the highlands, the Chavín florescence must be seen as the effect of an agricultural way of life, not as the cause of its dissemination. Agriculture and village life preceded the spread of the Chavín cult, and were necessary to its development and diffusion.[6]

> . . . the rational manner in which agriculture was carried on, and in particular the cultivation of maize, afforded a fair degree of prosperity and sufficient leisure to build temples and fashion stone idols, made in a laborious process with stone tools and sand.[7]

One difficulty with this "explanation" is the location of the grand American civilizations. The country around the ruin at Chavín is almost barren, good mainly as pasturage. In Sauer's brief summation, "the high-lands are miserably poor in fish, game, and fuel."[8] There is not even evidence of a substantial permanent population in the territory around Chavín, and scholars have had to postulate gangs of migrant laborers from far afield.

Why then did the magnificent temples, requiring surpluses of food for their construction, rise up in a steep land of scant soils and inhospitable climate? In Mexico, too, the high, arid plains surrounding the lake drove farmers to construct floating barges on which crops were grown--a com-plicated and expensive means of obtaining food. In his diffusion over the land mass of two continents man had encountered terrain of easy access, great fecundity and fair weather, but these areas did not serve as the cradles of civilization.

Some scholars have tried to account for this situation by arguing that it was the very circumstance of scarcity that stimulated early farmers to refine and intensify their methods, and their efforts were so successful they soon had the leisure in which to develop an advanced culture. A corollary of this explanation, implied and sometimes stated, holds that tropical climes, which otherwise would favor the development of agriculture, discourage the metabolism necessary for the advancement of culture. In the classic *Handbook of South American Indians*, Professor Gilmore says of the Amazonian rain forests:

> Most are correlated with a monotonous warm temperature and high rainfall, which are considered enervating to man and to other temperate mammals.[9]

> Mongolian man, like Caucasian man, probably is an organism of temperate ecology and climate; apparently he finds these conditions most agreeable and responds with high physical and mental activity.[10]

According to this line of reasoning, extremes of heat, cold, rain or drought inhibit development, since the struggle for subsistence leaves no time for invention, and a climate too convenient or regular dulls human faculties. Only a "temperate" region which provides sufficient potential resources and, simultaneously, a seasonal hardship can stimulate humans to the creative effort of civilization.

There are several troublesome aspects of this formulation. Those who believe that high cultures are based incontrovertibly on agriculture admit that domestication and hybridization of many common foodstuffs or fibers took place long before the appearance of stone temples. When the Olmec and Chavín cultures flourished, gardens were already producing corn, beans, squash, potatoes, peanuts, tomatoes, cucumbers, cocoa, cotton, peppers, ciruela, avocado, papaya, guava and palm. Some of these crops had been carried thousands of miles by trade, immigration or conquest, and had undergone considerable adaptation to a new environment. Most seem to have originated in tropical or semi-tropical regions, and some have living ancestors still native to those regions. To admit that human ingenuity could produce these plants and disseminate them, yet argue that climate and "temperament" could conspire to thwart any further improvements in crop-growing, until early farmers faced the challenge of chill, rocky and remote places, seems illogical. Indeed, the enervating atmosphere of a rain forest would seem neither a greater nor lesser challenge than the numb exhaustion that attends working poor ground on desert or mountain.

Some scholars have also been bothered by what they view as an inordinate gap--an abyss--separating the first signs of cultigens and the intensive, high-yield agriculture that is associated with the great pre-Colombian societies. There is general agreement that a dependence on

plant food developed very gradually, probably over a period of eight or
ten thousand years, proceeding from random collecting of wild fruits,
tubers and seeds to garbage-heap volunteer gardens and finally to selection and cultivation of favored strains. Some writers, to explain this slow
accretion of knowledge, assert the curious position that early tribes were
simply not interested in complicating their lives. Sauer says of ancestral
man: ". . . they were as sedentary as they could be and set up housekeep-
ing in one spot for as long as they might."[11] Horkheimer, like many others,
believes that the first Americans migrated only when population pressure,
weather, war or disease drove them to it.[12] In a recent article on economic
determinism as a spur to cultural advancement, Bronson mentions "a
simple lack of incentive" as a reason for the millennia spent in mere
hunting and gathering.[13] The implication is that the aboriginals were a
conservative, unimaginative lot. When circumstances forced them to it,
they made grudging, miniscule adaptations which were nonetheless
cumulative, so that in a final and apparently sudden surge they made the
transition--the neolithic revolution again--to a sophisticated agriculture,
hence the solid nutritional base from which rose the mighty stone idols.

However, our "ancestral" or "primeval" or "aboriginal" man is not
biologically distinguishable from ourselves; he is largely a professorial
construct. The actual ancestor is only thirty to forty Grandfather Ages
removed, and his own immediate forerunners had accomplished the
glorious feat of occupying two continents, adapting to every conceivable
environment, from icy wasteland to dense jungle. Over the next three or
four thousand years he creates, by careful manipulation, very nearly all of
the useful cultigens known to man--for humans have succeeded in
developing very few domestic plants since the appearance of "civilization." The "high" cultures have been, in this sense, remarkably sterile. In
the face of such a record it is hard to view these hunters and gatherers and
rudimentary farmers as doltish or soporific.

A final puzzle. In Professor Rowe's monograph on Chavín art there is
one sentence that ought to shock those who believe civilization springs
from agriculture.

*Plants and vegetable products are rarely shown in Chavín art and
then only as secondary figures.*[14] It might be argued that the people of
Chavín did not themselves recognize the central importance of agriculture, but took their food for granted, much as nowadays we ignore (at
least in our ceremonial and decorative arts) the primary nourishment for
our way of life--petroleum. But if crop production had become so
routine, why did no elaboration of culture occur earlier, in the first rush of
bountiful harvests, in areas where rainfall and rich soil would augment
human labor? And if the development of systems of cultivation, storage
and distribution was not haphazard, but a conscious application of human

reason, how could these first engineers fail to appreciate and celebrate the worth of their discoveries?

In fact, the iconography of Chavín suggests that the culture was preoccupied by an even more remote age, when hunting tribes roamed the jungle slopes and river courses. Of the four creatures prominent in Chavín art, all are associated with the rain forests of the upper Amazon: the snake, jaguar, eagle and caiman. Quite as Eliade suggests, our ancestors at the supposed "dawn" of civilization appear to have revered and yearned for a still more distant time, when tremendous events and beings set the cosmos in motion.

Rowe's monograph demonstrates that this preoccupation was not transient or arbitrary, for the stoneworkers executed designs of great complexity and elegance, in a uniform style that clearly required several generations to perfect. He ingeniously compares the integration of the reptile, feline and bird motifs to the kennings of Anglo-Saxon poetry, elaborate and sometimes cryptic metaphors that take on formal, conventional meanings. He points out the subtle variations in basically symmetrical designs and traces the Staff God represented on the Raimondi stele to the chief figure on the Gate of the Sun at Tiahuanaco--a temple a thousand miles away and two thousand years later than Chavín. Other experts have shown that the Chavinoid influence was immense and durable, penetrating all the subsequent major civilizations of the Andes.

The second of the mysteries of Chavín, then, is this coincidence of highly developed talent, the resources to support it, and a tradition of imagery--surely the imagery of articulated myth--reaching back into the jungle, back again into those long ages of "primitive" life. We lack, of course, the substance of the myths, but they can have been no less complex, structured, and compellingly styled than the art which expresses them. The power they held in the human imagination can be estimated from their duration and geographical range, and it seems logical to assume a mythology is prior in time to the temples at Chavín and Kotosh, that a body of story and song is the most ancient root of culture, and that this material, invisible and evanescent, would best illuminate and explain the development of culture in the Americas, had we only an archeology of the purely mental.

Donald Lathrap has outlined some provocative conjectures on the relation of Chavín to early agriculture. He finds designs on the Tello obelisk which appear to represent the yucca plant, the manioc that even today comprises the staple item in the diet of jungle dwellers. Thus the great cayman is connected to the vegetable world, and also to the riverine tribes who, Lathrap speculates, journeyed by canoe to the far reaches of the Amazon basin and ultimately migrated into the highlands. The first domesticated plants, in his view, were not foodstuffs but products useful in fishing: the bottle gourd for net floats, cotton for twine to make lines or nets, and barbasco to poison fish. Having learned methods of cultivation, these fishermen subsequently domesticated food plants, principally yucca, and settled in larger and more sedentary communities, but kept the beliefs and symbols of their nomadic past. Lathrap believes these symbols are of great antiquity. He relates the supreme cayman diety of Chavín to the Mayan god Itzamná, "who was also initially a cayman."[15]

Sauer remarks on the uniformity and wide dispersal of Arawak culture, a life based on dugout canoes, fish poison, pole and platform dwellings, small household gardens, fermented drink, and small game hunting with bow and arrow. This complex he traces across the top of South America and into the Caribbean, and then offers the daring suggestion that its ultimate origins are in Southeast Asia. During an especially warm period between glaciations, he believes, this essentially tropical mode of life could have passed from Asia to the Americas. Even without this final leap, Sauer and Lathrap can supply a coherent and credible background for the creatures graven on the stones of Chavín. These creatures were, like the peoples who raised the temples, of jungle origin. They hint at important transformations: fishermen became farmers; river nomads who secured plants as useful tools became villagers who raised them to eat. As stylized stone icons, they suggest also a long history of ideological adaptation, in which beings of earth, air and water were interwoven in complex metaphor, perhaps as narratives of generation, cosmic cycle, and final significance.

Lathrap believes agriculture is a "systematic distortion in human behavior."[16] He suggests that men first experimented with plants 40,000 years ago, and only as recently as 6 to 7,000 years ago brought the cultivation of bitter manioc to high efficiency, thus allowing the neolithic revolution to spread. For most of his history, then, man made occasional use of plants, but did not bind himself exclusively to a few of them. They furnished transportation, building materials, decoration, medicine, tools, hallucinations and supplementary nourishment. In his systems of thought, one may infer, he paid more attention to animals, especially the hunters like himself. But his brain was most likely busy, then as now, with schemes to make sense of both.

Already, in Lanning's discussion of Rio Seco and Chuquitanta, we have encountered a challenge to the belief in agriculture as the sole possible foundation of advanced culture.[17] Major settlements with impressive temple architecture have been nourished primarily from the sea. Very recently Dr. Richard S. MacNeish has excavated sites in Belize which indicate that the great Mayan civilization began in similar coastal fishing communities, some quite large.[18] These sites are now dated at around 4200 B.C., and endured until 2500 B.C. when the population expanded inland, planting corn, beans and squash. If crop cultivation was not indispensable as a means of supporting large, settled populations and providing the surplus necessary for extensive creation, if in fact leisured, communal life was possible well before any extensive development of cultigens for food, then we must look beyond agriculture for an adequate explanation of the sudden emergence of Chavín culture, and of other high cultures as well.

We confront now the last and greatest mystery surrounding these so-called high or advanced societies--the mystery of their very existence. So obviously full of grandiose self-regard and aspiration to hard-edged permanence, still portentous in their half-decomposed state, they are nevertheless all moribund. Nothing remains of their gods, their ceremonies, their intricate beliefs, but a few enigmatic pictures in cold stone. On the other hand their predecessors, the "primitive precursors," have endured in many regions, their traditional dwellings, tools, and customs still largely intact. The Asháninka, along with peoples elsewhere in the Amazon basin, in MesoAmerica, even in Indonesia, Southeast Asia, New Guinea and the South Pacific, have survived through very ancient techniques of fishing, gardening, and weaving fibers. Their "simple" and "undistinguished" way of life, often including a lively and complex mythology or folklore, is probably 10,000 years old and still viable. As Varese remarks, the Asháninka belong to a community of 200,000,000 people, inhabiting the 36 million square kilometers of tropical forest on the earth's surface, whose house-garden, slash-and-burn agriculture and fishing economies are generally, in broad outline, the same.[19]

The great linguist and ethnographer Franz Boas clearly stated the bias toward heapers of stone, a bias which unites most antiquarians and cuts across otherwise profound ideological and theoretical differences.

> We value a culture the higher the less the effort required for obtaining the necessities of life and the greater the technical achievements that do not serve the indispensable daily needs. . . . The more varied the play with techniques that furnish the amenities of life the higher we estimate a culture. Wherever spinning, weaving basketry, carving in wood or bone, artistic stone work, architecture, pottery, metal work occur we do not doubt that an advance over the simplest primitive conditions has been made.[20]

It would be foolhardy to deny the astonishing talent and sensibility of the stone-cutters of Chavín, or of Olmec sculptors, or of Moche potters and weavers, or of Inca engineers, or of Aztec city planners. The monuments of preColombian civilizations are awesome human achievements, and historians of art are justified in their claim that as examples of difficult craft they have not been surpassed. But to appreciate the artifacts of a culture is not the same as to "value" the culture itself, and it is fair to inquire into the meaning and function of the societies which produced these mighty emblems, but could not save them from ruin.

It is not surprising that many authorities refuse to speculate on the ultimate significance of Chavín iconography, or skirt the simple question of why a group of tribes would band together to perform such immense labor. As Lanning remarks, it is self-evident that an efficient system of procurement of food and materials was in operation, and that this system required a concentration of authority.

> Public works on such a scale are usually the product of stratified societies in which an upper class orients and controls the labor force of a fair-sized region.[21]

> It is more difficult, however, to explain why the surplus economy and community organization should have been dedicated to the build-ing of temples rather than to more secular activities or to ritual activities which did not require the building of such colossal, permanent mon-uments. . . .[22]

A few elementary observations may occur even to a casual visitor. All of the major figures in the temple of Chavín de Huantar are predators of legendary stealth or ferocity: eagles, hawks, condors, jaguars, alligators and snakes. The most outstanding feature of these figures is the mouth, especially the fanged cat's mouth. Claws are also prominent. As Rowe demonstrates, these elements were routinely stylized, detached and shifted about as pure motifs so that, for example, the Staff God's hair is a nest of serpents, some of which twist to form a small cat mouth. The great birds of prey seem to guard the portals of the temple, and deep in its bowels squats a composite creature, a being part human, part feline, part bird and part reptile, with a blood-groove into its jaws. A few entirely human heads, done in a style of strict realism, present expressions of extreme emotional force: the lips are drawn back, jaws spread, brows contracted. Perhaps rage, perhaps terror, perhaps a kind of demonic ecstasy--feelings at their most outlandish grow confused--have distorted these faces into silent screams. They appear possessed.

Professor Rowe notes the ubiquitous cat-mouth and ventures to suggest that it represents "power, perhaps spiritual power." My impres-sion is that this motif works as a sort of shorthand for an omnipresent fear. Every aspect of the temple of Chavín seems to incorporate or reinforce such fear. Its structure is that of a mighty gate (or mouth) leading to dark mysteries. The tenon heads that once jutted from the walls could hardly be construed as welcoming those who approached; they glare most balefully, and contort horrifically. The central icons all possess huge maws lined with fangs, and details of decor continually repeat this motif in small. The atmosphere of Chavín is that of dragon's breath; it is the lair of some ravening, devouring, monstrous force.

Like man himself the creatures of Chavín were born in the jungle. They thus evoke primal fears, for they carry us back to a time when the night swarmed with dangerous predators. It was a time, we might specu-late, when stark terror struggled--at least in some--with fascination, with an obscure impulse to conquer. Certainly human settlements learned to protect themselves from the big cats and reptiles, and hunters doubtless killed them fairly often, and even wore their teeth and hides as charms. But the fear of animals who can devour appears to run deep: the success of movies like *Jaws* suggests as much, and any reader of folktales, child-ren's literature or science fiction could cite additional proof (Grendel, the Sphynx, Cyclops, the Beanstalk Giant, the Sand Worm).

In the art of Chavín these jungle creatures are of course greatly transformed. They have become metaphorical and mythic, tremendous, stylized extensions of a merely physical threat. In our own tradition Gods have wielded lightning bolts and spoken from whirlwinds, but these crude forms of retribution were long ago supplanted by subtler psycho-logical instruments. The iconography of Chavín suggests that a similar transformation may have occurred there: the cult surrounding the *lanzón* and its "Smiling God" perhaps centered on divinities whose authority extended over all land, river and sky, and whose representation blended superhuman prescience with supernatural power, into a series of images of feathered, scaled, humanoid beings. The function of such images was then to inspire awe and obedience, if not terror, by inviting the imagina-tion to conceive, by analogy with the most powerful carnivores, an inexorable, overwhelming authority, an authority potentially malevolent.

These frightening icons are nonetheless human creations, attempts to render concretely the mighty forces that have always intrigued and startled us into ceremonies of worship and sacrifice. Always there are priests whose function is to refine and perform such ceremonies, and usually the aim of this special caste is to command a vestige of the great powers for themselves. Certainly the elaborate temples of the Americas--not only Chavín but Chuquitanta, Huaca del Sol and Huaca de la Luna, Chan Chan, Tikal, Palenque, Monte Alban, Teotihuacan, and so forth--imply the exist-ence not only of a priesthood, but of a whole hierarchy that included artists, warriors, administrators, merchants and slaves; and it is surely self-evident that this priesthood successfully directed vast expenditures to commemorate its gods.

It seems to me, then, that the temple of Chavín illustrates a systemati-zation of ancient, potent myths. They were rooted in an immemorial past, a time when a nomadic people feared the deadly predators of the jungle, perhaps also a time--if Lathrap is right--when men first succeeded in converting to an agricultural way of life, based not on corn but on manioc. But this group of myths was refined and interpreted by gifted individuals who, to strengthen it, developed a congruent art, ritual, and (we may presume) law. The force of this elaboration was to bind people to the new cult, and to exact from the community thus formed a permanent commitment to its glorification.

And the mechanism of this binding force, still plainly inscribed in the stones, is that of terror. It is of course no longer the terror of man crouched in the forest with his puny spear. It is religious awe, a cowering before beings whose power is supernatural--swifter than the eagle, more cruel than the jaguar, stealthier than the serpent. To function as the cement for a social order, the visceral fears of darkness and wild beasts must be transmuted into holy dread--terror with an intellectual and imaginative dimension, conditioned by ritual into an omnipresent element in the citizens' emotional life.

The priests' duty is to devise ceremonies that can instill, sustain, and exploit this terror, making it into a dynamo of creative energy. The temples of the Americas testify to their skill, and many modern pilgrims to these shrines have wondered at the governments that could keep so many of their subjects engaged in such arduous efforts for so long. In part, the explanation may lie in a single-minded dedication to self-perpetuation: the more awesome the temple, the more tractable and zealous the populace; the more diligent the populace, the more feasible the monumental scale of architecture.

Only a great concentration of political power and social prestige--a despotism--in the service of an ancient but vigorous faith could account for the huge and intricate monuments of the Americas. Thousands of laborers had to be locked into regular duty: cutting, polishing and setting stone, or cultivating and gathering food to feed the construction crews, or standing guard to see that the workers did not fall idle. Others had to design and lay out sites for temples and additions, arrange for transport and storage of materials, secure housing and tools. Still others had to organize and coordinate all these efforts, possibly in connection with policies of conquest or alliance.

It is intriguing to speculate on the sequence of developments that led to this new and highly complex structure. Did a surplus of food provide "leisure" in which some early messiah discovered principles of organization and persuasion--especially the power of imaginative horror? Or did insights into mass psychology allow a cunning trickster--a familiar form of god--to build a system to produce a surplus of goods and nourishment for his own benefit? Were the first priests inspired geniuses or colossal hoodwinks, or both? In any case what we know of our own culture would argue that, once brought into being, a comprehensive social, political or religious institution develops autonomy and tends to consume a community's resources to aggrandize itself.

In our own time the "military-industrial complex" manifests this trait: so-called superpowers are expending most of their wealth in the building of terrible weapons, thus sustaining the various devil-myths they project upon one another. The support of such cumbersome institutions becomes finally a society's whole task and justification and achievement; everything and everybody is commandeered, in one fashion or another, to serve the fearsome end of defending "national security" or "national integrity" or simply "our way of life." If propaganda is successful, tremendous fervor may develop in the populace and an era of prosperity and expansion may ensue. Fear, properly managed, is far from a paralyzing emotion. Thus the work of supply and organization and construction may be enthusiastic and efficient, whatever the ultimate goal of the project. The citizenry are caught up in pure activity; everyone is employed; the walls rise; there is food for all; the enemy is at bay; the trains run on time.

The underpinning of these periodic surges of civilization, a stratum deeper than foundation stone, is the principle of division between sacred and profane, along with its corollaries of obedience and order, which are in turn immanent everywhere in a hierarchy of subtle gradations. Inventing and codifying distinctions which bear various nuances of privilege, restriction, coercion, punishment, obeisance, malevolence, and purification--this is the traditional duty of priests. As these distinctions proliferate, a society tends to greater authoritarianism, to systems of effective slavery.

Lévi-Strauss argues that the art of writing, probably first used to keep accounts, to grade and measure, is the instrument of such slavery.

> During the neolithic age, mankind made gigantic strides without the help of writing; with writing the historic civilizations of the west stagnated for a long time.
> The only phenomenon with which writing has been concommitant is the creation of cities and empires, that is the integration of large numbers of individuals into a political system and their grading into castes and classes.
> My hypothesis, if correct, would oblige us to recognize the fact that the primary function of written communication is to facilitate slavery.[27]

There is truth in this startling proposition, but only partial truth. Behind the mere mechanism of orthography, of record-keeping and contract and law, one may perceive the signs of a major geological rift in the human mind. Intelligence and imagination, after thirty thousand years of creative freedom, conspired to exploit certain of their recent discoveries, and in a few centuries reached a narrow but intense focus on new goals: the concentration of power and wealth in the hands of an elite in order to foster the acquisition of all available human and natural resources, which are in turn expended to secure and celebrate the position of the elite.

The wellspring of "high" culture is therefore not corn or aqueduct or hieroglyph or bronze, however necessary these discoveries may have been to its success. To explain the astonishing temples of the Americas, and especially the divine fanged beast-men of Chavín, we must venture into human psychology; we must ask what could initiate and sustain such tremendous efforts. Surely "leisure" does not intrinsically entail such exertion. Surely human beings, once beyond mere subsistence, do not rush to sacrifice life and substance in order to realize the visions--perhaps mere fantasies--of others. Surely to live in one place, to work for years at a single task, to abide by a labyrinth of regulations, and to do all this in the shadow of sudden death--surely this is not intuitively recognized as the ultimate and desired destiny of life.

To account for such strange behavior it seems necessary to assume that either by design or by accident a shaman, seer, witchdoctor, prophet-- a form of early experimental psychologist--acquired the gift of inspiring or mesmerizing others to do his bidding. A combination of political astute- ness, persuasive poetry, and visionary power were necessary to evoke the tremendous chimeras of the imagination in a whole populace and yoke that populace to the business of representing and placating such beings. At the same time, a tendency in humankind that had been latent, a tendency to cede individual autonomy, to trade freedom for food and spectacle, to submerge self in order to achieve some grand glory of the whole--perhaps it was a common yearning for transcendence and immor- tality of sorts--some such tendency must have coalesced as a new and dominant social force, exploitable by priestcraft.

If speculations like these are held valid, our account and judgment of early civilizations must undergo great change. For one thing, time itself has made their implicit goal of permanence a monstrous mockery. The simple and lowly life of their forebearers has outlasted the stone gods. For another, it is fair to ask whether slavery and terror and human sacrifice, in the service of Boas' ideal of useless decoration, can be considered an advance of the human spirit. We may ask also if the development of huge settlements governed by a few powerful theocrats, often devoted to military ventures and human sacrifice, represent a progressive step over the "savages" who usually fought over water, salt, hunting grounds or women.

Doubtless the priests and kings of the Americas thought themselves a great improvement over the tribal chiefs they overcame, just as the Spaniard, charged with murderous greed for soft and useless metals, believed himself superior to any Indian. And both of them--the barbarian priest and the European Lord--repeat a paradox: committed to their own chauvinism and yearning for a final realization of their particular *Volksgeist*, they nevertheless turn for guidance, inspiration and vision to--that distant primordial past, the Sacred Garden or mighty Demigod or Divine Beast who began in all enlightenment and power and freedom.

The simple savage is with them here, for he too looks backward and finds the shadows of the past all around him. What is different is that he sees further, to the tremendous origins, and is nearer to that awesome time. His are the most complicated and sure accounts of the making of specific rocks and rivers and tribes, of the doings of beasts and supernatural beings, and his life still involves the same primary and direct activities of the original gods: the catching of fish, the making of fire, the gathering or growing of plants. So he is the most backward of men, and for that reason, perhaps, he is also nearest an ultimate goal.

28

The Tambo is a big, brown river, deceptively swift. It loops a good deal between hills and higher, sharper ridges that deserve to be called mountains. The banks are fine sand in shades of salt and pepper, and where the river has changed its bed there are expanses of boulders in all sizes, from some as big as a three-story house down to pebbles. The Asháninka have tales about the more prominent outcroppings: the steamboat-sized one just downriver from Otíka, for example, was supposed to be a craft full of white men and their goods on its way to capture Indians, when Aríveri, the trickster god, turned it to stone.

Behind the sandspits, or where the channel narrows to cut through bedrock, the jungle hangs, droppings roots and vines down to the water. The density and richness of the greens is overwhelming. There is every kind of leaf: huge, bright, and slick; dark, downy, and fern-like; frothy pastels and coarse, hairy clumps. There is every shape of tree too, though the uplifting fan variety predominates. The mighty caoba, cedar and palo amarillo rise and spread from trunks six feet thick at the base, but from a distance they appear delicate, almost spindly, with pale skeletons articulated in a generous space. Others send aloft, a hundred feet or more, a single thin trunk that ends in a puff of leaves.

Nearer the ground countless other plants spread or crawl or twine or spray. It is hard to tell whether some varieties are trees or bushes or vines. All kinds of palms--skinny, spiny, hairy, squat, gawky, jaunty and brooding--appear, and all sorts of creepers--from heavy, gnarled hawsers to others no thicker than twine. At certain seasons, some of the larger trees flower. In January it was a variety that blooms in a diaphanous cloud of white. Now another tree has a crown of blossoms of peach color with a strong red bias. Against the deep green hills, these islands of color are intense.

On the very floor of the jungle the profusion of vegetation is duplicated in microcosm. Out of a dark brown and black mat of rotting leaves spring narrow blade-like stalks and clusters of plump clover; lichens, of ochre, rust and mustard shades, and mushrooms, some a delicate pink and cream, shaped like ears, grow on stones and rotting branches. Small, tough runners snake in and out of the humus, bursting into leaf here and there. Sometimes a seed with a durable shell of brilliant scarlet or amber lies like a gem in the grass, and small flowers of yellow, white, blue, violet, or fire-red wink in the moving spots of sunlight, the spare scatter of gold coins--all that penetrates from that great conflagration in heaven above.

The tempo of the village has also changed with the seasons. The months of May, June, July and August are drier and cooler. It is harvest time for coffee, corn, cotton and cocoa. Every two or three days the Alas de Esperanza plane buzzes out the sacks of coffee and a passenger or two, for now villagers have the urge to travel, and the weather and crop payments permit it. Those who cannot afford even Alas' reduced rates move on foot or by canoe. In terms of our own plans, we have the opportunity to film in good light, and the people are active at the year's principal work: clearing land and burning slash, hunting, weaving, and visiting relatives.

On May 11 we board an *expreso* to Otíka. The little Cessna is loaded to capacity, for we are now a company of three. In Lima Dianne and I were fortunate to encounter a Fulbright student, Brian Ransom, who was in Perú to study ancient musical instruments, and he has joined our crew as soundman. An ebullient, bearded twenty-four year-old, he comes equipped with a studio-quality Uher recorder, several microphones, a case of tape, and a passionate enthusiasm for folk music. Our freight includes also a Polaroid, a Bolex hand-wound 16mm camera, a Nizo Super 8, zoom lenses for both, 8000 feet of film, a case of batteries, and the necessary tripods, light meters, and filters. At the market in Satipo we packed up provisions and trade items for a month's stay: rice, beans, tuna, raw peanuts, onions, coffee, sugar, salt, garlic, kerosene, soap, fish line and hooks, mirrors, hair clips, beads, shotgun shells, knives, and Chiclets.

Our plan, a sound one in the abstract, is to spend a few days in Otíka, running equipment checks and working out procedures, then to travel to Ovíri for a two-week stint, returning to Otíka for another week of work before departure. After a brief respite in Lima, we will come back for a final three weeks in the two villages, when the shooting and note-taking should be completed. For most small-budget cinematic enterprises, a seven-week shooting schedule, with another three weeks for preparation and logistical support, would be more than adequate, and my notebook grows at such an alarming rate that I imagine my chief difficulty will be that of excision. We will discover early, however, how naive and mis-guided are such assumptions, how our cargo of equipment and provi-sions obstructs the purpose it is supposed to facilitate.

We bank between the abrupt green hills and swoop down to the long, shapeless patch of darker verdure that is the airstrip. Already we see black dots at its edges, and after the bounce and rush of landing, when the Cessna wheels and taxis back, we watch the swarm of children, their chocolate and rust cushmas flapping about high-pumping knees as they run, bandy-legged and zigzag, pell-mell, their faces awake, intent, and ecstatic. As we climb out of the aircraft and begin unloading our gear the villagers gather. Martín, looking thinner and stronger, steps forward with his familiar smile, shrewd and shy; then Matías with his fine, sturdy boys. The children laugh continually, like a small waterfall, and some of them fall down in the grass in paroxysms of excitement.

The plane has ruptured a brake line in landing, so Matías and I collaborate to repair it; he supplies wrenches to remove the shoe and I give another few feet of my nylon cord to bind up the loose line. The pilot does not appear worried. At San Ramón he has enough runway to land without brakes, so he shakes our hands and roars off into the sky. The villagers have hauled everything to the large house near the river that will be our camp, and when I rejoin Dianne and Brian I find a gallery of perhaps twenty-five spectators perched like voluble brown birds in and around the building. As we unpack, each new item produced brings sighs and comments. When we turn away from arranging pots, lanterns, hair-brushes, or camera cases, the people edge closer, extend tentative fingers, and finally pick things up and fondle them gingerly. Brian looks up to find his sunglasses on the nose of a proud and delighted young man, and my Buck knife is passing from hand to hand with cries of admiration.

Pulling a wooden *quena* flute from his pack, Brian blows a few jazz riffs, pulverizing the children with joy, and he initiates a round of teasing, pinching, and wrestling that will go on for the rest of our stay. Martín, who lives next door, now arrives with a great chunk of fresh meat on a banana leaf. It is fish, he says, caught this morning. He was just cutting it up when the plane landed. Dianne and I step over to have a look and find his wife and daughter hacking at the carcass of an armor-plated leviathan at least five feet long. The flesh is a rich, dark red, and the women are handing out three and five pound chunks to youngsters who bear the gift away without a word. It is for everyone, Martín remarks. Dianne mutters that we were ten minutes too late; it would have been a fine scene for the film.

Finally our welcoming committee begins to disperse. The women shoo away their children, and old Rosa rises with an expostulation that I am able to interpret before Matías translates. She has worked hard welcoming us, and wants to know what we are going to give her in return. Dianne presents a hand mirror, which she examines with no great enthusiasm. An onion is thrown in and she retires, at least provisionally content. Matías directs us to a pile of tree trunks, our fire wood, along one side of the house, and tells us that he will return tomorrow evening and we can discuss our plans in more detail then.

We set about organizing our camp, perishables in sacks and jars placed in the overhead loft or hung from roof poles, sleeping bags and mosquito nets spread on the spacious platform, our cooking gear on the one narrow table at the front of the house. We have no walls, and are on a main pathway to the river where the canoes are docked, so we must get used to being observed at any time. For a few minutes, Brian cannot locate his sunglasses, and remembering the young man who tried them on with such obvious pleasure, we know a twinge of paranoia. But they were only misplaced, and aside from this oversight, despite all the handling and exchanging of our effects, all have been returned to their precise locations, just as we unpacked them. In subsequent weeks we forego security, leaving thousands of dollars worth of gear untended while we are off swimming or doing laundry. During the months of living with the villagers, we will be relieved of only two items: a pair of papayas at one corner of the platform disappeared one afternoon, but as a coffee-grower from the Chanchamayo observed, the Asháninka treat papayas as pig food and worth nothing anyway.

The very next morning our confident plans begin to go awry. We have become, literally overnight, the principal diversion of the villagers and a significant force in the local economy. As we are finishing our morning coffee and discussing a likely location for a certain scene, the schoolmaster appears, followed by a small troop of his charges. The professor bears with him his *tocadiscos*, a flimsy battery-powered 45 rpm machine, which he offers reverently to Brian. Even with new batteries it does not function, and he seeks our professional assistance. *Claro.* We have unloaded on the previous day more mysterious machines than he has ever seen, and must perforce understand the profound nature of electricity.

"Jesus," Brian mutters, "I don't know a thing about these outfits. What if I can't fix it?"

I advise him to try anyway, but the recommendation is superfluous. He is already digging into his tool kit, and the boys again form their ring of awed admiration around him. When the back cover is off, Brian clucks in satisfaction. "It's just got things growing inside. Plant and animal life." He scrapes away mold and a spider's cocoon that apparently interferes with a crucial contact. In a matter of minutes the turntable is spinning, and a test record produces a scratchy sobbing that is--though marginally--identifiable as music.

The professor's monkey face is aglow with gratitude, and the children jump up and down with this confirmation--quite expected--of their hero's omnipotence. Brian favors them with a series of owl calls made by blowing into his cupped hands, and they respond with a whole series of sound effects, some imitative of animals and some of gross bodily functions. Two of them speed off and return in moments with gourd bowls and sections of hollow reed. They dip the reeds in a sticky mixture at the bottom of the bowl and begin to blow bubbles, some of them quite large, irridescent and durable. Dianne dives for the camera case, and I abandon my coffee for a light meter.

For better than an hour they keep us furiously busy, and themselves immensely entertained. When I produce a string loop they perform figures, some of which I recall from Marcos' demonstrations. Two more emissaries return with little popguns, the barrel formed of a hollow papaya branch, into which is fitted a plunger of tough weed stalk. A plant on the riverbank yields a pulpy pith which is readily compacted into bullets. In and around the house and the cane thickets along the river they stage a mock war, flying down narrow trails, swarming up low trees, crouching in the shadows in ambush. Quick and sure-footed as squirrels, they are not the least camera-shy; in fact our bumbling about among our cases and cans, our peering and pointing, and whirring and clicking, inspire them to excesses of hilarity. After each session of filming and taping, when we load our machines, check our light readings and voice levels, they gather to observe--and to beg for replays.

We are interrupted finally by the arrival of another villager with a malfunctioning radio. Word has apparently spread. Brian rolls his eyes heavenward and gamely pitches in again. While our little gang of half a dozen performers watches his every move, I watch them. They wear nothing but a cushma, often ragged and filthy--probably a hand-me-down that has clothed several older brothers. Each has also a handwoven cotton bag slung from the shoulder, which may contain (when school is in session) a cheap notebook and stub of pencil, a little roll of twine, bright feathers from birds they have killed, interesting pebbles, a bit of baked yucca wrapped in banana leaf, perhaps a small knife. As often as not they bear in hand a light bow and three or four miniature arrows.

They appear sturdy and in good health. The Asháninka are well-proportioned, square-shouldered and upright, with slightly bowed legs. Obesity is rare, among men almost nonexistent. These boys have dazzling teeth, skin like polished, close-grained wood, and feet of dirty, tough, lizard hide. Their eyes, black and shiny as wet obsidian, strike with an intensity of humor, curiosity, and excitement that one must strive hard to ignore. We learn, on this first day, that we must ignore them or we would be forever distracted by their zany charm and accomplish nothing of our own purposes. In subsequent weeks we will acquire, gradually, a little of their Asháninka ability to work at a task while joking, flirting, or arguing with bystanders at the same time. Brian already possesses this knack, and as he pokes at the innards of the radio, whistling and muttering profane incantations, he trades words and grimaces with his gallery of spectators. A couple of the boys catch on very quickly to what he is doing, and when he misplaces a screwdriver or wireclip or bit of tape, they point it out to him immediately, understanding that the order of dismantling is now to be reversed.

By lunchtime a second radio has arrived, and we realize that we may have to establish some limits on our wizard's accessibility--especially since so far these encounters have led to success. A loose wire in the first radio needed only a dab of solder to bring us the blather and blast of Pucallpa. From the excited whispering that greets Brian when he opens his little kit, we know that he has already the reputation of a great healer, an Albert Schweitzer of transistors. It appears, however, that this third patient may not recover, and further operations are postponed until tomorrow. The owner is chagrined, but brave, and leaves his dearest possession in its disembowelled state, promising to return with a bunch of bananas.

We file along the trail that winds to the small tributary on the eastern edge of the village, where we spend the best part of an hour bathing in a clear, refreshing pool shaded by overhanging branches and vines. The gang of boys at our heels was gone by the time we reached the stream; they realized our destination and tactfuly left us our privacy. It is exceedingly pleasant to sit on the clean, warm, white stones that rim the pool, watching a buzzard wheel over the jungle that rolls away to blue mountains which vanish into clouds. Though confused by so much activity, we are elated that the morning's work has gone so well.

Late that day, in the last of the sunlight, the children are at play on the airstrip, booting a soccer ball or tussling indiscriminately, and we provide them with a final thrill. In a spontaneous stroke of genius, Dianne stuck two frisbees in her luggage before leaving California, and produces one of them now. Brian seizes it with a delighted oath and trots onto the field for a demonstration. He is gifted in this art too, and with a backhand whip sends the fluorescent pink disk far and high. The whole troop, boys and girls alike, screams and departs at a gallop to retrieve it. The small person who recovers it first tries his hand, with a tremendous fling, and succeeds in casting the thing perhaps five yards. Another child scoops it up and races back to Brian. He uncoils another all-college throw, flat, low, bullet-fast. There is an instant of awed silence as the children watch the frisbee scythe past, then pandemonium again.

A kind young man has brought us a three-pound chunk of fresh wild pig which Dianne has placed in a pot to roast, and we sit on one of our fire logs where we can occasionally check its progress and watch the action on the field at the same time. The previous evening one of the rangy, pugnacious old hens from Martín's almost robbed us of the fish we were steaming, pecking off the aluminum lid and grabbing a filet. We chased it into the bushes, squawking and beating its wings in rage, and endangered it sufficiently to force it finally to drop its prize. Now we toss a chip occasionally at one of these sharp-eyed renegades who feigns interest in some bug or seed and sidles too near, yearning for this sizzling pork, fragrant with onion and garlic.

On the field a pattern has developed. The children care most for distance and duration; they scream most wildly at those times when the breeze catches the frisbee and lifts it to hover seemingly for a hundred heartbeats high above them. Then they collect in a swarm beneath and jump wildly to reach it first of all. Brian has shown a few of the children the proper stance and handhold, and one of them, Zacarías, Matías' boy of ten, can produce a wobbly flight of perhaps fifteen yards. Now, whoever recovers the frisbee runs to give it to Zacarías, so that he may improve his mastery. The struggle to snatch the spinning disc out of the air remains tumultuous and anarchic--I fear for the tots of three of four who seem in danger of being trampled--but apparently by universal consent the children abandon their own hard-won advantage instantly in order to encourage another's talent. I marvel at this good-humored self-abnegation, and also at the occasional departure from it. Once in a while Zacarías is passed over in favor of his sister Heorihéna, who is so hopeless at the sport that the others collapse with the ecstasy of their glee when she tries a throw. Yet she appears proud to be the object of such fun, and there is no trace of malice in the laughter at her flubs.

The bright pink saucer is still readily visible sailing through the gloom, but Brian is afraid the younger children will run into something or each other in their mad pursuit. He returns to the fireside, waving away the last reluctant troops in his little army. He is himself in a child's state of happy exhaustion.

"The little buggers are crazy. They'd stay out there all night."

I grin at him. "Between the frisbee and the Polaroid we can probably destroy this town."

"They won't care as long as Brian keeps the radios going." Dianne hands us our plates, heaped with chunks of the wild pork, tender and savory. "And as long as we get meat like this, I don't care either."

As we eat we formulate plans for the morrow. Brian wants to record native instruments, especially the mouth bow whose eerie sounds I have heard on Weiss's tape and described for him. Dianne and I agree that some footage of the making and playing of instruments would be valuable. We know from our reading that anthropologists have also catalogued panpipes, flutes, drums and whistles in this area. In his research in Lima Brian has become interested in the controversy over the origins of the "high" cultures; he believes that certain musical scales, motifs and styles found in these cultures may be traced to jungle tribes, confirming Tello's thesis of the selvatic origin of highland civilizations. But he is also simply a music lover, and wants to hear and learn new songs.

As we are enjoying our evening coffee and Inca cigarettes, Matías drops in to discuss our plans, and incidentally to sample our *caña* and tobacco. He downs a neat half-tumbler of the strong, raw liquor and then lights up, inhaling luxuriously. He asks us if we are content with our quarters. We assure him that we are and thank him again for his thoughtfulness in providing for us. Then we mention our wish to record more music, and ask about local instruments and performers. At first he frowns and shakes his head, but when I mention the mouth bow he remarks that Carlos may be able to make one for us. He is simultaneously reminded to inform me that Carlos has prepared my hunting bow and arrows, as I requested him to do by a pantomime during the drunken party three months ago. It both pleases and sobers me to understand how staunchly the Asháninka hold to their word. The intuition I had about the young man, that his aloofness was a special dignity or pride, seems confirmed. Matías tells us that Carlos "knows much about the mountain." He came out of the forest only five years ago, having made the momentous decision to raise his family near the Otíka school. For whatever information we want concerning hunting or gathering, he is manifestly the man to see.

We chat idly for a time, watching the fireflies drift and gyrate in the shadows. Somewhere at the other end of the village masato is being consumed, and there are sporadic cascades of distant laughter. We have lit a candle or two as well as our kerosene storm lantern, and now and then a moth dances briefly in one of the haloes of light. Already, perhaps under the influence of the chorus of frogs and insects, we have begun to tolerate moments of tranquil reverie in the midst of conversation. The hectic impulses of Lima are fading from the bloodstream.

As Matías rises to leave we press upon him the remainder of the pack of Incas. Dianne has been relating to him the tale of the thieving hen from Martín's. These chickens of the selva, she exclaims, are bold, tough marauders, quite unlike any we have known in our own country.

Matías smiles slightly. "They are all brought from Lima," he says. "The chief place of robbers." And he vanishes with our laughter into the night.

29

At midmorning everything is ready, as Matías promised, and we walk to Carlos' houses, for there are two, each with its fire and pots, hanging baskets, masato canoe, wife and children. We are seated on the platform in a small third structure which seems to be a common living room, and one of the wives serves us the traditional bowl, while we discuss the details of our proposal. Carlos knows very little Spanish, so we must make every-thing clear through Matías at the outset. He first brings out my finished bow and arrows, stored aloft in one of the houses. I admire them and try them out on a banana treetrunk in the back yard. The bow shoots true, and is a little longer and heavier than the average, as I requested.

After I have paid the five hundred soles agreed upon, we quickly strike a bargain for today's expedition. Carlos listens carefully to Matías and examines the knife we have brought as proposed payment. He has painted his wide, flat face with bright achiote and wears a good cushma, tan with dark brown and black vertical stripes. His eyes are alert, expres-sive, and from time to time he glances at one of the wives, who have gathered with their children at the edge of our conference, and says something. It appears that the knife is ample payment, and Dianne seals the arrangement with the gift of a hair clip to each of the women.

We want to work when the sun is near its zenith, providing maximum light on the jungle floor, so we refuse a second bowl and indicate our eagerness to begin. Carlos slips an old knife into his cotton shoulder bag, picks up his machete and pads away, down a trail through clumps of banana trees and plots of yucca, across a small, clear brook and up the slope of the first hill. We struggle after him, our paraphernalia hung all about us and encumbering our passage, until we reach a sun-dappled stretch where we can get a shot of our native gliding through the forest. We call after Carlos, and when he returns we explain by gestures and a few words that we want him to retrace his steps here while we crouch in the bushes and operate our machines, though he must not look at us as he passes by.

He proceeds immediately to do as we have instructed and I have to stop him to explain the procedure of beginning the action after the sound of the camera is audible. He waits, secretly amused, until I wave urgently at him to commence. Then he walks, swift and sure, face blank as a blind man's, through the sunny spot and out of sight into the green gloom. Good enough, Dianne judges through the viewfinder, though we will need some more of this sort of thing, and a few cutaways. In the next takes Carlos grasps the essence of this odd business and performs perfectly: he stops whatever he is doing when we tell him, repeats phases of an operation, and otherwise goes about his task completely ignoring us, until the camera stops its whirring--at which point he grins hugely or utters his deep, idiot lowing.

When we are beyond the scatter of lime and coffee groves that hem the village and diffuse outward, running wild into the jungle, Carlos leaves the trail briefly and locates a thick vine that droops from the trees. He hacks out a section perhaps eighteen inches long and an inch thick, which he stows in his shoulder bag. Then he doubles back on the trail to a cluster of palms he evidently remarked during our first passage. These are the peculiar "walking palms" that Bodley described for me six months ago. They are slender, usually less than a foot thick, but quite tall--I estimate fifty feet or more--with a lush spray of fronds at the tip. About three feet from the ground the single trunk branches into anywhere from eight to twenty roots which fan out as a cone-shaped base, a many-legged stand. According to Bodley, the tree can migrate slowly on these root legs, an inch or more each year.

Carlos machetes through several of the legs and the tree begins to topple, but then hangs on the branches and vines that surround it. He murmurs something, clamps the machete in his teeth, and in a moment has walked swiftly on all fours up the trunk and into the tangle overhead. Forty feet up he balances with one foot on the precariously hanging palm, the other on a loop of vine, and swings the blade to cut away a single frond that drops with a whoosh at our feet. Then, in a series of swings and catches as graceful as a monkey's, he is back on the ground beside us to retrieve the long palm frond. There is no trace of self-consciousness in his transition from terrestrial to arboreal travel, and he leaves the tree hanging there to die in the air.

After slicing out the center spine of the palm frond, Carlos adds it to the section of vine in his bag and turns back toward the village. We retrace our steps until we have reached a section of recently cleared and burned land. There Carlos digs about at the base of a young palm of a different species until he finds two very long and thin fibrous roots. These he lays over a dead branch and taps with the handle of his machete, apparently to soften the outer skin, for he next strips off this covering to expose the white, string-like core. He has now all his materials, and sets them out at his feet to begin assembling the instrument. The light, however, is inadequate so we pull him up and direct him about our invisible frame until we are satisfied with the angle and illumination. By now we can treat him as unceremoniously as a trade actor, and he only grins, returning always during the actual take to his utterly preoccupied state. When we interrupt him, he shifts from concentration on his work to compliance in our strange drama with the same ease and grace with which he left the ground for the trees.

The assembly begins. Carlos uses only an old table knife sharpened on a stone. With it he first whittles two small bows from the section of vine, notching each at both ends, then strings them with the tough white root core. From the spine of the frond from the walking palm he trims a long, limber wand, a little larger in diameter than a matchstick. He works seated, catching shavings in the lap of his cushma, using his large, splayed toes as much as his hands to hold the bits of wood.

Running the wand between his lips he coats it from end to end with spittle, then takes the haft of the bow lightly between his teeth. One hand holds one end of the bow in such fashion that the thumb and two fingers touch the string and move along it, while the other hand saws the wand back and forth over the string. Instantly the soft, whining tone appears and shapes itself into a melody, agile but haunting. The trills and glissandos Carlos makes with his thumb and fingers are extraordinary. As far as I can tell, he manages near-perfect intervals, and a certain harmonic modulation seems to be accomplished by shaping the mouth cavity, as is done on the Jew's harp. The tune is not long, and Carlos finishes up with a few random saws of the bow, utters his deep, mindless laugh, and rises as if to go.

"*Otro! No, otro!*" We clamor around him as the children do, avid for tricks and treats. He is somewhat puzzled, but willing to indulge us. Once he has made the toy he does not seem particularly interested in what happens to it, but by playing back his performance Brian intrigues him into performing some half a dozen songs. All are intricate, subtle, and plaintive, with enough resemblances to suggest that here the artist works infinite variations on ancient, simple patterns. We are spellbound, Brian especially, and watch and whisper over his every move. Carlos is entertained by all this but not flustered. More than anything he seems secretly astonished that we could be so excited by such a plaything. After all, anyone can make one in a few minutes.

Finally Carlos indicates that he wishes to go home, so we reluctantly pack up our gear and follow him. At his house we drink another bowl of masato, and a wife gives me a beautiful necklace made from small black seeds and parrot feathers. I ask what she would like in return, and by dint of much gesturing and creative use of our tiny vocabulary we divine that it is beads. Gifts are the cement of this society. One gives trinkets, time, attention, food or drink as a sign of amiability and responsibility, and one may expect them in return. The aim seems to be balance, what is commensurate, but the equilibrium is dynamic. The knife has been exchanged for the mouth bow lesson; hairclips were given as well; now a fine necklace as a rejoinder, and I promise beads soon.

Collecting my bow and arrows, I ask Carlos if he will take me hunting. A simple request. I shake the bow at him, point to the mountains, and inquire *"Mañana? Tsámi? Arí?"* (Tomorrow? We go? Yes?) *"Arí,"* he says, and after holding his arm level with the horizon for an instant, he drops it a few degrees. I take the signal to mean that we must start before sunup. But I am elated, for if Matías is correct I can expect the best available instruction in forest craft. We leave, smiling and waving, content with our morning's work, but Carlos and his families are already turning back to the fire, to mending or minding of pots and children.

I rise in the first grayness of dawn, dress quietly without waking the others, and take my new bow and arrows with me down the path. A thin fog hangs in the air, and the leaves are slick with water that patters to the forest floor. At Carlos' all is dark; the firelogs in both hearths have burned back; only a handful of coals glows between them. I pause at the edge of the clearing and whisper, *"Vamos? Tsámi?"* In a moment or two I hear the platform staves creak and a figure moves out from the black shadow of the roof. He comes toward me and peers closely to verify my identity, then nods and beckons me to follow him back to the house.

He removes a shotgun from its perch in the roof braces, slips on the cotton shoulder bag, and without another word or look strikes off on the path leading across the creek to the mountains. We go swiftly for perhaps three quarters of an hour, often in deep darkness where the trail is overgrown. Shouldering through this vegetation soaks our clothing, and I hurry not only to keep in sight of Carlos' figure, but also to fend off the chill in the air. With the first touch of gold light on the hilltops, the last tatters of fog vanish and we can see at last the wet, glistening leaves, branches sharp as cracks, and a mosaic floor of moss, mushrooms and rotting wood. The varied chorus of birds has begun and now and then Carlos halts to listen carefully, then moves on. Sometimes he leans over to examine the trail too, but when I pause to inspect the same place I can see nothing but a scuff mark in the spongy humus or a few dislodged pebbles.

Carlos goes barefoot and like Marcos he has a swift, gliding step, pigeon-toed and straight, one foot falling directly in front of the other. He moves without sway from side to side, except when ducking smoothly under fallen logs or hanging creepers. As with Marcos, this pace is deceptive, and I find myself periodically trotting to keep up. The bow tangles often in the undergrowth, and my clothes catch on thorns or sharp twigs. The more I imitate Carlos' carriage the better my progress. My normal splay-footed stride has to be corrected, because the trail is scarcely wider than the breadth of a human foot, and to swing one's instep wide is to invite collision with the tough stalks of bushes, or stubs and stumps left by other travelers' machetes. The knee must come up rather high, and the foot reach straight or toed in slightly. It is also better to keep the head up, rather than tilted forward to watch the trail immediately in front, for there are as many hazards above as there are below.

Concentrating on these new lessons of physiological adaptation to the environment, I nearly blunder into Carlos who has stopped to listen, one hand extended behind him to signal the halt. I can hear nothing, and we stand motionless for what seems to me several minutes, before Carlos utters a thin, high whistle. A moment later, just at the threshold of audibility, I hear an answer. After another long pause, the call and response are repeated. I look inquiringly at Carlos and he nods solemnly and gives me an Indian word. *"Ave o animal?"* I whisper.

"Ave." He indicates with his hands a chicken-sized bird. Cautiously we proceed, and for twenty minutes the exchanges continue, the bird sounding always a little nearer. I remark that from time to time Carlos varies the tone structure, interval and attack, though a three-note, falling pattern is most frequent; the answer is sometimes not the same as his call. Finally he motions me to remain on the trail and disappears silently into the undergrowth. I wait for perhaps ten minutes, during which I hear the bird utter two more cries. After an interval of silence Carlos materializes a few yards further along the trail. *"Nada,"* he says softly and twiddles his fingers to indicate something running over the ground. We move on.

By late morning I have lost my bearings completely. We have crossed several ridges, branching from time to time on trails that appear to be only the faint track of animals, and small streams, which Carlos sometimes follows for a few hundred yards. I am surprised that he keeps up the swift, gliding walk. Since we more than once strike sign fresh enough to produce a grunt of solemn enthusiasm, I half expect Carlos to find a promising stretch of trail and wait in ambush. But the strategy seems to be one of covering the maximum territory for the day. It is true that in spite of his speed on the narrow, twisting trails Carlos remains observant and what I see I usually see because he troubles to point it out. Once, in a rather gloomy glade of the giant *ceiba pentandra* trees, whose bases spread out for fifteen yards or more in a star-like pattern of narrow root ridges, he stops all at once--another of his peculiar abilities, going without any transition from rapid motion to the absence of motion.

I look for a long time in the direction he indicates, into the pattern of shadow and flecks of light, through hairy vines and glossy leaves, at the soft humps of fallen and rotting trees. Nothing moves but the shadow and light.

"Donde?" I whisper. *"Lejos?"*

He shakes his head. *"Cerca, cerca."*

I strain to see the shape that must be near, the alien animal shape in all these loops and twists, stalks and blades. Carlos takes a step or two, his arm still extended and pointing. I ease after him, blinking, trying to refocus my vision at various planes. His finger seems to be trained on a small tree with corrugated and mottled bark.

"*Qué es?*" I hiss.

"*Mariposa.*" Butterfly. Carlos is fond of the word and repeats it. I stare at the tree, but I see no butterfly until there is the tiniest pulse of wing, and then it is there, huge and obvious, at a distance of no more than a yard. The camouflage is extraordinary. As big as the blue morpho, this insect has an intricate pattern of browns, blacks and whites embossed on the underside of its wings, each of which is as large as my hand. The central figure is a white ring around a black bullseye, which is surrounded in turn by whorls of dark and light brown; the effect is that of a knothole perhaps with a rich infestation of blight. It is certainly the most beautiful butterfly I have ever seen, but as with all butterflies I succumb finally to the temptation to touch, and just before my fingertip reaches the delicate wing the insect flaps softly away. Carlos laughs his laugh deeper than thought and glides on down the trail.

In early afternoon we hook north and pick up the small river that will lead us back to Otíka. We cross the trail of a *sachavaca* or tapir, the slick-hided, split-hoofed ruminant that can weigh as much as five hundred pounds. With a sixteen gauge loaded with birdshot we are decidedly undergunned for such a beast, but the stale tracks do not get Carlos very enthusiastic anyway. Then, perhaps forty-five minutes further down the river canyon, I hear at a distance a peculiar, grunting whoop that ends in a deep and echoing whistle. I think first of the tapir, then of jaguar, because there is something of a big cat's cough in the sound.

Carlos turns to grin at me and I ask *"Maníti?"* He shakes his head, and points into the trees. A bird then. I hold my hands apart to suggest a size, and he gestures no, much larger, something larger even than a vulture. We strike off in the direction of the sound, and in a few minutes hear it again, still far away. The resonance of the sound is awesome, and I imagine a thing with great wattles or air chambers to puff out its throat.

Then for some time there is quiet--or rather the endless variety of squawks, trills, bloops and whirrs that only deepens the spacious silence under the giant trees. Carlos strides swiftly along for a hundred yards or so at a time, then pauses to listen before proceeding. We are on a bench above the stream, the ground fairly open and thickly carpeted with damp leaves. It is early afternoon, and the intricate, dappled patterns of sunlight and green shade soon tease me out of thought. I am shambling after my friend, bow and arrows in hand, head as empty as the air around me, when all at once the sound comes again, now much closer. A tremendous, thundering shriek that stuns me in my tracks. Carlos flashes a grin over his shoulder and edges ahead, peering intently into the branches. Again it comes, and my mind is jarred into a comparison: the squeal of a pig and the whine of a jet liner warming up, lowered an octave and amplified through an echo chamber.

I stare into the trees, unable to imagine the source of such racket. A shaking of branches overhead, and a sudden flash of one small, black face through the leaves. Monkey! The famed Howler!

They are three, all a dark rust color with long curling tails and the shrunken leather faces of old men. They come swift and easy through the tree tops, making the whole mountainside boom and ring. Carlos is grinning now from ear to ear and gesturing at me to take up a position beside him, just below a tall tree where they seem to be settling. I do so and for some moments the primates watch each other, alert but without fear. Carlos breaks a branch from a shrub and begins thrashing it against his leg, making a hissing whistle between his teeth. Then he takes a shotgun shell from his bag and waves this tiny bright red cylinder at the gallery above. As they disdain to be silent, these creatures will take risks out of curiosity. They swing circumspectly down to the next level of branches, launching another cacophonous outcry.

After another attempt to coax them closer, Carlos slips the shell into the chamber and aims carefully. At the blast of the gun I expect to see them scamper away, but they only scream and retreat to their previous sanctuary. The birdshot, apparently, has no force after travelling thirty yards straight up. Another few minutes of branch-thrashing and the smallest of the clan aloft cannot resist venturing closer. Carlos loads his last cartridge and fires again. A shred of leaves floats down and the youngster flees to rejoin his fellows. He hops on a branch and beats his arms against his ribs, as if stung by bees.

"*Pique, no más,*" Carlos explains, regretful. He indicates the size of the shot with thumb and forefinger. "*No vale.*"

I am not entirely sorry. For a few seconds, in the excitement of smelling powder again, I knew an impulse for a rifle. It would not have been a difficult shot--the old twenty-two would do very nicely. Then I was ashamed. It would be too easy. A few rifles in this environment, in the hands of even an average marksman, and the game population would soon diminish dramatically. That would surely be a pity in the case of this creature, with its outrageous, bellowing whoops from the treetops.

Carlos beckons to me and relieves me of the bow and arrows. He tries to charm the monkeys once more, and for a time they lead us from tree to tree, until at last they reach one with low, drooping branches and Carlos decides to risk a shot. Twice he bends the bow and both times the arrows are deflected by small branches and careen away into oblivion. The third time he positions himself directly below the monkeys, and, arms trembling with strain, draws the arrow back to the very barbs of the point. The shaft hisses swiftly away and one of the howlers dodges, startled. A near miss. A second or two passes, while both of us gape upward. The arrow has vanished into thin air. We glance quickly at each other, and then hear it rip through the topmost branches of the tree. I try to retract my head between my shoulder blades and Carlos drops the bow and hugs himself, beginning the dance of a man caught in a hailstorm. He bellows his deep, imbecilic laughter and I too begin to hop about in anxiety and exhilaration. The expression we are mirroring for each other provokes us to hilarity, and even when the arrow drives into the loam a dozen feet away we continue to jump and shout.

Though the point needs no further proof, I have again clear evidence of the peculiar philosophy of the Asháninka: mishaps, failures, even near-disasters can provide as much merriment as their opposites. There is some automatic sympathy for and even delight in the unfolding of uncontrollable consequence; the instant of revelation, when we realize that arrows must come down (we know not where), yields a shudder of heightened vitality. These hunts, fruitless all so far, are like a long tumble of the dice, and every gambler reaches the final knowledge that his pleasure is in that tumble, not in the still die or its aftermath of despair or rejoicing.

But we do not return altogether empty-handed. Carlos notices a certain kind of small, dark green bush and underneath it we collect some seeds. They are the size of beans, bright red with a black spot, and as hard as rocks. Not to eat, Carlos indicates, but for hanging about the neck. We gather between us a couple of dozen, and I find also some brown ones, pecan-sized and shiny. With this pitiful harvest we make our way along the stream until we strike the Tambo at the northern boundary of the village. I am bone tired after what I estimate to be a tramp of fifteen kilometers, and the bowl of masato that a wife serves me tastes cool, rich and refreshing. Carlos regales her and the children with a brief account of our trek, and I gather by their reaction that I have again become a source of humorous anecdote.

Before I leave, understanding well now the Asháninka habit of sleeping in the afternoon, I ask if someday we can hunt again together, and Carlos nods. *Lejos*, he points. Further. We have only made the briefest of forays into the village's back yard. A little stroll to look at the butterflies and practice on small birds. He smiles and yawns. I hand back my empty bowl, nod at them, and leave without a backward look. Fatigue and the masato working through my blood have aided me greatly to imitate the curt departure so characteristic here.

30

After a long nap and a swim in the river, I dig a string of tiny glass beads from my pack and a length of braided sweetgrass from South Dakota. These small gifts I take to Carlos. The sweetgrass puzzles him, as I expected it to, but I do my best to explain its significance. From *Indios* of the north, it is a holy herb whose fragrance helps purify the participants in various Lakotah ceremonies that cure and regenerate. I can only light a strand in the fire to demonstrate its use as incense, gesturing at my breast and heavenward, and hope that some measure of its medicine power will endure here, eight thousand miles from the people who first blessed it. Carlos is still puzzled, but carefully stores the twined fibers in a basket hung from the rafters.

This quixotic presentation completes an obscure cycle for me. I obtained the sweetgrass during a filming expedition in Wounded Knee, during the occupation and defense of that monument by the American Indian Movement in 1973. This journey to the country of the Sioux brought me face-to-face for the first time with the grim reality of reservation life, and forced recognition of the sinister connection between our naive, romantic myths about the redman and the actual cultural suicide we have brought upon him.

This connection appeared most clearly in the way in which the entire struggle, which lasted two and a half months, was a function of the consciousness on all sides of its possibilities as televised drama, a live re-enactment of the massacre eighty years ago. The Indians, not only Sioux but Chippewa, Oneida, Cherokee, Kiowa, Paiute, Washo and many others, played their roles with old lever-action Winchesters, shotguns and twenty-twos. Many wore feathers in their braids, medicine pouches around their necks. The marshalls and federal troops were costumed in fatigues, packed automatic weapons, and travelled in armored cars and in helicopters. Had the cameras not been always present and inquisitive, the battle would have been very brief. A blanket of tear gas, a barrage of mortar or light field rockets, a sweep with the armored vehicles bearing fifty calibre machine guns, and the resistance would have been wiped out completely.

But the "dramatic" aspect of the Indian takeover of Wounded Knee prohibited any such action. The AIM war council played cleverly on popular sympathy for last-ditch heroism, announcing often that their forces were committed to a fight to the death. They invited the press daily to their camp and gave interviews freely, aware that their best weapon was this broadcasting of a stance of noble defiance, a public demonstration of potential sacrifice. They were of course not merely posturing. Everyone expected death, sooner or later; death of a high order of symbolism was effectively required by the scenario.*

For their part, the army of the state cooperated in this ritual. To unleash their full firepower would have been too ghastly and sudden an end, so they dallied with their adversary and made mock war, posing like actors in a B movie with walkie-talkies, field glasses, and ammo belts. Like professional soldiers anywhere, they enjoyed the added dimension of daily publicity, an authentication of their performance.

The attention span of the public is quite short, however, in the age of television. When the Indian spokesmen began to try to shift the focus of their propaganda to the issues of dispossession, alcoholism, suicide, and malfeasance in reservation politics, they lost exposure. Their lifeline of food, medicine, and contraband arms began to weaken; the ring of steel around them tightened. When the AIM leaders began to talk of negotiation the interest in their plight diminished markedly, and it became finally clear that the sympathy that had powered their early success had in fact a ghoulish tinge, that they had drawn spectators who wished to witness, via satellite, another desperate stand against the bluecoat charge, to root for a hopeless underdog over a cold beer in their own living rooms, to shake their heads, be appalled, mourn in comfort. The Indians were in fact being reminded that they were most admirable, most memorable, most *interesting* when howling their death songs into the blazing guns. As survivors, clamoring for schools and jobs, they were boring and unlovable.

I, too, came under the spell of this tainted myth. Watching television in California, I saw a homely, happy Sioux dancing in front of the burning courthouse in the town of Custer, a covey of burly policemen, as frightened as children, trying to hold an angry crowd at bay with their Mace cans, and a man on a horse with a gun, riding through the driving snow. It looked like a daring and desperate revolt to reverse the long tide of the century, and avenge in some way the original Wounded Knee massacre. I looked up the particulars that night in James Mooney's contemporary account, and suffered again twinges of rage and grief at the memory of that atrocity. More than a hundred women and children blown to rags in a few minutes by Hotchkiss guns firing two-pound explosive shells at a rate of more than fifty per minute. Three days later, after a severe blizzard,

---

*During the height of the occupation the soldiers on both sides traded tens of thousands of rounds—always at night, after the press had withdrawn. That only one Indian died in these salvos is little short of miraculous, for there were as many as 300 men, women and children quartered in the few flimsy buildings of the settlement.

troopers heaped the frozen bodies in a trench and covered them with raw earth. Wrapped in blankets by their dying mothers, four babies were dug alive out of the snow. One survived, clad in a small cap upon which her mother had embroidered an American flag.

The next day I determined to join the pilgrimage of those who wished to participate in the symbolic revival of this situation--though I believe few then understood this slant on the matter--and mustered hastily the minimal equipment for a filming expedition. I hoped that what resulted would be of benefit in portraying the uprising with greater insight and compassion than was evident in the few minutes alloted to the story in nightly newscasts. Near the University of California at Davis, where I teach, is DQU, a settlement of Indian and Hispanic students, and I contacted there a small group anxious to make the trip for their own reasons.

We travelled in my sedan and a microbus belonging to a Washo, and in our company were a huge young Pomo, a Hoopa, a quarterbreed Minneconjou and a fullblood Lakotah girl. I and the Minneconjou's girlfriend were the only whites. They were all students--bright, active and afire with purpose. I was self-conscious about being white, a professor, and most ignorant of the culture of my companions, but in the course of two days and nights of crosscountry driving we made the careful beginnings of friendship. They let me know by indirect allusions that they carried guns hidden in the doorpanels of the microbus, and that we would be staying in the home of one who belonged to the AIM underground responsible for smuggling reinforcements to the besieged militants "in the Knee."

The evening after our arrival we set out for the staging area, Crow Dog's camp, located on the Rosebud Reservation. It was a three-hour drive, all of us packed into the microbus along with the camera gear. The excitement of talking over the campaign with our host, an old Sioux woman whose face was twisted by some injury into an expression of demonic glee, had induced us to celebrate with a good deal of beer and some marijuana. I was driving while most of the others dozed in the back, and missed the turnoff to White River from Interstate 90. In this plainsland there are long reaches between connecting roads; I grew impatient and elected to cross the shallow depression of bare earth which divided the lanes of opposed traffic.

I had not reckoned on the South Dakota mud in March, a period of alternate freezing and thaw, and the bus settled at once over the axles in the ditch. When I gunned the engine the back wheels produced only a stream of mud clots the consistency of warm chocolate. With some difficulty I roused my companions and tried to make them aware of the gravity of our situation. Were a patrolman to stop, he would find four hulking Indians and one white woman in a vehicle with California plates, carrying concealed weapons, with open containers and controlled substances in abundance. We tried to push the bus out but the slippery ground gave no purchase for the feet and we succeeded only in covering ourselves with gobs of the mud. I felt miserable, aware that if all of us wound up in jail, mine would be the blame and mine the responsibility and expense of obtaining release.

We stood in the chill night wind, cursing periodically, cringing at oncoming cars, and trying to think. Headlights swerved, and a pickup truck stopped on the embankment above us.

"Y'all stuck?" A head came through the side window. The little tractor-driver's cap bobbed in the dim glow from the dashboard. He was an old man, his neck scrawny and wrinkled as a plucked chicken's, his eyes invisible behind the thick discs of his spectacles. "I guess you shore are. Anywhere off'n the road is bad this time of year."

He climbed from the cab and came to stand momentarily by the bus. "You boys are in there." He laughed, a quick wheezing. "California. Long ways from home."

I wondered what the old man must think, given the daily newspaper and television coverage of the armed confrontation only a few miles away. I half expected him to retreat cautiously to the safety of his truck and leave us. Instead he bustled to the tailgate and lifted out a chain.

When we were hooked together he took up the slack, gunned the engine to a high, roaring whine, back tires smoking and shrieking on the asphalt, and with all of us heaving on the rear bumper the microbus unglued itself and rolled up the embankment to safe ground. I dropped the chain into the truck bed and walked again to the window to express our gratitude, not unmixed with amazement.

The old man would not hear much of it. "People done the same for me. We got to help each other. You didn't know about this old South Dakota clay. Dust or soup, ain't no in between. Fellas have a good trip." He nodded sharply and lunged away.

Later, on the last leg of our journey to Crow Dog's, the Washo laughed in the darkness. "And we came here to shoot them," he said softly. "Is that what they call irony?"

Sun Bear was a Chippewa medicine man and trader with a small group of devoted followers, which included an indeterminate number of wives. He had come to the Knee as correspondent for his own magazine, *Many Smokes*, a mimeograph-and-staple publication that presented his gentle philosophy along with tips on herb preparations and wood lore. I met him at the Pine Ridge office of the Bureau of Indian Affairs, then decorated with sandbags on the roof, behind which men with guns stood guard. I hoped to obtain some kind of press certification from the Justice

Department representatives who had moved in to monitor official traffic in and out of the Knee.

Our expedition to Rosebud had ended badly: Crow Dog's encampment was a vortex of tension and confusion. The Washo and Pomo were told they would have to give up their guns, undergo a two-week trial period during which they would have to do kitchen chores and practice sentry duty, and only then, if cleared, would they bear arms in an attempt to run through the enemy lines. They were outraged; they had come to fight, not to be in boot camp. My offer to help by making a documentary film sounded irrelevant and silly, delivered in Crow Dog's rundown house at three in the morning, while a cold, silent, black man from Oakland strung field telephones around us, as if he were back in Nam. I was informed curtly that they needed food, ammunition, and men who were ready to die. So I confronted the fact that I had not come with enough zeal to warrant such a commitment, and withdrew to try a safer and more conventional approach, despite a feeling of shame and inadequacy.

Waiting on a bench in the hallway outside the Justice Department office, I explained all this to Sun Bear and his patron-companion, a Palm Springs screenwriter, perhaps Mexican, who was about to go through bankruptcy and put his Cadillac and credit cards at Sun Bear's disposal for his remaining days of solvency. As a polite, bearded young man in a suit beckoned us from the door, Sun Bear advised me genially to join his press corps as a photographer for *Many Smokes*. Of course, I agreed, and after a few minutes of sly and amused interrogation we were all granted cards good for one eight-hour visit the following day. The authorities clearly saw nothing to fear in a conspiracy which included an unemployed screenwriter, a medicine man and a college professor. I was jubilant that my pilgrimage would be in some sense completed. I had already determined that my film would concentrate on the people I was meeting through the old Sioux and her friends--mostly other powerful old women, families living in reservation shacks, and the editor of a small local newspaper--but a little footage of the actual scene of the conflict was indispensable.

Rapid City was at this time crammed with an assortment of people involved in the drama. Mark Lane had arrived with a contingent of legal workers; there were press teams from *Esquire, Playboy,* and CBS, NBC, and ABC; various hastily-formed committees (or individuals like Sammy Davis Jr.) had mandated convoys of supplies or technical help to the besieged Indians. The government had various kinds of personnel in the area: three hundred or so Federal Marshalls, Justice Department workers, FBI agents and sharpshooters, and Interior Department brass. A motley selection of unofficial visitors also passed through: Marlon Brando was expected momentarily; Angela Davis flew in for a press conference; there were no-nonsense lady anthropologists in thick spectacles and combat boots, dreamy young men with backpacks, a Hollywood producer complete with cigar and million-dollar talk, some high-spirited young women who came to give body and soul in support of the troops.

The press contingent was equally diverse. Just ahead of us in the convoy was a Dutch camera crew, for by now the occupation was international news, and behind us a carload of ecstatic Indian teenagers, representing a school paper in Arizona. We were searched by FBI agents, deferential young men with remote eyes who sniffed our thermos, examined my camera and commented on the weather. They did not find the candy bars and dried soup. Then we drove on down the narrow oiled road, past the bunkers and armored vehicles, over a rise to the Indians' checkpoint. One white man and two Indians with rifles emerged from behind the wrecked and burned-out carcass of an automobile, itself barricaded behind cinderblocks and sandbags. They examined our press cards perfunctorily, accepted a handful of candy bars, and as the shift was changing, one asked for transport back to headquarters.

The village of Wounded Knee lies in a basin surrounded by low bare hills. An old wooden church stands atop a knoll where the more than two hundred bodies of Big Foot's people were interred in 1890, and from this promontory we could see the Indian bunkers at the perimeter of the basin, the nearby trading post now converted to a mess hall and meeting room, and the scatter of buildings that composed the settlement. Except for the cinderblock trading post, these structures were pathetic board and tarpaper shacks, housing a population of perhaps a hundred souls. To take care of the occupying troops and AIM administration, some temporary tents, teepees and pickup campers were clustered near the post, and the parking lot was jammed with visitor's vehicles, camera trucks, and even a couple of horses.

We moved about with the other press teams for a time, under the loose guidance of an AIM guard, visiting the church and graveyard, a ceremonial teepee, a sweat lodge, and a sentry post. The bullet holes in the church and a pattern of burned patches on the hills--the mark of parachute flares sent up at night by the Federals, to inhibit night runs through their lines--proved to us that the casual informality and bland respectfulness of the agents at the government checkpoint vanished with the light of day. A group of guards at the church, young Indian men with a hard, sardonic look about them, told us that there were firefights every night. It was for this reason that only day passes were granted to visitors. They had already become accustomed to these barrages, although the loud thrum of "tumblers"--bullets that spin end over end--still interfered with sleep.

At a briefing following our tour, we learned that the most newsworthy event of the day was to be a symbolic march out of the camp, staged by a group of Indians from the East--Oneidas, Onedagas, Mohawks and Iroquois. They had come to express their solidarity with the Sioux and to discuss strategy, staying a few days in defiance of the regulations against remaining overnight. We decided to accompany them, and hurried to complete a few interviews with the occupying forces before the march began. I managed to persuade one or two of the Indian soldiers to say a few words into my microphone, but they were uneasy, suspicious. All of them would eventually face severe charges for bearing arms against Federal Agents, and preferred not to incriminate themselves on tape or film. They also mistrusted the flattery and adulation visible in many of their interlocutors. Having made a gesture of risk and sacrifice, they were offended to find themselves treated as material for hastily produced "human interest" dramas.

At the ceremonial teepee I had met Black Elk, a tall gentle Sioux (a descendant of the old man who dictated visions to Niehardt and Brown), and his wife Grace Spotted Eagle. While I stood in the churned mud at the entrance of the trading post, armed with my recorder, they approached. A few off-duty warriors lounged on nearby car fenders, and two men rested beside a wheelbarrow laden with a dismembered beef, its stiffened, blood-caked limbs covered with flies. I greeted the couple, fiddled with the knobs on the machine, and asked some awkward question about the purpose of the occupation and their feelings toward it. Black Elk spoke briefly and with dignity, saying that they were a free people in their own country, and that they desired only recognition and acknowledgment of their claim. "Now she will speak," he said, and gestured proudly at his wife.

She drew her blanket about her, fixed me with her black eyes, and spoke indeed. She began by stating that we stood here on sacred ground, near the bones of her ancestors who had been shot down on a winter's day eighty years ago. These spirits had talked to them and called upon them to recover and defend their land, now a tourist stop where beadwork, moccasins, and gimcracks were sold to the curious by a white man who owned the concession. Some of the postcards showed the corpses in the snow, arms rigid in a gesture of supplication. How would white people like to see pictures of their grandfathers, dirty and frozen, sold in the stores for souvenirs?

"They tell us Indians we are better off on the reservation. The government will take care of us. But what has happened for these eighty years? They give us the worst land in the country, and the food they hand out--the government commodities--the flour is full of weevils and the meat is rotten. Then the rich ones, the big shots, the white people lease what ground we have because we have no cattle. They are still getting rich off us. Nobody cares. Now we are fighting, and you all show up to find out what is going on. That is the only reason, because we are fighting. We will die here if we have to, but we don't want to die. We are just asking that you talk to us. We want President Nixon to come here and sit down--right here on this ground where they killed our people--and talk. He can fly around all over, to China and to France, why can't he come here in our country, and *sit down on the ground,* and talk to us?"

Some of the soldiers had gathered around us now, and at points in her speech, when she paused for a breath, they or her husband uttered the traditional *Ho!* of approbation. The force of indignation in this stocky woman and her chorus rendered me speechless, foolish, and finally ashamed. The microphone was a cheap talisman that could never transform such righteous rage into art, and in a helpless motion of atonement I shut off the machine and to my own consternation burst into tears.

"I have spoken from my heart," she said quietly, and the two of them moved off, the plump woman erect in her faded blanket, the gangling man in worn overalls with a pair of feathers in his hair. They were splendid in their pride, and for a long time I stood with the microphone dangling from my hand, wracked by an inexplicable grief. The two men with the wheelbarrow were highly amused. "She told you," one of them remarked, and they resumed pushing and shoving their bloody cargo through the mud.

Other adventures ensued during this pilgrimage: my automobile disappeared for three days, when it was employed to transport Dennis Banks and Russell Means to a makeshift landing strip; I narrowly escaped falling in love with a one-legged Sioux woman with a great and mighty heart; a Wyoming Highway Patrolman held a .38 at my ribs for several very long seconds. But only two other experiences had an enduring effect.

Late in the afternoon we walked out of Wounded Knee with the small band of Six Nation people: men, women and children. For part of the way we were escorted by Indian warriors, many of them teenagers proudly bearing their single-shot twenty-twos and old shotguns. On the brow of surrounding hills we could see the men in khaki crouched behind their machine guns, and our cheerful banter held a note of apprehension. But it was daylight and there were national press people among us, so our escort turned back without incident and we walked on.

For the last few hundred yards I walked beside a woman who bore in her arms a six year-old girl with a new tee-shirt. The decal on the shirtfront advertised the Independent Ogalala Nation, decreed only a few days ago by the AIM council. (Rather in mock seriousness: Banks and Means announced that, broke, surrounded, and almost out of food and ammunition, it was time to become a sovereign nation and declare war!) I said to the woman that when the new nation opened its office of immigration, I would request an application for citizenship. She looked at me in weary disgust and said, as if explaining matters to a slow child, "Application? Papers? There will be no papers." I was humbled. I saw how for us the simplest and most direct actions had become difficult. Our presidents never sit on the earth; our citizens exist only by virtue of their licenses and numbers.

The last enduring incident of this trip was Sun Bear's handing me, just before we parted, the little bundle of sweetgrass from his worn, battered suitcase stuffed with trade goods.

31

On the day of our departure downriver to Ovíri, Matías unbolts the Briggs and Stratton from the lawnmower in order to transfer it to Martín's canoe. This craft, now finished, is large, graceful, and perfectly sound. With the motor attached, Matías claims, it will bear us to Ovíri in little more than an hour. His wife and two year-old arrive soon, with a basket of provisions, for they are to accompany us. Brian's minions help us freight the gear to the river, where everything is stowed amidships while two of the boys quickly cut lengths of cane to wedge into the hull as seats. When we push off to the whoops of our escort, we ride high in the water, a light load for this municipal flagship, and with the engine bellowing we draw swiftly away.

The water is much lower than it was in January, and though still turbid it has lost the opaque chocolate hue of the flood season. Passage is easy now; the river does not bulge and froth as before. We can travel well away from the bank, where new rock formations are exposed, driving in the tongue of the current and rocking easily over an occasional riffle. The trip seems to take no time at all.

At Ovíri all is as Matías has promised. Professor Nicolás has prepared sleeping quarters for us in the large, enclosed building which was once the coffee trading post for the village, before the airstrip was in service. When we arrive, a crew is hurrying to complete the latrine nearby, a luxury construction of three walls, a canopy, and a floor of bamboo with a hole giving to the pit beneath. Only a few steps away bright globes of oranges and grapefruit hang ready to hand in their glossy green foliage, and a smaller house offers a roof, a table and benches, and a hearth for cooking.

The village organizes itself around the airfield and the Ovíri river, a clear, cool, rapid stream perhaps thirty feet across in the shallows. The Professor and a few other families live on the west side of the stream, while most of the village, including the school, perches on the east bank, a steep bluff formed by erosion at a sharp veering of the current. The river has dropped, exposing boulders that provide an easy crossing.

Although Ovíri, with more than three hundred souls, is twice as large as Otíka, there is no appreciable sign of this difference: the schoolroom is about the same size; a like number of canoes are drawn up on a sandbar at the mouth of the river; and we are followed by another half-dozen youngsters who have been enthralled by Brian's flute-playing and skilled buffoonery. Asháninka villages appear to be diffuse, a resident being effectively anyone who can walk to the node of houses about the airfield, visit and drink for a few hours, and walk home again. Given the Indian's reputation as a walker, this establishes for the town a perimeter of twenty kilometers or more. Later, on hunting trips with Carlos, I will find dwellings at the outermost edge of a hard, day-long trek. These are, so to speak, the suburbs.

While we arrange our effects for a long stay, Professor Nicolás pays us a call and invites us to accompany him on a visit to some of the village leaders, so we can discuss our project. He has donned a white shirt and the ubiquitous rubber oxfords, and is in an expansive humor, the gold teeth flashing and nearly every utterance bounded by rich, deep chuckles. On our way to the houses near the juncture of the river we begin outlining our plans. Nicolás recommends to us an interpreter, his nephew, who lives on a chacra upstream; he tells us that through such an interpreter we will have no difficulty arranging to meet a traditional family or finding a story-teller who can provide a few of the old traditional tales. On the morrow, he promises, he will send word to his nephew.

Next we meet briefly with important men of the village. Near our own quarters, in the orange grove, lives the keeper of the conch horn. He is a stocky, good-natured fellow with numerous children. There is a lively air around his fireside, much chatter and tomfoolery. Here the men of the village gather to make up work crews or to hold community meetings, Nicolás explains. The stocky man brings forth the large, smooth white shell that produces a deep and vibrant tone. Blown full strength it will send a signal for two kilometers in all directions. The conch shell is a very old and very widespread symbolic motif in pre-Incan art. By the respectful way in which it is handled, I infer that the shell has maintained here some of its antique authority. Perhaps this aura, or a touch of extraordinary deference in the shell-keeper's manner when he speaks to the Professor, evokes the word "factotum" and I consistently thereafter forget his name and think of him as Totum.

We next encounter the President of the Community, Luís, who lives in a complex of huts with his family and new relatives. Asháninka newlyweds generally go to live with or near the bride's parents, so the in-law relationship is an important one. One of Luís' daughters has recently married a man from the mountains and another is already raising grandchildren in his household. Luís is tall, affable rather than imperious, and the owner of a very loud Hawaiian-style sport shirt and a wristwatch of extraordinary proportions, as large as a silver dollar, with several control knobs at its rim. He knows a little Spanish and pretends to know much more, keeping up a fixed smile of understanding with periodic vigorous nods.

The new husband from the mountains watches us from several steps away, as we take the ritual gourd of masato and chat formally. He squats on the bare earth with his filthy dark brown cushma pulled over his knees, his skullcap of straight black hair rudely hacked with a knife, two slashes of orange achiote across his cheekbones. He gapes with a strange, tentative, half-smile whenever I meet his look, but his eyes remain wide and alert. He suggests immediately an old memory of a startled deer, with its almost paralyzing intensity of awareness.

In the course of our conversation and bowl of masato with the President, we are assured of full cooperation from the community. The Professor will help us arrange matters with the interpreter, story-teller and a family in the village, for we want a close view of mundane life. We are also invited to a party to be given in two days, and informed that the people will soon be constructing a fish dam--a major communal effort that we may want to record with our cameras. In another six weeks, the Professor adds, Ovíri will hold its own birthday party, celebrating fourteen years of existence. Nearby communities, including Otíka, will gather for soccer matches all afternoon, and there will be a great party in the evening.

We are all initially surprised at the ease with which our expectations are being met, excited at the prospect of going immediately to work, and pleased at the good will we have encountered. Nicolás and Luís are jovial, attentive, helpful. Indeed, it is all a little too easy. Our clearance from Weiss, the skill of Matías in handling foreign investigators, this display of inter- and intra-community cooperation--the smiles and bowls of fermented cheer--all these begin to diminish my sense of adventure and experiment, remind me of how many generations of "explorers" have passed this way. The Franciscans, gold-seekers, rubber crews, alligator hunters, surveyors, ethnographers and now writers and filmmakers. We are near the end of a long parade that often must have appeared terrifying or ridiculous to these river-dwellers, but that now moves them only to good-natured accommodation.

Our discussion is nearing its close, so I get out the Polaroid. Partly I wish to formalize this agreement, but I also want to get a shot of the son-in-law from the mountains. As usual when we pull out our gear the children push forward in expectation of some new miracle. When I press the button to record Luís and Nicolás, both rigid as smiling corpses, the camera growls and the youngsters start backward with gasps and cries of shock as the tongue of the film protrudes. Everything happens just as it did in Otíka. I tear off the photograph and coax them nearer to watch. When the faint outline of the image appears they are transfixed in wonder. The gray-green faces gain a tinge of color, shadows and leaves begin to materialize in the background. The children utter hushed exclamations. The smallest seem stunned.

As I cannot give Nicolás a picture without doing the same for Luís, I pose them again for a second performance, this time with an awed gallery of witnesses. A couple of boys race away to spread the news, and others keep looking from the first photo to the preparations for the next one, as if uncertain of the order of reality. I will come eventually to share their confusion.

At this point someone shouts "Avión!" and we soon hear the buzz of the new arrival. By the time the second photo is drying in Luís' hand, the plane has touched down and some of the children have broken away to welcome it. Meanwhile the man from the mountains has edged over to examine the Polaroid pictures, and does not seem disturbed by them. I indicate to Nicolás that I would like a picture of him also. When this information is relayed a long discussion ensues, the upshot of which is the gathering of the man's wife and child and his bow and arrows.

I position the group at the end of the airfield, the open green behind, and prepare to take the picture. Just then the pilot at the other end of the field guns his engine and as I am framing the shot the airplane roars toward me. The man and woman and child turn and look up at the winged monster lunging into the sky, including all of us in the deafening cave of its sound. They watch as it rises over the trees and the river, tilts and begins to shrink away in the sky. Then they turn again toward the camera, their faces blank, ravaged. I snap the picture, wait for the print to extrude itself, snap another.

This time there is a pause before people come forward to see the images develop. I too am momentarily disoriented, at a loss, unsteady in some gap or hole in time. The intersection of my arranged tableau, the airplane straining for release from earth, the pilot perhaps peering down at what must be for him only blurred dots, the man from the mountains standing somehow at the center with everything dear and meaningful to him on display--in all this I sense a slight shock, like the invisible grinding of continental plates of the soul, a movement of obscure but powerful forces far beneath the surface of things.

Hesitantly Luís' son-in-law takes the piece of paper. He and his wife glance at it, then away as if embarrassed, then back in irresistible fascination. Others gather around, laugh and point. We compare the photographs, identical visions of a family stock-still, and then everything seems normal again. We shake hands with the President and his retinue, and Nicolás leads us away, back toward our quarters.

There on our doorstep he lingers for a few minutes, and mentions that he wants to ask us something that has been on his mind for some time. A few years ago the radios announced that some American pilots had actually flown to the moon. When they got there, it was claimed, they found only rocks. Was this true, that the moon was in fact huge like a whole country--Russia or the United States--but only dead rocks, without inhabitants?

We tell him that it is true, as far as we know. The pilots returned with some of the rocks, and they appear to be like our own, unspiritual and valueless. They brought back pictures also, many pictures, and these reveal only a desert and bare mountains, without water or plants. The Professor looks unhappy beneath his constant smile. Nothing but rock. He shakes his head. It was not as we thought. He leaves us, with a gallant attempt at cheer, and we watch him from the bluff as he rolls up his pantlegs, holds his rubber shoes in one hand, and picks his way barefoot over the smooth stones to cross the river.

32

Next morning the Professor's nephew appears on our doorstep to introduce himself and to size us up. Wearing a clean sport shirt and cheap polyester pants, furnished with the usual wristwatch power symbol, with a barbershop part in the hair on his handsome head, he is the incarnation of a young man on the make. He is affable but shrewd, certainly familiar with making a deal in the manner peculiar to civilized peoples. His price is a flat 500 soles a day, and he guarantees introductions to a storyteller and a typical family, and thorough translations of all their material into Spanish. He will even throw in a few songs of his own. He has studied at the school in Atalaya and has been to Pucallpa, so even though we can detect an accent, his Spanish is more fluent and dependable than ours.

El Smootho, as I privately dub him, mentions that he can work for two-day stretches, but must occasionally visit a chacra he is clearing upriver a few kilometers. Then he asks us if we are writing about the Asháninka. When I indicate that this is the case, he reminds us that he should receive a mention in any such book. Already he is a professional collaborator who may have use for bibliographical references in the future. We conclude our bargain by fixing an appointment after lunch with the storyteller, a man named Kentikíri.

During this conversation we were visited by various villagers, not only children but curious parents, some bearing small items for sale or trade. They gathered just inside our door, or peered through the slats of the wall, whispering among themselves while we went on with our discussion. Among the first to arrive was Totum, whom we obliged by taking another Polaroid picture. Soon others began to appear, often entire families, to ask for "*el foto, lo que sale pronto.*" Our new employee quickly adds a clause to his own contract, requesting a family portrait, and departs with the amused remark that we will need lots of film.

Indeed we have made a tactical error of some magnitude by flashing this magic toy so early in our visit. All through the late morning we are besieged by petitioners, for word has spread throughout the village. Many are disappointed, if not miffed, at our refusal. Reasonably enough they argue that we have taken many fotos already and still have film, so we ought to take more. We decide on a policy of trade, and tell them that we can supply pictures in exchange for fresh meat or certain artifacts--a feather fire-fan or necklace, for example. This proposal is not greeted with notice-able relief or enthusiasm. The people know that we took the earlier pictures without charge.

One young man in particular is persistent. He appears first by himself, smiling uncontrollably, and we explain as carefully as we can our new policy. He responds that he will come back soon with a gift for us but we can take the picture now.

We hold firm to our decision, straight-across barter with no defer-ments. Above all we do not wish to unpack the camera anymore and take any pictures in front of other supplicants, for fear of creating a feeding frenzy. The young man retires and an hour later is back, this time dressed in his best clothes: polyester pants and loud cotton shirt--apparently the tuxedo of the jungle. He also wears a watch now, and carries a cheap radio.

He is ready for his picture, he says. The wife will be along any moment with our gift. Something about his ingratiating manner and this display of finery rubs us the wrong way, and we make two or three emphatic denials. He continues to stand at our door, the radio playing softly under a hiss of static, a smile flexing spasmodically across his face. "*Señor,*" he whispers from time to time, "*Porqué? Un foto, no más.*" And the like. Finally I point him back down the trail and insist that he leave us, telling him that if he comes back in the morning with a suitable gift we will take his picture.

At lunch we have a long conference on the moral bog the camera has gotten us into. It is not hard to understand the villagers' point of view, especially in the light of the paper Bodley presented to me a year ago. In his research the anthropologist uncovered in Asháninka communities a network of "deferred trading partners." This network establishes, as a central code of conduct, the exchange of food and tools and luxuries as a means of sealing friendships and family arrangements. According to this code an Asháninka gains esteem through generosity and dependable reciprocity, though sometimes a year or more may elapse between a debt and its payment. To many of those in this morning's crowd, our behavior must have seemed erratic and stingy.

At the same time we realize that the Polaroid pictures are a powerful barter item, not to be wasted, since we must pay in some way for the songs, stories and scenes of daily life that we intend to collect, and we must make graceful gestures to the leaders who help us. Nor can we turn away all offers that do not connect with our own motives. Such a course would seem narrowly selfish. In our own culture we set prices on desired things and believe that anyone with cash in hand can buy them. There is no way to obviate the damage we have already done by withdrawing from our first posture of open-handedness, but we can at least remain consis-tent from now on, asking for fresh meat or a prize trinket as our photo-grapher's fee.

We are all a little uneasy with this solution, and relieved when, in the next few days, our novelty for the villagers appears to wane, and our own work schedule consumes most of the daylight hours. Our chief activity during this period is a two-fold documentation: El Smootho introduces us first to Kentikíri, a lanky, dour old man who can tell us many folk tales, and then to Alejandro and his family, who have only recently moved into the village from the mountains. We hope to glean from Kentikíri a story that we can illustrate with footage of this traditional family, since we have encountered, in Weiss's compendium, many myths involving the routines of masato-making, weaving, fishing, and the like. The Asháninka deities, like the Greek ones, are very human: they travel by canoe, carry weapons, and oversleep; sometimes they drink too much, fornicate, and fly into destructive rages.

As things unfold, many of the tales the old man relates are variations-- usually inferior--of those Weiss collected, and others are so full of marvels-- trees changing height at will, a man-swallowing leviathan, shamans trans- forming themselves into hummingbirds and jaguars--that we have no ready way of representing them. We do pick up, we believe, one good idea. We learn that the Asháninka never let the hearth-fire go out, until someone in the household dies; then the dwelling is burned to the ground and the family moves away, so that the ghost of the deceased will not hang around. We are attracted to this bit of folklore mostly because of its potential for visual display, and because a few other stories also show that fire possesses, in this culture, a mystical dimension.

But the real surprise of the session with Kentikíri occurs in the ordinary, real and domestic world, not in the mythological one. El Smootho told us in passing that our storyteller married late in life, and at the end of our last session he urges Kentikíri to ask his wife to sing a song for us. The old man demurs at first. He is one of the tallest men in the village, string-muscled and hard as palmwood despite his sixty-odd years, and the bunches of wrinkles at the corners of his eyes give him a shrewd squint. His wife is shy, he claims, but our interpreter insists, and Dianne produces a hairclip as bribe. Finally Kentikíri raps on the slats of his wall and calls out a command. A small voice replies and a discussion ensues, its alternately wheedling and peremptory tone requiring no translation.

Ultimately, the hairclip works its magic, and the sack curtain on the other side of the house rustles and in a moment a girl steps around the corner, carrying a baby in her bone-fringed sling and looking fixedly at the ground. She sits on the edge of the platform. Her eyes skitter around us, and she watches Kentikíri's face carefully as he talks to her.

"Wait a minute. *Momentito.*" Brian gets to his feet and walks around the fire so the wisps of smoke will not interfere with his vision. "*That's* his wife?"

El Smootho confirms it to be so.

"Come on." Brian looks at us, at the girl again, and back to El

Smootho. "Be serious. How old is she?"

"Fifteen." El Smootho looks mildly surprised. "She is shy, but she will sing."

"Wait a minute." Brian approaches the interpreter and speaks more confidentially. "I mean, do they . . . you know . . .?"

El Smootho grins. "Of course."

"That's his kid?"

El Smootho laughs and says something to Kentikíri, who laughs too. A ghost of a smile steals over the girl's face.

"He got her when she was seven. An orphan. He took care of her until she was ready to marry. Last year." They are all happy, nodding.

"Wow." Brian sits down. "Far out."

The songs are lullabies, crooned in a soft, high voice, and again they seem melancholy. Perhaps the unaccompanied purity of the human voice has an intrinsic sadness. Anyway, we imagine that these lullabies serve, like our own, to comfort the babies swinging gently in their hand-woven hammocks. As translated by Matías later in the day, however, one of them demonstrates a rather different approach.

Go to sleep now little one,
Go to sleep now,
Or a terrible demon
Will come after you.

When the girl has finished three or four songs she suffers another attack of shyness and retreats into the house again, clutching the hairclip Dianne has pressed upon her. We pay Kentikíri his day's wages as well, and agree to return in the morning for a filming session; we will take footage of him as he spins his tales for a group of listening youngsters. He seems content with our arrangement, and bids us farewell with an expresion I read as one of sardonic cheer. El Smootho also takes his leave until tomorrow, when he promises to spend all day at our service, so that after a morning at Kentikíri's we can proceed to Alejandro's house to begin our work on domestic routines.

33

We are awakened the next morning by a soft hiss through the slats of our housewall.

"*Señor! Señor!*"

A row of shadows is etched by the new sun along the wall. Brian groans and turns away.

"*Momentito, momentito,*" Dianne mutters and I stumble out of my bed to investigate.

It is the young man desperate for a foto, now with his whole family in tow. His wife has donned a cheap frock, their three children are newly washed and combed out. He wears all his finery: trousers, shirt, watch and radio. He is beaming, confident that we cannot refuse him after such elaborate preparations, everything so presentable. Where, I ask, is the fresh meat? He commands and the wife steps forward and shows me the contents of a small basket. Yucca. I remind him with some exasperation that we have had this out before. No meat or red mountain papayas or firefan, no foto. He appears not to grasp my meaning. The foto, he repeats, they are ready for the foto which comes out right now.

I shout at him in English, Spanish and my limited Asháninka. We are not supplying him with any foto, unless he brings acceptable barter. The wife and children gape at me; the man looks deeply chagrined. They have come far, he says. They have put on their best clothes. He has been to Pucallpa and worked in the wood trade. He turns on the radio and there is a subdued wash of static and brass. I stomp back into the house.

We carry our hardtack, bananas and coffee to the little cookshed and fan the coals to heat a pot of water, pointedly ignoring the disconsolate family who drift along to watch these preparations. We discuss the tense situation, wondering again if we are violating some cultural code, have missed some important signal. It is unpleasant to talk about the people standing only a step or two beyond our hearth, to pretend that they do not exist. No clever resolution comes to mind, but Dianne at least clears the air of some worry and self-doubt. "He's a sponge," she says. "And he's trying to con us."

The group is still there when El Smootho arrives, and after inviting him to our table we explain our position, while the foto-seeker calls out his version whenever there is pause for breath. El Smootho points out that we have taken fotos earlier for nothing. We explain patiently that we are aware of this inconsistency, but have assessed our stock of film and feel that we cannot simply give away the pictures to all comers. Our gifts to Nicolás and Luís were expressions of appreciation for their help. This young man also wishes to help us, El Smootho says. Let him bring some meat or papayas then, we retort, and after this request is translated the family leaves, the young man waving and smiling as if nothing were amiss.

"He'll be back," Dianne warns grimly. "He's different."

I propose that we not give an inch, and we agree unanimously on this policy. We speculate that the problem stems in part from the young man's belief that his visit to Pucallpa, his polyesters and his radio, establish a familiarity that automatically obliges us to grant his request. On the contrary, our aversion to his faith in the dubious frippery of our own culture is precisely what turned us against him. We are guilty of both bigotry and niggardliness, in the cause of imposing cultural integrity on one who would prefer to lose it. But such is the strength of our desire to embrace the primitive and repudiate our own "cultural integrity."

Still, I believe we are right to discourage the direction this young man has chosen. He is representative of many elder sons in the river villages. Each season a few of them vanish, drawn into Satipo, Atalaya, or Pucallpa, and sometimes never return, stricken permanently by the virus of civilization. And civilization, in this region, is not a matter of tram lines, public hospitals, and art museums. Behind Mr. Fastfoto's sport shirt, blathering radio and ingratiating smile looms the specter of Pucallpa--a steaming, sulfurous vision of the future of the selva.

Pucallpa. Three months ago Dianne and I made a swift trip there in order to strike upriver on the Ucayali to the Pachitea; we wanted to survey the northern boundary of Asháninka territory, from Puerto Inca to Puerto Bermudez, a region humid and flat, a thousand feet lower than the upper Tambo country. My first clear image of the place, after an aerial view of endless, flat tin roofs flashing through ragged trees, was the fly-covered foreleg of some animal lying on the tarmac near the foot of the exit ramp of the plane.

Indeed, during the rubber boom in the first decade of the century, Pucallpa and Iquitos gained a reputation for the savage slaughter of men, plants and animals. The rubber trees, of course, were sacrificed in tremendous numbers. Several large varieties of the species *Euforbias*, especially the *Hevea Brasiliensis* or *"jebe fino,"* are native to the upper Amazon, along both the Marañon and Ucayali drainages, and this region became a prime source of rubber for the world.

The exploitation of indigenous people was soon notorious. On the Putamayo, a river claimed by both Colombia and Perú, the Arana family effectively ruled through their "Peruvian Amazon Company," which hired Colombian convicts and, through an English connection, Barbados Negroes to round up Indians and force them to harvest the rubber. In *vaporcitos*, small and maneuverable steam launches, they raided villages and took the healthy and young, men and women alike. The *caucheros* worked many of these slaves to death, but in Perú in 1900 that alone would have created no particular scandal. A journalist from Iquitos, however, published an appalling account of the company's work camps, where foremen routinely brutalized the captives for sport; they raped the women and set fire to kerosene-drenched malcontents in order to use them as moving marks in front-porch target practice.

The coercion of Indian labor would not have ended even with this atrocity, but the importation of *Hevea* trees to Ceylon and Indonesia, and their successful domestication there, ruined the market in South America. Even without this competition, the wasteful cutting of whole trees would have doomed the rubber trade for most Amazonian companies. Next, Pucallpa became a center for commerce in animal hides, pelts, feathers, and teeth. The many varieties of caiman were nearly exterminated to provide the civilized world with shoes and suitcases. In 1947 alone, 180,000 alligator hides were shipped from Perú, almost all of them from the Pucallpa-Iquitos corridor. In our travels along the Pachitea, a hundred-mile stretch of fairly remote river, we saw just three of these creatures, all of them less than six feet long.

Now the Amazon basin is being explored for timber, minerals, and oil, and the atmosphere of boom-town brutality and carnivorous greed persists. Mestizos move in from the highlands--often the most rapacious elements of that population--and hire young Indian men as laborers. The destitute from Lima are another source of cheap labor. Pucallpa is an in-land seaport, shipping cacao, coffee, bananas, rice and hardwood and un-loading manufactured goods: tractors, chainsaws, pumps, dry goods, and especially--by the appearance of things--tee shirts and motorcycles.

The city is on the Ucayali at a point where a loop of the river has formed a lake a mile or so across. The water in the channel is a turbid green, shading to khaki at the shoreline. On the inland edge Pucallpa is a maze of little shacks of palm and galvanized metal, each with a plot of yucca, a few banana or papaya trees, and perhaps a rose. Toward the center of town the vegetation disappears and only shacks are left, crowding in on each other. The streets are either mud or dust, constantly churned by cars, buses, trucks, and the omnipresent motorcycles. Some of these vehicles are incredible derelicts, a lazarus brigade of nations and eras, even more miraculous in motion than my San Ramón taxi.

Approaching the waterfront, one is assailed by sharp, organic smells-- urine, pigs, rotting fruit--curiously intermingled with the fragrance of gasoline. At the water's edge the chaos is complete. A long row of boats of all sizes and kinds--dugout canoes, motor launches, barges, fishing smacks and small ocean-going steamers--is matched by a wandering, scattered line of sheds, palm thatch or tin roofs held up by a few poles, where sacks of goods are temporarily housed, or where women are cooking on kerosene burners. People swarm around both boats and supply depots, and along dilapidated wooden piers that stagger well out into the river.

An apron of red clay soil--Pucallpa means "red earth"--lies between the street and the docks. It is so rut-scarred and ridged that it is nearly impossible to walk on, so rude wooden sidewalks have been laid down to cross it. The hubub is considerable: the shouts of boatmen negotiating their craft, the stevedores--a motley and sinister lot--heaving sacks and cans, the dockside taverns and cooksheds with blaring radios and boisterous drunks. By afternoon, the smoke from open fires and engine exhaust and the fine dust raised by the roaring vehicles on the streets has created a dense haze, and even before sundown one sees headlights flare in this murk.

In and through the turmoil of humanity move two ubiquitous creatures, the dog and the buzzard. Like many of the people hurrying by, the dogs are furtive, gaunt, and larcenous. They sniff and paw over the heaps of refuse that stink and smoulder at the streetcorners, and small boys torment them for sport. The buzzard, a bird that now appears to span the continent and thrive everywhere, is overlord of the city, and takes the richest offal with impunity. Here the bird is black except for a gray chevron at the tip of each wing. The spot of red on the crown, familiar on the North American vulture, is missing. The heads of these ugly creatures are a loose, wrinkled sheath of sooty skin drawn over flintblack eyes and a bill viciously hooked at the tip. They balance on abandoned crates floating near the docks or squat on the spars of boats, and in town they hunch on rooflines. When traffic thins they descend to the street and waddle in the gutters after delicacies.

SNAPSHOT

Busy morning near the waterfront. A large buzzard spots a dead dog in the middle of the street, but passing trucks keep him at bay. He stalks the shoulder of the road, the wrinkled head swaying to and fro, wings half-cocked. Verification of a bit of folklore: will he go first for the eyes? The wings beat in anticipation; there is a gap in the stream of vehicles. He sidles near his object, prancing with a peculiar gingerly stiffness, an absurd stateliness. He pauses at the dog's tail, under a cloud of flies. Then, with an obscene grace, his head tucks back and drives swiftly out of sight up the dog's anus. The wings jerk a time or two, and the head slides out again, shining, with a bit of intestine in the beak. The throat works, and the beak drives in again.

34

Alejandro's family lives a good twenty minutes' walk from the airstrip, and by dress and demeanor they appear more traditional than most of the villagers who border that symbol of progress. Alejandro is a short, shy man in an old and filthy cushma. His cheeks are thoroughly rouged with achiote. When he speaks to our interpreter he looks away, fixedly, at the surrounding trees where hummingbirds thrum and flicker. His wife keeps her eyes on the ground, and appears too thin to have produced the four children who hang about her. The youngest, a girl of perhaps eighteen months, has a bad infection on her face, which is swollen into a fixed expression of dumb pain.

We sit in the shade of their small hut, while from an adjoining structure another family--apparently an older daughter and her husband and her husband's brother, with various attendant children--regard us, unsmiling. El Smootho engages Alejandro in an extended desultory conversation, while the wife serves us masato. From time to time someone gestures toward us, so we know that our affairs figure in the discussion some of the time. The bargain is finally made; for three hundred soles a day we will film the family's daily routines.

We undertake, then, in the next few days, to capture the look and pace of domestic life, but as the midday idle time is usually upon us too soon, we finally suggest to the interpreter that he ask the family to repeat a few of the morning's simple tasks: fanning the fire, placing a pot in the blaze, leaving the house with a yucca basket. Alejandro's wife tries to make these motions, but our routine of giving signals for action to begin or end confuses her. When she does at last move on cue her face is deadpan, her posture wooden. One day El Smootho detects our dissatisfaction with the performance and speaks sharply to her, and though we try to counteract his influence by smiling at her and ourselves speaking sharply to him, warning him that he must be gentle and understanding (!), the damage is done, and we merely waste film in the next few takes. Our subject moves tentatively, in slow motion, as if in apprehension of some dark doom.

We shift to another scene. Alejandro is supposed to arrive home, seat himself and receive from his wife's hand a bowl of masato. He too moves a little jerkily, puppet-like, and with an aggressive purposefulness that is quite unlike his normal gait. After a third take of this action we call an intermission and huddle for a conference. We know things are not going well, and suspect that El Smootho has edited our diplomatic requests or added his own sting to our language in translation.

The family is holding its own muttered council, the in-laws peeping out at both groups, and when we turn to approach our task again Alejandro announces that he does not wish to go on. We are shocked into the realization that our success with Luís and Nicolás, the fluent Spanish of our interpreter, and our pocketfuls of soles will not carry us far enough with these people. Residents of the village are not employees or even "citizens" bound by any communal order. We have to deal with each one as an individual, and in the current situation we have clearly dealt badly. Perhaps our open disappointment and confusion, perhaps our offer to pay a day in advance and to supplement the salary with some gifts, finally reverses Alejandro's decision, though we decide that we ought to quit for the day and try to start tomorrow on the right foot.

When we have packed our gear we reiterate our promises, manufacture all the agreeableness we can, and depart with vigorous waves. The small man in the greasy sheath of an old cushma manages to turn his face toward us, but his eyes still angle up into the trees after hummingbirds and only the children stare openly in our direction. Months after these sessions with Alejandro I cringe with shame when I think of our behavior: how we must have looked arguing, frowning among ourselves, fiddling with our black boxes, and then turning toward them with ingratiating smiles painted over the strain. Plunging back through the jungle toward the heart of the village, we variously blame the time of day, cultural incompatibility, and each other for the morning's difficulties.

At the river we note that the fishdam has progressed. In the late sun a few men still work along the line of rocks breasting the current, adding boulders one by one. They tell us that by tomorrow afternoon the dam will close off one of the two channels created by an island which divides the stream. Then barbasco, a plant whose bark and leaves are poisonous, will be gathered in baskets and sunk in the pools left when the flow in this blocked channel ceases. We will have to film in the morning at Alejandro's, then move our gear to the riverside for the fish harvest.

Our interpreter agrees to meet us at sunrise on the morrow and takes his leave. Unslinging our various bags and cases, stretching and groaning, beginning preparations for a desultory dinner, we feel irritable and hard pressed. There is so much to do. Reborn, after an idyllic interlude, is a steamy complex of motives we know very well: ambition, anxiety for control, rivalry, responsibility, deviousness, deadline pressure, the forced reach for results. Work, as we define it and do it, has begun. Many months later, going over my journal for this day, I imagine Mr. Fastfoto grinning slyly at us from the shadows.

35

El Smootho is on time, and we enter Alejandro's compound while mist yet hangs over the mountains and keeps the gloom and chill of night on the forest floor. After exchanging greetings and presenting our gifts, we proceed circumspectly. First we film the wife and children as they huddle around the fire to breakfast on baked yucca and begin a batch of masato. When the sun finally reaches the open space around the house, we shift to a sequence that features Alejandro making arrows. This work we intend to intercut with the masato-making and cushma-weaving that constitute women's chief effort.

At first Alejandro appears relieved to be given so simple a task. He springs confidently to the platform of the main house and takes from the rafters a small bag containing feathers, handspun twine, and a lump of the tree resin that serves as glue. He takes a woven grass mat under one arm, spreads it on the bare earth, and places his kitbag on it. At one corner of the house stands a tipi of straight cane stalks, and he selects a handful of them. He examines each for warp and length, rejects a couple, chooses replacements, and returns with four matched shafts, ready to begin.

We are still fussing with the camera, taking light readings, and setting sound levels on the recorder, so we ask El Smootho to tell our subject to wait. Alejandro sits patiently, his materials before him on the mat, and watches us peer and listen and mutter. When we have everything ready, we indicate that he can begin. He asks what kind of arrow we want. I have learned already the several types: blunt wooden points for birds or small game, trident spears for fish and broadbladed tips for large animals. I explain that the simple, barbed chonta spike will do, the most ordinary style.

Alejandro nods and sets to work swiftly. Wait! I motion for him to stop and he is puzzled. The camera must be running, I remind him. He will hear its gears, then begin. He thinks for a moment, then acquiesces. Probably when we instructed him not to look at the camera the message reached him as an admonition to ignore it. I press the trigger and the burr of the turning reels is audible. Alejandro waits for long seconds.

"Tell him to begin," I hiss and of course through the viewfinder I see Alejandro look up directly at me. I shut off the camera with a sigh and Alejandro beams. "Now?" he enquires.

Several false starts ensue, before a procedure is ironed out: when he hears the camera, he must begin working; but he cannot look at it, or us, while the noise of its operation continues. We may talk to him and look at him, but he cannot respond. The machine clatters into motion and like a snake striking Alejandro seizes his knife and a feather to begin shaping the fletch. I try to anticipate his movements and pan slightly to keep the action in frame, concentrating until the spring has wound down and the motor stops. Alejandro too is concentrating and does not stop. While I hurry to load the magazine again he finishes trimming the feather and begins coating a length of twine with resin.

"Slower," I plead with El Smootho.

Alejandro looks puzzled and disturbed, and when I am ready to film I ask him to replace the twine and ball of resin on the mat, then pick them up and start anew. I want to overlap his actions, or at least cover each definitive juncture in the process--reaching for a new tool or material--with our single camera. This repetition alarms Alejandro. El Smootho resorts again to stern admonitions, and motions that moments before were swift and natural become spasmodic, the lunges of a frightened creature.

Brian and Dianne are groaning on the sidelines, berating me for bearing down too hard. We will ruin two days' work, they predict, and perhaps more if word gets around that we are so difficult to please. I become grim and defensive, but out of this discomfort--rather than good sense or intuition--I simply urge Alejandro to pay no more attention to the camera at all (his very approach to start with), finish his arrow and then make another. Stone-faced, he complies, and as I film I realize how simple the solution is. On the second arrow I capture just the stages I had to miss on the first when it was necessary to rewind. Except for one or two movements, I have it all.

The two completed arrows in his lap, Alejandro addresses a question to me. Are these good arrows? Are they well made? I tell him they are so, but I would like one more. What is wrong, he wants to know, with the two he has made? Nothing, I try to reassure him. I just want a third. Perhaps, he suggests, a different type of arrow. He can make all kinds. No, I shake my head emphatically, it must be exactly the same. He talks a little with El Smootho, and then sets to the task of making one more arrow. Although he does not flinch from his work, I can tell he is bothered by something. When I run off a few seconds of film to catch the small actions still missing I realize what it is. With each arrow the camera has growled less, more intermittently, and Alejandro has logically enough concluded that we are not pleased with his performance.

When we have finished I try to thank him profusely and laud his craftsmanship, but I detect that he does not believe me. Although I have sense enough to take the arrows, he rightly perceives that they are not prized for themselves. He knows that we wished to see the making of them, and believes we were not satisfied with the results; three times he strove to make a good arrow and each time our machine paid him less and less regard. The notion of fragmenting and reassembling reality is alien to him, as is our obsession with robot repetition. His last remark, after a glance at the camera and recorder, is that he could not operate such devices, does not understand them. I reply that I cannot make arrows as he does either. But without intent on my part, the residue of the experience has strong tinges of baffled and hurt pride.

We shift next to the women, who oblige us by carding and spinning some cotton. They perform these operations with the simplest of tools: wooden combs and a spindle with clay tip for weight and balance. When we have taken more footage of masato-making, including the mashing of cooked yucca in the wooden canoe and the chewing and spitting of purple sweet potato, the sun is straight overhead, and everyone is tired. We present another round of gifts, and as we are packing up El Smootho tells us he hopes we have secured enough material, for Alejandro has informed him that he does not wish to do any more of this work.

We know without asking that offers of higher pay or more trinkets will not tempt the family any further. We have obtained enough for a minimal sequence of domestic activity, and though we would have liked to continue, we must accept that we have failed to establish the proper rapport with this household, that not all Ashaninka are, like Carlos, natural actors, and that our knots of anxiety and frustration reverberate immediately among our hosts. And beyond these immediate circumstances there is a more general irony. A century ago our culture invaded this one with the gun, and now we arrive with the camera, a similar device, which we aim at people in a domineering gesture. I feel again a tremor in my mind, connected with the old man with his box camera on the plaza in San Ramón.

When we return to the riverbank at the center of the village the fishdam is nearly complete, and the river is aswarm with people, laughing and splashing, the youngest like colonies of naked brown frogs in the pools. A line of boulders has been stacked across one channel at a point where the stream divides around a small island. Now the men are hauling baskets of sodden leaves, moss and grass which they plaster along the inner wall of the dam to seal the cracks. Their heads disappear in a dash of foam as they submerge to reach the bottom row of stones. A couple of men also have baskets of the crushed barbasco plant, and as the flow of water diminishes in the channel they slosh these baskets about in the larger pools. Already a few ghostly white bellies appear in the murk, and boys dive and grab at the half-dazed fish.

No one pays us any mind on this location, and we shoot at will. It is a bright, clean afternoon, great puffy white clouds scooting across a dense blue sky. As the fish are trapped and the poison begins to work everyone takes to the water, and there are soon more glistening black caps of hair and brown bottoms than white stones to be seen. Feeling along the underside of large boulders or in crevices between them, the women and children catch a very small species of fish. They immediately cram the head of the wriggling thing into their mouths and crack its skull with their teeth. If the fish is small enough they leave it there, the jerking tail dangling from their lips, and with hands free pursue their underwater palpations. At the second or third catch they must return to the bank and spit the prey into baskets.

I examine one of these prizes and find it not an appetizing creature. The *hetari* (*carachama* in Spanish) is a hardscaled, mudcolored fish not over five inches long. It is a bony, plated head with a tail, and survives by means of a wide sucker mouth, useful for vacuuming algae from the rocks or for fastening itself firmly to them. We talk to one of the men bearing the barbasco, and he tells us the fishing has been bad for several years. Formerly another variety of fish, much meatier and tastier, was plentiful. He shows us an example: a ten-incher with a broad, silver-scaled flank and a mouth like a bass. The same is true of the big river, he adds; men must start before dawn and go far to reach good holes, for the places near the village are mostly fished out. Formerly the *hetari* was used mainly as bait for the big catfish, but now people settle for the scant mouthful it provides.

We have brought with us some large hooks and fifty yards of tough nylon line. Perhaps aroused by the excited cries and the frenzied flopping, Brian and I determine to finish the day by trying our hand at casting the big river for catfish. People have already pressed upon us a dozen of the *hetari*, and employing them as bait will relieve us of the responsibility of trying to eat them.

In the last light of afternoon the harvest appears to thin out, so we restore our machines to their cases and hurry to assemble our fishing kit. Totum shows us how to wind the line on a section cut from the branch of a small tree, and how to thread the bony little fish on the book, then twirl it overhead for a cast. With a bucket of bait and our simple line we set out for the river, passing by households where fires are leaping briskly and women chatter excitedly over baskets of fresh meat. The air is redolent with the scent of woodsmoke and fish guts, and when we reach a sandspit extending into the river, it is that time of perfect balance between day and night. All the durable things of the earth--stones, treetrunks, and sharp-edged leaves--take on a faint incandescence, so that their dying colors appear translucent; while the diaphanous and insubstantial forms--cloud, water, shadow--become dense and opaque. The river is like liquid metal, brighter than the sky, and the clouds have solidified in contours ruddy from a reflected glow. Now and again, searching for driftwood, people pass before fires or are silhouetted against the burning horizon. In their fluttering cushmas they look like dark, scavenging shorebirds, and from a distance their cries and laughter are musical as the night creatures that have begun to hoot and gabble in the jungle.

I make a feeble attempt to say something about this scene, but the words are submerged in a numbing ecstasy, an exhilaration that has an edge of fear. I have the definite sense that the beauty of this scene contains a new order of power, a power that could paralyze me, draw me with an overwhelming yearning into itself, forever. It is only a moment, a certain fleeting time when darkness itself seems luminous, but the effect is profound: the whole tremendous mystery of life seems immanent, so radiant that it is in danger of annihilating not only language but consciousness itself.

Then two small boys run toward us, zig-zagging over the rocky beach. They also have a fishing outfit, and point excitedly at the line wrapped around the branch in Brian's hand. My mood of spirituality is gone in an instant, the way a dragonfly disappears into thin air when it darts away. We exchange our gear for inspection and comment. Before showing us how and where we should cast, one of the boys spits on the baited hook, a gesture I recognize with a shock from my own boyhood. How ancient this rite must be, to be common to schoolboys from Idaho and from this remote tribe deep in another continent!

We set the line in a large eddy, and loaf on the bank. The usual fisherman's idle and sporadic dialogue ensues: we talk of our past, of the day's difficult time at Alejandro's, of the work to be done. We still must secure an abandoned house for our grand conflagration, and find places to film ordinary life to piece out the minimal footage we obtained at Alejandro's. We agree that tomorrow we must talk with Luís about our plans.

Then Brian says he is interested in locating a shaman who prepares ayahuasca, the notorious hallucinogenic potion of the selva. Under its influence, shamans chant special songs, and Brian wants to record them. In Lima we had discussed doing some work on this ceremony, but since the authorities claim it is conducted in absolute darkness we would have no opportunity to film.

"To hell with the film," Brian hoots at me. "Let's see what it's like." I warn him that a writer I know, a famous naturalist and explorer, found the experience utterly revolting, but Brian argues logically enough that the tribes of the selva have taken the stuff for thousands of years, so there must be a benefit to be gained. I confess to some curiosity myself, for many of the tales in our books make mention of the drug, usually in the context of a medicine man's transformations. It was the vehicle whereby Porínkari, even now riding into the eastern sky behind us, piloted his raft to a place among the stars. We resolve at least to press Luís on the issue when we visit him tomorrow.

It is nearly full dark now, and since the last cast our line has been inert in the water for long minutes. I sit up and stretch, and begin a joking remark about our foresight in bringing plenty of peanuts--Dianne has invented a delicious combination of roasted nuts, boiled banana, fresh cacao and rice--when Brian utters a strangled cry and gropes after the line, which I now perceive is uncoiling with increasing rapidity. He seizes the heavy monofilament and I hear a sudden hiss and a yelp of pain.

"Holy Jesus!" He is alternately wringing his hand and sucking his fingers. The line has gone limp again.

"What is it?"

"Something *big.*" He shows me his hand, where the line has blazed an angry red stripe. When we haul in the hook we find that it has been bent completely straight, a six-inch barbed needle.

We look at each other. "It could have been worse," I tell him. "You might have held on."

36

On the morrow Smiling Luís summons us to tell us that he has located an abandoned house, without dueño, and a local man who might be willing to introduce us to the vine of death. We can visit the house and talk to the man right away. Pleased at this speedy advancement of our project, we take a bowl of masato and then set out to make our arrangements.

The abandoned house is quite small, but not badly invaded by undergrowth. Only one major repair will be required. The floor platform has collapsed, and we want to place a few pots and baskets on this platform--the hypothetical deceased's possessions--to make the scene realistic. Brian and I estimate that we can devise a makeshift floor in an hour. We also want to film a family group departing from the house and putting it to the torch. We offer to pay well for this acting job, so Luís promises to ask someone in the village to help us. Our plan is to film the collection of the *Banisteriopsis* in the morning, the burning of the house just before dark, and the drug session at night.

We move on to the ayahuascero's house. San Tomás is stocky for a Campa: he has a belly, a wide, easy face and very alert eyes. He could be anywhere from thirty to fifty years old. The people here do not turn gray, and hard work keeps them muscular and close-grained. A life out-of-doors also bakes and creases faces at an early age, and numerous smile lines are practically a cultural feature. Certainly San Tomás does not look like a *sheripiári*, a shaman. His trousers, worn through at the knees, are mostly a patchwork of material from old flour sacks, bits of canvas and whathaveyou, the original garment having undergone an almost complete transubstantiation. Besides his pants he wears nothing but a black pullover that has been ripped off at the elbows.

After introducing us to his two wives and some of his fourteen children, San Tomás listens carefully as Luís explains our aims. He smiles quickly at us in turn, his eyes friendly but penetrating. Then he nods. "*Arí*," he says. "*Mañana.*" Could Brian and I accompany him to film the collecting and preparation of the plant? "*Arí. Mañana.*" He smiles again.

We stand, rather at a loss, expecting I suppose some touch of ritual or at least explanation or cautioning, but none is forthcoming. San Tomás understands very little Spanish, and I have mastered no more than a few dozen expressions in Asháninka, so our smiles gradually assume an idiotic fixity. The solution to our quandary is, finally, as simple as walking away. Luís and San Tomás glance at each other in relief and wave at us in that oddly wooden manner of those for whom the gesture is not natural.

The next morning around ten o'clock our ayahuascero appears at the door, bearing a capacious shoulder bag and a machete in hand. *"Tsáme? Vamos?"* he inquires, in a certain way the people here have, which seems to mean: "I am ready to go if you still feel like it, but if you do not feel like it, I am also pleased." We certainly do want to go, we say, indicating our recorder and camera packed and ready. He smiles and sets off immediately across the grass strip of the airfield toward the creek. We fall in behind and in a few minutes are on a narrow trail that winds upstream toward the hills.

At an opportune spot we cross the creek. It is turbulent after two days of rain, so San Tomás cuts sturdy walking sticks to help keep us steady against the current. On the other side we begin to climb and the trail enters thick undergrowth. Ahead of us we can hear the machete ringing, and I often have to crouch to get under heavy branches or vines. Before long my glasses are fogged with humidity and perspiration again, but as I want to get some footage of our subject moving through this terrain I hasten, half-blind, to catch up and capture San Tomás' squat form vanishing into the green mist.

After a thirty-minute trek, we reach a small coffee orchard, and a few steps beyond the berry-laden bushes our guide points into the jungle and smiles from ear to ear. "Ayahuasca," he says proudly. I look for a vine, but even in this few square meters there are many varieties, and some are bound intimately together, like mating serpents of different species. San Tomás takes from this profuse tangle a tough, dun-colored specimen about an inch thick. It has few leaves, and he strips these away before cutting out a ten-foot length which he then chops into sections that fit in his bag. He moves through the orchard to another spot, also only a step or two into the undergrowth, and takes another specimen. Examining the sections as he cuts them up, I perceive that the stalk is not perfectly round, but rather like two smaller vines that have grown together, so that a cross section looks like a figure eight--or perhaps more appropriately the symbol for infinity.

Next San Tomás collects the elongated leaves of the catalyst plant. When his bag is stuffed full, we turn back immediately. Before long a flock of yellow parrots with long tails crosses our path. San Tomás produces a sling made from an innertube and begins to stalk them. For his bulk he is amazingly graceful, light on his feet, and silent when he moves. After a couple of misses, he drops a bird, but that is only half the task of bagging game in the jungle. Though two of us saw the creature flutter down, and a yellow feather is discovered on a log in the general area, we turn up nothing more. The light and shade and leaf structures create a shifting maze from which a pattern can suddenly leap out--an insect, lizard, or bird--and as suddenly disappear. After ten minutes of chasing such optical illusions, San Tomás smiles again, calls *"Tsáme!"* and we are back on the trail.

When we arrive again in the village, San Tomás sets briskly to work. He unrolls a worn cushma and begins to scrape the bark from the sections of vine with a knife. The exposed yellow-white wood looks much like old bone. When all the sections are stripped, he picks through the leaves of the catalyst plant, discarding withered ones and removing bits of bark that have come off with the leaf stems. The bark debris he wraps up in the cushma and carts off down the trail. I suppose this is necessary because even these remnants might have some kick to them, and cannot be left about indiscriminately. It is also true, according to Weiss, that the Ashá-ninka are careful of refuse because in the hands of an evil brujo it can be turned to nefarious purposes.

Next San Tomás cuts the vine into still smaller sections, perhaps four inches long, and using one stick of hard wood against another, pounds them to pulp. These crushed sections and the leaves are then put with water into a large aluminum pot propped on the fire logs. After adding smaller branches and fanning the flames, our ayahuascero manages to convey to us, by gestures projecting the sun's path, that the brew will be cooking for three or four hours, and that we can come back then if we like.

During the afternoon we are preoccupied making arrangements for the burning of the house. Brian and I devise a makeshift platform and clean out the weeds surrounding the structure. With a couple of castoff baskets, a broken pot and some rags we furnish our set sufficiently for the camera's gross eye. When we have sought out Smiling Luís, however, our whole project is cast into doubt. He grows evasive when we ask about our actors. The family he had in mind has vanished. He can think of no one else for the part. People are fishing, or visiting, or drinking, and cannot be bothered. Still, he admits there are others who have not been asked. We begin to suspect that we are being avoided, that an imitation of a funeral burning is some sort of sacrilege. But Luís is still pretending, however tepidly, that the scene is possible.

Meantime, when we return to the site of the house, a number of children have understood what we intend to do and are excitedly await-ing the event. They perch on the makeshift platform and it promptly collapses, to howls of delighted surprise. Immediately they set about building it strong enough to last for years, even though we plan to destroy it in twenty minutes. A platform is only good to sit on, and to withstand sitting, it must be well made. I understand at last one of the problems we have been having in communicating with these people. We have been rigging "sets," working to get them to do things for the sake of appearances, for the camera, and this concept is utterly alien to them. Things are done for real, and for real only. I wonder if the word "fake" exists in the Asháninka tongue.

While the children in their wild enthusiasm fall over each other, collapse the platform a second time, and get in the way of our camera placement, President Luís and a few bystanders--including San Tomás, who has wandered by to see what we are up to--look puzzled and slightly nervous. We ask again, by word and mime, for someone to help us by carrying a few items out of the house and then, during this somber departure, by igniting the roof. Our answer is a row of averted eyes. We give up and announce with thinly veiled disgust that we will wait until we return in three weeks to do this scene. Even the children are now appalled into silence and downcast looks.

It occurs to me all at once that these people anticipate an event, but they have no notion of participating in "drama." It is not from lack of imagination: we know they possess a rich store of parable, myth and story. They know tales of flying balsa rafts, monstrous primeval crabs, and hairy one-legged demons. Perhaps they see no purpose in "imagining" such ordinary things as platforms and funerals. Alejandro, after all, had difficulty pretending to make an arrow even while he was actually making one, and in this situation we do not have a corpse to found our fancy upon. I look Smiling Luís squarely in the eye and demand to know if they really, really, *absolutely* want us to burn down the house, this house, right here and right now. Oh yes, he says, nodding emphatically, we all want to see that. The children brighten into smiles.

All right then, I expostulate, and begin to give orders like a general. *Pametakotena!* Help! Stand here. You kids over there. Pick up the basket. Leave. Come back and pick up that flaming brand. Fine. Now put the fire aside and we will do it again. Now again.

Dianne signals that she is ready to film. I bellow through my Von Stroheim imitation, and everything goes like clockwork. It does not, however, bear much resemblance to the scene of grief and pomp we had imagined. San Tomás, eyes merry, hurls the flaming palito into the thatch, then turns to the camera with a wide grin that is far from funereal. When the roof catches, spiders of orange flame race through it in a truly spectacular show. We film the inferno in the interior, the sparks cascading upward into the night sky, and the crossbeams collapsing in a shower of flame. It is exciting as all fires are. The bystanders are beaming, the children delirious. In no more than fifteen minutes nothing is left but the cornerposts and a heap of smouldering ashes. Most of the spectators drift away with the last sparks, nodding with gratitude for *our* fine performance.

San Tomás has already decanted the liquor from the boiled vine and leaves, and goes off now to fetch it. For the evening's occasion he has put on a clean cushma, and looks a little more imposing, but his broad, happy face and rounded form will never allow him to appear majestic. He returns in a few moments with his shoulderbag and a brown glass jug. Then he ushers us to a little house by itself on the edge of the airstrip. It appears to be tenantless, though clean and well maintained.

Already it is deep dusk, almost nightfall. We request and receive a lamp, the usual Nescafe tin of kerosene with crude cotton wick. It was our hope to capture at least a face in the glow, the gleam of the jug, on the highspeed color film. But after checking the light meter, Dianne announces that there simply is not enough candlepower, so we abandon the camera. The tape recorder, fortunately, we allow to roll.

San Tomás sits crosslegged inside his capacious cushma and takes a small bundle from his bag. He unwraps it to produce an old briar pipe and a pouch of tobacco. The pipe is stuffed and he strikes a match and puffs repeatedly, making a slight grunting sound. When the bowl holds a single red coal, he passes the pipe to me, belching as he does so. I puff manfully, then transfer it to Brian. The tobacco has a distinctive savor, pungent and slightly sweet.

Two others, a youth in his twenties and a boy of about twelve, also smoke, and then the round is repeated. This time, just before he passes the pipe to me, San Tomás makes a circle around his lips with thumb and forefinger, blows smoke at me, smiles, and then belches. I realize he is swallowing the smoke, which produces the grunting sound. I try it, and the results are immediate lightheadedness. The Ashāninka *sheripiāri*, I recall from my reading, is also called *tabacero*, and his most common intoxicant is a powerful tobacco syrup.

After one pipefull, however, San Tomás puts away his smoking materials and pours out enough of the ayahuasca brew to fill two cups one quarter full. The liquor is thick, of a burnt orange hue. "*Tome*," he says. "*Pametakotena*." And smiles. I notice that the cups, of cheap enameled metal like those we have purchased in Satipo for our camp, bear small decals of cartoon animals: a pig in a hat and vest, a fox in pants, a duck in bonnet and apron. The concentrate of the vine of death is intensely bitter, with an aftertaste that has a strange edge of persimmon sweetness. It is ninety-nine parts gall and one part nectar. I have sense enough to gulp the entire dose, as the stuff would be unsippable. San Tomás watches our faces intently as we swallow, and laughs in delight. He pours himself a double shot and downs it.

We sit then in the shadows, silent around the single, wavering tongue of the lamp, for perhaps ten minutes. San Tomás takes a few deep breaths, and spits two or three times over his shoulder. Finally he swings his legs over the side of the platform and poises ready to step out. I see him lift his hand and put a finger down his throat: then he steps swiftly out of the light and I hear him casting out liquid. It is not the sound of retching, but a kind of whooshing, as of blowing out a mouthful of water. Then with a low laugh he is back, light and swift, and resumes the cross-legged position.

He pours another draught for each of us from the jug, and we wait for perhaps another half hour. I feel drowsy and lie down. For some minutes I experience the wandering flow of memory and fantasy that often precedes sleep. The house is of the simplest type, a roofed platform open on all sides, and after a time the night chill grows uncomfortable. I sit up and ask Brian and Dianne if they need wraps.

Brian stares at me. "You don't feel it?" I shake my head. "Wow." He puts his hands on his brow. "I'll see you on the other side." He reclines again with a soft groan. Dianne says she too is a little cold, but feeling nothing else but a certain calm.

I take the flashlight and head back to our camp, a hundred yards away across the field. Threading the trail behind the white spot of light, I feel only a little dizzy, probably from the smoking, and a little hungry and tired, for we decided to eat only a light lunch, having read somewhere that ayahuasca acted as an emetic. I am disappointed so far in its effects, but not surprised.

During the sixties I experimented with peyote, LSD and psilocybin, taking these hallucinogens in controlled conditions, after appropriate readings from Huxley, Leary, Castañeda, and others. After a certain familiarity with these substances, I found their magic diminished, and their physiological effects uncomfortable. Probably, I presume, the vine preparation yields an effect far beneath my tolerance, which has been conditioned by these powerful and refined chemical agents.

After securing a pile of blankets and ponchos and a pack of Incas, I think of the ripening banana in our cookhouse. The drug is sitting easily on my stomach, or has already passed into my bloodstream, so I give in to what I feel as a mild hunger. The banana is slightly green, and its skin, when torn, oozes a sticky oil. Even as I eat it the hunger vanishes, or rather transforms itself suddenly into its opposite, the unease of surfeit.

When I arrive at the ayahuasca house, everyone is stretched flat; only the sound of breathing and the flutter of the lamp flame are audible over an increasing cacophony of cicadas. I put down the covers and sit again, and immediately feel a strong sensation of disorientation and internal somatic pressure. I recognize the combination of nausea and spatial disorientation that accompanies peyote, and prepare myself to weather a period of vomiting. The banana, clearly, was a rash decision.

The insect clamor has become incessant, and so loud it appears to come from inside my own skull. The body's natural response to a bombardment of sensations, internal and external, is to try to limit itself to one or the other. I try closing my eyes and putting my palms over my ears.

Behind the spangled darkness of my eyelids, creatures begin to take
shape. They are something like the technicolor monsters I have seen
before on peyote, but of a more liquid, fiery substance. They are definitely
of jungle origin, birds and reptiles that materialize out of dappled shadows and undergrowth, but they have the luminous translucence of fire,
water, and opal. Again, this dimension of hallucinatory reality I have
travelled through before, but only rarely has it been so intense a swarm.

The nausea has increased, and I manage to stagger away from the
house to the edge of the cleared ground around it. For a long time I hang
in the excruciating discomfort of being ready but not able to vomit. The
plumed and serpentine fire-beings writhe at the edges of my vision,
darting out sometimes to toy with my sanity. Finally what is left of the
banana, and the dregs of the ayahuasca potion--so bitter this time I nearly
faint at the odor--come up. As I heave, the creatures assemble on the
ground at my feet to receive the stream from my mouth, and I think in a
flash of the Siberian Koryak shamans who pass their urine, enriched with
the alkaloids of the fly-agaric mushroom, to others to drink. I become a
mother bird, nourishing her gape-mouthed brood; and mother wolf who
regurgitates half-digested food for her kits; and the Asháninka women
who chew and spit *camote* into the masato trough.

But the luminous horde has taken a distinctly demonic turn. Their
tongues and fangs look sharp, and they are swimming up the stream to be
swallowed and tear at me from within. I get out the last drop of bile, and
reel back to collapse on the platform. I hear San Tomás chuckle, and after
a few moments he begins to sing again. That is, when he starts this time I
am aware that he has already been singing for some time, but so faintly the
song is nearly lost in the sawing of the crickets. Now, fighting to keep the
ravening things from consuming my field of vision, I lie close to the lamp,
not far from San Tomás, and listen. I listen intently, even desperately, out
of some instinct and also out of necessity, as the voice is so soft.

Brian has explained to me that the music of the lullaby, masato songs
and the mouthbow is based on a pentatonic (five note) scale, which is a
minor mode, and has usually the mournful and haunting quality of
minors. It is also, at least mathematically, a simpler system than the
dominant twelve-tone scale of western music. But the songs that come
from San Tomás this night evoke not yearning or a sense of loss, or not
these feelings solely, but a rising, driving grace and power. They are sung
at the very threshold of audibility, constantly almost vanishing in the
steady droning of the crickets and the crashing of frogs. His voice plays
with silence, ducking in and out of hearing as rhythmically, as freely, as a
dolphin glides in and out of the waves.

He begins always with a simple phrase, with clear and definite
accents, almost like drumbeats, and these elemental patterns seem to me

to have something of force and pride in them. The notes, however, as one concentrates on articulating them out of the silence, contain controlled modulations, shifts in tone and volume, that are incredibly subtle, rapid and sensual. In the range of volume from silence to the lowest of conversations, and within this pentatonic form, San Tomás is creating--from flat on his back--the complexity of a symphony.

That comparison implies an abstractness and formality, on the other hand, that these songs do not possess. They are vivid and rich in sugges-tion: of the sound of water and birds, of war parties, of the movement of wind through branches. I think more than once, too, of the way a snake arrows through grass, over stones, across water, and the way a swallow folds its wings to sink and then opens them to lift again. But these comparisons disintegrate into the music. There is in each song an energy, a pure energy, that transcends any images left in its wake.

At some point, because of what the singing does to my own mind, I understand why he is doing it. The songs hold the monsters within at bay, conquer them, and then drive them for sport. Whatever creative power the ayahuasca releases, and it is considerable (volcanic, I would say), these songs provide a simple, repetitive and open form, capable of infinite elaboration, and fully accessible at any time. Their softness bends one's attention to them, and once one is focused on the variety and color of the music, they charm away all unease, all threat, all extraneous vision. What a lark sometimes does on a brilliant still morning--that brief but total trance that follows its explosive, liquid call--San Tomás did steadily for perhaps two hours. Near the end of this period I begin to join in, singing the rare words or syllables I know in the native tongue. The effort of trying to sing so softly, yet with full expression, absorbs me completely, and in this absorption, on the delicate, fierce crest of San Tomás' songs, I know an inner tide of strength, a sense that this knowledge will never leave me; that in whatever battle, or beset by whatever inner demons, even looking death in the eye, I will have this song, and if I can bring myself to sing it, I will not fear.

A small boy, like the shadow of a bat, passes swiftly in and out of the faint light from our lamp.

"*Vacas!*" he cries.

San Tomás sits up instantly and says something in Asháninka, fum-bling in his bag and producing a flashlight. It won't go on, and I manage to reach out and hand him mine. He is at once on his feet and darts away into the night, shouting at his children, or the cows, or both.

So the Professor's cattle are loose. Several tons of them are cruising through the moonless night at high speed, including a large, short-tempered bull. San Tomás has left his ayahuasca world of rare and subtle artifice to plunge out there and deal with them. And he left immediately, without a sign of apprehension. To lift my own head from the platform and push back the blanket is an immense effort, and my admiration for his feat is commensurately great.

As I gaze out two or three huge sides brush by the platform, perhaps four feet away, and I feel a fetid blast of cow-breath. The bright spot of the flashlight dances here and there, and shouts come from several quarters. There is a clumping of hooves, and then only the crickets again. Agile as a bird alighting, San Tomás swings back onto the platform. In the waver of the lamp he is smiling, and throwing a huge shadow on the palm-rib ceiling.

"*Se van,*" he says. "*Toman masato.*"

Indeed, as everyone tells us the next day, the Professor's cows have developed an incorrigible taste for the rich beer, and every few weeks go rampaging through the village in search of unguarded brew pots. They snap up whatever ripe bananas or ears of corn might fall their way as well, and make a general pest of themselves. But the next morning Brian has formed the unshakeable conclusion that our ayahuasca session, on a moonless night, roused not only the crickets and frogs, but sent the cows prowling as well.

San Tomás lies down, folds his legs inside his cushma, and resumes singing. Now the melodies seem simpler, more like lullabies, and the notes are held longer, sometimes almost a droning.... I float on them, as on clear, deep water, until I wake abruptly in the still, cold dark of very early morning. The lamp has burned low, the burr of the crickets is intermittent, and the first hesitant bird calls have not come yet. Thinking San Tomás is asleep, I gather up my poncho and the recorder. But he opens clear eyes, and after one stretch rolls over and sits up, alert as a cat. He reaches for the jug and pours out the last quarter of a cup of ayahuasca, then offers it with an encouraging smile. I take a symbolic sip, and hand back the rest. Brian and Dianne, awakening with yawns and scratches, also decline, so he drinks it down.

We stumble back to our house and fall into a profound and untroubled sleep. We all wake late, to a sparkling morning and a yard full of trash from the marauding cattle. The day is easy, if short, and all of us feel empty, clean and irrationally happy. On my way to draw water from the creek in late afternoon I see San Tomás returning home from a day's work in the field. A pudgy man with a sunny and slightly ethereal face, wearing only his ragged shorts, machete in hand. He lifts the blade in greeting, smiles broadly, and hurries on homeward to his dinner.

37

At the very moment of our struggles with the technology of cinema, a much grander conflict of the same kind is taking place five hundred kilometers to the north. Werner Herzog, the *enfant terrible* of the new German cinema, has undertaken to shoot a feature movie, a production which the publicity agents will characterize as "major," "titanic," "colossal," "epic," etc. His story concerns a quixotic Irishman--"Fitzcarraldo" the Indians call him--who in 1900 expends a fortune gotten in the rubber trade to transport a river steamer over a range of mountains, in order to build an opera house in the jungle.

Herzog chose the Aguaruna Indians in the Marañon drainage to represent the natives who harvested and hauled the rubber, and who were pressed into service to winch the great ship over the mountain by hand. But after months of battling the rain and rot, small and undependable airplanes, and a frightened and suspicious populace, the director found himself the object of formal compaints; the Aguaruna chiefs appealed to authorities in Lima to have the project stopped, charging that the epic movie had thoroughly disrupted the community. There were threats of violence, and troops were dispatched. Herzog moved the entire production to the upper Urubamba--Asháninka and Machiguenga territory--and for two more years he poured millions of dollars into the jungle. All this labor was to project the story of a man obsessed with an odd dream--the creation of a palace of art, in which Caruso could sing his arias, in the heart of the wilderness.

Another filmmaker, the documentarist Les Blank, accompanied Herzog's army of actors and technicians to record this colossal battle between art and nature, and Blank's film, *Burden of Dreams*, exposes the tension, confusion, frustration and despair that haunted the making of *Fitzcarraldo*. Many of the scenes in Blank's film are near duplicates of our own sessions with Alejandro, only magnified to an awesome scale--legions of puzzled or sullen Indians trying to grasp complicated instructions bent through three languages, moving stoically to accomplish the mighty, senseless task of building and then destroying a steamship, watching as the white men fume and squabble over the "quality of light," wasting in a few moments more money than their whole tribe will see in a lifetime.

This last incident, a scene which features hundreds of Asháninka moving downriver in their long canoes in the gloom of evening, I do not see until three years after I have left the jungle. I see it in a small art theater in Berkeley, California, surrounded by film buffs who are reveling in Blank's portrayal of Herzog's grand obsession, in his quiet ridicule of wasteful, pretentious romanticism. Watching the Indians glide, phalanx after phalanx of shadows, over the great river, I experience a sudden knotting of associations, a bewildering, intense complex of emotions that cluster around this scene and my memory of a similar one in Joseph Conrad's novella, *Heart of Darkness.* That resonant title, evoking as it does the whole moral confrontation of man and the wilderness, reveals another dimension of our trials with Alejandro and Mr. Fastfoto. I recall how on our fishing expedition at dusk, and again in our ayahuasca session, I was troubled by hints of an extraordinary beauty and power lurking near what professionals call the "latitude" of a film, the limits of exposure beyond which no image will register. As the shadow of night grows around the dying coal of the sun, or around the flame of a single lamp, some dimension of the soul is revived--even without the stimulus of the vine of death--and from this mysterious region come the spirits of poetic vision, nightmare and revelation.

The movies exist at the threshold of this primal dark. Convincing shadow-plays, they partake of primitive magic and religious fit. They begin in a darkened temple, where, after a hush of reverent expectation, we see bright apparitions take shape. As in a dream, these figures can be transported instantly from one context to another. They can blur and dissolve as dream-images do; they may, through "special effects," undergo strange distortions and transformations. We are often enthralled and troubled by these powerful images, which may recur with a hallucinatory vividness years after we first absorbed them, and even our laws reflect a concern toward the more threatening of them away from impressionable children. Like charms, or curses, or prayers, they are intense, magnetic, disturbing.

Thus the filmmaker, more than any other sort of artist, imitates God, for he fabricates a complete, kinetic world in full color, and draws millions of viewers--at least for two hours--into that world. As a movie unreels, if it works its magic successfully, we undergo the visceral reactions of a participant: we are possessed; we recoil at horrors that rush at us, laugh at the antics of characters, weep when tragedy strikes down one we have come to know intimately. As the historians invariably remind us, the realism of the cinema is such that when Lumière first projected footage of an onrushing locomotive, spectators cried out in terror and tried to dash from their seats. And in our own day, a young man was so impressed with a movie about a tormented taxi-driver, a would-be assassin, that he shot the President of the United States to impress (in "real life") the actress who played the part of the taxi-driver's beloved.

One does not imitate God with impunity. That is one way of stating the moral content of Conrad's story, and a way of aligning it with those other myths so potent in Western Civilization: Prometheus, the First Fall, and the legend of Doctor Faustus. It is of course a commonplace to view Kurz's expedition into the Congo as a metaphor: an extraordinary man's quest, in the depths of his own soul, for a moral purpose to guide his power, and his discovery that the quest itself is corrupting that power. Marlowe's journey to find Kurz, in an equally traditional reading, becomes a search for some illumination of this dark paradox, which applies not merely to a lone, maniacal ivory-hunter, but to the whole western industrialized world as it drives to penetrate and civilize the wilderness for a profit.

For Marlowe, the jungle comes to symbolize the shadowed labyrinth of the human heart, with its obscure and treacherous motives, as well as the impenetrable mystery of the natural world, which in our age may appear amoral, indifferent, overwhelmingly counter to our notions of meaning and value. The jungle, like the primal void, is both without and within: implacably it produces, then consumes, a riotous, terrible life. In such a context, man may run mad.

As Marlowe says of Kurz

> But the wilderness had found him out early, and had taken on him a terrible vengeance for the fantastic invasion. I think it had whispered to him things about himself which he did not know, things of which he had no conception till he took counsel with this great solitude--and the whisper had proved irresistibly fascinating. It echoed loudly within him because he was hollow at the core.
>
> But his soul was mad. Being alone in the wilderness, it had looked within itself, and, by Heavens! I tell you, it had gone mad.

Kurz's quest has a monstrous irony about it, for he began, at the behest of the "International Society for the Supression of Savage Customs," with the intention of bringing the benevolent light of progress to the Congo; but at the end of his grandiloquent pamphlet devoted to this noble project, after succumbing to "monstrous passions," he scribbled the phrase "Exterminate all the brutes!" Worshipped as a god by the aborigines, surrounded by human heads on stakes, the most "successful" of the ivory agents, he must confront the horror of his own depravity and the vicious hypocrisy of the colonial system that sustains him.

Many of our most talented moviemakers, the tormented geniuses of this twentieth-century art, have lived out Conrad's melodrama. As the technology of cinema and the apparatus of its distribution developed, financed by ever-huger sums of capital--accumulated by the colonial industrial nations--directors found themselves indeed in the position of gods. They sought locations in far corners of the world, and their realized fantasies were projected everywhere. In some countries, the industry was nationalized by rulers who recognized the power of the new medium as propaganda. In others, the individual was at liberty to build an empire around his own moral and political vision, an empire rooted in the public's thralldom, its appetite for dreams.

George Méliès, a professional magician who became the first major artist of cinema, sent his brother with a great retinue of assistants and valuable equipment to film in the South Seas, and this enterprise ended in financial ruin. David Wark Griffith, the first great American filmmaker, was tempted to try to surpass his own epic *Birth Of A Nation*, the story of the white Klan's victory over dark "savages." He launched *Intolerance*, a dramatization of man's inhumanity to man, a stupendous movie that consumed all his resources, personal and financial, and finished his career in exhaustion and failure. Von Stroheim, the brilliant eccentric, met a similar fate with *Greed*, the tale of a man destroyed by his passion for gold, a man who dies alone and mad in the wilderness. Orson Welles, the boy genius, came to Hollywood sporting a lush beard for the role of Kurz, for he had determined to launch his career by directing and starring in *Heart of Darkness*. When RKO studios balked at so unorthodox and ambitious a proposal, he turned to another story of a great man corrupted by his obsession for power--*Citizen Kane*--but after making this extraordinary film, Welles never again reached such incandescence, in command of both his own talent and the resources of a major studio.

Finally, in 1979, Francis Ford Coppola brought a version of Conrad's story to the screen. For a setting he chose the United States' disastrous attempt to maintain a colony in Southeast Asia, an attempt which began with earnest and noble pronouncements and ended in disgrace, the nation's soul lost in the jungle. This movie, *Apocalypse Now*, expended unprecedented sums of money, upwards of thirty million dollars, and nearly destroyed its creator's career, for it was an enterprise of colossal size and difficulty, bedeviled with delays, accidents and false starts. Dennis Hopper, an actor who played a small part in *Apocalypse Now*, had already imitated its theme by directing a film called, fittingly enough, *The Last Movie*, the tale of a Hollywood stunt man who becomes a god to the natives in a South American jungle. The film failed and Hopper has not directed another major production.

Herzog is thus only the last in a long series of filmmakers who have been irresistibly, and often fatally attracted by the prospect of making the movie to end all movies, the final and highest statement of some universal, moral theme, or the most tremendous display of cinematic resources--or both. Astute as they are, many of these directors have grasped the logic of portraying just this yearning for an ultimate personal power as the subject of the film, and often enough, the tragic outcome of this quest has thrown its shadow over their own lives. In some cases, the downfall of the protagonist is made symbolic of the failure of a whole society, especially in those dramas enacted against the backdrop of the wilderness.

This dangerous parallel between art and life is not really surprising. In the very act of mustering the vast sums of money, the hordes of "extras," the cumbrous technical armament necessary for a feature production, the filmmaker may create the conditions for his temptation, corruption, and defeat. In the popular imagination, Hollywood is Babylon, city of over-powering lusts and opulent display, of meteoric rise to fame and precipi-tous decline; but unlike its ancient counterpart, it is capable of projecting everywhere its values, or its obsessions (they are often the same), as brilliant larger-than-life dreams.

These are clichés in the popular mind, of course, but no less accurate for being so. Hollywood, the "dream factory" of the world, has a well-deserved reputation for gathering and consuming immense reservoirs of money, beauty, and talent, and for driving the too-innocent or too-sensitive to debauchery or despair. The most cynical of its workers maintain that this expenditure has no other aim than profit: "entertain-ment" is merely manufactured and sold. But this view is myopic in the extreme. Our finest and most serious artists have been attracted to cinema, or have had it visited upon them. Even Conrad, living into the third decade of this century, collaborated on scenarios based on his work, and collected some £4000 for film rights to his books. The Bible, Homer and Shakespeare have been "done" repeatedly. Hemingway, Faulkner, and Steinbeck sold major works to Hollywood, and it is rare to encounter a modern author who has not flirted with the producers.

The modern artist succumbs most of all, I believe, to an ancient temptation. If we retrace our path to a time when the distinctions between rulers, priests, and artists were not so clear, to a time when there were ceremonies that unified magic, drama, religion and secular authority, we may recover the memory of a heart-shaking thrill: the act of creating and manipulating an imaginative world *that has greater force and meaning than the actual world!* Those charlatan-artist-priests who founded the cults from which sprang the mighty stone temples surely summoned such marvelous worlds in a convincing way. Out of the "unconscious," that fecund, primal inner void, the first "directors" spawned a fantastic array of supernatural beings, and the images of these gods rose over the wilder-ness, dominating and repelling it, cowing the savages who lived there, putting them under a spell that often enough exacted their very lives as consummation.

It is the prospect of wielding such power, the power to "civilize"--thus begetting a "new world"--that attracts and corrupts Kurz, and tantalizes the makers of movies. For the cinema, an art with an aura of magic and religion, allows its creators to fetch images from that private, interior jungle and articulate them with tremendous, compelling, life-like energy. The beams of ten thousand projectors strike into the blank of a vast, public mind: *Let there be light!* A world ablaze with color and resonant with complex sounds starts forth, a torrent of new life that sweeps us away from our everyday existence, immerses us in the creator's vision, limns his values, ideas, obsessions in our own souls.

Writing on still photography, Susan Sontag has accused modern artists in that medium of inaugurating this dangerous shift of sensibility. Only through the two-dimensional copy of a selected image, a frozen moment in time, do we apprehend, appreciate, *validate* experience. Only when the wedding, reunion and christening pictures are shot are we satisfied that the "occasion" has been legitimized, that an event has actually occurred, in the fullest sense. Only when an official verifies the passport photo can the visa be granted, or the check cashed. This attitude ends, Sontag says, in the substitution of photographic reality, with its necessary reduction and distortion, for *understanding*, which strikes through visible appearance to seize the essence of things. Rephrasing Mallarmé, she adds: "Today everything exists to end in a photograph."

But there is another step in the process, most obvious when the photograph is kinetic, a "moving picture." This substitution of kinetic, photographic art for real experience is precisely what characterizes our age, and in particular the latter stages of colonialism. We rake the planet for resources which we can smelt into products, but the bare, factual existence of these products--autos, appliances, houses, cosmetics, medicines--is not enough. We must transmute them into images, into "advertisements," into a glorified dream of themselves, before they are consumed, and the citizens of this modern order find more and more of their time is spent in the foreplay of absorbing these images, for without them the industrialized world would present itself, cold and unadorned, in all its grimy, frenzied, and brutal actuality. Thus, even those most high and serious functions of society--political campaigns, coronations, public addresses by world leaders--are now carefully managed dramatic productions. They are real and meaningful *because* they are broadcast as electronic images. Humans, like toothpaste or shampoo, are transformed into chimeras of light and shadow, and are thereby rendered glorious and potent as talismans.

In this scheme the "documentary" film may be cited as a corrective, an attempt to render "honestly" the reality which is elsewhere so badly distorted. This superior stance is, however, suspect. Despite its commitment to sincerity, the documentary film must involve itself in the burden of its own technology, in the potentially sordid economics of production and distribution, and more importantly, in the peculiar warp in perspective these factors may entail for both maker and subject of a film. Like other kinds of photography, and also the phonograph and radio, it substitutes itself for "live" experience, renders the spectator passive, a voyeur. Insofar as we accept the "truthfulness" of the documentary, we are discouraged from making our own voyage into the heart of darkness. Others take that god-like risk and return with their splendid catch: the aborigine in his jungle fastness, the natural man apprehended, subdued, reproduced for our delectation.

The sequence of Alejandro making arrows, for example, can be edited to show a man busily engaged in fabricating a humble object. It will appear a unified, continuous action, or if there are slight breaks in the sequence, these can even enhance the apparent "realism" of the scene--a certain hand-held shoddiness is sometimes cultivated for just this effect. The viewer will see nothing of Alejandro's disgruntled uncertainty between takes, of his damaged self-esteem, of his speculations on the ultimate meaning and purpose of the whirring black boxes. To make reality manageable for the camera, it is necessary to reduce, falsify or destroy it.

So even with our pitiful hand-wound Bolex and little Uher recorder, we share a kinship with Herzog, and therefore also with Kurz, and all of us--ivory hunters, rubber pirates, gold seekers, movie makers--participate in the Pishtako myth. We invade the jungle, driven by curiosity, ambition, noble purpose, in search of new and peculiar essences which our own culture avidly consumes. In this odd brotherhood I uncover the snarl of motives that made me, often enough, restive and snappish with the Asháninka, an image-hunter blind to the dignity and mystery beneath the surfaces of quotidian life, to all that lay beyond the register of mere daylight. My aim had been to translate this reality into "art," to transport what was here commonplace into my own culture, where it would appear exotic enough, and by so doing to ennoble myself, to render myself a preserver, an educator, a transmitter of cultural perpectives. And at a final, baser level, I of course hoped to sell this art, to accumulate the capital and reputation necessary to launch yet more ambitious projects, in the great Faustian tradition. I saw myself at the lecture podium--explorer, writer, filmmaker--summoning concern, compassion and commitment from audiences, raising funds for more impressive ethnographic work, conveying the rare pathos and charm of the remote tribes of the world.

Fool! Soon enough all these fantasies would be turned topsy-turvy, and in the process I would photograph--but not for my own aggrandizement--every grown man and woman in the two villages we called home.

38

In July Brian was forced to leave our crew in order to record highland *huaynas* at a festival in Huaraz. We separated in Lima, with great regret, for his good-humored pranksterism had charmed many hearts in the villages. For a few days Dianne and I recuperated in the city, and prepared for our next stint in the jungle. We packed away exposed film, made small equipment repairs, and put some order in our notebooks. On June 11 we flew back to Satipo, spent one long day buying provisions and gifts, and rode Alas to Ocopa the next morning.

Through the good offices of Padre Castillo we obtained a few gallons of petrol and commandeered a canoe for the journey downriver. Before noon on the 13th, we found ourselves underway, travelling fast. Then, just after doubling the mouth of the Ene, we pass three canoes, long ones with families aboard, headed upriver. Those in the first craft look at us strangely and cry out. Our boatman glances over his shoulder, grins and points. But it is not until the second canoe is almost by us that I recognize Martín poling mightily in the stern. He pauses for a stroke and regards us with a rueful expression, and gives what I interpret as an ironic little whoop.

"They're people from Otíka!" Dianne exclaims. "There's Margarita and her daughter. . . ."

But in moments the current and the motor have swept us out of earshot. We are left to speculate on what circumstance has motivated such an arduous voyage. The rest of our trip is easy, a swift glide along the boiling green fringe of jungle, past intricately scalloped and honeycombed sandstone, the rapids now tame, a mere joyous see-sawing now and then. During the last two hours, however, the mist on the peaks spreads to form a canopy overhead, and a fine, dense rain begins. In this season the clouds throw a chilling shadow, and we huddle under a poncho in our coats.

Then the boatman cuts the engine back and we ease into the shallows. The river has fallen so much now that we must pack our gear over fifty yards of smooth stones to reach the high sand bank. When we arrive at the main pathway by the airstrip, one of Martín's girls greets us, friendly though offhand, and waves us toward our old quarters, the big, empty, open-sided house by the river. While we are unpacking and distributing our gear, Matías arrives, his countenance uncharacteristically glum. He tells me first, straight out, that he has had a very bad dream.

MATÍAS' DREAM

*I dreamed you were sick, Señor Weel, very sick. Then I was walking
in the trees and met a man, a demon. I fought him with my machete,
and cut him into pieces. But the parts of him went back together, so I cut
him up again, and again. But every time he went back together as if
nothing had happened. It was very frightening. I am glad to see you are
all right, Señor Weel. I am relieved.*

In the week we have been gone, he continues, the whole village has
been thrown into a turmoil. They have been afraid for years that a new
wave of colonists will push down the Tambo and take up chacras in their
territory. A few days ago an official from Lima passed through, called a
community meeting, and told them that in order to resist this pressure
they must have an official tribal identity and some sort of organization.
Only then can they make claims to the government according to certain
laws regulating the disposition of native communities. To exist legally,
they must make up a roster of residents in each community, and these
residents must then obtain identity cards from the government. There are
special red cards for *analfabetos*, illiterates, but to apply for them the
Indians must present a birth certificate, or a document of registration as a
village resident. Many of those who have come into the villages from the
mountains have no such papers, and the president or professor of a village
must devise some makeshift certification. Then the villagers must travel
long distances, on foot or by canoe, to Ocopa or Atalaya in order to obtain
their *analfabetos* card. The three canoes we passed in the morning, Matías
says, were on just this pilgrimage.

He tells us next that the government has set a time limit for the
applications, after which the delinquent will be liable for a fine of 500
soles. Many people, therefore, will be travelling in the next month to
comply with this deadline. I am touched and appalled at the situation so
described: a man must take his wife and of course any very small children
on a voyage of from two to five days simply to obtain a scrap of paper that
certifies that he is who he is. If he fails to do so in time, he is fined the
equivalent of two or three days' wages, and he still must obtain the card.
Nor is all this effort going to earn the Ashaninka any benefit, in the form of
increased government services. It is for them a simple defensive manoeu-
vre: if they fail to negotiate the hurdles the government plants in their
path, they will not be recognized as a valid community at all, and settlers
from the highlands may take what they wish.

Now, Matías sighs, yet another problem has emerged. Now it appears
that the special cards for *analfabetos*, though signed by a government
functionary at Ocopa, are still not fully operable. They do not have
photographs. Matías shows me one of the cards, and points to the small

blank square where the mugshot should go. But to get such a picture they would all have to go to Satipo--an even more expensive and time-consuming overland trip--and pay a street photographer. For many of the older women, the Alas plane would be the only feasible transportation. It is in fact a quite impossible requirement, and many villagers are upset.

Of course we see his drift and volunteer immediately to take the photographs. When we reach Lima again, we will have them developed and printed and send the finished portraits back via Alas. Matías is grateful, and cracks a smile. He will spread the word, he says, and people will come to take advantage of our offer. He mentions casually that Carlos has just returned empty-handed from Ocopa, and must make a second journey. Since he came from the mountains, he has no existence in any community register. He had no certificate to supply to the functionary, so he was sent back to get one. The schoolmaster will have to write out, painfully, a notification of Carlos' status in the village, a list of his wives and children; then Matías will oversee planting of a thumbprint on the document; and then Carlos will have to pole a canoe another three days to return to Ocopa.

After breakfast I pay a visit to Carlos and his close friend Andrés, a short, muscular young man who never lost the brilliant grin of childhood. They are lounging together drinking masato, whispering and giggling, heads together and hands entwined. The scene recalls to me immediately the intimacy of Moslem men, often mistaken by newcomers as homosexuality. Carlos' two wives bustle about, in no way perturbed.

That Carlos only glances up and nods at me I take as a sign that we are on familiar footing. He addresses me as "grandfather" and we all laugh. I ask when in the future he might be able to hunt again. He suggests a short jaunt this afternoon. Does he not need rest, after a four-day canoe trip, travelling by the power of his own arms? He rested last night, he says, and tomorrow will be ready to start out again. A little hunting in between would be no trouble. His good humor and physical stamina are astonishing; he seems to bear no resentment at bureaucratic stupidity or adverse circumstance. He will again put his shoulder to the drive upriver and present his tattered paper to the official with equanimity. Probably the official will not even remember the first visit and rejection, and Carlos would never remind him of it.

I explain to both men that we will be taking the fotos for their cards, and they can present themselves and their wives when they wish. Then I take my leave, and when I arrive in camp again I find a gathering of villagers on our doorstep. Dianne is taking light readings, having already loaded the camera and set the tripod.

It is a tedious business, requiring much patience and tact. The people both want and don't want their picture taken. Some are clearly disappointed that this variety of camera does not buzz and produce in a few seconds a visible image. Others require the presence of husbands or sons to cajole them into standing sulkily on the right spot. Each person's name and origin--already we have a few arrivals from Anapati, a village downstream--must be recorded and matched with the number of the exposure. Every few minutes, another group arrives, and we must postpone our own work to serve them.

The camera has an immediately sobering effect on most of these subjects. The natural ebullience and openness of the people vanish the moment they must step before the lens, and they stare impassively at me through the viewfinder. Some positively glower. Apparently, they recognize that these pictures will be "official." I try a time or two to demonstrate another expression, pointing at my bared teeth, uttering a hollow laugh, but they doubtless conclude that this is some series of spasms that are part of the photographer's ritual. In the end I must work to maintain a polite efficiency and not allow myself to grow officious and irritable, pulling and pushing the shy wives into position.

By midday the traffic dwindles, and we announce that the studio will be closed for the afternoon. A number of people have brought bundles of yucca, papayas or bananas, which we add to our larder. After half a papaya, still chill from the morning, and a few crackers, I recline to doze over my notebook, but have only scratched in the date and an observation or two when Carlos appears, shotgun in hand.

I know the routine now. I hand my companion four of the cartridges I have brought from Satipo, and in my own shoulder bag I place the Super 8 camera, two rolls of film, a lime and a length of string. In my new cushma, bearing the bow and arrows, I feel quite the dashing figure when we set out across the airfield to wind though the village. We cross a few streams and again keep just west of the small river that feeds into the Tambo on one border of our settlement. The day is cool, with a thin cover of cloud, and for the first time I am able to travel at a good pace without a cursed film of moisture on my spectacles. Carlos, moving in his pigeon-toed glide, still vanishes into the trees ahead of me without appearing to hurry, but he seldom has to wait.

Occasionally he bends over to study tracks and grunt with greater or lesser enthusiasm. We climb sometimes gradually, sometimes sharply for an hour or two. Now and then Carlos utters a bird call. When his back is out of my view, I cannot tell whether the sound comes from him or from a nearby bird. Once he stops still, in mid-stride, and moves noiselessly forward in a crouch. There is a tremendous thunder of wings and a large, heavy bird coasts away deeper into the forest before Carlos can bring the gun to his shoulder.

The afternoon repeats in other ways the pattern of our earlier hunts.

Carlos points to various spots where the leaf humus is churned, and finds droppings or, at one point, a single bristle from a wild pig. This is a feat surely on the order of detecting the needle in the haystack. Once a flock of *Paloma* sweeps into some nearby trees, and I lose three of my five arrows to them, on the last try coming close enough to win a squawk from one. In a deep, overgrown draw Carlos again succeeds in seducing a band of black spider monkeys to perch for a few minutes in the canopy overhead, but a little out of range of the gun.

The sunlight is nearly horizontal through the trees when we reach a small, clear creek and stop to rest. I am a little worried, forseeing a trek back in the dark over these already indistinct trails. I share the lime with my partner, and its puckering, slightly bitter taste is greatly refreshing. Then from a few yards away Carlos grunts and beckons to me. He is standing on the gently inclined bank of a shallow pool, a natural watering place, and points to the earth at his feet. In the dark red mud is a single track, as broad as my hand, with the five smaller pads of the claws neatly marked.

"*Maníti*," observes my instructor. "*Tigre. Grandasso.*" He shows me how high the cat would stand, almost to his waist.

"*Sí,*" I agree. "*Grandasso.*"

We regard each other a moment, and then he moves his chin slightly in the direction whence he came.

I gesture at the shotgun. Carlos nods, but circumspectly, and points to his head, then at a spot perhaps twenty paces away. "*Cerca, sí,*" he says. If you are close and get him directly in the head. Without hurry, but definitively, we turn from this fresh track and set out for home. The darkness seems to come swiftly, and I am bone-tired. The half papaya and handful of crackers were poor fuel for this journey, though I know it is only a stroll for Carlos.

During the next hour, tracking Carlos like a dim ghost moving through the gloom, I muse over what I have learned of the hunter's life. So far, in terms of metabolic efficiency, it has been a dead loss. We have garnered a handful of pretty seeds, and no protein at all, only hoots, rustles, wing-beats and squawks. Now we have been reminded that we are ourselves more than a hundred kilos of fresh meat, earthbound and slow, with a few sticks and a loud noise as protection. Still, even stumbling along in this dark, dense undergrowh, we have not lost our enthusiasm. Now and again I hear Carlos' deep chuckle, and smile to myself. A clue, perhaps, to why our ancestors dallied in this "primitive" stage for so many millennia.

39

The human spirit is enthralled when it confronts these bowers and labyrinthine corridors of greenery. When light begins to fail, and shadows move within, the lone walker may see half-obscured monsters (bears, wolves, dragons) or nymphs, smooth of limb and graceful of body, starting forth from the leaves. His thoughts wander, and encounter forbidden or exotic wraiths that have hidden themselves in his brain, which has its own deep forests.

In a long essay on the connection between nature and art, John Fowles has drawn out this conceit in intricate and suggestive detail. Our tangled and unmanageable unconscious, from which art takes its energy, contains a mythical Green Man, an anarchic and creative self who must not be tracked and hunted from his glades, for he works his magic in concealment, and can be protected and encouraged by our forays into the actual forest. The forest exerts its power to charm away our faculty for identification and analysis, and in this empty-headed, summery mood we allow this rare and beautiful creature to approach and stimulate us. But only as a green shadow, that we must avoid turning to regard or catch.

It is not only the artist who receives a vital impulse from the wilderness. If *desarollo* links the Asháninka villager to the New York financier, a half-conscious yearning for escape to paradise is also common to both. In August all across the Western States of America the highways grow crowded with "recreational vehicles"--the chariots designed to carry the family into the wild wood, to be created anew as pioneers, hunters and fishermen and berry gatherers living in the open country. In the Pajonal region this is the cooler winter season when long voyages are made into the mountains, for visiting about the fire, singing old songs and telling old stories. In industrial, in agricultural, and in hunting and gathering cultures alike there are seasons of freedom and rejoicing, of worship and ritual, in which a psychic renewal takes place.

In our own society there is little or nothing left of formal ritual or spirituality connected with recreation or vacations, yet the importance these hold in the lives of workers is immense. Americans will purchase large, expensive machines equipped as houses--with refrigeration, showers, commodes, lounges--to bear them hundreds of miles from the city to a campground by a lake, where they will spend a few days. We have all seen these vehicles of re-creation, sometimes towing boats or horses (!) or motorcycles, grinding up the hillsides or remote mountain chains in the summer, and for the rest of the year squatting in the driveways of suburban homes. It is obvious that whether accompanied by a somber ritual or not, this exodus for renewal is something sacred.

There are grotesque ironies involved in this quest, to be sure. The incineration of gallons of petroleum (the ancient forest), the transportation of television and radio entertainment into secluded glades, the deafening pursuit of pleasure over the surface of quiet waters, the murder of "wild" creatures imprisoned and marked even as eggs--these would seem to make a mockery of Rousseau's notion of the "natural man," freed from the falsity of his arts and sciences.

Yet in the very heart of this brutal assault on the forest lurks a real yearning, a sincere desperation, a deformed hope, a motive purer than its continual perversion and disappointment. The simple, crude rewards of clean wind and an open fire continue to draw us from home, whatever the cost.

Why? Etymology may be of some help. Words are very old, older than the bones, baskets and pots in our museums. Hidden in them are meanings we have forgotten or ignored, meanings that bind us invisibly to ancestors for whom the formation of language was a magical, world-creating experience. In the beginning, we are told in the legends of many races, there was only the breath: *spiritus, logos, at-man,* a divine presence.* A puff into clay, and man was, and his first task was to name. So man made the world with his tongue. A tongue of flame, for fire, with its eternal, frantic, mysterious analogy to passion and life, brings forth light out of wind. However worn or vacuous our language may appear to us in its "advanced" state, there is in it--the poet proves again and again--an echo of that power that energizes the world.

vacation: From Latin *vacare,* to empty, to free.

wild: From Old Norse *villr,* bewildered, astray;
    and Old English *wildru,* wild deer.

To vacation in the wilderness, to hunt the wild deer, is to seek to go astray, become dizzy with freedom, to lose oneself in the wood where alien creatures are the only company. It is also to forget names, to empty oneself of words, to bewilder oneself beyond speech, to recover the intense moment when the world was not, or not quite, but existed in a

---

*"The term *tasórenci* is a critical one, for it contains within it reference to the manner in which these great spirits exercise their power. It is the substantive form of the verb root -*tasonk-* (to blow). The Campa belief is that the tremendous creative acts of these most powerful spirits are effected with no more than a puff of breath."

—Weiss, *Campa Cosmology,* 266

state of terrible, inarticulate potential. We say we go to the mountains or the beach *to get away from it all.* We mean also to recover it all, transformed, the act of "recreation," achieved by returning backward to that condition before things *are*, as we usually see them and say them, backward to the border of the wilderness.

We may arrive at that border with a purpose--as hunters, say, with our binoculars, map and compass, and high-powered rifle--but when we cross it, the purpose will not serve. Once in the wood there is nowhere definite to go. The trails are many. Rain may wash out a spoor. A sudden snow can drive the game from high ridges to the valleys. Deer are shy, evasive creatures; they alter their ways in response to subtle changes in wind and weather, bloom or frost, their own biological urges. He who sets out to climb a certain slope, reach a certain watering spot, cover a certain territory, is likely to get nothing but exercise; the hunter who wanders, not "after" but *in* the world of the wild deer, may find them.

This fact was known to many North American Indian tribes, who sought first of all to know the deer through dreams. Sometimes an especially gifted shaman would have a vision that located, or even charmed the animals, propitiated their spirits and summoned them. Such a deer dreamer was often not allowed to participate further in the hunt, or eat of the meat. To do so would have given him motive and purpose, intruded human will and calculation into a world--a thicket--whose forces are alien to thought.

> *wander.* From Old Saxon *wandlon* and Old English *wandling,* to change; probably from Old Teutonic *wend-* to turn, to see.

> *deer.* From Old English *dior,* derived from Pre-Teutonic *dheuso.m,* from the root *dhus,* to breathe (as in *animus*-animal).

Here is the spirit-breath figured as animal, not human, as the animal that has no voice, but moves like the wind or the fog, a shadow that is gone with the shifting of a branch. To track, and circle, and stalk this being is to win nearer and nearer a spirit. It is finally done by abandoning that consciousness we know as our own, in favor of an emptiness or bewilderment--not even a waiting, but an absence from our selves, a release again of the puff of breath that is our deer-being and our life. In that instant, no longer human, we are capable of change. In earlier times such transformation was expressed as becoming an animal: crow, lion, wolf, eagle, or bear. The Machiguenga, neighbors of the Asháninka, believe that at death their souls enter the red deer. At least this much is true: moving at last in the world of the deer, moving as breath moves, we may turn, suddenly, and see.

They are there, perhaps watching us, perhaps not. Sitting on a branch, an eye still and unblinking as a small moon, or the only moving thing among twenty snowy mountains; or poised in the shade, head aloft and riding the air, a tense absence of motion. The creatures who spend their entire existence in this wordless universe of spirits beyond mind are aware of a presence, a being they recognize, once familiar to their ancestors. The animal man has returned.

There is nothing beyond this recognition. In a flash and rustle they are gone again. At the moment of sighting, the hunter may recover his purpose, revert to ordinary consciousness, aim and fire. Or--a phenomenon well known to seekers of game--he may find himself mesmerized, unable to raise his rifle, bewildered beyond the reach of his own will. "Buck fever" my father and uncles called it: a joke, an occasion for ridicule, diagnosed as the nervousness of one too astonished to make the kill. Yet they marvelled at the event. They had all suffered from it at one time or other and been mystified by this strange lapse in the skill of seasoned woodsmen. It was one of the tales that belonged with those others concerning the prescience of animals, the legendary giants that haunt certain mountains, the oldtime hunters who simply knew where the game would be, long before sign was found.

The first deer I killed is memorable now not for the violent shock of its death and the trembling, triumphant moment afterward when I rose with dripping knife to count myself a hunter. What burned itself into my being was the moment of mutual awareness. I had turned back from a day-long walk, alone, my heart sour with defeat. My father and a companion had made kills the day before, while I was driving to the mountain camp to meet them. Grim with determination, refusing their urging to return home with the game we had, I struck off on my own, into the highest and most remote country I could locate. I was sixteen, from a family of hunters, passionate for first blood.

Near an outcropping of gray basalt fringed with stunted pine I awoke from my despair and began to step quietly. An inexplicable apprehension gripped me. There was a silence broken only by the faint tinkle of a spring on the other side of the rock. Unconsciously I moved the rifle into both hands. There was a small sound, muffled in leaves. I reached the brow of the outcropping in a few swift strides on an ascending curve of excitement.

The doe bounded from the brush that choked the little draw below me, her hooves gathered under her belly. She is suspended there forever in my memory, in a way the rapid sequence of subsequent images--a stumbling run, working the bolt of the rifle, seeing her disappear, reappear in the trees, aiming, firing--has never been, because at the apex of that leap her ears were cocked and one eye was full on me. And in that instant time stopped. I felt the force of her being, totally aware of mine. In that awareness was the possibility of trance, and I brushed the experience the old hunters talk of. An amplification of that shock could have paralyzed my intent, left me gaping after her as at a star disappearing behind a cloud.

But I had felt her before I reached the crown of the rock, before the sound of her moving in the willows. Of course there may have been a subliminal odor, or the hunch could have been entirely coincidental, but I think not. There was a presence, indefinable but certain, that I apprehended before any physical stimuli confirmed it. The common expression puts it best: you feel these things in your bones. Even if, as some research indicates, our sensory apparatus is far more subtle than our consciousness of it, and constantly feeds us clues we ignore, the effect is quite as magical as telepathy or witchcraft.

The distinction is trivial. What is important is that accurate information can simply appear in the mind. I am speaking of that information that transcends specific perceptions--scat signs, rustlings, startled squirrels-- and calculations derived from them. Too great attention to such perceptions, in fact, may blot out the subtler messages, and make the difference between the very good and the inspired hunter. And beyond mere apprehension is some obscure realm of psychic echo, a contact with a non-human but conscious and sympathetic being. It is something we need very much--our dogs and cats and horses are proof enough.

The domestication of the dog, brother to wolf and coyote, a hunter of deer like ourselves, must have entailed more than mere cooperation. At the outset, surely, they were competitors, fierce enemies. In the period of the retreat of the last glaciers they both sought bison and reindeer and mammoth, and at times those were doubtless scarce. One can imagine a band of neolithic hunters rousing themselves from the fireside at a distant yapping and howling, seizing spears and setting forth to investigate. They find the wolves have downed a calf, have the cow at bay. They move in to take the kill for themselves. When they depart, the wolves return to scavenge a few scraps and gnaw the bones.

Gradually some dim sense of interdependence--call it shrewd gratitude--encourages the wolf to keep close to man's camp, especially in time of plentiful game. Man tolerates this shadow at his heel because of its acute senses, which, when he obtains the young and raises them as stepchildren, become an extension of his own. Something we may call respect develops between them. To man, the wolf's senses appear magical; and the wolf must be enthralled by the ability of this slow, hairless being to hurl his stone fangs and bring down mighty beasts.

They go further. Man tries to imitate wolf, understand him, be him. He takes the name, wears the fur, dreams of his companion as a teacher. Wolf changes too, learns to love his new family and keep a wary eye on strangers. He appears sometimes to smile or frown, and mourns the dead.

And always, together, they hunt deer. One day the man notices that wolf-dog is at his feet, eyes frantic with anticipation, before he himself even realizes that this is the very moment to take up weapons and seek game. He must admit that his brother at times knows him better than he knows himself.

So wolf, by a great stroke of intuition, made himself into dog. Man was unable to take a corresponding step toward wolf, but he has a dim recollection of a time when understanding was developed between them. For this reason their companionship endures, and results sometimes in those sentimental sagas of courage, fidelity and intelligence that are peddled in popular magazines. The amazing element of these tales, it is claimed, is the degree to which the animals manifest "human" behavior. This unconscious arrogance is touching, even pathetic, in the light of the superhuman performance of so many creatures, even fish and insects. These stories are nevertheless quite true: in certain circumstances animals become the guides and teachers of men, and so save their lives.

For some years I have worked in the summer on a cattle ranch in Montana, and in that part of the country there is a keen estimation of horses. They are indispensable in the cowhand's work, but they are legends as well. Like Coyote in the cycles of Indian tales, the western pony can be an infuriating trickster, a cunning demon, a being of unexpected strength, a performer of miracles. An old wrangler who no longer broke stock, but did routine chores on a neighboring ranch, told me of a night when a plug, an old workhorse, saved his life.

He had taken a sled loaded with hay to a distant pasture in wintertime. The wind whipped up sudden and fierce and drove the light snow into a blizzard. In minutes the fencelines were drifting over, and in the gathering dark the wrangler lost his bearings. He was afraid, for without shelter no creature could long survive such a freezing gale. Finally he found what he thought was the road and started along it. But the normally docile old horse kept veering off the track, always in the same direction.

Near panic, the man jerked and beat the animal again and again. Soon there was no mark at all to steer by, only the treacherous, lashing veils of snow, and the old workhorse--after fifteen years of service--refused to obey. Patiently, inexorably, he pulled his own way. The wrangler was confronted with a final choice: he could let the horse and sled go and try to flounder back to the ranchhouse by himself, or he could suspend his own judgement and trust the animal's sense of direction.

He did the latter, and as he said to me with his drunken blue eyes brimming with tears, that was why he was there to tell me the tale. Had he persisted in following what he thought was the right road--an abandoned logging route that wound for some miles into heavy timber before dead-ending--he would have perished. We toasted the memory of that plodding "dumb" animal, and I thought of the plains Indians' respect for the horse, an oracle of wisdom, the teacher in the visions of Black Elk.

The Sioux were dependent on the horse not merely for travelling and hunting, but for extraordinary knowledge. This great and powerful being allowed itself to be controlled, would give its life to save a weak two-legged creature that could be destroyed by a single blow of its hooves. But in dreams and visions, mighty ghost-horses came, swift as thunderclouds, and gave instruction to man, told him of the true way, of freedom, of strength that comes from uncompromising attention to spirit. It was an extension into myth of the cowhand's tale: somewhere in us is a stream of power that can only drive one way, the way of harmony with all things living, of mutual survival, and it draws us again and again, often against the remonstrations of intellect and judgement. Black Elk's great grief was that he did not trust the vision of the spirit horses enough; he felt that he lost the red thread of the right way, and his people drifted away from their sources of strength and became like the white men, drivers of beasts of burden, butchers of tame meat.

The cowhand's tale in a Montana bar also evokes a quite different Indian story. Not far from my home in California is a tiny settlement, a few dwellings gathered near a grocery store, a cafe, one old saloon and a filling station. Our narrow valley is given over to orchards and hayfields watered from a small river that originates in nearby mountains. It is scrub oak, digger pine and manzanita country, hot and arid in the summer. Because the land is too poor and hilly for the rich row crops of the central region, most of the farms remain small and dilapidated, surrounded by abandoned, rusting machinery from an earlier, inconstant time of prosperity.

The Wintun, a tribe closely related to the larger and more powerful Pomo nation, lived here once, and since the valley was never a prime object of settler's greed, a miniscule reservation remains: a cluster of half a dozen mobile homes on eighty acres of river bottom. The land was actually acquired recently by trading the useless hillside which the Indians had been granted a century earlier. They do well on the new place, farming intensively to raise tomatoes and corn. Already the mobile homes have a coat of paint and a fringe of fruit trees.

After spending a day on the tractor in dust and searing sun, the two Indians who do most of the work on the land come to the saloon to drink. There one summer night, after a period of alternate comradeship and pugnacity, the older of the two told me this story. He had been talking of his military service in the Philippines during World War II, mingling these reminiscences with other anecdotes of bar fights and amorous conquests far and wide. He wore thick glasses on his brown moon face, and laughed a great deal, his squat body rocking on the stool.

Oh yes, he related, he could ride. Soon after they landed in the Islands their company took a small town and found themselves in possession of a terrified horse. The colonel descended from his jeep to see the show, and singling him out, said all right Indian, let's see you ride. So he caught the horse--no saddle or bridle--and mounted him. And rode. Rode that horse like hell, up and down the road. The whole company was laughing, cheering. The colonel was laughing too, laughing a lot.

And just then, the Indian said, snapping his thumbnail on his fore-head, a sniper got him. Shot the colonel while he was laughing so hard, right here, between the eyes. He rocked on the stool and hit the bar with his fist. They hunted that sniper all day. Seven hours. When they found him they blew him right out of his tree. So I went back, he said, and shot that horse right here, behind the ear. He put his head down then, one moon cheek flattened on the bar, the glasses askew on his nose, and I could see that he was crying.

We see the carcasses on the freeway, guts drooling out, the identity of the animal nearly gone, only a stain, a fringe of hair remaining. Or others in the supermarket, blocks and strips of meat chemically colored a garish red, wrapped in styrofoam and polyethylene. Or the horses, old or wild or merely unwanted, ground up to feed the dogs who are confined to a piece of rug in an apartment except for a single stroll to a narrow green where they must relieve themselves of wastes they have been forced to retain all day long. Noble dog. Noble horse.

A few escape. The naturalists report that the western Coyote shows signs of interbreeding with domestic canines, and the wild horse herds in the great deserts of Nevada, Utah, and Arizona have replenished them-selves. Perhaps one day we will find ourselves again at the beginning of the cycle, stalking out from the bleak ruin we have made of our world, seeking the secrets known to those alien renegades, sharp-muzzled and slant-eyed, long-maned and swift, secrets forgotten by our poor poodles and ponies long before we exterminated them.

Matías

Hermania

Carlos

President Martín

Rosa

Margarita

San Tomás

Kentikíri

40

For three days our labors are frustrated by the periodic appearance of people from outlying areas who need fotos for their cards. Word has apparently spread to villages downriver, and a few come from Oviri. We tell these latter to inform their neighbors that we will be coming to town for the birthday celebration, so they need only wait and we will take pictures there. We had also a plan to film Rosa as she gathers, prepares and serves masato, but by pretending some ailment or other the old lady has conned the Alas pilot into flying her to Satipo, so we must await her return.

To get away from what has now become a passport mugshot studio, I leave camp one afternoon to wander about, record a few village sounds, bathe in the river and visit various people. In the yard of the schoolhouse I stop to chat with Natalia, the Professor Miguel's wife, and as we exchange small talk--her Spanish is quite good, for she lived some years in Atalaya--there is a commotion two or three houses away. I hear guttural cries and a thrashing in the bushes, then a babble of voices, but hedges and trees screen whatever is transpiring. Natalia listens for some moments, and then goes on with our conversation. What is the matter there? I interrupt. Manuel has tried to kill himself, she observes matter-of-factly.

A man and his son come from the direction of the noise at a half-trot. They exchange a few rapid remarks with Natalia as they pass by.

"What has happened? Is he dead?" I fiddle foolishly with the knobs on my recorder and take a hesitant step toward the hidden uproar.

"I don't think so. He couldn't get it down. The barbasco." She hitches up the baby in her sling and moves off with a casual nod, toward her own house.

I stand for some moments, irresolute, and then the voices subside or draw away. On my way back to camp I remember Martín's claim that the people of his village have no worries, no problems. Until this moment, there has been little to gainsay him. Only the day before, in fact, we went by canoe with some of Matías' children--Heraldo, Heorihéna, Zacarías, Antonio--to a nearby orange grove to pick fruit, and I had thought myself in paradise.

Happy brown children swarmed into the trees to pick ripe mandarin oranges and coconuts, making a game of throwing the bright globes at those on the ground. Then the younger boys stripped off their cushmas at the river bank and dove in with shrieks of glee. From a vine their sister picked a huge, succulent flower the color of flame. After stripping away the petals she withdrew a corkscrew-shaped core from the stamen, then split the stamen and put it in her mouth. By drawing breath through this fibrous husk she made a shrill whistle, and they all laughed at our surprise--that same wide-open-to-heaven whoop that from the first gave me a pang of wistfulness, a longing for what our civilization seems to have lost.

Dianne too is shocked, not only by the incident but by my description of Natalia's reaction. From our doorstep we see no sign anywhere in the village of unusual activity or concern. There are no worried faces, no subdued children, no hurrying figures. A gang of boys is booting a soccer ball on the airstrip, shouting lustily, and I see women gabbling away as usual around the fire at Martín's--who is, after all, the President here. When, at last, Matías drops by to visit, I ask him directly about this suicide attempt.

"Manuel," he says, shifting his feet. "He is only a boy. Seventeen. A bad thing to do."

"He is all right now?"

"He will be sick for a while, but he is all right. He did not really want to eat enough."

"Why did he eat barbasco?"

Matías utters a mournful, soundless chuckle. "He is a foolish boy."

"But that's all? Foolishness? Didn't he say anything?"

Matías sighs and turns one hand up. "He said a woman told him he could not cut wood properly."

We regard him expectantly, but he looks away with the same soft, sad laugh.

"And that's all? Just what she *said?*"

"*Sí.*"

Matías leaves soon after an exchange of polite wishes for good days ahead, and we sit by our kerosene lantern, scribbling in our notebooks. We can conclude that seventeen year-olds are everywhere sensitive and turbulent, but a shred of mystery remains. The community does not overtly register this "problem," even though everyone knows everyone else, and most of them are related by blood to several families. Margarita and Matías are cousins, for example, of Rosa's and Martín's lineage. Of course there may be much talk around campfires about all this, but there is always much talk about something, and Matías has made no mention of doctors or *sheripiáris* or medicines or calling for Alas to remove the young man to Satipo. All these responses, which might be "natural" for us, clearly do not occur here.

On the following day Rosa returns and when we visit her she barters shrewdly for a machete as recompense for her job of preparing a batch of masato. And then we will drink it, she says with a sly look, and Dianne and

I will dance. If she has heard the news of Manuel's eating of barbasco it clearly has had no dampening effect. In fact she suggests we begin immediately. If she prepares the brew today it will be ready enough tomorrow night. She claims to need the blade badly, and we strike the bargain. Only as we are leaving to fetch our gear do I notice, impaled in the roof supports of her house, two old but quite serviceable machetes.

The ensuing three hours are a remarkable display of female energy. Rosa must be well over sixty, but she remains erect and active, a rangy workhorse of a woman. She descends into a yucca grove with the new machete and a large handwoven basket, until she reaches a stand of mature plants. Grunting and muttering to herself, she lays about lustily with the big knife until the stalks and foliage are reduced to a heap of refuse, then uses the point to dig around the roots that remain. When the earth is loose, she seizes the stubs of stalk, her leathery arms tensing, and puts her back into wrenches and heaves until the long, brown roots tear loose. She trims them with practiced whacks, and heaps the basket to the brim, a load of perhaps forty pounds.

This burden she packs back along the trail to her house, Dianne and I scrambling behind, alongside and ahead to get our pictures. At no point in her labors has she bothered to look at us and our machines, and we have learned from our experience with Alejandro not to interrupt. Her conversation to herself I imagine as a sardonic reflection on people who would give away a brand-new machete merely to watch someone else do what she would be doing every few days in any case.

At her fireside she places a large pot of clear water. Squatting with the full basket beside her, she begins splitting the tough hide from the yucca, throwing the bone-white inner core into the pot with hearty splashes. When the pot is stacked nearly full, she places a layer of banana leaves over the top and covers the pot with a lid before placing it in the fire.

While the yucca steams, she sweeps up the husks and casts them out of the yard, secures another pot and begins removing the rind from a second batch. After a time a granddaughter or grandniece shows up to help with this assembly line, and before long they are mashing the smoking yucca in the trough with wooden mallets, chewing the more fibrous chunks and spitting them back into the mass. Occasionally a bold chicken tries to alight on the rim of the trough and steal a beakful, but Rosa routinely backhands them away.

When the water has been added and the canoe covered with banana leaves, our light is failing, going red, and Rosa under her black head shawl is hardly visible but for the touches of bright achiote on her cheeks and her eyes brilliant as a bird's. The fire cracks sharply and we draw near it to pack up our gear. A monumental batch of masato, augur of a considerable party on the morrow. Now the old lady is up and around to bake a few of the yucca roots set aside, and the tiny great grandson plays in the dust underfoot. We depart with a word or two, but Rosa looks up only briefly, as at a pair of chickens or dogs passing out of her yard.

The party is a typical one, though perhaps longer and more populous than most--a simple function of the quantity of masato available. One has the impression that if a month's supply were on hand, the seasoned drinkers in the village would rise to the occasion. We have learned to pace ourselves, keeping the bowl two-thirds full for a good while, and dozing occasionally for a few minutes between conversations. Rosa and various granddaughters or nieces circulate the brew, and when the womenfolk have been sufficiently primed, the first quavering songs begin.

Before long the dances are also underway, and the whoops of merriment come thick and fast. Dianne is dragged to her feet again and again to lurch about the yard. Rosa and she have become soulmates, a relation sealed by an exchange of gifts: Dianne has given the old crone hairclips and onions and beans, and Rosa has responded with snakeskin bracelets. They lean into each other, rounding the corners of the house, with the familiarity of kin.

I am rather glad to be a privileged male, who merely lifts his bowl when it runs dry, and is otherwise free to sit like a stone. I stay on, mildly and pleasantly drunk, until most of the company has gone. Night has come, moonless, and the exhausted dancers and most of their children have stumbled home. Rosa herself is snoring, stretched flat on the platform. Only a handful of men sit, feet tucked inside their cushmas, still conversing and sharing a last bowl of drink. I can hear women talking and three or four young boys scuffling about beyond the circle of light or crawling underneath the platform. Matías is still beside me, and we converse sporadically, looking into the red caverns of the fire.

I become aware after a time that a figure has moved to sit huddled on one of the fire logs, as if chilled. I can see only the silhouette of a man with hair longer than usual, and the pale sheen of a white shirt. In a few minutes Matías rises, steps to the man's side and puts a hand on his shoulder. They speak in low tones for a while, and then Matías resumes his seat beside me.

"Is he sick?" I ask casually.

"Better now. Only a little cold. It is Manuel. Who took barbasco."

"Ah." I am careful not to glance at the man.

We sit in silence, and then Matías begins to talk to Manuel again. He speaks softly, steadily, with very slight stresses. Around us the small boys are playing some game like hide and seek, and one of the women speaks sharply to them. They ignore her. One, who has crept beneath the platform where we sit, tries to tickle my feet. In a last spasm of celebration, a foursome of young women and girls begins a snake dance, though with something less than wild abandon.

Pancho, a slender man in his early thirties, moves toward us as the group of men breaks up. He sits beside me and joins in the easy current of talk. One of the girls arrives with more masato, the brew now thick and pulpy with fibers because we are at the very bottom of the tub. Then Matías' youngest daughter becomes entangled in something, trying to follow the boys through the struts under the platform, and sets up a howl. He calls to his wife, who emerges from the shadows, rubbing her eyes, to tend to the child.

Because I am curious, I have noticed that Matías and Pancho have skillfully maintained a conversation to include all four of us, though I must rely on occasional asides in Spanish from Matías, and Manuel has so far said nothing. But now in the confusion of extricating the bawling child and receiving fresh drink, we are distracted from all other concerns, and Manuel murmurs something that sounds like the most ordinary of remarks --a "yes, that's how it is" or "I guess so." The two men beside me nod and begin again to weave the conversation around us. Then Matías' eldest son approaches and launches some questions in Spanish about the soccer match planned for Ovíri's birthday party a few days hence.

I interject a remark about the number of pretty girls I have seen in Ovíri, who will be watching the important match, and everyone laughs. Matías gives a brief lecture to his son about the need for good conduct when one is a visitor on a football *equipo.* You must remember, he says, that you represent us here in Otíka, and you must drink your masato properly and if there is dancing, then you dance. Heraldo looks embarrassed and dubious, and nervous too, when I intrude again to say that I will be there to see that he dances. He retires to a far corner of the platform to brood on his responsibilities.

I light a cigarette and after a puff or two hand it to Matías. The conversation resumes in idioma, the tone effortless, calm, attentive. When the cigarette returns from Pancho I lean over and offer it to Manuel, and he takes it. All three are now talking, and Manuel has moved close enough to the glow from the fire so that I can make out a narrow cheekbone and large liquid eyes. There are long lulls in the discussion, and some time later I am roused from a reverie of my own to realize that the pattern around the fire has altered. Heraldo is asleep behind us and Rosa's tiny great grandson stands at my knee, watching my blank face. Only Matías remains beside me. Pancho and Manuel have vanished. I pick up the child, a handful of wren-bones, and set him on my knee.

"What were you talking about?" I ask Matías.

"What he did."

"So?"

"He said he does not want to drink barbasco anymore."

"What did you tell him then?"

"Life is short anyway. There is nothing after it."

"Nothing?" I think of Weiss's thick book with its many tales of spirits and ghosts.

"Nothing. We just disappear from here. So it's better to wait. Death comes soon enough anyway."

"That's all?" I shake my head in disbelief. The conversation, after all, lasted more than an hour.

Matías shrugs. "That's all. We all told him."

"Ah."

We stare a while longer into the last coals. My stomach and mind are both heavy, tired of stretching.

"I am falling asleep."

"Better go to bed."

"Yes. *Hasta mañana.*"

"*Hasta mañana.*" Matías tugs his son's foot and gives him a command.

When I lurch out of the circle of bare earth surrounding the house, the beam of a flashlight glances along before and I hear the soft padding of bare feet behind. At the edge of my own living area the beam flicks away and Heraldo, politely if a little distantly, bids me goodnight.

In the morning I think of the two times in my life when suicide occurred to me, not as an abstract notion to be debated as the existentialist philosophers do, nor as an empty fantasy founded on self-pity, but as a series of actions imagined with a hallucinatory concreteness: sliding the deer rifle from its case, inserting the cartridges cool against the fingertips, the small dark eye of the barrel, the twitch of one tendon and then something like a quenching, sudden and ecstatic, after crossing an impossible desert, something immensely fascinating in its horror. Both times, and only those times, I had gone to see the shaman of my own culture, the psychiatrist. I learned, this past night, what had been missing from those sessions--which I very soon abandoned--missing from those offices with their polished wood, filing cabinets, soft lighting and black leather. There was nothing to drink. There was no singing. There was no ring of honest old friends with a yen to talk. There were no small boys to occupy the lap, or to tickle the feet.

41

During the next two days we finish our mugshot work. We have recorded every able-bodied man and woman in the village and its environs, keeping a log of names to match the pictures. Except for one afternoon when I managed to catch a gang of small boys on a lizard hunt, we have done little of our own work, and now it is time to leave for the monumental soccer match and birthday party in Oviri. Our subjects, in any case, have undergone startling transformation.

In one canoe for the trip downriver we see some of the soccer *equipo*, and each boy has a tee shirt, nearly new, with a printed design on the front. There is a Muhammed Ali, the ubiquitous John Travolta, a Case tractor, a Dracula, and a spaceship. Hair is plastered tight and shiny to the skull, and they wear the fixed, idiotic grins of nervous adolescence. There is a great deal of giggling and whooping at nothing in particular, and a pink flag snaps proudly aloft on a stake at the rear of the canoe. It is the last thing we see as they round the steamboat rock below their village.

We travel more sedately, Matías having agreed to strap the Briggs and Stratton to Martín's canoe and motor us to Oviri, with a luncheon visit to Kenchori along the way. Andrés has included himself in our group, having taken a fancy to me, and we talk at some length on the first leg of the journey. He squats on his heels in the prow of the canoe and grins intently at me, chattering away and sometimes grasping my wrist with one hand. Once, without warning, he rises to a crouch and points at the bank with a hissed exclamation. We peer in the direction of his gesture and spot the white caiman, a fourteen-foot monster. It is asleep until we are quite near, and then Andrés claps his hands and shouts. The crooked snout lifts from the sand and the thing waddles swiftly to the river where it disappears with one mighty thrash of the tail.

Andrés resumes his talk, excited and happy after this interruption. He is telling me how much he would like to have the nylon fishline and the hooks he has seen in my pack, for these are valuable and necessary things he does not possess. I tell him I would trade him something for the hooks and line. He nods and goes on, telling me now that he once had a beautiful young wife but a man travelling down the river in a big boat took her away. An Indian or a gringo, I ask. A gringo, he says, from Pucallpa. He was very sad, he says, and cried for her, but his father helped him find another woman, now his wife, and he is content.

And so on. There is something child-like about the directness, intensity and variety of this conversation. The frank revelation of the loss of a wife invokes a new degree of intimacy, and one of its implications is that Andrés does not harbor resentment against all whites for this one transgression. It is, I think, as when we were children, and sealed our friendships with the confession of secrets: what we wanted most, which relatives we hated or loved, what we wanted to be. Only many months later, glancing over my notes, do I brush the suspicion that perhaps the story of the abducted wife might be an oblique strategy to earn the coveted line and hooks and the "child-like" confession of this native might be the mask of a very astute fisherman.

Our arrival at Kenchori's riverside chacra is much more dramatic than anyone expected. He lives on a partially formed oxbow lake separated from the main channel of the river by a sandy shoal. When we enter this oxbow of slack water, perhaps two hundred yards long but no more than forty or fifty in width, a patch of the surface suddenly crepitates, as if at a squall of rain.

"Ainiro shima!" Andrés shouts. Fish! I see pale slivers of light in the green water, then another dimpling of the surface.

Our canoe, nosing into the shore, wobbles as Andrés and Matías both stand up, and above us on the bank we hear an answering whoop. Kenchori peers down at us, his narrow hawk face full of glee. We unload hurriedly and scramble up the bank, Andrés remaining with the canoe to keep it in readiness.

The conflicting priorities create a very comic scene: we shake Kenchori's hand, greet his wife and oldest son, accept a bowl of masato, in a quite un-Asháninka way, moving at a jerky, silent-movie speed. Matías, after the barest formalities, races back to the canoe and fetches a small package. Andrés continues to shout from below, giving a running report on the location of the school.

Matías and Kenchori and the son huddle over the package. I see it is a single stick of dynamite, a coil of fuse, and a few metal caps wrapped together in newspaper. Matías apparently bought the explosive from a *regatón* who came through a few days earlier. By wedging an occasional question into their excited chatter, I find out that the stuff is incredibly expensive, greatly coveted as a fish-getter, and especially effective on schools of the variety now cruising around the oxbow, if the charge can be delivered in the midst of them.

While Matías cuts a length of fuse and crimps it tight to one of the metal caps, Kenchori seizes the stick of dynamite, lays it out on one of the firelogs, and chops it cleanly in half with one blow of a machete. He then splits one of the halves at the top and holds it while Matías jams the metal cap and fuse into the raw granules exposed in the split. This most primitive bomb is encased in the newspaper, folded tightly in several layers, with only a tip of fuse protruding. The whole is bound securely with twine, and in the last few turns a flat stone the size of a man's hand is tied to the paper package.

Matías scoops up a handful of wooden matches from Kenchori's wife and sprints back to the canoe, our host and his son close behind. Andrés pushes off as soon as Matías has one foot aboard, pointing excitedly to the spot where he has last seen fins break the water. From the bank we watch as they move slowly to the center of the oxbow, Matías poised in the prow with the weighted packet and his handful of matches, Andrés propelling the canoe with small, quiet stirrings of his paddle. In a few moments Andrés utters a little yelp and points, then drives a hard stroke. I too see the slight shattering of the calm surface, the moving raindrop pattern.

Matías scrapes a match on the stone and even at this distance I can detect a thread of smoke. The canoe lunges again, and this time the water boils just to one side of them. Matías touches the match to the fuse; there is a puff of smoke; he hesitates for an excruciating second or two, estimating his timing, and then the packet arcs into the water with a healthy plop. The canoe glides over the spot, and Andrés turns it carefully. It seems to me that several heartbeats go by, and then there is a dull thud. For another second or two I see nothing in the water, but then a muddy cloud blossoms and all at once a half-dozen slashes of silver appear, white fish-bellies. The wives on the bank raise a cry of enthusiastic appreciation.

Kenchori shouts with laughter and launches his own little canoe, bow and a dozen arrows in hand. Andrés has maneuvered his craft into the center of the spreading blossom of silt, and he and Matías are grabbing the fish with bare hands, raking them into the boat, many still shivering and flopping. More and more of the silver bellies are visible, but some still glimmer intermittently, and I can see many of the fish are only partially stunned, swimming aimlessly near the surface. Kenchori is soon tracking this still mobile prey, especially the larger ones. He fits an arrow into the bowstring, draws and a shaft zips into the water, then bobs free. A miss. He tries twice more before one of the arrows seems to stick, jerking, in the water itself. He plucks it back and there is a shuddering, foot-long fish impaled on the point. He whoops lustily and turns to wave his prize at us on the bank.

In fifteen minutes the harvest is complete. The water, though still roiled, is clearing noticeably, and Kenchori has taken his last long shots at the survivors. The canoes return to the bank, where the women wait with knives, buckets and salt. The fish are poured into the buckets, and the women haul them up the bank to the house. There they set about immediately cleaning, splitting and salting the catch, draping the new white flesh of the split carcasses over a log in the sun. The fish resemble bass. There are three or four dozen, and the larger ones might run three pounds.

As there is already a pot of yucca boiling, four good-sized fish are beheaded, split and the filets dropped on clean fire coals to roast. By the time the whole catch is drying in the sun we sit down to a fine lunch; the meat is succulent with only a little salt as seasoning, and we have just-ripe bananas for dessert.

During lunch I have asked Kenchori to tell us a story or two, since he is mentioned in Weiss' book as an informant, but he demurs. He can think of nothing, he says, and the tape recorder makes him nervous. But after another bowl or two of masato I try again, this time inquiring specifically about a tale concerning cameras. The reference strikes a responsive chord, and Kenchori tucks his legs inside his cushma, hugs his knees, and begins to talk, pausing often to laugh at himself. This is the story he tells us about God's camera:

"Our God Tscorenci was our Father and created the sun, which is like a mirror. He sees us from up on high, and makes photographs of our reflection. When we die the photograph disappears. Many have been lost. So now, if our hearts are good, we may go to the sky, but if we do evil we cannot go. If you marry your sister or your mother you cannot go. We can see our Father Tscorenci in the sky, which is called the place of the young people."

A polaroid picture seems a fitting recompense here, and after I have taken it Kenchori launches into another story, this time a variation on the account of the exodus of Porínkari into the sky by means of his magic rope. Then a third tale, and Kenchori remarks with a loud laugh that with masato and time these things begin to come back to him. Matías, however, is anxious to push on to Ovíri, and the fish has already crisped enough in the sun to allow the women to pack half the catch into baskets with banana leaves. We take our share to the canoe and push off, full and content. Moving out onto the bright face of the river, I have a fleeting vision of a distant God, for whom I am a tiny doll on the viewfinder, as He grinds out the ultimate motion picture, the final documentary, which merely by fixing all our acts invokes the awesome doom of judgment.

42

On the sandy beach below Ovíri a number of canoes are tied up, including a large one belonging to a *regaton*. A group of children receives us enthusiastically, and helps us transport our supplies to our lodgings--the same large, walled structure with adjoining cook shed that we first occupied. The village is a-buzz with activity. One crew is setting up benches alongside the section of the airstrip that will be the field of battle tomorrow. Teams are scuffling over balls here and there on the greensward. The children are delirious. At every fireside we pass there are women stolidly mashing yucca, or chewing it, to make ready the great quantities of drink that will be consumed over the next two days.

We greet old friends, and find everyone cheerful until Nicolás appears. He is more vociferous than usual, and his new white shirt is mottled with dark patches of perspiration. His wife has been weak since her operation a few months ago. Last week Alas promised to send a plane for her, so that she could be given a checkup in Satipo, but the plane has not come. It is so that they treat us, the Professor declares. They care nothing for Indians. Now his wife has overworked, preparing for the celebration. She has made special steamed fish and rice cakes, at her own expense. Then, two nights ago, she had a great pain, a seizure.

There is little time, however, to be distraught. Nicolás must greet the new arrivals, direct them to the homes of villagers where they will be fed and lodged, and see to arrangements for the match and banquet. He asks me if quick fotos are possible for the winning teams, and I volunteer to perform this small service. It will be a considerable celebration, he says, taking on a glow of proprietary pride. I have ordered from the *regatón* three cases of beer--Peruvian beer, in bottles--at an expense of 3000 soles, for the players' refreshment after their hard-fought matches. There will be record-players and much dancing. You two, he points at Dianne and me, will show us how to do the Tweest, as they do it in your country.

Truly a magnificent party, we assure him, and we will certainly attend. A wonderful day, Nicolás sighs, if only the Alas plane had come and I were not preoccupied about my wife. She has made all the food. And the beer is very expensive. But those things we must accept, and be glad in the birthday of our community, now fourteen years old.

I offer to contribute one of the cases of beer and Nicolás laughs his deep belly laugh, eyes closed. Of course he would be grateful. I have learned something of Ashaninka ways. A generous people. Tonight we must come with him to Totum's house, along with Miguel and Natalia, where we will drink and talk and have a preliminary celebration. His wife will perhaps be well enough to come. The diversion might do her good. Compensation in a small way for the perfidy of Alas.

Then he is off, his fellow professor Miguel and Totum also in tow, joking with the visitors and villagers when he passes them. There is enough excitement now to keep everyone occupied, and we are miraculously by ourselves, able to lounge in our quarters or stroll by the creek without arousing interest. In late afternoon I encounter the *regatón*, a skinny, angular man with very thick spectacles. He is the first half-breed I have met on the river, for the mix of mestizo highlander and river aborigine appears rare.

It is clear that the villagers like and respect him. He has a small, frayed notebook in which he makes careful entries, when a customer buys on credit or wishes to count purchases against profits from a rice or coffee bean sale. A few plastic buckets, a sack of chiclets and cheap cotton shirts and dresses constitute his inventory at the moment, and he allows the women to finger these items and comment as they will. He makes change deliberately and exactly, and the people smile and nod their trust. The Asháninka are notoriously bad at arithmetic, since their own language has limited ways of expressing computation, and Padre Castillo has told me that they are often cheated by unscrupulous merchants.

When I mention my wish to contribute to the cost of the beer, he says that Nicolas has spoken to him about the matter, and my half of the bill is 1700 soles. I must break a 5000-sol bill to cover this new access of generosity which the professor has conferred upon me, so we walk to the large canoe on the beach to make change. As he pulls back a tarpaulin and rummages about for his cash box, I note that the canoe is a very well-kept craft. The ancient Evinrude motor lost its paint years ago, but the bare metal is scrubbed bright and there are no oil or exhaust stains. The floor of the canoe is dry and clean, and the cargo neatly stacked amidships. I spot our three cases of beer: liter bottles of Arequipena, one of the better brews.

Around us now a gang of youths has gathered, the oldest perhaps sixteen, and we watch together as the merchant opens his plain wooden box, which is secured by a metal hasp without lock. The thick wads of pale green, blue and pink paper bring gasps of wonder from the spectators. I hand over my bill and the half-breed lays out my change methodically. Apparently this simple box holds all his investment and profit for a trading expedition of many days-- perhaps 50,000 soles--and such a sum constitutes fabulous wealth here. But the *regatón* merely shuts the lid, slides the box back under the tarp, and walks away, picking up our conversation where we left it before the transaction. I glance over my shoulder and see that the youths, after a final moment of reverent contemplation, are returning to their games.

43

Just after supper, in early dusk, one of Totum's boys appears on our doorstep with an invitation to join a gathering at his home. When we arrive we are ushered to folding chairs that have been purloined from the schoolhouse, filling in a circle that includes Miguel and Natalia, Nicolás and his wife, and two or three of the coaches of visiting teams from downriver. We are warmly greeted, and everyone appears to be in high spirits. The conversation turns at the moment on school matters, and Miguel and Nicolás are holding forth on the corruption and favoritism of the central administration. The Peruvian office in Pucallpa which was established to oversee the jungle schools is worse than venal, they declare: it is malevolent. There are tales of extortion, even of demands for favors from young Indian girls.

These rumors of exploitation remind Nicolás of his troubles with Alas. Manolo the pilot, an immigrant Spaniard, was supposed to be a friend, and promised unequivocally to fly his wife to the hospital in Satipo. They waited yesterday all day long, twice crushed by false hope when the Linguistico's plane droned at the edge of the horizon. So it is they think of us Indians, the Professor says mournfully. I stand ready to do everything for my Señora, whatever the expense, but without the airplane what can one do? A murmur of sympathy runs around our circle. Then after a pause Nicolás laughs. But this is our time of celebration. He turns to Totum and commands him to fetch half a dozen bottles of the beer.

Now the discussion moves to international politics, the United States and Russia, Perú and Chile. Then Israel and Egypt--and here the Professor has specific questions that first amuse and then disturb me. He wants to know why "the Jews are still being killed." He wants to pass correct information on to his students, but though he can carry the story as far as the flight from Egypt to Canaan in the Bible, he is uncertain of events thereafter. At the end of a moment's reflection, I realize that I have little more than the Ottomans, Lawrence of Arabia, and King Farouk to pour into this three thousand-year gap. To these scraps we can add only a supplement from our last reading of the international issue of *Newsweek*-- the Palestinian problem, the U.S. sale of arms to both sides, Israel's occupation of Arab territory.

Totum has opened three of the bottles at a signal from the Professor, and the young team captains have swiftly dispatched the first. I have been watching Nicolás' wife covertly, and note that she does not drink. Except for an occasional polite exchange in low tones with Natalia, she remains quiet. Her blue polyester dress, obviously her best, is set off by a string of cheap glass beads. She sits with arms folded, looking at the ground except for an occasional quick glance of her large, liquid brown eyes. Although her expression is a little drawn, she does not appear feverish or in pain. At some point another party of visitors arrives to stand by the fire and greet us, and one of the newcomers inquires about her health. Two operations are mentioned, and I ask as tactfully as I can about them. The first I am told was a hysterectomy, the second a repairing of spleen or liver. After the second, she began to experience fits, fainting spells, the sudden access of delirium.

Again Nicolás berates Alas de Esperanza, dwelling bitterly on the phrase. Wings of Hopelessness should be their title. They have lied to him. The newcomers also express commiseration, and at another gesture from Nicolás Totum pulls three more bottles from the wooden case. This genial henchman says little in these conversations; he stands beaming beside the beer, turning the bottle opener idly in his hands, ready to laugh with the rest when the Professor makes one of his sallies.

The young men have reached the stage of inebriation that produces more laughter and whooping than talk, so our discussion becomes shiftier, more fragmented. We are reminded that it is our duty to dance the Tweest tomorrow after the game, for everyone will be watching to learn the fashion *comme il faut.* The subject of our gringo dollars, always fascinating to Peruvians and by now tremendously boring to me, comes up again, and we recite again the amazing sums we earn and pay. The mere word "dollar" seems to have the effect of a magic spell, and some of the men repeat our figures with an almost religious awe. Inevitably this litany entails mournful head-shaking over the state of Perú's desarollo.

At some point idioma has replaced much of the Spanish spoken in deference to our ignorance, and the Professor's wife says something in her own language, stands up and walks away. Laughing with everyone else, Nicolás tells us that his wife thinks him a liar. He resumes the anecdote he was telling, and with a wave at Totum decrees a move into the second half of the case of beer. The hilarity of our circle has attracted a few of the players, who stand or squat just behind their coaches and now the bottles circulate among them too.

I know pangs of guilt and unease at this turn of events. The beer was clearly designated--Nicolá has bragged of it publicly--for the after-game celebration. Now nearly one-third of it has been consumed here, and I have a nagging suspicion that in part this spontaneous and somewhat imperious gesture has been made for our benefit. We are the only white people in town, the sole representatives of the distant land where dollars and airplanes and bottled drink and radios and the Tweest originated. The deference shown us troubles me, and so does the cluster of young men in their Yamaha and Travolta tee shirts, drinking at the Professor's pleasure, and all the talk of dollars and exploitation.

The conversation has grown boozier, lurching from primitive metaphysics to estimates of the point spread in tomorrow's football matches. Dianne and I agree in whispers that it is time for us to leave, and after some outburst of merriment from the young hangers-on we rise to make our escape. Nicolás shakes his head and points at the second case of beer. We cannot go yet. Totum needs no instructions now; another bottle is out and open with gleeful dispatch. Another drink while the Professor outlines for us a slightly fuddled philosophy which involves the rate of robbery in Lima, the strength of the dollar, the amazing small breasts of white women, the backwardness of Indians and how the festival tomorrow will show the open-hearted way of his people, though they have very little, because this festival has been decreed in his wife's honor, for she has contributed not only this beer but the *juanas*, the rice and meat wrapped in banana leaf, for the dinner tomorrow in honor of the players.

With firm handshakes, a symbolic swig or two, and perseverance, we manage to disengage ourselves and make off into the darkness. Wending our way along the airstrip to our quarters, we can hear other informal celebrations going on at the outskirts of the village. The training rules in this river league, clearly, are not stringent, and coaches and players alike will carouse the night away, and--most probably--compete ferociously on the morrow. And after the final goal the celebration will of course continue.

Tired of talk and heavy with beer, I roll into my poncho and fall immediately asleep. In my dreams a tree frog, the kind that makes a resonant thunking sound, grows from his normal dimensions of perhaps two inches in length to the size of a man. His calls are insistent, ever louder. On a jungle trail I confront him and notice a resemblance to the Professor. The whunk! whunk! from the bellows of his throat is deafening, and all at once I am awake. Someone is indeed pounding on our house. It is pitch dark around me but a flashlight glints through the slats of the wall.

"*Señor Weel! Señor Weel!*"

Dianne groans from her bunk in a tone of mingled irritation and apprehension.

"Who is it?" I croak, and fumble out my own flashlight.

"*La señora se pone loco!*"

When I step to the door and snap on the beam I see Miguel, his face stricken, both terrified and apologetic.

"*La señora-un attaque de... no sé. ...*" He waves his arms in mimicry of someone struggling.

I know without being told that he is talking about Nicolás' wife. It feels like three in the morning. Miguel urges me to bring my medicines, which might help calm her. I shake my head, for I have only aspirin, tetracycline and quinine, none of which seems relevant. On the path I wonder if they have all been drinking since we left, but when we arrive at Totum's the atmosphere of revelry has certainly evaporated. Two wicks are burning to illuminate a ring of solemn, intent faces. The eyes of the small children are huge and dark as the night itself.

Nicolás is attempting to hold his wife, who writhes in his arms and emits at intervals a high moan.

"An attack. Like the others," the Professor says. His face, without its usual expression of devilish humor, is small and glum. "I told the pilot and he said he would be there in the morning, and now she is like this. This is how they treat us." His voice breaks, and tears start down his cheeks.

"She just began crying and throwing herself about," Totum says in awe. "What can we do?"

All of them, the children alert as nocturnal tree creatures, the distraught professor, Miguel and Totum and their wives--all of them look at me expectantly, hopefully. The white man, the maker of aircraft and master of the Tweest, has come with his medicines.

The weight of this expectancy is more than I can bear, so I begin an act, a performance, a pure fakery. Since no one else appears to know what to do, I must pretend competence and authority. I put my hand on her brow and ask a few questions: How long has the attack lasted? What symptoms are there besides the cries and thrashing about? Where was the incision for the second operation? I place my hand on this spot, but detect no swelling or sensitivity, nor is her brow feverish.

I sit beside her, nonplussed, and watch the others murmur and touch her hesitantly. It seems to me that she resists all efforts to restrict her movement, but relaxes a little when her brow is stroked. I call for water and a cloth, then motion for the others to draw back and give her room.

"The pilot should have come," Nicolás says again, and sobs.

I press the rag soaked in cold water to her temples and begin to chant the usual banalities: this will help, you must be calm, you feel better, the water is cool. Doubtless these bedside rituals are rendered more absurd in my unskilled Spanish, but I have the impression that she grows quieter. Occasionally her back arches in a slight spasm, but there is nothing like a convulsion, no trembling of her limbs. After a time my position becomes uncomfortable and I gesture at Nicolás. I place his hand over mine, intending to transfer the damp rag to him, but the woman moans and begins again to twist from side to side. Totum and the Professor seize her arms and she cries out, attempts to sit up.

I warn them to release her, and when we draw back she squirms more slowly, almost sensuously. Totum, looking worried, appears at my elbow with two huge white tablets in one hand and a gourd of water in the other. One of the visiting coaches has supplied these, he says, they are *calmante.* I eye the tablets apprehensively. Barbiturates? Codeine? Valium? He is sure they are only for the nerves, for delirium. I lean over the Professor's wife and speak slowly and clearly. We have some medicine, I tell her, but she need take it only if she wants it.

Her eyes open, and she speaks for the first time, pressing her side with one hand. "I hurt here," she says. "Inside." She sits up and rocks back and forth. When I extend a hand to steady her she drops her head against my shoulder and I put my arms lightly around her. After a bit Totum asks again if she wants the medicine. She nods and takes both tablets, washing them down with a drink from the gourd. Then she lies down again, and I resume my work with the dampened rag.

In the twenty minutes or so that elapse before her breathing becomes slow and rhythmic, I think hard about the complexity of this community, about parallels between witchcraft and our kind of therapy, about Weiss's belief that this culture is collapsing. All these matters intersect, I am convinced, in the case of this woman and her fits. Her movements have reminded me of three things: the struggle to break through a net, the labor of childbirth and--though more distantly--the seductive gyrations of lovemaking. All three of these metaphors connect with intuitions I have about the place of this couple in their community.

The hysterectomy, in a culture where children are supremely valued, must have been a great trauma. Nicolás, however, has been preoccupied by the blow to his pride dealt by the treacherous Alas pilot. His power in the community should have been sufficient to insure the airplane's arrival, thus demonstrating his concern for his wife. It would also, however, have confirmed his control, and her reaction to his attempts to restrain her argue that she resents and fears that control.

And if she has indeed contributed not only the food for the feast but the beer as well--the beer we so churlishly drank earlier in the evening--would it not be insufferable to see her husband, incorrigibly jolly and politically shrewd, mingling with the celebrants, charming the ladies, dominating the whole affair? Would she not shrink alongside Dianne, tall, white and regal, and Natalia, voluble, flashy and still fertile? Shrink away as barren and forgotten, shrink finally into a defiant, dramatic illness? This interpretation would go far toward explaining my role in the drama. I was the white witchdoctor who touched her with comforting, strange hands, who replaced her oppressive mate, who held her both as father and lover, reaffirming her womanhood.

Or did I suffer from a hyperactive imagination? I thought not. I saw no signs of a purely physical disorder. Perhaps there is no "purely physical" disorder anyway. One school of modern medicine, I am told, has questioned our reliance on needles, knives and pills. They believe in the influence of attitude, and speak of "energy fields" and "centers," of the place of diet, exercise and proper posture in maintaining health. Usually I side with the brain-scanner and penicillin in this controversy, but here the issue seems not so clear-cut.

There will be little opportunity to test my thesis, I know. Whatever the foundation of the Professor's wife's attacks (Why did I not register her name!), I have neither the resources nor the time to prepare any plan for treatment. My advice would not be consulted, I suspect. The Professor is too proud, his place in the village too exposed. To bring him from the wandering of Moses all the way to Freud would be too much for both of us.

But I have the definite conviction that I am face to face, in this remote Indian village, with the classic problem of the ambitious, domineering executive with an intelligent but misunderstood and neglected wife. We have a vocabulary for this problem, and special situations for its discussion--the couch and the bar--but perhaps the Asháninka do not. They cannot quite believe it is the work of a demon, which a *sheripiári* could handle, but they have as alternative only a tentative faith in the bottled nostrums sold in Satipo. In a less "advanced" community like Otíka, where the problem was a suicide attempt, a context still exists for offering counsel and solace.

Myself I feel a need to recede faster in time, to acquire more of the ways of the *sheripiári*; for the pressures and tensions at work here will not be resolved by flying in serums and gas-powered generators. The vanishing game animals, the yammer of radios, the fatal attraction of dollars, a creeping sense of inferiority before the marvelous beings who command and operate the airplanes--these entail powerful anxieties, addictions and self- deceptions. Powerful inner demons. I believe there is one at work under the ribs of the Professor's wife.

It occurs to me suddenly that I have been so sure of this particular demon that I have not even bothered to take the woman's pulse. I should have done so, and like many an old-time family doctor, I should have listened especially to the silence between heartbeats.

44

We are roused early, groggy and hungover, to face a line of supplicants on our doorstep. The visitors from nearby villages have heard that we are taking photographs for the *analfabetos* cards. We gulp down a cup of coffee and set to work, shooting pictures and taking down names. This time the line moves smartly, for the people are anxious to have the job done and get on with their celebration. When we have taken care of most of the crowd a man comes to remind us that we have promised fastfotos also for the participating teams, so we take the Polaroid and abandon our studio.

The airstrip is dotted with young men performing drills or scrimmaging, and with small children, naked or in tattered cushmas, imitating them. Logs have been dragged to the sidelines to serve as benches, and a few families are seated there or on the grass, visiting and quaffing masato. A table has been set up at midfield under a rude sunshade of thatch, and here the team captains have gathered, summoned by the half-breed *regatón* who apparently acts as timer and game boss. On the table are the coveted trophies: the largest, for first place, is a golden frog mounted on a black plastic base; the consolation award is the more traditional player kicking a ball. Beside these monuments there is a large bag of jelly beans and toffees, which the *regatón* seems to employ as a repository of surprise mini-awards and a portable concession.

We take pictures of the game boss and team captains, then of each team. The boys fall automatically into stiff and sober postures of self-importance, a stance that lasts until the camera buzzes, then instantly dissolves. All assemble with giggles and guffaws to watch themselves emerge through the turbid emulsion, and the *regatón* passes out jelly beans in a seizure of munificence.

Then it is time to put up money for the cash pool and to draw for position in the tournament. The captains step forward and stand in a semi-circle about the *regatón*, who has prepared folded scraps of paper with numbers on them. When he extends a hand with these scraps in the palm, a tiny child, having wedged himself through the wall of legs, mistakes the proffered paper for toffees and reaches swiftly to take his share. The *regatón* pulls back to whoops of laughter, and the little marauder is shooed gently away.

Positions established, the Professor steps forward in clean white shirt bearing the game ball and the first contestants take the field. There is considerable milling about, since obstreperous younger boys must be run off the field, as well as a few chickens, and spectators cross the field to take up seats on the sidelines. One Ovíri boy begins to tap on a home-made drum of wood and boarhide, and the women gather in their babies to keep them from the field of battle. There is much fresh achiote on the cheeks of young women, and a few families--Mr. Fastfoto's among them-- are wholly garbed in western-style clothing. They do not clap or shout, but sit sedately and watch with impassive faces.

Otíka plays in the first round against a downstream village, Océni. The tempo of combat changes often, sometimes appearing relaxed and hum-orous as an afterschool informal match and at other times escalating into fierce skirmishing. Rules are also flexible. Except for the two goals-- bamboo and palm frond nets--there is no boundary but the wavering border between mowed and unmowed field. The Professor nevertheless shows consummate skill in discriminating between balls too deep in the long grass to retrieve and those that a skilled toe can still root out. Occasionally a hard, wild kick sends the ball off the field and over the bluff into the creek, and the obstreperous small boys have their moment of heroism then, streaking to retrieve the bounding ball from the rapids before it is swept away.

At halftime Otíka is two goals down, and there is a considerable intermission to allow the first canoe of masato to be drunk. Thereafter the game grows leisurely and indefinite, and I wander away to amuse myself. Others I notice are doing the same. A couple of modest parties are already underway in the village; some children are in the swimming hole; and I see two men asleep under a radio playing to itself.

In midafternoon the tournament ends, or rather peters out, and I yield to their beseeching and take final fotos of the happy, sweating victors with their great gilded frog. Then everyone adjourns to the schoolhouse, where tables have been set up and the banquet will be served. We are invited to dine first, along with the teams, and sit down to a plate of the specialty the Professor's wife has cooked. The dish is delicious: banana leaf packets stuffed with rice, pork, chicken and chopped olives, seasoned with aji. The Professor and *regatón* sit at our table, and when Totum arrives with the beer, a dispensation ritual begins again.

Nicolas' wife moves from table to table, seeing that the pots of rice and meat cakes are distributed to all. She is smiling evenly, showing no trace of the past night's anguish. The Professor holds forth on the usual range of topics, and with an occasional magnanimous wave, confers a bottle of the warm beer on a band of petitioners, or dismisses them with a reminder that this treat is for the players and chief attendants. Soon the record machine begins to throb, and President Luís enters, beaming, with his teenage daughters in tow.

Once more I am matched with the plump young lady of thirteen, while the President spirits Dianne away. The players gather in the doorway, and other village youths line the clearing to watch us perform. I work to display a sedate version of free-style rock-and-roll dancing, a blend of rusty memories. The effect is ambiguous; some of the spectators appear awed or fascinated, but a few--especially the younger boys--undergo severe convulsions of hilarity. At least some are energized into imitation or competition, and soon the schoolyard is full of crazily bobbing figures.

After two more numbers, we excuse ourselves and retreat inside, but it is not long before a line of suitors begins to form. Dianne must emerge again and again, to general acclaim, and dance for her dinner. I have apparently acquitted my responsibilities by the token gesture of squiring the President's daughter, but the young men of the various teams have egged each other into this final rite of initiation into the modern age, and there is no convenient and fair way to deny them the chance for such an act of courage and gallantry. Meanwhile, the Professor, the *regatón*, a few of the players and myself grow garrulous with drink. As the afternoon ebbs away I notice how stray, shy villagers edge into the building and cadge the last scraps of food or stand wordless and expectant at the outer fringe of our circle hoping to intercept one of the last bottles of the beer as it makes its way around.

There is a lull in the dancing while someone changes batteries in the record-player, and Dianne indicates tactfully but firmly that she is retiring from her position as Queen of the Ball. I am ready to flee also, disturbed again by the skeletal hierarchy I have seen take shape around the bottled beer, the artificial music, and the ridiculous golden frog. I want to walk by the river at sunset to purge myself of the thick-headedness of food and drink, then scribble in my notebook by lantern light before the phantoms I have glimpsed vanish.

When we excuse ourselves I see disappointment congeal in the faces of the Professor and the President and their retinue. Nicolás is insistent that we return, and I say it is possible, knowing as I do so that it is not true, and a mistake. We stroll into the dusk along one edge of the airfield, where a group of small boys dart about a ball, replaying perhaps some glorious exploit of the afternoon. At the far end of the grass field we hear voices and laughter, in the vicinity of San Tomás' house. We venture toward his fire and are greeted happily and handed our bowls. Here the party is only the usual neighborhood gathering, with perhaps a downriver relative or two. Everyone seems tired, but comfortably so, and content to relax and merely talk. We stay perhaps a half an hour, trading the few words in our common stock or simply sitting quietly, and then leave, Asháninka fashion, without a backward look.

The very next day a plane arrives from Cutiveréni, a mission on the Apurimac north of Puerto Ocopa where two priests from the United States have mustered large support contributions. The pilot tells us that Manolo, the Alas man who regularly flies this route, developed severe sinus trouble and had to be hospitalized. So the Professor was not forgotten or betrayed after all. The Cutiveréni pilot had his own responsibilities yesterday, but was contacted by Alas in Satipo and dispatched today to pick up the Professor's wife.

A boy arrives soon after the landing to inform the pilot that Nicolás and his wife are hurrying to the airstrip, and in a few minutes they appear, out of breath, clearly happy to see the agent of possible salvation. The wife wears her cheap blue dress and a shawl, and carries a plastic shopping bag stuffed with a change of clothes, toilet articles, and--probably--some baked yucca wrapped in banana leaf. She looks preoccupied, a little anxious, but hopeful. Nicolás is beaming, a film of perspiration on his broad face, and explains at great length to the pilot how concerned he was the previous day, when his wife suffered another attack, how relieved and grateful he is now that she can be taken to the doctors in Satipo.

Following these formalities and the loading of a sack or two of coffee beans, the wife boards the plane, we step back, and in moments it has roared off again and over the horizon. The Professor lingers with us, apologetic for his previous condemnation of the Wings of Hope, and optimistic about the chances of a cure. I do not share his confidence, given my diagnosis, but I must admit that merely the fuss and thunder of flying her off seems to have improved the spirits of both of them.

We are soon ourselves caught up in the ambivalence of departure, an exhilaration strangely hollow. Our last few days in Ovíri are packed with visits, last exchanges of gifts, and exposing all but a few hundred feet of film. For one of these last sequences I ask a friend, a boy named Virgilio, to assemble for me a favorite toy: a crudely carved balsa airplane with dry leaves for a propeller and tiny chonta spikes as landing gear. Virgilio is a serious lad. His expression and his broad, rather large head give him the appearance of a miniature adult. He has taken to sitting beside me in the cook shed as I write, and from time to time we talk about quirks in the Spanish tongue, or about Lima or about my country. He is observant and intelligent, and from him I learn that the Professor is a good teacher, but that people in the village grumble because he does not distribute much of the milk from the cows to those who help mend the fences.

When I ask Virgilio to make an airplane for me, promising twenty-five soles for the job, he assents. But the next morning he appears empty-handed, and despite the smile I tack on to my reproach he looks downcast and soon withdraws. Two hours later I look up from my pages to see Virgilio at the head of a small gang of boys, and each bears like a talisman one of the carved planes, new-made, propellers fluttering in the breeze. I am touched in more complex ways than I can name, and hurry to gather my equipment to film the procession. With a little urging, the boys soon enter into their normal play, running with the planes twisting in their uplifted hands, and manufacturing their own quite convincing sound effects.

I pay all of them twenty-five soles, and they present me with the planes. Two or three I accept. Virgilio is proud that I select his--a two-engined craft. I will hold on to it through many packings and unpackings, until it hangs from a beam in my living room in California. Like Carlos' arrows or the wild pig teeth Kenchori gave me, it can suddenly pull me back in time to the little hut on the edge of a jungle river. This wooden image of flight can transport me, more swiftly and surely than a jet, to the brightness and laughter of late morning, the odor of oranges and sour masato, and the still figure of the boy who watches me carefully as I write, or lift my coffee cup, or smile at him. An interesting reversal of the Pishtako myth: the artifacts of the aborigines--rude bows, hand-woven cushmas, these curious balsa models-- are born back to the tourist's homeland where they consume his dreams with the memory of another kind of existence, a life swift as an arrow, sweet as water, and simple as laughter.

One day we move our packs and cases to the river, the usual band of small porters carrying most of our burden. The Professor himself has commandeered a peki-peki and volunteered to freight us to Otíka. As we stow our gear and Nicolás pours petrol in the tank, a small group assembles as if by accident. Felipe the snake-skinner is there, some younger men, and San Tomás with a few of his children. They talk as the youngsters skip a stone or two, not paying us much heed. Our only clue, and not a wholly convincing one, that this may be a farewell gesture is San Tomás' new shirt. A garish concoction of color, it was probably purchased from the *regatón* for the birthday party.

The Professor pushes away from the bank and leaps into the canoe. The engine catches after a few jerks of the cord, and we swing into the current, pulling rapidly away from the group ashore. The children have caught on to our custom, and wave and shout. We return the gesture, but only meet the eyes of the men. San Tomás wears his calm, self-satisfied smile, and nods at us, seeming to approve this departure with the same tolerant good humor with which he first greeted us. The last thing we can see of the village is his shirt, a dot of outrageous color, against the green wall of the jungle.

45

A day or two later we wait through a long morning for the Alas plane, our gear lashed and taped for the journey to Lima. The hollowness at the heart of me has reached its maximum expansion and has begun to contract into the familiar grief at parting. The Asháninka suffer from no such disorder. Villagers arrive and grow joyful at our brave smiles and gestures of friendship; they stand about a little awkwardly, eyeing our goods, clearly hoping for last-minute gifts. Ecstatic, Andrés collects his line and hooks, and Rosa--not without grumbling--seizes a trinket or two and departs. Doubtless she has tasks to perform with her new blade. Matías, Martín and Carlos have already received tokens in private, informal meetings, including 5000 soles I present to Matías for a kind of community fund. As Minister of Tourism, he recognizes our custom and stays to bid a formal farewell, along with Andrés who has been overcome with our generosity, and of course the children.

The night before we were entertained at a fine party, and there too we encountered no trace of regret, no hint of sadness, no backward-yearning. We drank and laughed; Dianne was spun about by Rosa and Margarita in the usual dances; the women got into a water fight and I taught the men how to arm-wrestle. As always a few of the old, drunken men insisted that I repeat my vocabulary in their tongue, and children stood near to peer at or touch us, and occasionally a young man or woman would be sent into paroxysms of mirth at the mere sight of us. As the afternoon waned people drifted away, the masato grew thick and pulpy, and we found ourselves suddenly, again, at the end of an ordinary day.

Now another such day has begun, and no one is disturbed by our departure. Martín's daughter ignores us as usual on her way down the path to draw water from the river. The chickens come to investigate our hearth, the embers now dead. Children appear to idle away a few minutes under our roof, forever curious and hopeful that on this last morning we will produce some entirely new and unforeseen miracle from our packs.

We have an impulse to capture what is soon to vanish for us, and snap pictures indiscriminately of the house, the chickens, the children--all that was yesterday so commonplace. Even when the Cessna arrives in its drone, rush and roar, and our things are quickly stowed, Dianne keeps the shutter clicking. The door swings shut and the engine races. The adults and a few older children step back to stand almost at attention. Matías is blank-faced, staring at something on an inner horizon.

The last photograph blurs. Framed by the window of the plane, faces are only brown smudges against a band of green streaks. The plane is already in motion. This last desperate picture best captures my experience for the next few weeks. The moment the propeller roared into its perfect, shimmering circle time began to accelerate; the selva rushed away and Lima, Los Angeles and Sacramento bore down upon me. In Lima we were submerged in the turbulence of last minute preparations for leaving the country. Dianne was to fly first with the film, while I had a few days to clear up my reports to the Fulbright Commission. The pictures of the villagers were printed and sent off to Matías; items left in storage with friends were unearthed and packed; we went to market for final purchases of gifts for friends at home. Woven through this rush--taxis and buses and dinner parties and farewell embraces-- were sudden inner visions of the Asháninka, of birds crying high over the river at dusk, of a bed of coals under blackened husks of yucca root.

As the avalanche of civilization gained momentum, these flashes of memory became like the intermittent lightning of hallucination: illuminating all at once, in a lurid glow, a single scene lodged in one of the mind's caves. Waiting at a crowded airport boarding area, loudspeakers booming and the stench of fuel already strong, I would remember wind and current in an open canoe, the slap of rapids, Matías and I lifting our poles in rhythm. Or at a dinner gathering, amid cut glass and candles, I would see a fire and small figures in cushmas crouched on the bare earth beside it. The shock and poignancy of some of these momentary juxtapositions was paralyzing, and beyond my ability to explain; simple contrasts of past and future, primitive and technological, or the like, sounded ludicrous, the fatuous blather of travelogues at their worst.

Soon after my return to the United States a series of events conspired to bring me nearer to an understanding of one of these persistent images. When I arrived in San Francisco Dianne broke the news to me that at least half of our footage was badly damaged by heat. It was certain that the movie we had planned--a full-scale ethnographic documentary--could not be made, and at best we would have only a few good scenes to tack together. Our hope of providing a powerful work, that might someday serve to muster support for the Asháninka and their efforts to retain tribal identity, was apparently dashed. Both of us were dejected and bitter; I was particularly to blame for not having refrigerated the film in Lima during my first foray into the selva, and I cursed my stupidity in a fury of despair. During this bleak period I set out for a visit to my birthplace in Idaho, and in a motel in Lovelock, Nevada, I awoke at three in the morning with a high fever. By the next day I had a confirmed case of malaria.

One image that had haunted me for months--the portly gentleman in the plaza at San Ramón with his box camera and buckets of developer--

recurred as I sat in my mother's home, alternately sweating and shaking, watching the television premier of *Holocaust*, the enormous reenactment of the Nazis' extermination of six million Jews. The ghastly crimes of that era seemed an appropriate accompaniment to the raging parasites in my own blood. In some obscure way I believed the jungle heat that had fogged our emulsion and turned it sickly yellow-green, and the anopheles mosquito, tiny and deadlier than the jaguar, were visiting vengeance on me for such perversions as the gas chamber, and further, for the queasy business of reenacting these perversions as a form of entertainment.

Certainly the horrible was presented in colorful, close-up detail. Interruptions for commercials were rare (reviewers found this strategy "tasteful"), and at the end of the ten-hour program the producers made solemn pronouncements to clarify the message of the program: these terrible events must be resurrected, through art, so that we do not forget our potential for evil, so that we hold ever more tenaciously to our tradition of humanism, so that such transgressions--felt to be beyond the limits of human nature--may never occur again.

It should have been easy to recoil from these visions of horror: the long lines of emaciated bodies, the sadistic guards who watched the writhing victims for diversion, the lampshades of human skin, the soap from human fat, the ovens that worked overtime to rid the world of evidence so foul. But I kept recalling the groups of villagers filing before our little Pentax, as we snapped each visage for a government document, a tiny symbolic incarceration, a beginning of the process we call registration, or enrollment, or induction, or identification, but which may be simply the subtle machinery of slavery and genocide.

An aberration in history, my mother said, that must not be repeated. Those people were mad. Arthritic, unable to walk more than a few yards at a stretch, reclining in a padded chair that looks like those men are strapped into for voyages into black space, she for years has absorbed television with a gargantuan appetite. She takes in everything: news, comedy, extravaganza, travel, public service programs. She worries about the state of the world. She sends small amounts to the addresses flashed on the screen. She grieves over the misfortunes of the characters in soap operas. She adds her own acid embroidery to the self-puffery of political speakers. I have always thought of her as a cultural seismograph, an oracle of what good, common-sense folk in my country would think. So, then, an aberration that must never be repeated. Except as a television spectacular.

It is of course no aberration. The techniques of extermination have reached a new order of sophistication in our century, but genocidal war appears to be as ancient as human history. Our oldest national epics (*Beowulf*, the *Chanson de Roland*, *Sigurd*, the *Iliad*) are invariably battle-songs, crammed with bloodthirsty rant, and the earliest religions--to judge by the fanged maws of the gods--were hardly more compassionate. What makes our era most sinister is not the awesome body-counts of our wars, or the terrible power of weaponry--thermonuclear bombs, lasers, toxic gasses, deadly germs, sound waves--but the subtler force of the industrial monoculture, which is spreading everywhere on the planet, not merely as the iron axe, powder and shot, machine-woven cloth, railroads and aircraft, but as a tapestry of glorious electronic images and sounds, visions manufactured to invade and possess the soul and hence, ultimately, to realize themselves as fact.

In earlier centuries white men came to the new continents charged with unmitigated greed. They killed and enslaved the aborigines with few qualms, as any reading of early chronicles makes obvious. Finally people of conscience (and business sense) put a stop to most of these atrocities. But for the last half-century there has been no serious opposition to the philosophy of "economic development" of the land and its last rag-tag bands of indigenous peoples, for these survivors themselves generally welcome, fascinated, the new way of life. The visions are much more penetrating than bullets. The aborigines beg to be infected. Mr. Fastfoto and El Smootho become the most zealous apostles of the new order.

To my mother, a Mormon, it is important to bring to the pagan primitives not only penicillin and disinfectant but also the true word of God, salvation for the spirit as well as health and cleanliness for the body. Missionaries of all faiths have believed in this two-pronged assault for centuries, but I think it is a duplication of effort. It is necessary only to ship the tools, trinkets, and pictures--especially the pictures. Within a generation the pagan ideologies will disintegrate in the face of these powerful totems.

Nor are there villains in the piece. The Fascist, Communist, Christian and Capitalist are working together here: all belong to regimented industrial states that convert life into fuel, and justify--even deify--the process by broadcasting propaganda fantasies literally from heaven. The power of this vortex of vision, pulling all of us into the future, seems insurmountable, and we are all its helpless agents.

Viewed from this perspective, the oil, mineral and agricultural interests that flock to any hemorrhage of valuable material on the earth, and the philanthropists who send medicine and equipment to remote tribes are engaged in a common task. Even the scientist and artist who may think themselves mere witnesses must learn that they carry the virus of civilization quite as much as the old conquistadors. The terrible irony is that unlike these earlier expeditions, modern inquiry brings compassionate curiosity, a reverence for the subtlety and fragility of culture, and the high motive of preservation. Our own visit was in the name of fixing, in printed and filmed record, a people's way of life before it completely disappears, but we ended like functionaries at Dachau, abetting a government bent on grandiose schemes of exploiting its natural resources.

In one haggard moment of delirium I remembered Matías's dream. He saw me stricken by a sickness then. In the same nightmare a faceless assailant fought with him, and each time he cut the intruder apart, the pieces magically reassembled. I saw now that I was the menacing figure too, one of a faceless chain of them stretching over four centuries: the gold seekers, rubber pirates, missionaries, cattle and coffee bosses, students and tourists who have streamed into the green heart of the selva.

Slash at these demon-wraiths and they reveal their composite nature. Cortés and Pizarro disguised their greed for gold behind an iron cross; the Jesuits often burned what the compassionate Franciscans collected and translated; the Baron Von Humboldt, with his scholarly accounts of the flora and fauna and ruined civilizations of New Spain, drew to the region fresh hordes of adventurers and speculators; in our time the profits of great corporations are funneled into foundations which encourage research into tribal life. I wrote and photographed in one small corner of the greatest jungle on earth because my culture is so bloated with earth's riches that it can afford to indulge the curiosity of irrelevant romantics.

Watching the small, shimmering screen, my blood on fire, I knew that I had passed well beyond curiosity. I imagined that our own film, were it skillfully done as a tiny, tame holocaust, might intrigue and temporarily sadden the viewer, elicit from him honest sentiments like my mother's: Terrible, terrible, what happened, so many people gone! It must not happen again! But it will happen again, is happening again, and with enthusiastic popular support. For our viewer will brighten in relief to see so many Indians left alive, will hope that through education, improved diet, modern medicine. . . . Soon the new archetypes--El Smoothos, Mister Fastfotos--will be watching old movies about their former life, and perhaps training to make their own films of a new life, in universities carved out of ancient hunting grounds. And the overwhelming majority of mankind will rejoice in this transformation as both necessary and agreeable.

For we conceive of time and humanity as rushing forward, and the past, with its disturbing rumor of a lost Eden, serves primarily as romance, as a dream seen through an electronic window. Much of our experience, in fact, must be transformed into a ghostly swarm of electrons and fixed magnetically or chemically, as videotape or filmstrip or slide, in order to be valid, even significant. We shoot pictures of new babies, of weddings, of assassinations and wars and holdups and rocket launchings; fame and power are measured in almost direct proportion to the number of times an individual is broadcast, amplified, multiplied, blown up. Once so fixed, trapped in the ghost-world, persons and events may be manipulated, studied, enjoyed, re-enacted, as they never were in actuality, and the past is thus drained of its mystery.

The function of this spirit-world of electronic images, like the older one of clay and stone, is to stimulate in all people a passionate desire to enter and partake of that world. To be among the stars, a modern Porínkari, one must own and operate the same machines, use and throw away the same expensive toys, drink the same euphoric potions, listen and sway to the same throbbing music as the happy, beautiful people in the pictures. Each season the style or beat of these bright phantoms changes, so that the new and the now is always the new and the now, so that the effort to pass from the actual into an ideal, from past to future, is continuous, so that the desire for transcendence from one material order to another is always incandescent. The planet is now ablaze with this desire; and the black goo of the ancient jungle burns night and day to power a dynamo of dreams.

At the furthest reach of modern cosmology, at its most primitive, archeological level, stands the austere gentleman on the plaza at San Ramón, the old Zeiss box camera beside him on its polished wooden stilts. He is first to hand the last of the Indians a self-image, a crude negative of a negative, a study of a momentous afternoon: the trip to town after a season of hard machete work, an initiation into the vast store of delights we call civilization. They stand, broadly smiling under chopped black hair, barefoot but clad in cheap new clothes, proud to enter at last this new spirit-place. This is what it is, to become someone.

And of all the transactions that will ensue, this is perhaps the fairest and most honorable. For a fixed price the client takes away a picture, which will curl and grow yellow on the wall of a palm hut, and that is the end of it. No copies, no archives, no books. No quaintness, no anthropology, no identification. One picture at the cost of two days' hard labor.

That haunting image should have been our clue. The Polaroid was our grandest and safest instrument, the gentlest and slowest poison, a simple gift not compounded by high and possibly hypocritical designs of documentary salvation. The rumble of its workings and the swift apparition of images were an unfailing treat, and the slip of film an immediate possession. If its magic was evil, it was at least open and direct, whereas the machinations of motive behind our proposed books and movies were more treacherous.

If the import of this process of infiltrating and transforming souls was contained in the Pishtako myth, and we are all, photographer and photographed alike, being consumed in a petroleum devil-dance, a conflagration of spirits, then we ought to heed the advice Matías gave the young man who ate fish poison in despair. Death comes soon enough. There is no need to hurry.

NOTES
(Chapters 25, 26)

1. Claude Lévi-Strauss, *Tristes Tropiques* (New York, 1978), p. 253.
2. Hans-Dietrich Disselhoff and Siguald Linné, *The Art of Ancient America* (New York, 1961), p. 149.
3. Edward P. Lanning, *Perú Before the Incas* (New Jersey, 1967), p. 78.
4. Julio C. Tello, *Chavín: Cultura Matriz de la Civilización Andina* (Lima, 1960), p. 26.
5. Frederick Kaufman Doig, *Arqueología Peruana* (Lima, 1971), p. 160.
6 Lanning, p. 106.
7. Disselhoff, p. 164.
8. Carl O. Sauer, *Agricultural Origins and Dispersals* (New York, 1952), p. 53.
9. Raymond M. Gilmore, "Fauna and Ethnozoology of South America," *Handbook of South American Indians* (New York, 1963), VI, 354.
10. Gilmore, 355.
11. Sauer, p. 12.
12. H. Horkheimer, *El Perú Prehispanico* (Lima, 1950), 156-57.
13. Bennet Bronson, "The Earliest Farming: Demography as Cause and Consequence," in *Origins of Agriculture*, Charles A. Reed, editor (The Hague, 1977), p. 32.
14. John H. Rowe, *Chavín Art: An Inquiry into its Form and Meaning* (New York, 1962), p. 11.
15. Donald Lathrap, "Our Father the Cayman, Our Mother the Gourd," in *Origins of Agriculture*, p. 742. See also "The Moist Tropics, the Arid Lands, and the Appearance of Great Art Styles in the New World," in *Art and Environment in Native America*, Mary Elizabeth King and Idris Traylor, Jr., eds. (Lubbock, 1974), Special Publications of the Museum, No. 7, 115-158.
16. Lathrap, p. 715.
17. Lanning, *loc. cit.*
18. Boyce Rensberger, "The Old Mayans Weren't Farmers," *San Francisco Chronicle*, May 14, 1980, 6.
19. Stefano Varese, *La Sal de los Cerros* (Lima, 1968), p. 16.
20. Franz Boas, *The Mind of Primitive Man* (New York, 1938), p. 200.
21. Lanning, p. 78.
22. Lanning, *loc. cit.*
23. Lévi-Strauss, p. 299.

Will Baker was born in Idaho in 1935, and grew up in small logging and farming towns in the Payette and Boise River valleys. He attended the University of Washington, the University of Hawaii, the Sorbonne, and the University of California at Berkeley, where he received a doctorate in English Literature in 1964. For several years he made experimental films, including the prize-winning shorts *Spider God, Pun-Ting, Three Colloquies,* and *Adults Only,* and taught courses in film theory and filmmaking. He has taught at Reed College, the University of Montana, and the University of California at Davis.

His books include *Jacques Prévert, The Syntax of English Poetry, Dawn Stone* (novella), *Chip,* and *A Little Lady-Killing* (under the pseudonym Victoria Webb). He has also published poetry and short stories.

In 1979 he received a Fulbright Grant to do research in Perú, and in 1982 he was awarded a National Endowment for the Arts Writers' Grant.

Da MAY 15 84